Queen's University
Belfast

Language Planning and Education: Linguistic Issues in Northern Ireland, the Republic of Ireland, and Scotland

Edited by

John M. Kirk and Dónall P. Ó Baoill

Cló Ollscoil na Banríona
Belfast 2002

D1513383

First published in 2002
Cló Ollscoil na Banríona
Queen's University Belfast
Belfast, BT7 1NN

Belfast Studies in Language, Culture and Politics
www.bslcp.com

For the production of this book, the publishers gratefully acknowledge the support from the Cultural Diversity Programme of the Northern Ireland Community Relations Council, which aims to encourage acceptance and understanding of cultural diversity, and to promote a pluralist society characterised by equity, respect for diversity and interdependence.

British Library Cataloguing-in-Publication Data
A catalogue record for this book is available from the British Library.

ISBN 0 85389 835 9

Typeset by John Kirk in Times New Roman

Printed by Optech, Belfast

The papers in this volume were presented at
Third Language and Politics Symposium
18-20 September 2002
Queen's University Belfast
In collaboration with Iomairt Cholum Cille
An event of the AHRB Research Centre for Irish and Scottish Studies

CONTENTS

PART 3: LANGUAGE PLANNING FOR SCOTS: STATUS AND STANDARDISATION

PART 4: SCOTS AND EDUCATION

Contributors

Pádraig de Bhál is Senior Lecturer in Education, Trinity College Dublin, with responsibility for Irish-medium teacher training and a Member of the Board of the Ulster-Scots Agency.

Dr Cordula Bilger studied at the University of Zürich where she completed her PhD entitled "War Zone Language: Language and the Conflict in Northern Ireland" in 2002.

John Corbett is Senior Lecturer in Scottish Language at the University of Glasgow. His books include *Language and Scottish Literature* (EUP 1997) and *Written in the Language of the Scottish Nation: A History of Literary Translation into Scots* (Multilingual Matters 1999).

T.P. Dolan is Professor of English at University College Dublin. His website www.hiberno-english.com was launched in November 2002 and his *Dictionary of Hiberno-English: The Irish Use of English* will be published in a second edition in 2003.

Dr Sheila Douglas is Scots Language Tutor on the Scottish Music Degree Course at the Royal Scottish Academy of Music and Drama in Glasgow. Earlier papers have appeared in the *Language Links* and *Travellers and their Language* edited by John M. Kirk and Dónall P. Ó Baoill.

John Edmund, an Ulster-Scot, is a free-lance market consultant who advises Tha Boord o Ulstèr-Scotch and drew up the Language Development Strategy for Ulster-Scots.

Dr Anthea Fraser Gupta is Senior Lecturer in English at the University of Leeds and has published widely on minority language issues particularly in Singapore and Malaysia.

Carmel Hanna, MLA, was, at the time of the Symposium, Minister for Employment and Learning in the Northern Ireland Executive.

Dr John Harris is Senior Lecturer at the Institiúid Teangeolaíochta Éireann (ITÉ), Dublin. His most recent book, *Teaching and Learning Irish in Primary School*, co-authored with Lelia Murtagh, was published by ITÉ in 1999.

Dauvit Horsbroch is Honorary Research Fellow at the Research Institute for Irish and Scottish Studies, University of Aberdeen. He has contributed to each of the two previous volumes of symposium papers: *Language and Politics* (2000) and *Linguistic Politics* (2001).

Dr John M. Kirk is Senior Lecturer in English at Queen's University Belfast and has published widely on linguistic topics pertaining to Scotland and Ireland.

Margaret MacIver is Education Officer with Communn na Ghadlig, Inverness.

Iain Mac Ille Chiar, who was formerly a Lecturer in Education at Northern College, Aberdeen, with responsibility for Gaelic, is Head of the Gaelic-medium Unit at Inverness College.

Seán Mac Nia is the Principal Officer with the general responsibility for Irish-medium education at the Council for the Curriculum Assessment and Examinations, Belfast.

J. Derrick McClure is Senior Lecturer in English at the University of Aberdeen. His most recent book, *Doric*, was published by John Benjamins in 2002.

Irene McGugan, MSP, is an MSP for North-East Scotland. She is an SNP spokesperson for Children and Education and Convenor of the *Cross-Pairtie Group i the Scots Pairliament on the Scots Leid*. Her paper "Scots in the Twenty-first Century" appears in the earlier volume of edited symposium papers *Linguistic Politics*.

Dr Eugene McKendry is Lecturer in the Graduate School of Education, Queen's University Belfast. An earlier paper "Modern Languages Education Policies and Irish in Northern Ireland" appears in *Language Links. The Languages of Scotland and Ireland* eds. J.M. Kirk and D.P. Ó Baoill, 2001.

Dr Wilson McLeod is Lecturer in Celtic Studies at the University of Edinburgh.

Janet Muller is Príomhfheidhmeannach of Scátheagras Phobal na Gaeilge i dTuaisceart na hÉireann (POBAL).

Jacqueline Ní Fheargusa is Príomhfheidhmeannach of GAELSCOILEANNA – Eagraíocht chomhordaithe an Oideachais lánghaeilge.

Dr Gabrielle Nig Uidhir is Lecturer in Irish-Medium Education at St. Mary's University College, Belfast, and author of *In our Own Words* (Macmillan 1996)

Liz Niven is a former teacher of English who now works as a freelance consultant for the preparation of teaching materials. For her collection of short stories *A Braw Bree*, she has prepared a coursepack. Her most recent collection of poems, *Stravaigin,* was published in 2002.

Dr Dónall P. Ó Baoill is Professor of Irish at Queen's University Belfast and has published on all aspects of language pertaining to Ireland.

Seán Ó Coinn, who previously worked on the Northern Ireland Place-Name Project, is Príomhfheidhmeannach of the Chomhairle na Gaelscolaíochta / Chief Executive Office of the Council for Irish-medium Education, Belfast.

Helen Ó Murchú is a Founder Member and past President of the European Bureau for Lesser Used Languages and is currently Stiúrthóir / Director of Comhar ma Múinteoirí Gaeilge. Her paper "Language, discrimination and the Good Friday Agreement: The Case of Irish" appears in the earlier volume of edited symposium papers *Language and Politics*.

Ian J. Parsley is Corporate Director of Ultonian Solutions, a professional language consultancy firm, which advises *Tha Boord o Ulstèr-Scotch*, Media Relations Director with *Stormont Access*, a lobbyist and PR company, and runs a website on Ulster Scots: www.geocities.com/parsleyij/ullns.html, including the electronic discussion list *Ullans-L*. He has contributed to each of the two edited volumes of symposium papers: *Language and Politics* (2000) and *Linguistic Politics* (2001).

Stephen Peover is Under-Secretary at the Department of Education, Northern Ireland. An earlier paper "Encouragement and Facilitation: A New Paradigm for Minority Language Education" appears in in the earlier volume of edited symposium papers *Linguistic Politics*.

Dr Robert Phillipson, who was born in Gourock, is Research Professor of English at the Copenhagen Business School. His book *Linguistic Imperialism* (OUP 1992) has received high critical acclaim. He edited *Rights to Language: Equity, Power and Education: Celebrating the 60th Birthday of Tove Skutnabb-Kangas* (Lawrence Erlbaum, 2000). His latest book, *English-only Europe? Language Policy Challenges* will be published by Routledge in January 2003.

A G Boyd Robertson is Senior Lecturer in Education at the Jordanhill Campus of the University of Strathclyde and author of *Teach Yourself Gaelic* (Hodder & Stoughton 1996) and numerous official reports.

Lydia Rohmer is a lecturer at the Glasgow College of Building and Printing.

Dr Tove Skutnabb-Kangas holds several professorial appointments in Scandinavia and is one of the world's leading experts on minority language education and linguistic human rights. Her book *Linguistic Genocide in Education – or Worldwide Diversity and Human Rights*, which sets out much of her expertise, was published by Lawrence Erlbaum in 2000.

Dr John Walsh is Lecturer in Communication and Media Studies at Dublin City University. His book *Díchoimisiúnú Teanga: Coimisiún na Gaeltachta 1926* was published in Dublin by Cois Life in 2002.

Mike Watson, MSP, was Labour MP for Glasgow Central from 1989-1997 when he was made a life peer as Lord Watson of Invergowrie. He is now Labour MSP for Glasgow Cathcart and Minister for Tourism, Culture and Leisure in the Scottish Executive. As such, he can be described as both the Minister for Gaelic and the Minister for Scots. His diary of the first year of the Scottish Parliament is published as *Year Zero: An Inside View of the Scottish Parliament*. He is also a contributor to *Being Scottish* edited by Tom Devine and Paddy Logue (Polygon, 2002).

Introduction: Language Planning and Education: Linguistic Issues in Northern Ireland, the Republic of Ireland, and Scotland

John M. Kirk and Dónall P. Ó Baoill

Welcome to the edited volume of papers arising from Third Language and Politics Symposium at Queen's University Belfast, which we organised on behalf of the Forum for Research on the Languages of Scotland and Ulster as a constituent project within the AHRB Research Centre for Irish and Scottish Studies, and also in collaboration with Iomairt Cholm Cille.

The primary focus of the series of these symposia is the three jurisdictions of Northern Ireland, the Republic of Ireland, and Scotland on the one hand, and the overlapping linguistic continuums of Irish and Gaelic (the Gaeltacht) and of Scots and Ulster-Scots (the Scotstacht), as shown in the cover map. This year's main themes included education and language planning, language policy particularly with regard, yet again, to the status and standardisation of Scots, and the issues of linguistic human rights and linguistic diversity in an international context – and these are all reflected in the present volume.

By bringing together identified key stakeholders from Northern Ireland, the Republic of Ireland, and Scotland, and now with these edited papers, we aim to facilitate and enrich an exchange of ideas and critical debate about the issues affecting and affected by current language policy and its development. From this book, readers will acquire a greater awareness and clearer understanding of the problems arising from and the solutions needed for the successful implementation of current language policy in each area. In particular, readers will have a clearer understanding of the nature of as well as the differences between the implementation of Irish-medium education in Northern Ireland and the Republic of Ireland and of Gaelic-medium education in Scotland. And readers are also introduced to new approaches to the teaching and assessment of Scots.

Irish-medium and Gaelic-medium Education

All papers dealing with Irish and Gaelic-Medium education give a very concise overall review of strategies pursued by various government agencies, university and third level college departments and voluntary organisations and summarise research results emerging from work done by individuals and others in several research organisations, in Ireland and Scotland. There is a large amount of uniformity of purpose to be seen in what has been reported. Furthermore, a commonality of approach to the provision of education through a minority language is evident, which has also lead to an identical range of problems ranging from lack of different types of teaching resources, to teacher shortages and third level training provision. The impact of various policy decisions emanating from government departments have also been discussed in some detail by several authors and they show clearly that in many cases these changes have far-reaching implications for the future prosperity of minority languages and their cultures, particularly within the educational sphere and in society generally.

The central issues in Irish-medium and Gaelic-medium education raised in this volume are structures, teacher training, and assessment. To teach through another language (e.g. through Irish in Northern Ireland and the Republic of Ireland or through Gaelic in Scotland) what structures do we need to have in place? Is teacher training the only structure and where does it exist? What is missing from present structures? Even if we had ideal structures in place, would they work? If not, why not? In both parts of Ireland, there are Councils for all-Irish education: can they be overlooked? Does the Government or the political system help or hinder? How is Politics an obstruction to the implementation and smooth running of education through another medium? Why doesn't the government better support such a policy? What is Government afraid of? Why is it worth the trouble and effort? These issues are discussed with regard to the Republic of Ireland by **Jacqueline Ní Fhearghusa** (Gaelscoileanna), Northern Ireland by **Seán Ó Coinn** (Comhairle na Gaelscolaíochta) and Scotland by **Margaret MacIver** (Comunn na Gàidhlig).

Ní Fhearghusa delineates the development of All-Irish Medium education in the Republic of Ireland (ROI) in the last three decades. The rapid growth of schools at primary level teaching through Irish and the decline in the usage of Irish in many Gaeltacht areas have brought enormous pressures to bear on teachers and administrators alike, and despite supportive government policies in general, there has not been proper recognition of the practical difficulties encountered by teachers, administrators and pupils in finding appropriate teaching resources, assessment procedures, evaluative techniques and how teachers are meant to deal with pupils with learning difficulties. The greatest difficulties arise at secondary level where the provision of textbooks, educational resources and the availability of properly trained teachers with competence in the Irish language and in teaching through the medium of a minority language, is severely acute. She states that it is increasingly obvious that there is a enormous need for a well planned programme to deal with second level provision in a minority language, which will involve the government, third level teacher training institutions, teachers, school administrators and parents. Parents are more demanding and selective when it comes to post-primary education and they need to be convinced that their children will not be disadvantaged if they continue with their education through the minority language. The setting up of An Chomhairle um Oideachas Gaeltachta agus Gaelscolaíochta, which in many ways parallels Comhairle na Gaelscolaíochta in Northern Ireland, will bring cohesion and co-ordination to all aspects of Irish-Medium education - from classroom activities, curriculum development and applied linguistic research projects. A similar provision for the production of textbooks and other educational resources, which will parallel the Áis-Aonad is St. Mary's University College in Belfast, is also being provided for. The role of GAELSCOILEANNA (the co-ordinating body for All-Irish Medium education until now) will continue in the form of an independent non-governmental body assisting teachers, administrators and parents within established schools. It will also continue establishing new schools where the demand exists, liaising with school patrons and in proposing new developments in support of Irish-Medium education.

Ó Coinn's contribution focuses on the current structures appropriate to the development of the Irish Medium (IM) education sector in Northern Ireland (NI).

In doing so he also outlines the various contributions other institutions such as Gaeloiliúint, Altram and GESO (special needs in IM), Iontaobhas na Gaelscolaíochta and teacher training at St. Mary's have to make to the larger picture in order to give due recognition and full support to Comhairle na Gaelscolaíochta's own strategic plan for IM provision in the foreseeable future. The educational, financial, resource and training issues, which all of these structures have been and continue to address, are duly outlined and discussed. As some issues are more pressing than others within the sector as presently constituted, he advocates that priorities need to be rationalised along certain parameters in order to achieve a satisfactory degree of effectiveness. In those circumstances, he is advocating that the major problem to be addressed is the poor supply of properly qualified teachers to teach in the IM schools; furthermore, he stresses that Gaeloiliúint must have more strategic focus, that the government and Department of Education must become more pro-active and provide additional financial support for the resource unit and GESO, that ALTRAM needs to alter its focus to training and support in relation to competence in Irish and in second language acquisition in a minority language. The IM Education Trust is being asked to move away from supporting schools without Department of Education funding to a policy of ensuring that all new schools are capable of getting funding from day one. All of the interested parties must engage in fruitful and constructive debate, if we are to ensure that the future of IM education is to achieve its potential within a well-organised and planned programme of development.

MacIver outlines the structures that are needed to properly underpin a well-directed and planned Gaelic-Medium Education (GME) programme. Her starting point is parent education and support and she outlines the necessary structures needed in order to enthuse parents into action and to give them the confidence they need to carry through with a programme of language regeneration. These structures include the Pre-School Council, playgroups, nursery provision, Gaelic language courses specifically designed for parents and appropriately prepared and attractive promotional materials. There is a great shortage of teachers, including special needs, support and supply teachers, to address the current needs in GME Units and schools. This shortage results in many schools reverting to teaching though English at certain points. There is a dearth of trained psychologists and speech therapists to engage with children with specific needs. A teacher recruitment strategy is called for as a matter of urgency to overcome the appalling shortfall of qualified teachers at primary and secondary level. Training provision at third level must be fully addressed and a programme of practical supportive research undertaken to direct and focus the work undertaken in schools. A strong community and media dimension needs also to be developed and co-ordinated across the entire spectrum. Government support and co-ordination of effort to secure status for Gàidhlig is necessary to enhance its potential and guarantee its future.

The next three papers by **Pádraig de Bhál** (Trinity College Dublin), Northern Ireland by **Gabrielle Nic Uidhir** (St. Mary's University College), and Scotland by **Boyd Robertson** (University of Strathclyde) address teacher-training issues at third level. Their approach, while having certain shared features, is on the whole complementary as they have decided to focus on different aspects of the topic informed by their own day to day experience of teacher training programmes in their own institutions. To us, the central questions which we posed at the outset are these: How is training for teaching in another language to be carried out? Where is it done? What politics are involved in getting good teacher training practices accepted and up and running?

De Bhál advocates an admixture of different models in the preparation of teachers, from the practically oriented through one focusing on the development of specific competencies in language and teaching methodology, to a reflective model of analysis of the art and science of teaching. Applied linguistics and the findings of research, whether observational or analytical, must form a core element of training. Student quality at the initial access point also has a significant impact on the success or otherwise of the training provision. The three basic requirements for a teacher intending to teach through the medium of a second or minority language are (a) a high degree of language competence, (b) a high competence in classroom skills and teaching methodologies, and (c) an appropriate qualification in the subject/subjects through which the teaching is to be imparted. Careful classroom placement and a lifelong perspective understanding of education needs are essential components in the training of competent teachers. He goes on to discuss specific aspects of content based language instruction. Most approaches to language learning assume that language is learned most effectively by using meaningful, relevant content in class. The type of integration whereby an additional language – usually a second or third language of the pupil – is used as the teaching medium has definite advantages. This approach is well documented in Harris (1984) where pupils in All-Irish schools score highest, followed by those who are exposed to some Irish medium teaching. The value of content-based language teaching needs to be advocated and highlighted within the type of socio-political context in which Irish and other minority language are being acquired. Lack of textbooks and resources and problems arising from language difficulties are issues that need to be addressed. The involvement of parents, the awareness of policy makers, educationalists and teacher training personnel of the value and benefit of this approach must be our first priority if the resources to support it are forthcoming. It must become a central part of language planning and policy making.

Nig Uidhir outlines the development of specialist training at St Mary's and the importance of supportive infrastructure and environment in its application. The aim of the training is to produce and nurture an additive bilingual situation. Irish is a teaching functional medium which students use and develop as they acquire competence in the language within their year group. A creative and innovative approach was implemented in order to develop teaching methodologies and openness to pedagogical development. When students have direct access to the Irish immersion experience, they benefit from the social coherence it affords. It also encourages the use of Irish as a functional medium. Despite careful control of the number of students admitted to the programme, the IM sector is having acute staff shortages in 2002. This is due mainly to many of the qualified teachers taking up employment in the Republic of Ireland. This, however, is only one of a cluster of factors which contributes to this situation. Student placements, proper resources and quota allocation are some of the constraints which have emerged and they have been a hindrance to the healthy implementation and development of a language policy. School placements outside NI, in the ROI and in the Gaeltacht might have a favourable impact on student numbers. Key staff are also needed to expand the teaching staff at third level and consequently the extension of the range of subject areas available. Resourcing constraints and underdeveloped strategic recruitment continue to restrict further expansion and development in the area of IM Education at present.

Robertson describes the provision for teacher training education in Scotland in general and for Gaelic-medium (GM) in particular. Teacher education in Gaelic takes place within the context of the BEd and PGCE courses. There is not as yet any parallel GM versions of these courses and the Gaelic element within them is quite limited and optional. Recruitment and the continuing shortage of GM teachers is the highest profile issue at the moment as the demand for teachers has far exceeded supply. Access to training is a further hindrance to the efforts to address the acute shortage of competently trained teachers. The main Gaelic speaking areas are in the West Highlands and far removed from Teacher Education Institutions, which does preclude certain sectors of the Gaelic speaking community's participation in teacher training and distance learning may alleviate this problem. At present no specific qualification is needed to enter GM education; there is no formal recognition given to special training undertaken by students and no benchmarks have been set. A recent General Teaching Council for Scotland (GTCS) report outlined some of the major deficiencies in the provision of GM training – Gaelic language competence, limited placement opportunities and under-developed classroom skills vis-à-vis the entire curriculum being delivered through Gàidhlig. Other deficiencies identified include non-compulsory nature of Gaelic courses and Gaelic related electives; provision over the four years of training uneven; school experience in GM classes limited and inadequate preparation in terms of methodology, bilingualism studies and pedagogical implications in immersion programmes. Teachers in GM education feel isolated which is further compounded by the lack of opportunities for professional development. A new national professional development initiative has recently proposed the introduction of a new category of Chartered Teachers and this may open the way for the introduction of modules and in-service courses leading to a qualification allowing teachers to engage in GM teaching. Politically, the focus has been on recruitment and the acute shortage of trained teachers and educational personnel. Local authorities perceive a need to establish some training provision to recruit a pool of students unable to go to TEIs in the larger cities. Inter-agency co-operation is needed if improvement in the provision of GM education is to be realised and strategic planning is necessary. Implementation of the GTCS Report would resolve many of the issues. All in all, a concerted programme of action is needed to bring about the necessary improvements in provision; awarding of certificates for GM teaching at primary and secondary level would be a major advance. The availability of adult immersion courses and appropriate access to them would certainly increase the pool of people available to GM education. Nevertheless, it is still felt that a sustained and co-ordinated marketing campaign directed at recruitment would produce dividends. It is hoped that Bòrd Gàidhlig na h-Alba will accord the highest priority to recruitment and that resources and the financial power to implement the relevant changes will be forthcoming.

Several papers address the thorny issue of assessment and curriculum in IM and in ordinary schools outside Gaeltacht areas in NI and in the ROI and in GM in Scotland. How is assessment in another language to be carried out? What standing will such outcomes have in society? What politics are involved in getting assessment practices accepted and up and running? These issues are discussed with regard to the Republic of Ireland by **John Harris** (ITÉ), Northern Ireland by **Seán Mac Nia** (Northern Ireland Council for the Curriculum, Examinations and Assessment), and Scotland by **Iain Mac Ille Chiar** (Inverness College). Their contributions bring to light many interesting facets of these topics and they reveal patterns of development and progression that should underpin further discussion and planning within these different but related sectors.

Harris has extensive experience in research assessment exercises over the last three decades. His contribution, therefore, is a significant one as he places a large amount of evidence before us. He is particularly concerned in his paper about how evaluation and monitoring are illustrative of learning processes and help identify ways in which teaching programmes could be made more effective. His results reveal various facets of the success and failures of government policies and therefore indicate in a practical way what lessons we have learned. The results of research show achievement of curricular objectives is quite variable but relatively unchanged over a period of 20 years or so. A new more comprehensive survey was carried out in April and May 2002 in 200 schools, covering ordinary, IM and Gaeltacht schools and the results of this survey when published will provide a yard stick for comparison with previous national surveys in the 70s and 80s, General academic ability and social class background are positively linked to general educational outcomes and achievement and this has been supported by various research results reported on by Harris. Furthermore, gender differences, regional/locational factors, home use of Irish and the use of Irish in target language outside the language lesson proper does influence proficiency in a positive way. The role of parental and pupil attitudes and interests on language outcomes and process-type information about classroom activities, including classroom observation, were subject to detailed analysis in what the author calls *The Twenty-Classes Study*. Its ultimate goal was to provide an explanation for pupil-to-pupil and class-to-class variation. Results showed pupils well disposed towards the language, parental support lacking in many cases but having a strong positive effect when present and pupils have a poor estimation of their own ability in Irish vis-à-vis other subjects. Courses are felt to be boring and old-fashioned and repetitive. Greater emphasis on communication and communicative activities in class shows pupils having higher achievements and less anxiety. Negative outcomes are associated with traditional language practices such as drills, etc. Pupil participation is higher when real communication is involved, those with lower language ability speak less often and are less attentive in class. The introduction of innovative materials followed the analysis of the previous project and on two fronts - The Communicative Materials Project and The ITÉ Teaching through Irish Project. The central goal of the former was to produce positive attitudes to learning Irish and communication and meaning negotiation was paramount. Correction of errors was not permitted during communicative activities but focused on afterwards. The latter project was initiated and tested in 50 third and fourth-grade classes (9-10 year olds) Lessons were original and not translations of English-based materials. The subjects chosen were Art and Science and pupil understanding and enjoyment of the subject were paramount considerations. This project also provided access to content-based teaching which incorporates elements of other subjects into target language teaching. It is quite clear that policy responses to the research results reported in Harris's paper must take into account the socio-linguistic context in which Irish is used and taught. Identifying contexts and situations where the use of Irish would be 'natural' has proven difficult and the level of authentic material available to teachers and pupils bears no comparison with that available for the major European languages. In conclusion, we need a more pro-active approach to the teaching and learning of Irish, a support system for teachers, parents and pupils, co-ordination of textbooks and other educational resources, adequate in-service training and the development of a more supportive out of school environment for the use of Irish.

Mac Nia offers some insights and opinions about assessment within the IM sector in NI. Achievement in IM schools in Irish, English and Mathematics at each Key Stage as compared to attainment by mainstream pupils are given and discussed. All in all, the IM schools are quite close to meeting the DENI targets as set for 2002. Level 2 performance in IM schools is on target, while a drop back occurs at level 3. This may be due to a natural developmental process in bilingual children. The problem is probably more acute in NI as the majority of children come from an English-speaking background with little or no support outside school. The dearth of material resources and the shortages of specialist subject teachers, especially at secondary level, influence outcomes. The reality of immersion programmes is that they produce bilinguals who are communicative in two languages, but lack the depth and breadth in their weak or minority language and this is reflected in attainment in current assessment arrangements. The Transfer Test (TT) is probably the most controversial area for IM pupils and teachers. The nature of the issues is quite complex and the validity and reliability of the testing of bilinguals is a hotly debated topic. The main arguments by IM proponents are that IM pupils should not be tested using instrumental techniques or on content that have been designed for monolinguals and that their bilingual 'competence' should also be considered vis-à-vis their weaker/stronger language. This debate is likely to continue and while the number of pupils taking the TT in Irish (less than 1%) remains low, it might seem more reasonable to suggest that the IM schools should adapt and meet the criteria of the TT, rather than the reverse. Much has been achieved by schools in recent years and, as they grow, curriculum provision broadens. Inherent difficulties, however, must be addressed in order to improve outcomes. Solutions must and can be found by mutual recognition of the existence of a problem, and a resolution found through co-operation with all parties involved, in an atmosphere which will allow openness and a realistic evaluation of common objectives and outcomes. The recently established CCEA IM advisory group should provide a real opportunity for constructive dialogue. As one of its briefs is the assessment of IM pupils and the development of materials, it is incumbent on all to take up the challenge and become involved in finding a mutually agreeable resolution to the on-going problems of assessment in All-Irish Medium Schools in NI.

Mac Ille Chiar gives a very personal account of his own experience in teaching Gàidhlig and his attitude towards assessment procedures. As a long-standing teacher of Scottish Gaelic at various age and ability levels, Mac Ille Chiar bemoans the fact that the Scottish educational establishment is obsessed by assessment, and that the situation has now reached breaking point. He discusses an independent report commissioned by the Scottish Education Department, which has recommended, in his view, sensible and substantial changes to the assessment of Gaelic immersion courses. He regrets that, so far, the report has not been implemented.

European Charter for Regional or Minority Languages **Part III**

The above papers show clearly that not only are there many needs not being met, but that these needs are not met by Part III of the *European Charter for Regional or Minority Languages* which, however worthily aspirational, reflects only the present deficiencies and does not offer the solutions – policies and structures – which are needed. A set of papers focussing on Northern Ireland as a case study are presented by **Stephen Peover** (Department of Education – DEL), **Janet Muller** (POBAL: Scátheagras Phobal na Gaeilge) and **Eugene McKendry** (Queen's University Belfast). Poever and Muller focus on Part III of the European Charter for Regional or Minority Languages but from very different perspectives, not totally exclusive, as we will see.

Poever is concerned with whether or not the needs of what he calls 'other-medium' education are being met by Part III of the Charter. This relates in particular to pre-school, primary and secondary education. Although his conclusion is that in terms of education a 'safety net' exists for minority languages, nevertheless, that same net may be spread too thinly along the ground. This provides very little dynamism for future development or for a resolution to some of the problems encountered synchronically. DEL has a statutory duty to encourage and facilitate development in IM education since 1998, which has led to significant changes to the criteria necessary to create new IM schools. Nevertheless, establishing a unit or a new school is still fraught with difficulties and is therefore a daunting task for parents and others to undertake. Institutional co-operation should be facilitated by the establishment of Comhairle na Gaelscolaíochta, which has representatives from the main educational partners. The main objective of the whole education system is the provision of high-quality education and the IM sector is no different. The central priority of minority language education in NI as elsewhere is to deliver a quality product thereby establishing a larger and critical mass of fluent Irish speakers to form the basis for a healthy and stabilised bilingual community. A clear long-term strategy must be put in place to recruit teachers who will deliver a standard of teaching and learning on a par with English-medium schools. The governance of schools in the case of minority languages can also prove to be contentious and fraught with difficulties. The transition of IM schools from being parent-led to being professionally managed is an area of difficulty if not handed properly. Schools are complex entities and require a range of skills and perspectives not always available within the parent body. Partnership between parents and management should prove more effective in the long run. DEL has, however, identified the whole area of governance as one which requires fundamental review and a consultation exercise is to be initiated in the near future. Co-ordination within the IM sector is to be ensured through Comhairle na Gaelscolaíochtana and the scale of difficulty facing CnaG in achieving and maintaining a consensus on the way forward, is not to be underestimated. The momentum created by the IM sector must be maintained and strengthened with the proviso that the pace of development does not outstrip the system's capacity to meet the needs of schools. Stagnation is to be avoided and ambition and realism is to be encouraged at all levels. These is an increasing emphasis on the creation of units rather than free standing schools over the years, and consequently a growing level of co-operation between the IM sector and CCMS has been created. The creation of a stable bilingual society in which Irish-speaking families have a need to have their children educated in the mother tongue is a legitimate goal of IM education. Achieving this goal will be the ultimate success to which we all aspire.

In her contribution, **Muller** is concerned with the success or otherwise of the provisions in Part III of the *Charter for Regional or Minority Languages* as it has been applied in NI. Education has a key and pivotal role in the promotion of minority languages. There are many gaps in the support system necessary for the development of IM education, teachers, in-service courses, teaching resources etc. It is unclear as to what exactly the British Government agreed within Part III of the Charter. There is no provision whatsoever to deal with the special requirements of pupils in IM schools, remedial resources, psychological assessment, and access to speech therapy etc. The Charter provides no supportive mechanism to investigate this lack of provision and addressing the lack of services. The creation of 'diglossic situations' proves insufficient in getting responses in Irish from the Public Service. It transpires that an answer in Irish to a letter written in Irish is not forthcoming, although several departments have ignored the Charter's own recommendations and have replied in Irish to correspondence received in that language. However, DCA, the department responsible for application of the Charter do not reply in Irish to correspondence in Irish. Providing employment for able bilinguals has been on the cards and every effort it seems has been made within the provisions of the Charter to arrest the use of minority languages within the Civil and Public services. The British Government's White Paper on Broadcasting does not even mention Irish, although Welsh and Scottish Gaelic are mentioned. On the whole it is felt that it is too early to surmise what the effect of the Charter will have on the long-term development of the Irish language in NI. Legislation from Westminster is required to activate the various proposals made within the Charter. We do not want this to become a checklist, as this would hinder development and change. The Committee of experts is still to report on the application of Part III of the Charter with reference to NI during the past year. It is hoped that they will deliver on the many issues that have arisen and that have not been responded to.

McKendry's paper addresses issues arising from curriculum review in NI and its consequences for the teaching and learning of Irish at secondary level. Curriculum review is on the agenda in Britain and NI. Research on Key Stage 3 languages provision has shown great variation in the study of languages and cast languages in general in a very bad light. Languages and creative arts were seen as 'least useful', Irish, RE, Drama and Art as becoming vocationally less relevant, and languages were seen as one of the most difficult area of the curriculum. Current language provision in NI is identical to models in existence in Britain, ranging from one modern language, to two or more languages offered in Year 8, a modular provision whereby students are exposed to several languages and a dual provision where all pupils in Year 8 study 2 languages (say German and Irish). 30% of schools in NI we are told follow the dual model as compared to 10% in Britain. This provision has both advantages and disadvantages, more exposure to different languages but less time to study either one. GCSE figures for post-16 examinations are useful markers of language health and outcomes and they are subjected to detailed examination in this paper. What they show is the overall strength of French and the increase in the numbers taking Irish despite it being available mostly in maintained schools. By 2002, however, the trend is away from Irish and towards Spanish. It can be claimed that approximately 10% carry Irish through to a-Level, compared to 15% for German and 20% for Spanish. These figures for Irish could indicate a worrying prognosis especially in light of the current CCEA curriculum review proposals. This move from knowledge and content to a skill-led curriculum is a fundamental shift and is a challenge to language learning in general and is a particular threat to Irish. It is up to Irish language interests in NI to take up the challenge.

Status and Standardisation of Scots

The theme of 'Language Planning and Education' conveniently embraces the papers on Scots. **T.P. Dolan** (University College Dublin) had been invited to address the issue of Scots in the Republic of Ireland. Far from being a distinctive linguistic entity, he shows that it is inextricable from the continuum of spoken English which he calls 'Hiberno-English' for it contains features transferred from Irish as well as others retained from Elizabethan English and different regions of England whence seventeenth-century planters inevitably came. "The voice of the nation," urges Professor Dolan, perhaps echoing his literary predecessors, "is Hiberno-English", and his focus is as much on a 32-county as 26-county nation. Dolan is by no means the first linguist to recognise the inter-relationship between Scots and Hiberno-English, and the predominance of the latter. But he is probably the first to raise the issue in the explicit context of the post-Good Friday debate. Whereas northern activists have been successful in obtaining new legislative provision for Scots in Northern Ireland, it is they – and not southern politicians – who are seeking similar arrangements in the South. The presence of Scots in East Donegal since the seventeenth-century settlement of Ulster is the exclusive basis upon which the argument for recognition for Scots in the South is based; by contrast, Dolan looks at the nature of that Scots and shows that its distinctiveness is not of itself but as a formative component of Hiberno-English and overall bounded-upness within the English system. Nowhere is this better demonstrated than in Dolan's dictionary of contemporary speech: *A Dictionary of Hiberno-English: The Irish Use of English,* first published in 1998, with a second edition due early in 1993, and now incorporated into an interactive website www.hiberno-english.com launched on 27 November 2002. Yet again, another distinguished linguist views Ulster-Scots as a form of English. Dolan's paper is therefore a major challenge to political activism throughout Ireland.

In Scotland, the situation is moving forward constructively – nowhere more so than within the Scottish Executive. In the discussion following his symposium address, both included in this volume, the Minister for Tourism, Culture and Sports, **Mike Watson**, accepts that he is the 'Minister for Scots' as he is also the 'Minister for Gaelic' – he is just not called by these titles. (A Minister for Scots is one of Dauvit Horsbroch's demands.) The Minister further accepts that Scots should be upgraded to Part III recognition by the *European Charter for Minority or Regional Languages* – who better as an advocate? He confirms that he has invited the Cross-Party Group on the Scots Language in the Scottish parliament to produce a strategy for Scots, and that there is a need for a 'Meek Report on Scots', but whether these will be the same document and, if different, how each will be organised remains to be worked out. These are all welcome contributions to the debate on Scots. Watson has yet to acknowledge that the United Kingdom created a policy for Scots by including Scots in the international legislation which it drew up with the Republic of Ireland over the future governance of Northern Ireland. We are eager for all those concerned – the Westminster Government, the Scottish Executive, and the Ministry of Tourism, Culture and Sport formally to recognise the existence of and applicability of the Westminster legislation to Scotland and to act upon them and provide appropriate funding. As we write, we await the feasibility study about an Institute for the Languages of Scotland and the outcomes of the talks being conducted by the Scottish Arts Council with Scots Language organisations, but these together with a strategy from the Cross Party Group, the CPG's thorough-going, far-reaching and irrefutable *Statement of Principles on the Scots Language*, now due to be launched in early 2003, all reinforce the need for immediate recognition by the Scottish Executive that the Westminster policy on Scots exists and that it is their policy, too, and also for urgent action, including the upgrading of Scots to Part III recognition of the *European Charter for Minority or Regional Languages*.

Not to do so only extends what **Dauvit Horsbroch** (University of Aberdeen) rightly describes as 'linguistic apartheid' or the treatment of Scots-speakers as third-class citizens, without any language-speaking rights. Horsbroch's strong paper shows how the case is compelling and in terms of equality and rights irrefutable. As Horsbroch urges:

> *Whit's gauin on is the UK govrenment is signin up tae Scots speakers alane - oot o aw the hamelt leids o the curn in the isles o Britain an Irland - tholes the brunt o discriminaition aff o officialdom. The Executive o Scotland an its pairlament haes biggit a langage apairtheid in Scotland the day whaur the richts o the Inglis-speakin communitie, an - til a faur lesser extent - the Gaelic ane, is upheld, but at the same tyme latsna the Scots speaker get a shot at onie richts. [...] Whit's gauin on is the UK govrenment is signin up tae Chairters ettlin at proveison for Scots (an ither leids) whyle the Executive an pairlament in Scotland is de facto nae-sayin thir obligaitions tae fowk on the grun. Regairdless o thair ain narra-nebbit opeinions politeicians maun tak tent o the UK govrenment's official ratificaition o the Chairter. Sae faur ceivil servans haes*

> *made licht o Scots; but it's no a licht maiter ava becis it taks tae dae*
> *wi aw leids, wi democracie an human richts.*

It is now time for the Minister in particular and the Scottish Executive as a whole to end this linguistic apartheid by signing Scots up to Part III of the European Charter, from which so much has to – and will inevitably – follow, and to create and implement a report and strategy for Scots.

By contrast, in Northern Ireland, **John Edmund** shows that with policies, an infrastructure in the form of the Ulster-Scots Agency / tha Boord o Ulstèr-Scotch, and good funding in place, strategies and plans can be formulated and wish lists considered. Although the classification of Ulster-Scots as a language or a dialect differs categorically between political activists and genuine linguists, the envisaged language development no more than listed in Edmund's paper will require the assistance of linguists for it to be carried out, so that in the furtherance of linguistic development in Northern Ireland there is a real prospect of fresh opportunities for research into Scots which can only be welcomed.

Planning for Scots is not restricted to status – it includes standardisation. Whereas, as Mike Watson acknowledges, it is not the job of the Scottish Executive to standardise Scots in a top-down way, and whereas, as a direct result of the legislation signed between the UK Government and the Republic of Ireland, the Ulster-Scots Agency has a remit for the standardisation of the language, the Scottish Executive does have a duty to recognise this policy on standardisation and to have it implemented by delegation to an appropriate body. Standardisation of Scots is far too important to be left to Northern Ireland – Scotland simply has to be involved. Furthering the demonstration of standardised Scots in *Linguistic Politics*, which contains six chapters, the present volume contains four more (Douglas, Horsbroch, Macafee, and Parsley), two of which deal with the issues and choices head-on. **Caroline Macafee** (University of Aberdeen) looks critically at the issue of Latinity in Scots prose style in the context of the voluntary shift towards Anglicisation. Although Romance borrowing was shared with English, Macafee shows that the distinctiveness of the Scottish mind comes out in lexical items not shared with English and possibly not of Latin origin. In support of the latter, Macafee describes and commends as a model for the present day what is traditionally known as Older Scots 'plain style' – *auld plain Scottis*. And **Ian Parsley** (Ultonian Solutions) urges that all standardised Scots should be authentic – not synthetic – and authenticity entails unavoidably a mixture of Scots and English vocabulary and grammar.[1] The papers in *Linguistic Politics* and here suggest to us that the standardisation of Scots is now within reach, and that the form which will emerge as the standardised variety will be that which comes to be used most often and accepted

---

[1] We regret that Marace Dareau's paper 'The Role of Dictionaries in the Standardisation of Scots' was not submitted for publication. It showed that, on the basis of recent collections from throughout Scotland during the 1980s and 1990s, clear spelling preferences were emerging. Whereas Dareau recognised that dictionaries are merely descriptive of practice, she nevertheless expected the preferences identified by the dictionaries to be followed by writers in the future – if, indeed, writers consulted dictionaries of Scots for guidance.

by all concerned, including native speakers, as 'authentic'. It will be a form which can cope with variation within limits. The creation of a *Dictionary of Parliament Terms in Scots*, currently in progress, has all the promise of setting an example.

Scots and Education

The second approach to Scots was that of education about Scots.[2] **Derrick McClure** (University of Aberdeen), who for so long and in his numerous works of advocacy[3], has championed the recognition of Scots as the language of the nation, rightly chastises the contributors to a volume showing how Scottish literature can be used in schools for the over-simplification of many of their statements about Scots. If Scots is to be taught in any shape or form, it has to be taught – and written about – accurately. **Sheila Douglas** (Royal Scottish Academy of Music and Drama) reflects upon her long and varied experience as a teacher and finds that she, too, has to be critical of other teachers providing interesting insight into the sociolinguistic attitudes about the Scots of schoolchildren prevailing in the classroom. For her, education about Scots amounts to "freeing Scots people from the inhibition against using their own tongue". **Liz Niven** summaries her Mercator Education pamphlet on *Scots: The Scots Language in Education in Scotland* (Ljouwert/Leeuwarden: Mercator-Education, 2002).[4] The pamphlet provides a useful overview of the educational provision – or serious dearth of provision – for Scots at all levels.

At the core of successful teaching is successful assessment and examining. Awareness-raising sessions may be fine, but it is through the institutionalisation of an examination process conducted nationally that a subject comes of age. It is therefore very encouraging to hear of the new realities for examinations on Scots at the Higher Still level. It is more important that the provision is now in place, than that the uptake is still low. **John Corbett** (University of Glasgow) shares his experience as a setter for those parts of the Higher Still examination in which Scots features or where material in or on Scots can be used. **Lydia Rohmer** (Glasgow College of Building and Printing) describes her experience as a teacher preparing pupils for such examinations. The inclusion of Lydia's experiences alongside those of John makes a very attractive combination, and we are privileged to be able to publish them.

---

[2] We regret that it was not possible for Jim Allen, of the Jordanhill Campus of Strathclyde University, to accept our invitation. In his degree course on primary school education, he includes a short compulsory session on Scots.

[3] J. Derrick McClure, *Why Scots Matters* (Edinburgh: Saltire Society, 1988, revised edition 1997), *Scots and its Literature*, (Amsterdam: Benjamins, 1995), *Language, Poetry and Nationhood: Scots as a Poetic Language from 1878 to the Present* (Edinburgh, Tuckwell, 2000), *Doric* (Amsterdam: Benjamins, 2002), (with A.J. Aitken and J.T. Low) *The Scots Language: Planning for Modern Usage* (Edinburgh: Ramsay Head, 1980).

[4] Copies are available free from Mercator-Education, PO Box 54, 8900 AB Ljouwert/Leeuwarden, the Netherlands. and www.mercator-education.org.

The growing experience and expertise on Scots in Scotland should almost certainly find a favourable response in Northern Ireland. We welcome the establishment of a unit at Stranmillis University College to prepare materials about Ulster-Scots for classroom use. Although education about Ulster-Scots must be the most constructive way forward, none of these approaches are addressed in **John Edmund's** paper on Ulster-Scots. There, the focus on education is about learning Ulster-Scots and the aspiration of a bi-lingual and tri-lingual society. But beyond assertions that such societies exist elsewhere and that, pedagogically, bi- and tri-lingualism are good things, it is not clear why those would work in Northern Ireland. How soon Northern Ireland might become a bi- or tri-lingual society, if ever, is hard to predict, but it might be useful to consider the issue of preparing for bi- and tri-lingualism at a future symposium.

Linguistic Human Rights and International Linguistic Diversity

We were absolutely delighted that **Tove Skutnabb-Kangas** (Roskilde University) and **Robert Phillipson** (Copenhagen Business School) accepted our invitation. We had long admired their work and knew that we could all learn from their rich experience of minority languages worldwide. Her presentation serves as an introduction to her monumental book *Linguistic Genocide in Education – or Worldwide Diversity and Human Rights.*

Skutnabb-Kangas offers very fresh and original analyses about Ireland and Scotland. She begins with an introduction which stresses the importance of mother tongue education as a human right – the most important linguistic human right – for (to summarise her reasons) it counteracts illiteracy, counteracts linguistic genocide, maintains the world's linguistic diversity, it reinforces the insufficiency of only English, it substantiates creativity, and it is correlated with biodiversity.

Skutnabb-Kangas then turns to Part II, Art 8 of the European Charter which deals with levels of provision in mother tongue education and considers the provisions for Scottish Gaelic and Irish through a serious of comparisons with Sweden and Finland with regard to Swedish, Finnish, Saami and Meänkieli (a type of Finish in Sweden, which suddenly came into existence when Sweden ratified the *European Charter for Regional or Minority Languages,* with which she considers parallels can be drawn with Scots). Her general conclusion is that "much official rhetoric of the EU and its member states endorses a commitment to linguistic diversity, but in practice many of the member states are perpetuating linguistic hierarchies in ways that counteract multilingualism and linguistic diversity, and represent a threat to many languages."

Skutnabb-Kangas then considers sign language in the context of the European Charter, from which it is excluded, and the Good Friday Agreement. In her view, the Deaf are a national linguistic minority to whom the European Charter should apply. Moreover, sign languages are completely independent languages and have nothing to do with the official (or other) oral languages of the countries where they exist. *All* languages, written, spoken and signed, are 'means of communication', even if there are other means of communication too, like pictures, dress, jewelry, and so on. Using visual signs rather than oral signs as a means of communication does not make a language less of a language.

Furthermore, Sign languages are historical languages in the same way as oral languages are, and some of them may have a longer pedigree than many oral languages. Sign languages thus fulfil all the requirements for being minority languages for the purposes of the European Charter.

Skutnabb-Kangas raises many pertinent questions for the glotto-political debate in Northern Ireland. She helpfully raises questions about new languages such as Meänkieli or Ulster-Scots, and further questions about languages of which the majority are second language speakers.

For all the diversity of languages in Europe, it appears that Europe has the poorest record for dealing with linguistic diversity. Skutnabb-Kangas urges the need for more protection of minority languages, more minority language education and more linguistic human rights, and that these are all directly linked to the democratisation of the world and defence of everybody's human rights.

The debate about Irish/Gaelic and (Ulster-)Scots is greatly enhanced by these many searching questions which Skutnabb-Kangas has posed.

In the context of our interests, and mindful of the European context, it is highly appropriate to look at the other end of the perspective and to consider the growing dominance of English in Europe, and its threat to national languages – not merely minority languages. Whereas, at the outset, the EU placed considerable emphasis of parity for the languages of the participating states, this is now changing – certainly in practice. In the context of language policy within the EU, and recognising that English is an integral dimension of ongoing processes of globalisation and europeanisation, **Robert Phillipson** addresses the following questions: Do the policies of the European Union, in its own institutions, and in affirmations of multilingualism, represent a real counter-weight to English as the linguistic Tyrannosaurus Rex? Do member states, transnational corporations, and professional associations have clear policies for ensuring that English is in harmonious balance with the heritage and rights of speakers of other languages? Where will current efforts in educational circles to promote English as a 'European lingua franca', stripped of Anglo-American norms, lead?" In his answer, Phillipson addresses the very real set of tensions and paradoxes which has come to exist between a very predominant common linguistic denominator or "lingua franca", which is also the language of the United States, the reality of multilingualism and the maintenance of its associated needs in an increasingly expanding and linguistically diversified Europe, and the possible preferencing of some languages over others as "working languages". Phillipson envisages that the fundamental paradoxes in EU language policy can only be tackled by implementing policies and practices which respect linguistic human rights and strengthen linguistic diversity, which in turn will mean more equitable multilingual communication and, in a word, change. His recommendations – 45 in total – are set out in his latest book *English-only Europe? Language Policy Challenges* to be published in January 2003.

In the debates in Ireland and Scotland, English is often assumed as uninteresting or left out of the equation. We welcome Phillipson's discussion of English within its new habitat in Europe for it is conducted in the same terms of linguistic human rights and respect for linguistic diversity in which the minority language debates are conducted in Northern Ireland and Scotland.

There follows responses to the last two papers by **Helen Ó Murchú** (Comhar ma Múinteoirí Gaeilge) and **Wilson McLeod** (University of Edinburgh).[5] **Ó Murchú** in her response to Skutnabb-Kangas and Phillipson's contributions to the symposium, outlines the implications of the facts and policies presented in their two papers and relates these, in particular, to educational matters with regard to the Irish language. They are expressed under six different headings. The first of these relates to language rights or more precisely human language rights. Legislation is often deficient due to political compromises as expressed in Part III of the Charter already mentioned. Application of the various instruments attached to legislation is what is important. Arguments based on democratic liberalism are often used by states to escape from their obligations. They may play a neutral or a concessionary role, but in each case they are inactive. The concepts of nation-state, monolingualism and uniting linguistic communities into single political entities are still pursued. Reference is often made to language – not language community. Secondly, the issue of differential power is discussed in the context of economic power. Thirdly, bilingual education must be of the highest quality and additive if it is to be successful. Immersion education means the development from an early age of new appropriate methodologies and proper pre-training of teachers to ensure they posses the highest linguistic skills and the educational training to teach content through the minority language. Our purpose is to create a fully bilingual context in which the two languages can play their part. Allegiance to local varieties and to different registers will be to the fore and the greatest challenge facing teachers in the class is to employ a variety of teaching methods and approaches to facilitate pupils with a wide range of academic abilities and an equally varied competence in the target and home languages. Mental colonization is to be avoided and authentic biculturism is to be cultivated throughout the entire educational programme. Fourthly, the problem of language versus dialect must be solved to consolidate communities. Fifthly, it is apparent that many of the minority languages are dependent on second language learners to make up the deficit arising from erosion of the native speaking population and this is a problem that needs to be addressed. Sixthly, the idea of language disadvantage is discussed. The power of English throughout the world is the greatest threat to all languages, including minority languages. Language rights can be argued for primarily within services provided by the state. However, these services are more and more likely to be available in the private sector, and hence the range of available services is on the decline.

In his reaction to the same speakers, **McLeod** focuses on the monolingual mindset, which is prevalent in Scotland and emerges in debates about language policy and planning. The debates tend to be on a low level. Scotland on the whole, he fears, identifies itself with the larger English-speaking world and has no particular interest in the spread of English throughout Europe or elsewhere. The European Charter already referred to in previous papers, has important implications and ramifications for the future survival of Gàidhlig as a minority language. It will not resolve many of the major problems already adhered to (shortage of trained teachers, inadequate third level teacher educational provision,

---

[5] A third response was given by Mari FitzDuff (University of Ulster), to whom we are grateful.

the fall in the native speaker population etc). The exact policies being pursued by the UK Government are minimalist in nature, poorly focused and quite confusing as shown in its First Periodical report in July 2002. It may prove significant in the long run that the Government's provision will henceforth be judged by international criteria and by international experts. This will undoubtedly create new opportunities for the Gaelic community and their campaigners to engage with authorities and Government agencies for the betterment of the Gàidhlig linguistic community.

Finally, the volume is completed by three research papers: 'Privileging Indigeneity' by **Anthea Fraser Gupta** (University of Leeds), 'The Irish Language and Socio-economic Development: Tradition, Modernity and Modernisation'' by **John Walsh** (Dublin City University), and 'War Zone Language: Language and the Conflict in Northern' by **Cordula Bilger** (Universität Zürich).

In the on-going political debate about regional and minority languages, **Gupta** refreshingly considers several central issues such as languages vs. people in the context of power, support and privilege, languages vs. people as domains of morality or deserving moral support, and the native vs. the migrant vs. increasingly the local nativisation of new language varieties. She addresses the myth of indigeneity operated by many nations which considers the 'indigenous' as more worthy than the imported. She acknowledges that an ideology of indigeneity establishes certain groups of people (usually determined by ancestry) as having a particular link with a piece of territory; and that a language linked to these people is in turn seen as an indigenous language. Many of the recognised regional and minority languages are privileged by indigeneity. Yet the privileging of these languages is not based on a need to ameliorate an underprivileged *group of people,* but on a sense of the cultural and affective importance of the *languages* – the European Charter for Regional or Minority Languages, after all, is carefully addressed at languages, as Ó Riagáin (2000, 2001) repeatedly stresses. She rewords the customary definition of regional or minority language in *European Charter for Regional or Minority Languages* to the following: "languages traditionally used by part of the population of a state that are not dialects of official languages of the state, languages of migrants or artificially created languages".

Gupta is sympathetic to efforts to redress the injustices and oppression of the past, to efforts to benefit underprivileged groups, and to efforts to answer the linguistic needs of as many members of society as practicable. But she does not consider these aims are answered by distinctions between 'indigenous' and 'migrant' languages, which can only be based entirely on a quasi-genetic territorial system that gives high values to the indigenous. She does not see that there can be any human rights or linguistic justification for prioritising groups defined as indigenous over groups not so defined (e.g. migrant).

Rather, she considers that speakers are active creators of their own sociolinguistic identity, and that languages are nothing other than social constructs, with human behaviour at the centre. For her, languages are not things that need or deserve protection – grammatical rules are not things worthy of preservation. She is prepared to agree that there are circumstances in which groups of people may need to take action to enable themselves to continue performing language in a desired way. She urges new exploration of the ethics and the pragmatics of privileging some languages over others. She concludes her critical deconstruction of indigeneity with the following challenge: "If language shift and language change are both inevitable (perhaps natural?) aspects of human behaviour, then efforts to direct linguistic behaviour will benefit from exploiting the pragmatic and ideological motivations of the people whose behaviour they wish to change, but must also recognise the inevitability and moral neutrality of language shift and language change." There is much here for the current glotto-political debate on Irish, Gaelic, and (Ulster-)Scots to reflect upon.

Walsh's contribution addresses the issue of the interaction of language, culture and economic development. He compares two Gaeltacht Commission reports published in 1926 and 2002, respectively. He found the 1926 report reticent about the introduction of modern processes and therefore that many of the recommendations made related to 'traditional' industries such as agriculture, fisheries, the seaweed-processing and the clothing industry such as weaving. They opposed the prevalent economic policy of the time known as laissez-faire, which formed a central component of the modernisation policies developed by classical and neo-classical economists. The Commission insisted on reliance on government intervention strategies on a fairly extensive scale. Indeed, the Government followed a policy of non-interventionism in Gaeltacht affairs. Idealisation of the Gaeltacht played no part in the 2002 commission's report as the decline in the intervening period was on such a large scale. It focused instead on theories about bilingualism and bilingual societies, language planning and language rights for Irish speakers. Development of the Gaeltacht is seen as being wholly language-centred. It supports the right of the people of the Gaeltacht to become stakeholders in the process of intervention by Governments and hence gives due recognition to the importance of various successive community-based initiatives that have helped stem the decline of the Irish language and emigration since the early 60s. The author argues that Government bias against modernisation policies throughout most of the 20th century has fostered a perception that Irish is of very little practical use but important only as a symbol of Irish identity. The linking of language, culture and economic development within new theoretical frameworks in the application of the recommendation of the 2002 report, may help form and develop more meaningful and workable strategies which will place language, and in this case Irish, at centre stage in any new initiatives.

As a critical linguist, **Bilger** is interested in how people from different communities or people with different political backgrounds speak 'different languages' and in the relationship between social structures, ideological processes, and language. She wants to show that every act of linguistic expression is somehow 'ideologically' motivated, that there is always a reason why somebody says or writes something in one particular way and not in another. She illustrates her ideas by examining how the British and Irish Governments managed to find sets of words on decommissioning acceptable to the republicans, but still carrying the other parties along. One of the key claims of Critical Linguistics is that language does not only encode power structures in society, but that language is itself instrumental in enforcing power differences. Language is never a mirror of reality. Language is "a refracting, structuring medium" because presenting anything through language always involves selection – not just at the level of lexical choice and terminology, but also in syntax since it is the latter which determines the perspective in a statement. Her analyses of how agentivity, passivisation, and nominalization, can be explored to produce vagueness and ambiguity impressively reinforce that considerable care has been taken with the drafting in English of crucial Troubles documents.

Conclusion

The accumulation of these summaries in this short overview provides a not too uncritical insight into the state of some of the current glotto-political issues in Northern Ireland, the Republic of Ireland, and Scotland – the archipelago – at the end of 2002.[6] To all our contributors, to whom we are deeply grateful, we have tried to give a fair hearing, not least to those who wrote in Irish and in Gaelic. To bring together so many key stakeholders between the same set of covers and to shape their outcomes into a reasonably coherent volume – now for the third year running – has proven deeply satisfying. We are committed by the AHRB grant to a fourth symposium in 2003 and look forward to welcoming as many friends and colleagues old and new from 10-12 September 2003.

---

[6] We regret that the papers from the final session on Research Needs did not materialise for this volume.

Symposium Address

Carmel Hanna, MLA

Thank you for the kind invitation to attend this dinner in this magnificent hall – so well refurbished last year. I am delighted to give this brief and rather personal talk on the Government's role and my role in some of the issues which you have been discussing the past few days.

For those of you who are strangers to the governance of Northern Ireland, I should explain that my role as Minister for Employment and Learning encompasses all of the post-16 education and training issues outside of the secondary school system. At the time of devolution, we brought together the functional responsibility for higher education, further education and vocational training to provide a comprehensive and coherent approach to lifelong learning.

I have been aware of previous symposia on this general theme of language and politics. Indeed I am pleased to note that one of my predecessors, Seán Farren, has spoken at one of the previous symposia.[1] And that many officials from the Northern Ireland Executive and officials from agencies, financially supported by the Government, have taken part in this event and on previous occasions.

As you are all aware, the background to the present upsurge of interest in language and the promotion of culture has been given new life by the Good Friday Agreement and the subsequent setting up of the North-South Implementation Bodies – in relation to Irish and Ulster Scots. These agreements were inspired and informed by the European Charter for Regional or Minority Languages. I am glad to see that you launched here yesterday a research report on the outcomes for Irish arising from the ratification of that Charter by the UK/Westminster Government a year ago. I know that my colleague, Michael McGimpsey, at the Department of Culture, Arts and Leisure, has taken a keen interest in that issue.

It is also heartening for me to see that John Kirk and Dónall Ó Baoill have edited and published a series of proceedings arising from the previous symposia and I see from the brochure of their imprint, Cló Ollscoil na Banríona, that they intend to publish several other volumes by the end of 2002. These publications which are obviously filling a much-needed gap, have been well received and received critical acclaim. Professor Donald MacAulay has written that "the publication of these volumes from Queen's University Belfast has greatly added to the stock of information and comment available on questions relating to the languages of Ireland and Scotland in their linguistic, social and political aspects".[2]

---

[1] Seán Farren, 'Institutional Infrastructure Post-Good Friday Agreement: The New Institutions and Devolved Government', in eds. John M. Kirk and Dónall P. Ó Baoill *Language and Politics: Northern Ireland, the Republic of Ireland, and Scotland* (Cló Ollscoil na Banríona, 2000, 121-125.

[2] Donald MacAulay, Review of *Language and Politics: Northern Ireland, the Republic of Ireland, and Scotland, Language Links: the Languages of Scotland*

I welcome that one of your main topics this year has been Irish and Gaelic-medium education. The growth of Irish-medium education has brought into sharp focus the practical requirements of teaching and provision of adequate teaching resources. I have provided resources to St Mary's University College for teacher training in this area.

I do appreciate that other issues were to be addressed, such as availability of teaching resources including books and these days computer-based learning packages, technical, adult and parent training. Above all, it needs appropriate assessment tools – a topic which I gather was discussed yesterday. For assessment has a lasting impact for future generations in employment and access to further education and in their capabilities and their contributions in the workplace. It is the Executive's intention to again address Irish Medium education on targets in the Programme for Government and I am certain that the Education Minister, Martin McGuinness, will consider the reports of this event most closely.

One of my major tasks in this area is to address the issue of transfer of young people from the Irish Medium schools to third level education and the world of work. This poses significant questions of continuing academic or vocational learning. The practical difficulties facing us are considerable and finding the balance between enhancing more general learning and supporting and protecting Irish language skills, will prove an interesting challenge.

We are already aware of the need for tertiary-sector provision in certain areas – especially the need for high-quality translators, competent bilinguals in the media; the Good Friday Agreement commits us to enhancing Irish language broadcasting; not to mention the need for such translators in public services such as the health services and law. It has great potential for growth. My Department has been working closely with the Department for Culture, Arts and Leisure on these issues.

Job opportunities in an Irish language environment, whilst expanding, will remain relatively limited in the medium term at least. I will be consulting with the Irish Language groups here over coming months to try to determine a clearer policy in relation to vocational learning and in that context have been seeking to benefit from the experiences of the South and of Wales.

Considering the heated debate in certain public arenas in Northern Ireland and at this and previous symposia, it remains to be seen what level of support and provision comes to be adopted for Ulster Scots.

One has the feeling that a lot more research needs to be undertaken about so many different aspects of this policy.

These symposia are important because they are not only North-South, but also East-West, and they stress above all historical, linguistic, cultural contexts between Ireland and Scotland. The ongoing research reported at these events makes a worthy contribution to a better understanding of ourselves as people ... where we have come from, and where we are going. I am delighted to see Mike Watson, the Scottish Minister for Tourism, Culture and Sport here, for I consider

and Ireland and *Linguistic Politics: Language Policies for Northern Ireland, the Republic of Ireland, and Scotland*, each edited by John M. Kirk and Dónall P. Ó Baoill, in *Scottish Language*. 21: 2002: 73-77.

it a good thing that the devolved Governments in Scotland and Northern Ireland can now deal more directly and more easily with one another, particularly when the issues are shared than was previously possible. This event continues the linguistic and cultural links between Scotland and Northern Ireland which have gone on in both directions by different groups of people over centuries and show that no-one side can really monopolise that special relationship. In other ways, these relationships help with economic development and cultural enhancement and promote valuable tourism.

It is important to me as Minister that people from overseas participate in the work of our local universities, as demonstrated by the participation in this event of people from many different countries. In this case, I believe the furthest travelled has come from the University of Waikato in New Zealand demonstrating that we share more than a love of Rugby football. Part of the normalisation of Northern Ireland society, following the ceasefires and the Good Friday Agreement, has been its growing internationalisation.

It is good to see John and Dónall through events like this working in an interdisciplinary way – and supported by two of the biggest schools in the Humanities at Queen's. This kind of co-operation is for our mutual benefit. Leaders are needed in all societies, but while John and Dónall have clearly shown the way, it is clear that the contributors to the symposia and resultant publications have evidently responded to their call …. We all hope to see more in the future.

More Progress for Scots in the Twenty-first Century

Irene McGugan, MSP

Thank you for your warm welcome. I very much appreciate the opportunity to update delegates on two of the initiatives I mentioned at the Symposium last year.

I have to say it is still a bit awesome as a politician to speak about language to a room full of experts. My authority to speak to you comes only from the fact that I am a Member of the Scottish Parliament and convene the Cross Party Group in the Parliament on the Scots Language – a group whose membership and contact list increases with every meeting. Since you would not expect us to agree on everything, we compromise and negotiate, and so far, this has allowed us to be recognised as a powerful, united voice advocating for the language.

Of course we don't just act collectively. Individually, some of our members are making substantial progress of their own. In the last few weeks, we have seen the publication of the *Dictionary of the Older Scottish Tongue*, the launch of a *Scots Language Learner* by Colin Wilson, and the first 4 of 16 titles to be published under the Itchy Coo imprint (Susan Rennie, *Animal ABC* and *Kat an Doug on Planet Fankle,* Matthew Fitt et al. *The Hoose o Haivers*, and James Robertson, *The Scottish Parliament* – see www.itchy-coo.com). The Itchy Coo series is specifically for use with children and young people in schools. At a time when the Parliament is considering how best to support Scotland's languages, and some might say, doing precious little to take forward that aim, it is very apt that one of these books is effectively a history textbook in Scots about the Scots Parliament.

I know there have been other recent achievements by members of the CPG – but I mention these particularly because they are good examples of printed material in Scots – something still in short supply.

I will come shortly to describe the Cross Party Group's efforts to encourage the language and secure its status as a national language of Scotland, but first I want to outline some of the recent political contexts, which has shaped our actions and intentions.

Firstly, the *National Cultural Strategy*. Published in August 2000, it may have gone some way towards promoting the ongoing debate about the Scots language, but it is widely agreed that, two years on, there is little evidence of a cohesive policy, even less evidence of progress in turning the objectives into practical reality, and that far more needs to be done.

Secondly, delegates will remember that despite the urgent need for statistics on how many people speak the language, and where, the Parliament rejected a question on Scots in the 2001 Census. During the summer of 2002, requests that Scots be featured on the signage in the new Parliament building were likewise refused, in favour of English, Gaelic and Braille.

Finally, with regard to the *European Charter on Regional or Minority Languages*, which is the focus of our discussion this morning, the fact that Scots has been designated as a regional language under Part II rather than Part III is, I would suggest, indicative of the fact that Scots is viewed as an inferior language.

This means that there isn't as much onus or impetus to implement specific measures in terms of education and culture. If further proof were needed, when I asked the Minister directly in a Parliamentary Question what action would be taken by the governments of Holyrood and Westminster to comply with the terms of the Charter in respect of Scots, I was advised that no such action was required.

Indeed the recently published *Initial Periodic Report* outlining UK compliance (or otherwise) with the Charter reveals that, against a number of questions, there was no response in respect of the Scots language. The UK Government was unable to indicate any measures taken to make better known the rights and duties deriving from the application of the Charter, or to indicate the means by which they have facilitated or encouraged the use of regional or minority languages in speech and writing, in public and private life.

Indeed not – because they have in reality done nothing. Contrast this with Liechtenstein, who printed a report about their application of the Charter, despite the fact that regional or minority languages in the sense of the Charter *do not exist* in their state. Liechtenstein ratified the Charter in order to underline the importance it attaches to the Charter as an instrument for the protection and promotion of regional or minority languages as a threatened aspect of Europe's cultural heritage, and to contribute to the entry into force of the Charter.

However, it is entirely valid to look to Europe for examples of policies adopted to support lesser-used languages and examine how they might be applied in Scotland. And the European Charter is not the only tool from Europe, which we can use.

The *Universal Declaration of Linguistic Rights or Barcelona Declaration* was, you will recall, drawn up in the 1990s, and contains in a single document an inclusive body of principles for governance which can be put into practice for upholding, promoting and respecting language diversity throughout the world today.

Using this as a basis, the Cross Party Group has set about drawing up its own 13 Principles, or Statements of Intent for Scots. Generally speaking, each of our Statements of Principle takes as its starting point an article from the *Universal Declaration of Linguistic Rights*, either in full or in part, which we hold to be applicable to the situation for the Scots language today, practicable for use in addressing the relevant issues around the language, and requiring to be urgently actioned in order to protect and further a thriving Scots language.

It starts by asserting that Scots is a language and demanding an end to prejudice and discrimination – straightforward and achievable we thought – and then it goes on to make particular suggestions in respect of education, heritage and indeed politics. One of these is that "a kennin o Scots is necessar tae an understaunin o Scotland." Government, educational institutions and the people of Scotland in general, working together, all have it in their power to put together a language policy that includes recognition of the validity and status of Scots. Such a policy would chime with the wider and ongoing transformation of the political and cultural attitudes that make for a well, whole and equal multicultural and multilingual society.

It is written in a register of Scots which does not suit everyone – but that is what I meant when I referred to "compromise" within the group. We wanted the language to be accessible to the widest range of people, so its vocabulary and common origins with English are readily identifiable.

We are not saying that this is the way Scots should always be written – we are saying that this is appropriate language for this particular document. We intend to launch the document – at our own expense – in November 2002.

You might wonder where exactly that will take us, but at our Cross Party Group meeting in September, the Minister for Tourism, Culture and Sport accepted our invitation to attend, and impressed members with his willingness to listen to our concerns. He went so far as to suggest that the group should draft a strategy for Scots to inform the Scottish Executive what changes are needed. Our intention is that the Statement of Principles will provide the basis for this strategy statement, which should, in my view, encompass the requirement for an Agency or Board for the language, and adequate funding.

Coinciding with that will be the presentation of my own report on languages to the Education, Culture and Sport Committee of the Parliament. My task was to inquire into the role of educational and cultural policy in supporting and developing minority languages in Scotland, and that is the second initiative I want to mention. In common with the Statement of Principles, it also has taken a long time to put together.

Without giving too much away about the findings and recommendations, there was overwhelming evidence pointing to the need for a language policy for Scotland. Someone else who came to this conclusion was Professor Joseph Lo Bianco – a languages expert from Australia, whom I had the pleasure of meeting on his last visit to Scotland. He said that a country which has no specific language policy for its indigenous heritage language(s), does in fact have a covert policy. Its policy is to let the languages die out. I think that is a very powerful argument.

In this report, I also want to highlight the benefits of bilingualism and multilingualism, rather than monolingualism, which has been looked upon by British society as the norm for a very long time. Multilingualism doesn't need to be viewed as having everyone fluent in every language, but rather it should be seem as striving towards the capacity to use a number of languages fluently.

In its publication *A Vision and Mission for 2000-2005*, the Welsh Language Board states that:

> There is now a general acceptance in Wales that bilingualism is beneficial for individuals and communities. For individuals, bilingualism provides wider communication opportunities, giving access to two windows on the world by being bicultural, enabling access to two literacies, raising self-esteem, enabling a secure sense of identity and widening employment opportunities. For communities, bilingualism provides continuity with the past, cohesiveness for the present and a source of collaborative endeavour for building the future." (Welsh Language Board: *A Vision and Mission for 2000-2005*)

Other recommendations will, include consideration of the Cross Party Group's Statement of Principles as an overarching policy for securing the future of Scots, and I will, of course, draw attention to the terms of the European Charter. In particular, attention will be drawn to the extent to which the government falls short of its current obligations under Part II, and the case will be put for upgrading to Part III.

I don't want to present an overly optimistic view of the future of our language, especially when I am not convinced that the political will is there. However, what I hope I have done today is illustrate where developments are taking place. And we should welcome these, however insignificant they may seem to some. There was even an article supportive of the language in the *Guardian* earlier this week. Can you imagine that?

Finally, I was pleased to note Derrick McClure's comments about the language no longer being simply the province of language scholars and men of letters. I agree with him that it is a very good thing that the issues around Scots have come out of the ivory tower and into the workaday world of politics, education and social work.

I have always maintained that we will never achieve all that we want for the language until the arguments are taking place not in Universities or even in the Parliament but in the pubs and workplaces and schools of Scotland. That remains one of my ambitions for the language.

Towards a Language Policy for Scotland

Mike Watson, MSP

Introduction

It is a genuine pleasure to be here, partly because, as Dr Kirk said, it is the first time that there has been a Scottish Minister with responsibility for culture and language development. That comes largely as a result of devolution. Equally, however, it gives me the opportunity to say a little about what we are trying to do in the Scottish Executive. I will also say something about the groups that have established themselves for the Scots language — and, indeed, Gaelic — in the Parliament, something I feel is a strength of devolution. It is a pleasure to be here and to have been asked to address such a distinguished symposium.

I should first of all give three caveats. First, while I was an education lecturer for a time, I do not regard myself as an academic, and I am not going to speak in the breadth or depth undoubtedly possible for those of you who have studied the languages of Scotland and Ireland. Secondly, it is not my intention to stray into the politics — or the linguistic politics — of Ireland or Northern Ireland; obviously, anything that I say about Scotland is not necessarily intended to be extrapolated to the situation here. Thirdly, as I am speaking in Northern Ireland — and this might disappoint Dr Kirk just a little — I am not going to be making any new policy statements concerning the languages of Scotland or, indeed, any other matter, for that would be a discourtesy to the Scottish Parliament. However, I will be happy to take what I learn here back to my colleagues in the Scottish Executive and, where appropriate, to the Scottish Parliament.

I know that your conference is now in its third year, and the fact that it has attracted so many people from Scotland — and I met a few yesterday evening — shows that languages are a very important part of the cultural heritage of the country and are valued as part of our cultural wealth. In Scotland, of course, we have two predominant indigenous languages, Gaelic and Scots, and it is interesting to see points of similarity as well as points of difference. Gaelic and Scots are defined as regional or minority languages, and both language communities feel with some justification that they have suffered over the years from the dominance of English. To a large extent, of course, the political position is defined by reference to English. As the dominant language not only of the rest of the UK but in many international contexts, English casts a shadow over everything done for the development of either Scots or Gaelic. For anyone in Scotland to go about his or her daily life, to appreciate films on television, never mind benefit from education or international business, fluency in English is essential. Those who speak Gaelic or Scots still have to accommodate their languages to a culture in which English is inevitably dominant.

The Gaelic Language

While there are similarities in the situations of Scotland's two languages, there are also many differences. Gaelic is spoken by around 70,000 people in Scotland. That figure was announced in the results of the 1991 census. The 2001 census results are due out fairly soon, and most people feel that the figure will have dropped, though I hope not too substantially. Gaelic-speakers will still represent around 1·5% of the population of Scotland. Part of the language's difficulty is, as it was described to me, that it is effectively incomprehensible to non-speakers in the rest of the population — quite unlike Scots, of course.

Like other minority languages in Europe, Gaelic will be in danger of ceasing to be a spoken community language if certain actions are not taken. I am aware that it is my responsibility to ensure that that does not happen. Most people in Scotland agree that, if Gaelic is to survive, it needs some degree of public support in the learning of the language and its transmission to the next and future generations and in the provision of opportunities and incentives for people to use it. The question is how much and what degree of public support is necessary, and I have never found anyone who could give me a quantifiable figure. We are also increasing the resources that we are putting into language development and cultural aspects of Gaelic. It is never enough, but we will continue to do what we can as an Executive, and as far as possible that will be informed by the Gàidhealtachd, the Gaelic-speaking community itself.

In contrast, the Scots language is widely spoken in Scotland — I suppose it is difficult to estimate how many people use it, since it is on a linguistic continuum with English; many of us literally use Scots words and expressions in sentences that are otherwise English, and, indeed, vice versa, and in many cases we do not appreciate that we are doing so. There are thousands, if not millions, of Scots who use the Scots language in their daily business in a manner which, I suspect, speakers and advocates of many other minority languages would envy. However, I appreciate that there are issues concerning the status of Scots and its general lack of visibility in Scotland. The different circumstances of the two languages have naturally meant that public actions in relation to them have been quite different. I will talk first about Gaelic before moving on to Scots, finally mentioning what we are doing in relation to our obligations under the *European Charter for Regional or Minority Languages*.

The Scottish Executive — and before that the Scottish Office — have had a programme of support for the Gaelic language. Gaelic-medium education was first supported about 15 years ago and is now available in about 60 primary schools, with around 1850 children been taught in Gaelic-medium education at primary school. There are a dozen secondary schools in Scotland, with around 300 pupils having some of their subjects taught through the medium of Gaelic, though not the entire curriculum, and I freely admit that not enough are taught in Gaelic-medium secondary schools. There is obviously a big gap between the 1850 pupils in primary and 300 in secondary education, and that is a matter of concern for me. However, there is obviously a limit to what can be done.

My general view of the situation is that there should be provision wherever there is demand for Gaelic-medium education; where parents want their children to be taught in Gaelic-medium settings, that choice should be available. The question is, 'What should trigger it?'. Should there be 5, 10 or 15 pupils before the facility is made available? I currently live in Glasgow, where there is a dedicated Gaelic-medium primary school. Of the 150 or so pupils at that school, 60% of their parents do not speak Gaelic, but they want their children to be educated through Gaelic, and they are clear on the educational benefits of doing so, quite apart from the cultural benefits. That is an important point to make.

The Executive supports a number of organisations to promote Gaelic or particular aspects of it. We also provide funding for the Gaelic Broadcasting Committee. That has a budget of about £8·5 million a year out of a total budget for Gaelic of around £13 million.

Two years ago, a ministerial advisory group on Gaelic was set up by the Scottish Executive under the chairmanship of Professor Donald Meek, whom I expect many of you will know; It is nice to see Ken MacKinnon here today. The group published its report in May 2002, recommending, among other things, that the Executive set up a new public body for Gaelic, which it referred to as 'Bòrd na Gàidhlig'. In June this year, when I spoke at the Comann na Gàidhlig congress in Nairn, I announced that we would be setting up the new public body. The positions of chairperson and members of the board have been advertised; applications have now been received and are being considered. It is my intention that the new body will be operating before the end of this calendar year. I feel I have moved quite quickly on that.

Another suggestion was that steps should be taken to secure the status of Gaelic in Scotland. That terminology is not precise and has certainly been difficult to pin down. I have not been able to announce that the Executive is moving on that, for example, in the shape of a Gaelic Language Act, but the door is not closed on it. I have not gone far enough, I am aware, to satisfy most people in the Gaelic community, but it is something that we are moving towards, and I have no hesitation in saying that in the next session of the Scottish Parliament — as in Northern Ireland, we have elections on the first of May next year — there will be movement on it. It is my intention — and I can currently give you only a personal commitment on it — that there will be some form of legislation in the second term of the Parliament. I am already in discussions with political colleagues — for it will have to be a party political step — to make some commitment for that in the election next year. I accept that we have not yet moved on that part of the report from Donald Meek's group, but it is clearly something of which I am aware. I am also discussing it with the Cross-Party Group in the Scottish Parliament on Gaelic, which, as the name suggests, does not have a party political bias. It involves Members of the Scottish Parliament who have a genuine interest simply in advancing Gaelic language and culture.

Although the largest part of the Gaelic budget is spent on broadcasting, most people see education as a key to the future survival and health of the language. Gaelic-medium education has been reviewed by a team led by Professor Richard Johnstone of Stirling University, and the conclusion — not surprisingly, to my mind — was that pupils in Gaelic-medium education clearly gained broad educational benefits from growing up bilingual and having access to two cultures. There are clear benefits, not least in further language skills when they move to secondary school. Even so, the progress of Gaelic-medium education has not been as sustained as I had hoped. It continues to grow in numbers, but that increase has slowed somewhat, and the intention is certainly that that it should be restored. Therefore, the Scottish Executive are taking action in two areas to promote Gaelic-medium education, the first being measures to increase the number of teachers. The number of new graduates qualified to teach in Gaelic-medium education this year was 17, which compares to an average of 11 a year over the past five years. We are also promoting the production of teaching materials in Gaelic. Both those measures, I hope, will help give confidence to the Gaelic community that Gaelic-medium education is now an established and successful part of the Scottish education system; there is funding to underscore that commitment.

I do not have time to say very much about the Gaelic organisations. The ministerial advisory group recommended the production of a plan for Gaelic to which the organisations could contribute. That plan should lead to a more effective co-ordination of measures and support for Gaelic. Bòrd Gàidhlig na h-Alba will be the umbrella body overseeing all the actions of the various Gaelic organisations.

Part of the Gaelic programme is support for the Columba Initiative, with which many of you will have had contact; it is among the sponsors of this symposium. We consider the links between the Gaelic-speaking communities of Scotland and Ireland, both North and South, as valuable both in their own right and for the future well-being of the language in Scotland. It is immensely encouraging to young people growing up in a minority linguistic community to see that there is another related language which has a valuable and lively culture as well as an active social life; that is not to be understated. I hope that the schools' exchanges, the youth parliament and the arts visits will prove enduring and of increasing value to young people from Scotland and Ireland over the next few years.

The Scots Language

The Scots language, as I said, is widely spoken across Scotland, and it is therefore an important part of our country's cultural heritage. The poetry of Robert Burns is one of the most distinctive and unifying factors for Scots in Scotland and, indeed, in our national image internationally. Dr Kirk suggested that I might want to speak about the standardisation and revival of Scots. I may not meet his hopes, for it is not really my responsibility or that of the Scottish Executive to standardise the Scots language.

I can see that there is a point of weakness, in that the language does not have a standard written form, varying from place to place across the country. However, different people obviously have different views on the matter, and I suggest that it is not a matter on which a Government — not even a Scottish Government — should set about promulgating rules or laying down the law. If it happens, it will happen because of the various communities speaking the Scots language; that is where the lead should come from. A top-down approach might be counter-productive in that respect.

In other aspects, however, I hope that I can be more encouraging. The guidance which the Executive gives to schools and teachers is that pupils should be encouraged to understand and appreciate writing in the Scots language, whether in the classics of literature or in contemporary newspapers, and that they should be encouraged to develop their abilities to express themselves, whether in English or in Scots. In the past, teachers were often considered to be a source of prejudice against the Scots language. I can remember myself having certain aspects of the Dundonian with which I grew up literally squeezed out of me by teachers who said that there was no prospect of getting any meaningful employment if I retained the Dundee accent or some of the Dundee terms. That was common across Scotland and, indeed, in many cases, as I hear now, is still the case. However, more teachers are now much more sympathetic to recognising that Scots is a language which most Scots schoolchildren bring with them to school and use in the playground and among themselves. Why should that be different from the way in which they are taught, the interaction they have with teachers or, indeed, the way in which the language is used in examinations? That case is now less difficult to sustain, because there is a great deal that is positive for the Scots language in our schools. When I met the Cross-Party Group on the Scots language in the Scottish Parliament on 10 September 2002, one of the main demands was simply that the Executive should make a suitable public statement recognising that a great deal is being done in support of the Scots language.

The second main area of public support comes under the remit of the Scottish Arts Council. It supports the dictionaries of the Scots language, the Dictionary of the Older Scottish Tongue, which was completed last month after 75 years of work, and the Scottish National Dictionary, and both those projects are being taken forward by a new body, Scottish Language Dictionaries, supported by the Scottish Arts Council. The Arts Council also supports other bodies concerned with the Scots language, and it supports new writing in Scots. That includes awards for writers such as Janet Paisley, who is a member of our Cross-Party Group in the Parliament, literary magazines which publish writing in Scots, and projects to produce new work for schools, such as 'Itchy Coo'. That project recently produced four books for young people, and I am sure that you have seen some of them during the symposium.[1]

As ever, it will be argued that not enough is being done, but it shows that the public body concerned with literature in Scotland is giving serious consideration to that part of our culture and helping to ensure that it remains living and vigorous.

It is fair to ask where the Executive goes from here in relation to support for the Scots language. In his speech yesterday evening, Dr Kirk suggested that there should be a Scots language agency along the lines of the Ulster-Scots Agency, and that may indeed be what is decided as the most appropriate route for the Scots language. I learned a great deal about the Ulster-Scots Agency this morning in a meeting with Dr Linde Lunney and her fellow board member, John McIntyre, together with Professor John Wilson of the Institute of Ulster-Scots Studies at the University of Ulster.

There are indeed lessons to be learnt from the progress being made by the agency regarding Ulster-Scots, but I would be open to the charge of failing to consult widely enough if I were to say at this juncture what I intended to do to develop Executive policy on the issue. What I will say is that I want to hear the views of the people in Scotland who are at the heart of efforts to promote the language and properly establish its status. There is an effective cross-party group

---

[1] Susan Rennie, *Animal ABC* and *Kat an Doug on Planet Fankle,* Matthew Fitt et al. *The Hoose o Haivers*, and James Robertson, *The Scottish Parliament* – see www.itchy-coo.com .

in the Parliament, which is an example of the Parliament's accessibility and its ability to link with and benefit from the expertise of groups in civic society in our country. That group is involved in producing its statement of principles, and I will want to consider them in due course before resuming discussions with it. When I met it last week, I also invited it to harness that expertise by consulting on and producing for me a strategy for the development of the Scots language — not an attempt to duck the issue as far as I am concerned — and the group agreed to do so. I welcome that enthusiasm, for there is no greater body of knowledge on the Scots language than that group, and it seems to me to make sense to look no further for the drafting of the strategy which will take the language forward.

I am certainly willing to assist in using that strategy, which is produced as a means of developing the Executive's policy on Scots. In the longer term, a key will be investment in education, which is not strictly my responsibility, but, once again not trying to duck the issue, we have a very firm policy of cross-cutting between Departments in the Scottish Executive, between Ministers, and between officials in the various Departments, something that in my experience works effectively in a number of areas in my portfolio. I will develop that with my education colleagues and take forward the argument.

Statements by the Executive of our good intentions regarding the status of the Scots language will, I hope, signal our commitment to building on the recognition which has already been accorded to the language. That stems from the *European Charter for Regional or Minority Languages*. The UK Government, as you will be aware, signed the *European Charter for Regional or Minority Languages* two years ago, and ratified it last year in respect of Welsh, Gaelic and Irish. Ratification commits the member state to implementing at least 35 of the 65 paragraphs in Part III of the Charter. We are able to do that for Gaelic in Scotland, and the UK's first report indicates the measures that we have already taken.

In relation to the Scots language, there was some debate as to whether it should be considered a language or only a dialect. I dipped my toe in that water at the Cross-Party Group last week, and my ears are still ringing, but the view had been taken, when the UK Government announced its intention of signing the Charter, that Scots will be firmly regarded as a language. As far as I know, that represented the first official recognition of Scots as a language. I note that the Government in Northern Ireland has similarly recognised that Ulster Scots should be considered a language in its own right. That is only natural, and it is very much demonstrated by the events which have followed the Good Friday Agreement.

Part II of the European Charter requires a member state to remove discrimination against the indigenous language and to take measures to support it, and that we are doing through treating Scots as a regular part of educational and cultural life in Scotland. In Scotland, the curriculum is not prescribed nationally. It is up to local authorities to develop according to their own priorities, and even my colleague the Education Minister cannot lay down what will be in the curriculum across the whole country. Similarly, the Executive funds literature and arts through the Scottish Arts Council, which is at arm's length in the Government.

I know there are people who think that we should take more direct or even directive action. That would set a difficult precedent, and I am bound to say that it would not necessarily prove more effective for the language in the long run, for ultimately the language will thrive because people in Scotland want to use it and continue to do so, not because of some form of Government directive. However, I accept the benefits of Government support for Scots. What form that support should take should be the subject of discussion with those of you taking the Scots language forward.

Conclusion

I would like to reflect on the interactions between Scotland and Ireland, especially Northern Ireland, which have shaped our linguistic heritage. The Ulster-Scots Agency board members whom I met this morning certainly had several interesting things to say to me. Though I was born, bred and educated in Scotland, I had very little knowledge of the interaction in both directions between Scotland and Ulster over the centuries. That is a failing of our education system and the content of Scottish history taught, an issue regularly raised. It was raised with me as recently as yesterday [19 September 2002] in a debate in the Parliament on culture and education. It must be examined, and I will certainly be speaking to my colleague the Education Minister about it.

The Gaelic language in Scotland is generally believed to have been brought to us by settlers from Ireland, and for a millennium there was no distinction between the language on each side of the sea. My forebears have been traced to the island of Islay, which was one of the places to which settlers from Ireland came. Many arrived centuries ago, and the links between Islay and Ireland were cemented just a month ago when the Columba Centre was opened on the island with considerable representation from Ireland. I was very proud to be able to perform the official opening because of my links with Islay.

One important aspect is that I have no knowledge — or had no knowledge until less than a year ago — of any Gaelic heritage in my family. My forebears came from the island of Islay to mainland Scotland, settled in the Glasgow area and then moved to Dundee, and all aspects of Gaelic were somehow ironed out of the family — just airbrushed out — and I had no knowledge. None of my grandparents made any mention of it at all. That is very sad, to put it at its mildest, and I would not want that to happen to anyone else. I know that it is happening very widely, of course, but it is important that we rediscover the past — that we learn not just where we come from, which informs us of where we are and where we are going, but also the fact that heritage is a very important part of us all. If a part of that as important as language and culture is completely lost in my generation — I am only going back three generations of my family — there are huge blanks in our history which must be filled. The language is certainly an important way of doing that, and it has stirred an interest for me in Gaelic language and culture for a very personal reason that, until recently, I would simply not have considered.

The Scots language in Northern Ireland was of course brought by settlers from Scotland, notably in the plantation of Ulster. What is not so well-known is that some of those settlers were Gaelic-speakers and that, for a time, the north of

Ireland had a newspaper in Scottish Gaelic. Emigration across the Atlantic was of course extensive in the eighteenth and nineteenth centuries, especially to the United States, and one of the largest and most influential ethnic groups in the melting pot of North America was a group referred to as the 'Scotch-Irish'. Of course, there has been a great deal of migration in the nineteenth and twentieth centuries between Scotland and Ireland, even if the effect on the languages has not been as fundamental as earlier movements.

The links between Scotland and Ireland remain extremely strong in all sorts of ways, linguistic, cultural, sporting and in tourism. In the long view of history, the people of Scotland and Ireland, Scots-speaking, Gaelic-speaking or monolingual English, have more in common than is often realised. I have taken much from the discussions which I had last evening and this morning. I am here to listen, and I look forward to hearing more from fellow participants in the symposium in the session which now follows. I simply say that this is the start of a process. We are learning that devolution in my country, as in Northern Ireland and in other parts of the UK, has many benefits which were perhaps not considered when the legislation which brought it about was passed. An initiative on language development is clearly one of those ways in which devolution can aid what you are doing and, indeed, what the Government in various parts of the UK are doing as well. It is a discourse which I know will continue apace, and I hope I can make a useful contribution to that process.

I would like to finish by thanking you once again for giving me the opportunity to address you this morning. I look forward to the remainder of the session. I do not know if there is to be a question and answer session, but I will do my best to respond if that is the case. I am happy to discuss general aspects of Gaelic and Scots language, and I look forward to doing so now. Thank you very much.

Discussion following Mike Watson's Address

Ken MacKinnon: I should like briefly to describe what we feel is a necessity at this time. There have been various proposals for secure status, and in the press various impressions of what the legislation implies have been given, mainly grossly misleading, misinformed and, I feel, deliberately misleading public debate. The recommendations of our group are coming forward; what they seek is a very simple Act indeed, one which says merely that the Gaelic language is officially recognised as an national language of Scotland. I believe that to be important because there is a great deal of misinformation about what constitutes an official language. There are two Welsh Language Acts. The Acts reiterate that Welsh is an official language, and now equal publicity will be given to English and Welsh in Wales. That was necessary because there had been a sixteenth-century century Act which removed official status. No such Act has ever been passed in Scotland, but nevertheless public agencies say to Gaelic organisations regarding the delivery of public services, "Gaelic is not an official language." Charitable bodies which might give money to Gaelic say, "We cannot do that because Gaelic is not an official language." The reason is that you do not have an Act. As long ago as the early 70s, a previous Conservative Government said that there would be no need for a Gaelic Language Act because the Government recognised that English and Gaelic were of equal validity in Scotland. Nevertheless, I believe an Act is necessary merely to reiterate what might be the status quo. It would have no financial implications for the Government; it would commit the Executive to no commitments other than those to which they have already committed themselves. Mentioning what they have already committed themselves to, such as the Gaelic Language Board and various other measures, would merely reiterate the fact that the Government recognised the Gaelic language in those measures and in signing and ratifying the Charter. It would give tremendous confidence to the Gaelic community, and it would be a tremendous clarification of the debate. It would sweep away all the misinformation which is currently being perpetrated through the media. It would be a simple Act stating merely that Gaelic is a national — not *the* national — language of Scotland. That is our view; we put it forward. We will be meeting you again and discussing this further, and we are greatly heartened in the responses which you have given.

Mike Watson: I do not particularly want to respond to Dr MacKinnon, since, as he mentioned, we will be getting into discussion with the group again. I should not disagree with what Dr MacKinnon said about aims. My difficulty is that I must deal with a great deal of the misinformation. I have even been accused of contributing to the misinformation surrounding what a Gaelic Language Act might involve. My view is quite clear: it is about building on what we are doing at the moment. It is not — and this is where I have been misquoted in the past — about forcing people in the Borders or Fife to have bilingual road signs and produce all the reports in both languages. It is not about that at all. It is about building on the numbers of people — not necessarily geographically, although I hope that happens too — who are speaking and using the language. I accept that, and I am sure that, when we are discussing matters with the group, with which I have a very good relationship, we can take that forward.

Wilson McLeod: Dr MacKinnon's point is that a Gaelic Language Act has been the number-one demand in the Gaelic debate for some time, and it is very frustrating that there has been so little response from the Executive, and previously from the Scottish Office, as to the substance of those concerns. You mention misinformation in the media, but much of the misinformation has come from senior figures invited to speak. Way back we had Donald Dewar making some very unhelpful remarks about a Gaelic Language Act — 'deliberately misquoted'. Some key people, perhaps in London rather than in Edinburgh, seem to have a personal agenda against Gaelic development. We see that with regard to broadcasting. What are the real objections to a Gaelic language Act? What problems are you fighting? What are the difficulties in getting a serious commitment? If we do not know what the issues and concerns are, and the only problems aired concern bilingual road signs in the Borders, it is very hard to have a serious debate. What are the issues as you see them?

Mike Watson: There are two aspects to this. The first concerns what an Act might contain. The other is the question of building support in the Executive, which is the Government in Scotland, and in the Parliament for action to be taken. We are in the business of the so-called 'bonfire of the quangos' — getting rid of non-departmental public bodies — and I had to argue not just that we should have a Gaelic development agency, but that we should swim against the tide and establish a new non-departmental public agency. I am pleased to say that I won that argument, essentially because a great many people with negative attitudes towards Gaelic language and culture base them on a complete misconception. I do not even have the heritage of my predecessor, who was a Junior Minister for Gaelic, for he was a Gaelic-speaker himself, but I was able to get arguments across at a senior level. The fact that the First Minister of Scotland has given Cabinet status to culture, which of course includes Gaelic, is a sign itself that things are changing. I am doing what I can to win support. What would the Act itself involve? As far as I am concerned, Dr MacKinnon makes a very important point when he says that there would not be substantial additional resources required. So in terms of resources necessary, Dr MacKinnon, if it can be established that it is about building on what we have, it is about according a status which may just be a statement – Dr Kirk, you talked about a statement on the Scots language last night. Statements can be important, depending on who makes them. We are not very far away from achieving what you have suggested, Dr MacKinnon. If we can establish statements of principle and a statement about the status of the language, that will be a useful starting point. If we try to get into matters too deeply, we are likely to get bogged down, Dr McLeod, and not make much progress. My personal view of anything in politics is that it is about viewing and changing things. Let us try to make progress and keep it simple. I will work with Dr MacKinnon and his colleagues to do that.

Marace Dareau: Marace Dareau, Editorial Director of Scottish Language Dictionaries. You mentioned in your talk that Gaelic and Scots are treated very differently, but I should like to draw to your attention a feasibility study being written up at the moment on the question of an institute for the languages of

Scotland, which would cover all the languages, Gaelic and Scots, but with the obvious exception of English. One of the great advantages is that the experience and knowledge of those in each field — the supporters of Gaelic in how to defend and build up support for an embattled language and, on the other side, the experience on the Scots side in much more academic fields, including the dictionary tradition — can cross over and support each other, rather than the two being seen as in conflict. I feel that it would be an extremely good way to go forward, and we should very much like to see some support from the Executive for the idea.

Mike Watson: That is an interesting proposal. It seems similar to developments I heard about this morning at the institute established in Magee College of the University of Ulster. That is the way you put it across — that there should be input from an academic level to bring things together. I am also aware that it has been achieved with the substantial resources made available to the Ulster-Scots Agency. It would be misleading of me to say that we can put in similar resources. I can see the benefits, but, equally, I think I am right in saying that there was matching funding from the university for agency resources. It will be a collaborative venture with an academic institution. I am afraid that there may be more than one academic institution. All I am saying is that I am willing to consider the idea and should welcome future discussions.

John Kirk: I should like to comment on your willingness to receive a strategy from the Cross-Party Group. That strategy could well recommend both a language agency like the Ulster-Scots Agency and an institute for the languages of Scotland, the one being academic, the other far more social and community-based. Those could certainly go hand in hand if we had the strategy, and we are beginning to move towards that.

John Law: Mr Watson, you are currently consulting on guidelines that you plan to issue to local authorities on the implementation of cultural strategies. Do those draft guidelines contain advice on Scots, and is there an intention to provide them in the final version?

Mike Watson: Yes. We issued the document this week for a consultation period lasting until January to ensure that the national cultural strategy introduced in Scotland two years ago is taken forward effectively. It is quite a wide-ranging document.

Tove Skutnabb-Kangas: Tove Skutnabb-Kangas, Roskilde, Denmark. I have one comment and one question. The comment has to do with the difference between an official and a national language — what you want from the Act. In my latest book [*Linguistic Genocide in Education – or Worldwide Diversity and Human Rights*, (Lawrence Erlbaum, 2000)], I have a very long subsection where I compare constitutions from various parts of the world and specifically whether they have national languages, official languages or both, and what that means. The meaning of 'national language' is extremely unclear and can vary a great deal. From my point of view, it is surprising that you say 'national language' and want to keep the Act very simple, for next time around you might have a Minister who is not as supportive. Then having an Act which only says 'national language' without in any way defining the responsibilities, duties and rights that go along with that — and especially not defining whether any kind of resources are involved — may change a great deal. Then you may have a situation where there is a nice symbolic Act, but nothing goes with it, and everything can be swept away in one day with the next election.

I thought that some of what you said about the need for legislation, especially in education, was a little contradictory, since there is a great deal in the European Charter for the other languages but nothing about Scots, especially in article 8 of Part III, which covers education; Scots does not figure there at all. Why should the other languages be there but not Scots? I should like to hear the background to why Scots is not there.

Mike Watson: I am afraid that I am not the person to give you that background, for I was not involved at the time when the languages listed were decided. I should certainly say that Scots should be listed for Part III. I do not know the basis on which the decision was taken. For Scots to be categorised and designated as a language certainly seems a step forward. I realise that it has been accepted as such. I cannot give you an answer; I do not know why that happened. It seems to me to be contradictory, not just relative to my comments, but contradictory per se. I will certainly examine that. I do not know the history. Perhaps I might briefly comment on the earlier point. I notice your book is called *Linguistic Genocide in Education — Or Worldwide Diversity and Human Rights.* I take the point, and to some extent I hope that what I said in relation to education reflects the fact that, essentially, unless action is taken on education — and that is why what we are doing on Gaelic is so important — the Scots language will continue to be seen by some people in Scotland as just the 'bad language' of people who do not speak very well. It is very important to be able to tell where someone comes from, not just in a country, but within a country. Regional accents are very important, but a language is more than just a regional accent, and that is something that is not got across too widely, although, as I said, increasingly teachers are involved in Scots-language groups, an example being John Kirk and his colleagues in our Cross-Party Group in the Parliament.

Last — and it is an important point — comes continuity of policy. That is why, within political parties, policies are developed so that they outlive the tenure of the person who happens to be holding a ministerial position at any one time. I am a member of the Labour Party, and I can only talk about that party — it is important that we have discussions so that you develop policy and get that established as the party policy. Then it is implemented if your party is in power, irrespective of who the Minister is. The level at which language or culture as an issue is placed within any political structure of government is important in the extent to which it can be developed.

Tove Skutnabb-Kangas: Can I answer that? I should suggest a forward-looking strategy, since it is possible to add to the UK's or any country's ratification of the European Charter, whereby you would work to get Scots mentioned in the educational article and get sign language into the Charter.

Mike Watson: Those are all issues that have been brought to my attention for the first time, and I should certainly welcome submissions on them to ensure that, when I get involved in discussions, I can do so on an informed basis. If you would like to do that, or if anyone else would like to do that for me, perhaps through John Kirk, I should find that very helpful.

John Kirk: Part of the strategy that you have invited the Cross-Party Group to submit to you would include the extension of recognition of Scots from Part II to Part III. That would be an obvious component of the strategy, and it would be a mechanism to get that to the Minister.

Ken MacKinnon: Perhaps I might argue the point about why Gaelic should be recognised as a national language? We take one step at a time, and if we wish to get over the fact that there is recognition without getting into endless legal fankles about what 'official' means and what it does not, a first Gaelic Act recognising it as a national language will be the way for us to achieve that status. We very much look forward to the board and its work. We feel it will be essential to them to have such an Act.

John Kirk: I think the point is valid. We must move in ways that secure the continuity of policies and initiatives without regard to the tenure of a particular Minister, though we wish you well — and long life in your present position.

Margaret MacIver: Margaret MacIver, Cumann na Gàidhlig. In addition to the Act which has been mentioned, I am interested in the powers to be given to the new Bòrd na Gàidhlig. What powers will the new Board have that Cumann na Gàidhlig does not have and never had?

Mike Watson: I met Cumann na Gàidhlig and all five main Gaelic organisations, and on each occasion — this was before the decision to establish the board had been made — I tested the extent to which the various organisations were willing to give up part of their responsibilities for the greater good of the board, which will have a strategic role to draw up the plan for Gaelic — the strategy to take forward the development of the language and the culture. It has not been fine-tuned to the extent to which we can say that we will take those responsibilities from individual groups and give them to the board, but it is fair to say that there has been a general acceptance that the various organisations will be happy to pass on some of their responsibilities to ensure that there is no duplication, not least of resources, but of effort as well, so that there is a strategic view and people, by and large, subscribe to the same policy for that development. I am aware that there will be individuals who have a long association with the various Gaelic organisations and perhaps do not want to see that, or the influence of their organisation, weakened, but I think that Bòrd na Gàidhlig will prove to be an example of the whole being greater than the sum of its parts and that some of the co-ordination that has not been possible so far will be possible with the board, which will have full responsibility for planning and implementing that strategy. It is not yet down in black and white, for, until the board itself is established, and then establishes a relationship with the other organisations, I cannot be more precise. That is the general intention, however, and if Dr MacKinnon will bear me out, that is the way in which the ministerial advisory group envisaged it when it recommended the establishment of the board and its support.

Liz Niven: I am delighted to see you here, Mr Watson. What has come over from the last few days is the overwhelming lack of information, research and development materials for the Scots language. I come as an educational activist for Scots, and what troubles me is the shift through from the Culture to the Education Department. It is vital that we get to speak to Cathy Jamieson. It seems to me that a massive amount needs done, and sometimes I find difficulty in seeing just where to go. We hear amazing niceties about Gaelic and the stage that has been reached for it and Irish, yet we are so far away from that. For example, one thing that bothers me — and I have watched this for many years — is statements that come out declaring support from the Executive. In reality, that is not happening, and this week, to check statistics before I came to this conference, I telephoned Learning and Teaching Scotland. All the literature declares that there is continuing support for the teaching of Scots and for the production of materials through Learning and Teaching Scotland. In fact there are very few materials being produced by it. One of the major successes for Scots and Gaelic in the last few years was *A'Chiste / The Kist*, an anthology of materials with worksheets and tapes. All the worksheets and tapes are completely extinct. There is no prospect of their being reprinted; we have only an anthology without back-up material for the teachers. We have seen the volume of materials rise through the 70s and 80s, and now, as a result of lottery money — not education money — we see the materials come and go. Many teachers are as baffled as ever and are waiting for some sort of nod of approval about the language. Finally, would it be possible to have a Minister for Scots as well as Gaelic?

Mike Watson: That is meant to be me. There has been criticism that Gaelic is not named in my title — Tourism, Culture and Sport — but it obviously very much includes Gaelic, Scots language, the lottery, heritage and various other things too. I take the point that it is not explicit in that way. I understand what you are saying. As far as Learning and Teaching Scotland is concerned, it is a very important organisation because of the resource material that it produces, and I have been in contact with it recently. It produces for the creative industries and the teaching of creativity in schools, which is very good. On the point you make, if materials are out of print, a point of which I was not aware, I will certainly have to take that up directly. I can do it with Cathy Jamieson, the Education Minister, but I can do it directly as well, because it is a direct link with my responsibilities, and, once again, I hope I am not just taking what seems like an easy way out. If there is information on that, please give me the details, and I will follow it up, because I cannot know what I do not know.

Michael Hance: [recording is unclear]

Mike Watson: I do not doubt that there will be some prejudice against both Gaelic and Scots language. I feel lack of interest is a bigger problem. People say that it is not important. 'Prejudice' suggests doing something to suppress a language deliberately. I cannot say that that has not happened. However, when I talk to people about Gaelic or Scots language, there is a feeling of "I hardly use it. What's the point? Oh, we don't do that because it's the wrong thing to do." I have used my time as a Minister to try to talk up the importance of Gaelic as a language and a culture, as well as the Scots language and a broader Scottish culture, and I am meeting resistance not so much in terms of "I do not want that to happen," but rather "Why should it happen? Tell my why it is important." When I get into discussions with people, as many of you will, I feel I can win people over quite easily. I find that people have just not thought about it; it has never occurred to them that it was an issue. You could characterise that as prejudice, and, it is in any case the effect rather than the intent that counts; I accept that. But I find it is largely a question of lack of interest. I am taking that argument on. I tried to outline what I did arguing for Bòrd na Gàidhlig. That argument had to be won. The important thing is that the argument *can* be won – if it is argued cogently and sustained, it can be won. That is my approach to life in general: if you believe in something, you argue for it. I take what you say on board, but you are in danger of conjuring up some kind of conspiracy theory — that there is a blanket attempt to dampen everything down. More schools and more teachers are being responsive to Scots language now, and, provided we can get the teaching materials out, we can build on that. You might be overstating the case, but I do not deny the thrust of what you are saying — or the effect, however it is dressed up.

Boyd Robertson: Boyd Robertson, Strathclyde University. One of the frustrations of people such as myself who have been involved in the production of reports over the years has been the lack of action and co-ordination on those reports. One on which I worked was essentially shelved by people resistant to the idea of encouraging more Scottish culture. [rest of the recording is unclear]

Mike Watson: The question of teaching and education is fundamental to the growing strength of the language. I do not doubt that, and I tried to make that clear earlier. I want to ensure that, where there is demand from parents for their children to be taught in Gaelic-medium education, that such demand can be met. That needs a certain number of teachers, but it also needs teachers prepared to go to the parts of Scotland where there is a demand. A newly built school, Ardnamurchan High, opened only last month, and there are places there for Gaelic-medium teachers, but it is impossible to attract enough teachers to go to what is a very remote part of Scotland. You can only ensure enough places for teachers to be trained and then encourage them to go to certain places. It is a fact that, if you are teaching, particularly young people, for example, in their early 20s, they may not want to go to a remote part; they may prefer a part of Scotland where it is more organised, for whatever reason. I do what I can to ensure adequate provision for teachers to be trained, but one of the things we are also doing — and I will be making an announcement on this quite soon — is that we are going to ensure that it is easier for people, particularly women whose families are now at a stage where they may have left home, to re-enter the workforce, either through training or retraining, as teachers who can teach in Gaelic. There is considerable untapped potential, and that would be particularly attractive to people already living in remote areas. That is one aspect which we are examining. I have discussed it with Lews Castle College staff in Stornoway, who of course have links with your university. There are things we can do to try and increase the number of people available to teach in Gaelic-medium education, but ultimately they must be willing to go to the places where that demand exists, and unless we are going to incentivise people seriously to move there — and that has been advocated — it is very difficult to know what else we can do. Get the numbers of people coming through the system equipped to train right in general, and that will deal with most of the problems.

John Kirk: I think the general point is that people with good intentions, backed by all those institutions in Scotland, write reports deemed necessary to produce a programme for action, and nothing happens. It is very frustrating if someone like Mr Robertson has to come back again and again, having very willingly produced a report in the hope of a better and more inclusive society.

Mike Watson: I am not aware of that specific one. I cannot comment on previous reports for which I was not responsible. I have only begun to implement the one for which I have direct responsibility, and I intend to do my best to work through the other points recommended by Professor Meek and his colleagues.

[At this point the recording ended.]

Struchtúir Éagsúla an Ghaeloideachais

Jacqueline Ní Fheargusa

Nuair a bunaíodh GAELSCOILEANNA (Comhchoiste Náisiúnta na Scoileanna Gaeilge mar a tugadh air an uair sin) i 1973, bhí an ghaelscolaíocht ó dheas ar an dé deiridh lasmuigh den Ghaeltacht. Cé go mbíodh polasaí rialtais i bhfeidhm go mbeadh scoileanna ag múineadh trí Ghaeilge ó bhunú an tSaorstáit sna ficheadaí bhí an córas sin á bhrú agus á chur i bhfeidhm ag an Stát ní ar mhaithe le cúrsaí oideachais nó forbairt na bpáistí ach ar mhaithe le polasaithe polaitiúla teanga.

> The schools were used as a means to an extra-educational end, and schooling was directed not at developing the potentialities of the individual pupils for the pupil's sake but at developing certain cultural traits for the nations sake.[1]

Bhí na polasaithe seo dírithe ar an nGaeilge a athbheochan mar theanga cumarsáide mhuintir na hÉireann tríd an gcóras oideachais. Bhí sé i gceist go mbeadh an oiread de chóras scolaíochta na hÉireann déanta trí mheán na Gaeilge agus ab fhéidir ionas go ndéanfaí cainteoirí líofa Gaeilge as páistí na tíre. Chabhródh seo leis an tír a ghaelú agus an Ghaeilge a chur ar ais i mbarr a réime arís.

> Inspired by the ideology of cultural nationalism it was held that the schools ought to be the prime agents in the revival of the Irish language and native traditions which it was held were the hallmarks of nationhood and the basis for independent statehood. Many people held that the schools in the nineteenth century had been a prime cause of the decline of the Irish language; under a native Irish Government the process would have to be reversed.[2]

Níor éirigh leis an Rialtas nó leis an Roinn Oideachais a n-idéil maidir le hathbheochan na Gaeilge a thabhairt i gcrích, cé gur éirigh leo a chinntiú go raibh eolas agus tuiscint ar an nGaeilge ag céatadán áirithe de na glúnta a chuaigh tríd an gcóras oideachais idir 1930 – 1970.

Ba léir faoi thús na seachtóidí go raibh teipthe ar an gcóras an tír a athghaelú agus faoin am sin ní raibh ach dornán beag scoileanna fós ag seasamh an fhóid ó

---

[1] Akenson. D. H. (1975), *A Mirror to Kathleen's Face Education in Independent Ireland 1922 – 1960.* Montreal: McGill- Queen's University Press. Montreal. Lch. 41.

[2] Coolahan J. (1981) *Irish Education history and structure,* Dublin: Institute of Public Administration. Lch 21.

thaobh múineadh trí mheán na Gaeilge de agus bhí lagmhisneach ar dhaoine faoin chóras scolaíochta trí Ghaeilge i gcoitinne.[3]

.... By the 1960s the schools-based revival had become discredited. At most, the generality of students received a passing oral knowledge of Irish and a more indepth written knowledge of it.[4]

Ag deireadh na seascaidí agus tús na seachtóidí thosaigh grúpaí beaga tuismitheoirí ag teacht le chéile chun scoileanna lánGhaeilge nua a bhunú. Tharla seo don chuid is mó i mBaile Átha Cliath ar dtús, áit go raibh céatadán beag áirithe de thuismitheoirí ag tógáil a bpáistí le Gaeilge agus a bhí ag lorg tacaíochta ón gcóras oideachais. Bhí tuismitheoirí eile ann ar ndóigh a bhí mí-shocair faoin easpa Gaeilge, mar ba léir dóibh sin é, sna ghnáth bhunscoileanna.

Ghraf 1: Fás ar an nGaelscolaíocht sa Ghalltacht: 1972-2002

Fás ar an nGaelscolaíocht sa Ghalltacht / The Growth of Irish Medium Schools outside the Gaeltacht : 1972-2002

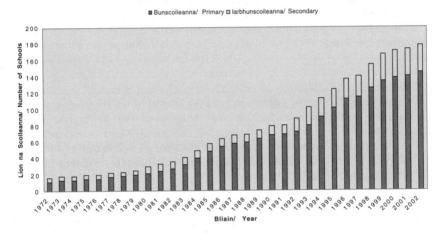

Mar a léirítear sa ghraf 1 tá líon na scoileanna méadaithe as cuimse le tríocha bliain anuas. Bhí an eagraíocht GAELSCOILEANNA ann chun cabhrú leis an bhfás seo. Chabhraigh siad le grúpaí tuismitheoirí ar fud na tíre scoileanna nua a bhunú, chuir siad brú leanúnach ar an Roinn Oideachais maidir le tacaíocht don ghaelscolaíocht agus chinntigh siad gur lean an fás agus an fhorbairt le linn na

---

[3] Ní Fhearghusa J. (1998) *GAELSCOILEANNA Stair na heagraíochta 1973 – 1998*. Tráchtas neamhfhoilsithe
[4] Kelly A. (2002) *Compulsory Irish Language and Education in Ireland 1870s – 1970s,* Dublin: Irish Academic Press, Lch 141.

mblianta sin. Throid siad ar son grúpaí tuismitheoirí ar diúltaíodh cead dóibh scoileanna a bhunú agus chabhraigh siad le grúpaí a bhunaigh scoileanna ar bhonn neamhoifigiúil aitheantas a bhaint amach. Chinntigh siad gur éirigh le geall leis gach grúpa a thug faoin obair seo, gaelscoil a bhunú agus aitheantas a fháil di. D'éirigh leis an eagraíocht é sin a dhéanamh le heaspa mór airgid agus acmhainn foirne.

Níl aon cheist faoi anois ach go bhfuil an ghaelscolaíocht thuaidh agus theas ar an ábhar dóchais is mó agus is láidre do thodhchaí na Gaeilge sa tír. Tá tionchar ag na scoileanna, tuismitheoirí, daltaí, múinteoirí agus aon duine a bhíonn bainteach leis na scoileanna ar an saol ar fad timpeall orainn. Éilíonn na scoileanna tacaíocht, seirbhísí agus cainteoirí Gaeilge idir múinteoirí agus daoine eile a bhíonn bainteach leis na scoileanna. Cuireann siad sruth leanúnach (atá ag dul i méid in aghaidh na bliana) de chainteoirí líofa Gaeilge ar fáil. Ar an iomlán aon uair a labhraíonn polaiteoir nó oideachasóir faoin nGaeilge déanann siad tagairt do fhás agus forbairt na gaelscolaíochta mar chomhartha go bhfuil spéis ag pobal na hÉireann sa teanga agus mar chruthúnas go bhfuil todhchaí i ndán don teanga.

Is léir mar sin go bhfuil tábhacht leis an ngaelscolaíocht agus le fás leanúnach na gaelscolaíochta sna blianta amach romhainn ar roinnt cúiseanna a bhaineann go dlúth le sábháil na teanga mar theanga a labhróidh céatadán áirithe de phobal na tíre seo. Ní dócha, go bhfuil sé réalaíoch a bheith ag caint ar athbheochan na teanga mar theanga cumarsáide iomlán phobal na tíre. I measc na bhfáthanna go bhfuil gá ag gluaiseacht na Gaeilge leis an ngaelscolaíocht mar bhunchloch áirím na cúiseanna seo:

1. Cruthaítear sruth leanúnach de pháistí ar maith leo an Ghaeilge, a aithníonn í mar theanga bheo ina saol féin agus nach bhfuil eagla orthu roimpi,

2. Éileamh leanúnach ar mhúinteoirí a chuireann brú áirithe ar an gcóras oideachais tríú leibhéal na múinteoirí seo a sholáthar agus a chinntíonn áit na Gaeilge sa chóras go fóill.

3. Tacaíocht leanúnach don Ghaeltacht agus dóibh siúd ar suim leo an teanga

4. Léiriú do pholaiteoirí agus dóibh siúd atá i gceannas ar an saol gnó agus an saol riaracháin go bhfuil an Ghaeilge tábhachtach agus lárnach i saol na mílte mílte tuismitheoir agus gur léiriú é ar bhá náisiúnta i measc cuid suntasach den phobal.

É sin go léir ráite, tá fadhbanna móra sa chóras gaelscolaíochta mar a fheiceann an eagraíocht é agus is cinnte gur gá don eagraíocht grinnstaidéar a dhéanamh ar fhadhbanna an chórais ionas gur féidir léi a chinntiú go leanfaidh an córas go barr foirfeachta.

Bunaíodh os cionn 100 gaelscoil agus 25 iarbhunscoil le tríocha bliain anuas. Go fóill, tá easnaimh sa chóras maidir le téacleabhair, áiseanna oideachais, fístéipeanna agus cd-romanna agus áiseanna teicniúla eile. Is léir go raibh na heasnaimh sin ann ó bhunú an Stáit agus beag beann ar pholasaithe tacaíochta an

Stáit do mhúineadh trí mheán na teanga níor léiríodh riamh tacaíocht phraicticiúil maidir leis na riachtanais oideachasúla:

> In conclusion, it may be said that despite the availability of grants, there was never a satisfactory number of Irish language books produced to facilitate the language revival.... The lack of books was particularly evident in the education system where Irish was compulsory as a subject and where there was active encouragement of Irish as a medium of instruction. Despite the schools-based revival policy, successive governments consistently refused to recognise that there was a shortage of Irish language text books, resulting in even enthusiastic schools having to revert to English as medium of instruction.

Ach anuas ar easnaimh maidir le téacsleabhair srl. tá fadhbanna móra praicticiúla eile nach bhfuil tuismitheoirí agus múinteoirí an lae inniu sásta glacadh leo:

1. Níl aon chóras measúnaithe ann do na páistí a fhoghlaimíonn trí Ghaeilge gurb í an Béarla a mátharitheanga.
2. Ní dhéantar measúnú ach an oiread ar pháistí a thógtar le Gaeilge atá sa chóras tumoideachais atá dírithe ar pháistí a thógtar le Béarla.
3. Tá easpa taighde ann agus tá easpa tuisceana ann maidir le cad is cóir a dhéanamh le páistí le deacrachtaí foghlama sa chóras.
4. Tá easpa soiléireachta maidir leis an gcóras tacaíochta foghlama sa suíomh tumtheagaisc.

Tá ag éirí go maith leis an ngaelscolaíocht ar fud na tíre agus an cruthúnas air sin ná líon na scoileanna atá bunaithe agus líon na ndaltaí atá ag freastal orthu. Tuigtear do na scoileanna go bhfuil tuismitheoirí ar an iomlán an-sásta leis an gcóras go ginearálta. Mar sin féin, is léir anois go bhfuil fadhb ollmhór ag an ngaelscolaíocht go mbeidh ar an ngluaiseacht i gcomhar le GAELSCOILEANNA dul i ngleic leis agus is é sin nach bhfuil ag éirí linn ar aon bhealach cuimsitheach na páistí bunscoile a mhealladh le dul ar aghaidh chuig an dara leibhéal trí Ghaeilge. Tá an fhadhb seo ag éirí níos soiléire le blianta beaga anuas, toisc go bhfuil cuid mhaith de na gaelscoileanna a bunaíodh ag deireadh na n-ochtóidí agus tús/ lár na nóchaidí tagtha in aois ó thaobh rang a sé a bheith san scoileanna. Os rud é go bhfuil cuid de na gaelscoileanna ar fud na tíre beag go leor níl na huimhreacha iontu a chinnteodh todhchaí iarbhunscoile neamhspleáí. Níl an Roinn Oideachais agus Eolaíochta sásta scoileanna neamhspléacha ag an dara leibhéal a cheadú mura bhfuil cúpla ghaelscoil ann ar a laghad ag soláthar páistí don scoil sin, cé go bhfuil cúpla eisceacht ann. An rud a mholann an Roinn go hiondúil ná Aonad lánGhaeilge laistigh de mháthairscoil Béarla. Bunaíodh an chéad Aonad i lár na n-ochtóidí i dTrá Lí, Co. Chiarraí mar chomhréiteach idir scoil neamhspleách agus sruth. Tá tuairim is 14 d'aonad lánGhaeilge bunaithe ó shin. Feidhmíonn na hAonaid seo laistigh de mháthairscoil a mhúineann trí Bhéarla. Tá difríochtaí móra idir an méid neamhspleáchais atá ag aon cheann acu, agus dá bhrí sin idir an leibhéal dul chun cinn a dhéanann siad. Éiríonn níos fearr leis na hAonaid a chinntíonn gur Aonaid neamhspleácha iad laistigh de chóras eile. Bíonn fadhbanna ag na hAonaid atá ró-lag lena gcearta a éileamh agus slogtar isteach sa mháthairscoil iad de réir a chéile. Ní léir do thuismitheoirí go bhfuil aon rud ar leith ar fáil do na páistí san Aonad seachas roinnt ábhar trí Ghaeilge. De réir a chéile cailltear spéis agus laghdaítear ar an líon daltaí a théann isteach san Aonad agus ar deireadh i roinnt cásanna dúntar an tAonad ar fad laistigh de chúig bliana.

Tá sé níos soiléire anois ná riamh go bhfuil géarghá leis an soláthar ag an dara leibhéal a phleanáil i gceart. Tá tuismitheoirí agus páistí i bhfad níos éilithí nuair a thagann sé chuig an dara leibhéal. Tá oideachas den scoth ag teastáil uathu agus níl spéis acu a bheith i seomraí réamhdhéanta gan áiseanna spóirt srl, ar mhaithe le roinnt ábhar a bheith á soláthar trí mheán na Gaeilge. An rud atá tarlaithe ó dheas ná go bhfuil Aonaid bheaga bunaithe i mbailte atá réasúnta gar dá chéile seachas iarrachtaí a dhéanamh na tuismitheoirí ó na gaelscoileanna a thabhairt le chéile agus iarracht a dhéanamh Aonad mór amháin a bhunú nó scoil neamhspleách. Caithfear a rá áfach gur seo an t-idéal agus i gcásanna áirithe de bharr cúinsí eisceachtúla agus tráidisiúin láidre áitiúla ní bheidh páistí sásta taistil. Ba chóir gach iarracht a dhéanamh an t-idéal seo a bhaint amach ach is gá a aithint go bhfuil eisceachtaí ann freisin ar gá freastal orthu. Tá géarghá le díriú ar an bpleanáil seo mar ábhar práinne. Tá gá freisin le breis tacaíochta do na hAonaid le cur ar a gcumas ábhair éagsúla a sholáthar do líon beag daltaí. Is gá freisin a chinntiú go gcuirtear córais éifeachtacha taistil ar fáil le deimhniú nach gcuirtear constaicí taistil ar dhaltaí a rachadh chuig an Aonad dá mba rud é go raibh córas éifeachtach ann. Is fadhb í seo a chránn na scoileanna neamhspleácha chomh maith.

Tháinig GAELSCOILEANNA agus na coistí Gairmoideachais le chéile bliain ó shin le plé a dhéanamh ar na fadhbanna sa chóras. Cuireadh plécháipéis le chéile, le cur síos ar an gcóras, deacrachtaí agus roinnt moltaí. Cuireadh é sin faoi bhráid na Roinne Oideachais agus Eolaíochta i mí Meán Fómhair 2001. D'aithin an Roinn go raibh fadhbanna iomadúla praiticiúla agus struchtúrtha sa chóras agus d'iarr siad ar an gCoimisiún um Chóiríocht Scoileanna an cheist a iniúchadh agus teacht ar ais chucu le moltaí.Tá an Coimisiún i mbun na hoibre sin faoi láthair. Tá aighneachtaí ó bhéal á éisteacht agus aighneacht scríofa á scrúdú agus beifear ag réiteach tuairisc agus moltaí le cur os comhai na Roinne.

Go dtí seo is GAELSCOILEANNA agus GAELSCOILEANNA amháin a bhí ag iarraidh freastal ar riachtanais agus ar fhadhbanna na hearnála gaeloideachais ag an dá leibhéal. Gan amhras, bhí an cúram seo i bhfad ró-dheacair agus ró-leathan d'eagraíocht bheag dheonach cé gur dhein an eagraíocht gach iarracht thar na blianta dul i ngleic leis na fadhbanna. D'aithin an eagraíocht féin chomh fada siar leis na hochtóidí go raibh gá le tacaíocht fhoirmeálta stáit agus go raibh struchtúr tacaíochta de chuid chóras an stáit de dhíth. Ní fhéadfadh GAELSCOILEANNA na heasnaimh go léir sa chóras a leigheas gan tacaíocht agus struchtúr ceart. Tá an eagraíocht ag feidhmiú mar chompháirtí oideachais ar chomhchéim le compháirtithe oideachais eile. Tá an eagraíocht in ann feidhmiú, áfach, ar bhonn neamhspleách, rud a thugann cumhachtaí áirithe di agus í i mbun eadarghabhála agus plé leis an státchóras ar son na scoileanna agus na gluaiseachta.

Tar éis deich mbliana de stocaireacht ag GAELSCOILEANNA, Comhdháil Náisiúnta na Gaeilge agus Eagraíocht Scoileanna Gaeltachta aithníodh go raibh gá le struchtúr tacaíochta don ghaelscolaíocht agus do na scoileanna Gaeltachta. Is fiú a rá ag an bpointe seo go raibh na fadhbanna céanna ag na scoileanna Gaeltachta, agus castachtaí eile anuas orthu siúd, is atá luaite leis an ngaelscolaíocht. Cuireadh foráil san Acht Oideachais (1998), – Alt 31- a chuir ar chumas na Roinne Oideachais agus Eolaíochta An Chomhairle um Oideachas Gaeltachta agus Gaelscolaíochta a chur ar bun. Féach Aguisín 1 le haghaidh foclaíochta Alt 31 den Acht Oideachais. Cuireadh an Comhairle nua seo ar bun le tacaíochta a thabhairt do scoileanna Gaeltachta agus do ghaelscoileanna oideachas trí mheán na Gaeilge a chur ar ar fáil ar an slí is éifeachtaí gur féidir.

Ar ndóigh, de bharr comhaontú Aoine an Chéasta cuireadh Foras na Gaeilge ar bun mar cheann de na sé Forais tras teorann. Bunaíodh Foras na Gaeilge chun an Ghaeilge a chur chun cinn ó thuaidh agus ó dheas. Leagadh dualgais reachtúla ar an bhForas i leith an ghaeloideachais freisin. Féach Aguisín 2.

Tá grúpaí eile ag plé leis an ngaelscolaíocht agus leis na scoileanna Gaeltachta ar bhealaí éagsúla agus seo mar a bheidh na línte cumarsáide eatarthu amach anseo:

Na forais/grúpaí/eagraíochtaí éagsúla a bheidh ag plé leis an ngaeloideachas

26 Contae

An Roinn Oideachais agus Eolaíochta

GAELSCOILEANNA

Foras na Gaeilge   An Chomhairle um Oideachas Gaeltachta agus
                     Gaelscolaíochta

An Gúm

Aonad Oideachais i mBaile Bhuirne

Grupaí Deonacha: Muintearas, Gaeil Uladh agus soláithreoirí beaga eile

---

Na Sé chontae

DENI (Department of Education Northern Ireland)

Gaeloiliúint

Altram

Comhairle na Gaelscolaíochta   Foras na Gaeilge
                                 An Gúm

An t-Áis Aonad – Coláiste Mhuire, Béal Feirste

An Comhairle um Oideachas Gaeltachta agus Gaelscolaíochta

GAELSCOILEANNA

Foras na Gaeilge
An Gúm

Aonad Oideachais i mBaile Bhuirne

Muintearas / Meitheal Chorca Dhuibhne / Gael Uladh

Soláthróirí príobháideacha – Prim Ed. / Fios Feasa/

Páirtnéireachtaí le grúpaí / eagraíochtaí sa Tuaisceart

Comhairle na Gaelscolaíochta / Gaeloiliúint / Altram / an tÁis Aonad

---

Is gá dúinn a chinntiú go bhfuil rólanna soiléir ag gach grúpa, go bhfuil comhoibriú agus comhthuiscint eatarthu agus nach mbeidh gach duine ag iarraidh a gcuid a chosaint agus a mhéadú. Is gá don Chomhairle nua a chinntiú go bhfuil comhordú aontaithe cuimsitheach ar siúl idir na grúpaí go léir atá ann anois idir eagraíochtaí faoin státchóras, eagraíochtaí deonacha agus soláthróirí príobháideacha agus foilsitheoirí. Braitear anois go bhfuil féidearthachtaí iontacha ann don chéad uair riamh ó bunaíodh an Stát a chinntiú go bhfuil an ghaelscolaíocht agus na scoileanna Gaeltachta forbartha i gceart agus go bhfuil tacaíocht fholláin cheart ag an dá chóras scolaíochta.

Tá a macasamhail ar shlí de na córais thacaíochta ó dheas bunaithe ó thuaidh chomh maith. D'fhéadfaí a rá go bhfuil cosúlachtaí móra idir Comhairle na Gaelscolaíochta ó thuaidh agus An Chomhairle um Oideachas Gaeltachta agus Gaelscolaíochta ó dheas, cé nach bhfuil a rólanna agus a bhfreagrachtaí iomlán mar an gcéanna. Tá ionad oideachais le bunú i mBaile Bhuirne a sholáthróidh áiseanna teagaisc srl. mórán mar a dhéanann an tÁis - Aonad i gColáiste Mhuire, Béal Feirste, cé go mbeidh cúraimí i bhfad níos leithne ar an Aonad Oideachais i mBaile Bhuirne mar a bhaineann sé le hoiliúint agus inseirbhís leanúnach do mhúinteoirí. Tá cosúlachtaí freisin idir GAELSCOILEANNA agus Gaeloiliúint cé go bhfuil Comhairle na Gaelscolaíochta tar éis cuid mhaith de sheanchúraimí Ghaeloiliúint a ghlacadh orthu féin (tar éis mórán plé agus comhaontaithe idir na páirtithe cuí) agus ní bheadh a chomhionann fíor faoi GHAELSCOILEANNA agus an Chomhairle nua ó dheas. Leanfaidh GAELSCOILEANNA ina ról mar cheann de na príomhchomhpháirithe oideachais a bhíonn i mbun plé díreach leis an Roinn Oideachais agus Eolaíochta ar réimse leathan ceisteanna oideachais agus bainistíochta. Leanfaidh GAELSCOILEANNA ina ról mar bhunaitheoir scoileanna, mar ghrúpa a thacóidh le hiarrachtaí nua oideachais mar a bhaineann siad leis an ngaelscolaíocht. Leanfaidh siad ag réiteach fadhbanna inmheánacha i scoileanna i gcomhar le pé pátrún atá ar na scoileanna sin, na hEaspaig nó an Foras Pátrúnachta, ag cabhrú le réiteach coimhlinte agus forbairt comhréitithe. Is é GAELSCOILEANNA a bheidh lárnach agus ceannródaíoch mar a bhí go dtí seo, ina aon fhorbairtí nua a bheidh chun leasa an ghaeloideachais. Beidh an eagraíocht ann chun tacú le tuismitheoirí, bainistíocht agus múinteoirí na scoileanna. Troidfidh an eagraíocht ar son an chórais agus ar son cearta an chórais sin agus beidh, mar a bhí go dtí seo, saoirse níos mó aici de bhrí nach bhfuil sí mar chuid den Státchóras cé go ngníomhaíonn sí go leanúnach laistigh de.

Aguisín 1: Alt 31.

(1) Bunóidh an tAire comhlacht daoine:
    (a)   (i)   chun soláthar téacsleabhar agus áiseanna d'fhoglaim agus do mhúineadh trí Ghaeilge a phleanáil agus a chomheagrú,
           (ii)   chun comhairle a thabhairt don Aire maidir le beartais a bhaineann le hoideachas trí mheán na Gaeilge a chur ar fáil agus a chur chun cinn i scoileanna aitheanta i gcoitinne agus i scoileanna atá suite i limistéar Gaeltachta,
           (iii) chun seirbhísí taca a chur ar fáil do na scoileanna sin trí mheán na Gaeilge, agus
           (iv) chun taighde a sheoladh ar aon ní nó ar gach ní lena mbaineann an mhír seo, agus
    (b)   chun soláthar téacleabhar agus áiseanna d'fhoghlaim agus do mhúineadh na Gaeilge a phleanáil agus a chomheagrú agus chun taighde a sheoladh, agus comhairle a thabhairt don Aire, maidir le straitéisí a bhfuil de chuspóir leo feabhas a chur ar éifeachtacht mhúineadh na Gaeilge i scoileanna aitheanta agus i lárionaid oideachais.
    (2)   Féadfaidh an tAire, le hordú arna dhéanamh le toiliú an Aire Airgeadais, aon cheann dá fheidhmeanna nó dá feidhmeanna i Leith na nithe dá dtagraítear i *bhfo-alt*
    (1)   a tharmligean chuig an gcomhlacht a bhunófar de réir an fho-ailt sin agus déanfaidh an comhlacht sin na feidhmeanna sin a chomhall faoi stiúradh agus faoi rialú an Aire.
    (3)   Maidir leis an gcomhlacht a bhunófar de réir *fho-alt* (1):
        (a) déanfaidh sé, le toiliú an Aire, coiste a bhunú chun cabhrú leis na feidhmeanna a thugtar dó faoi fho-alt (1)(b) a chomhlíonadh, agus
        (b) féadfaidh sé tráth ar bith, le toiliú an Aire, coiste a cheapfar faoin bhfo-alt seo a dhíscaoileadh nó comhaltas den sórt sin a bhaint de chomhalta coiste.
    (4) Déanfaidh an comhlacht a bhunófar de réir *fho-alt* (1), ó am go ham, de réir mar is cuí leis, comhairle a thabhairt don Chomhairle Náisiúnta Churaclaim agus Measúnachta maidir le nithe a Bhaineann:

        (a) le múineadh na Gaeilge
        (b) le hoideachas a chur ar fáil trí mheán na Gaeilge, lena n-áirítear nithe a bhaineann leis an gcuraclam do

bhunscoileanna agus d'iarbhunscoileanna a chuireann
oideachas trí mheán na Gaeilge ar fáil agus le nósanna
imeachta measúnachta a úsáidtear sna scoileanna sin,
agus

(c) le riachtanais oideachais daoine a chónaíonn i limistéar
Gaeltachta,

agus beidh aird agan gComhairle Náisiúnta Curaclaim agus
Measúnachta ar aon chomhairle den sórt sin le linn di a feidhmeanna
a fheidhmiú.

(3) Féadfaidh an tAire, le hordú, aon ordú arna dhéanamh faoin
alt seo, lena n-áirítear ordú arna dhéanamh faoin bhfo-alt seo, a leasú
nó a chúlghairm.

(4) I ngach bliain airgeadais, féadfaidh an tAire le comhthoiliú
An Aire Airgeadais deontas nó deontais a thabhairt, as airgead a
sholáthróidh an tOireachtas, don chomhlacht a cheapfar de réir *fho-
alt* (1) chun críocha caiteachais ag an gcomhlacht sin i gcomhlíonadh
a fheidhmeanna.

(5) Féadfaidh an tAire cibé tacaíocht rúnaíochta agus riaracháin
a mheasfaidh an tAire is gá a chur ar fáil do chomhlacht a bhunófar
faoin alt seo.

Aguisín 2: Dualgais reachtúla ar an bhForas i leith an ghaeloideachais

1. Na dualgais a bhí ar Bhord na Gaeilge i leith cur chun cinn na Gaeilge (iad
go léir aistrithe go dtí an Foras teanga nua)
2. Measúnú a dhéanamh ar áiseanna tacaíochta don churaclam san oideachas trí
mheán na Gaeilge - soláthar téacsleabhair agus áiseanna san áireamh
3. Taighde ar sholáthar oideachais trí Ghaeilge agus múineadh na Gaeilge i
scoileanna eile - modhanna múinteoireachta san áireamh, an curaclam atá á
mhúineadh agus meaúnú ar na modhanna atá in úsáid
4. Foilsiú a dhéanamh ar thorthaí an taighde (aon mholadh ag éirí as an taighde
san áireamh)
5. Leanfaidh siad ar aghaidh leis na dualgais a bhí orthu ag cur foilsiúcháin
oideachais trí mheán na Gaeilge ar fáil - tríd *An Gúm*
6. Leanfaidh siad ar aghaidh leis na dualgais a bhí orthu ag cur téarmaíochta
agus foclóireachta ar fáil as Gaeilge - tríd an g*Coiste Téarmaíochta*
7. Déanfaidh comhoibriú leis an gComhairle um Oideachas Gaeltachta agus
Gaelscolaíochta a bunaíodh faoin Acht Oideachais 1998 (Alt 31)
8. Ag éirí as an taighde a dhéantar is féidir leis an bhForas teanga moltaí a
dhéanamh maidir le hoideachas trí Ghaeilge agus múineadh na Gaeilge.

Struchtúir na Gaelscolaíochta i dTuaisceart Éireann

Seán Ó Coinn[1]

Réanhrá

Is é Comhairle na Gaelscolaíochta an eagraíoch ionadaíoch do chur chun cinn na gaelscolaíochta i dTuaisceart Éireann. Bhunaigh an Roinn Oideachais i dTuaisceart Éireann an eagraíocht sa bhliain 2002 mar gheall ar a dualgais faoi Chomhaontú Bhéal Feirste. Faoi láthair tá naonúr fostaithe ag an Chomhairle agus Bord Stiúrtha aice de 23 ball. Tá oifig na Comhairle i mBéal Feirste.

San alt seo dearctar ar na struchtúir atá ann faoi láthair don ghaelscolaíocht agus na struchtúir atá de dhíth agus léirítear an tuairim gur gá anois na struchtúir sin agus feidhm na struchtúr sin a athdhíriú leis an earnáil a bhogadh chun cinn go héifeachtach.

Seo a leanas cuntas ar an na struchtúir ghaelscolaíochta atá againn faoi láthair ó thuaidh leis an ghaelscolaíocht a fhorbairt. Tá oiliúint fochéime agus iarchéime á cur ar fáil i gColáiste Ollscoile Naomh Muire, tá áiseanna teagaisc, téacsleabhair agus aistriúcháin ar théacsleabhair Bhéarla á gcur ar fáil ó Áisaonad na Gaelscolaíochta faoi mhaoiniú ó Fhoras na Gaeilge, tá Gaeloiliúint ag forbairt na gaelscolaíochta agus ag bunú scoileanna úra, tá an Gaeleagras Um Shainriachtanais Oideachais (GESO) ag riar ar shainriachtanais oideachais na gaelscolaíochta, tá Altram ag tabhairt tacaíochta agus oiliúint d'earnáil na réamhscolaíochta, tá Iontaobhas na Gaelscolaíochta ag maoiniú gnéithe den ghaelscolaíocht nach dtagann faoi chúram maoinithe na bhforas stáit agus tá Comhairle na Gaelscolaíochta ag pleanáil chur chun cinn na gaelscolaíochta, ag tabhairt faoi fhorbairt iomlán na gaelscolaíochta idir bhunú scoileanna agus ardú caighdeán, ag cur comhairle ar fhorais stáit agus ag comhordú eagrais agus acmhainní na gaelscolaíochta.

Cuireadh na struchtúir seo ar bun le blianta beaga anuas le tabhairt faoi nithe a bhí ag cur sriain le fás na gaelscolaíochta dar le lucht na gaelscolaíochta.

B'iad seo a leanas na nithe a síleadh ar ghá tabhairt fúthu: na caighdeáin teagaisc a ardú sna scoileanna trí bheith ag oiliúint múinteoirí don ghaelscolaíocht; an ganntanas áiseanna don earnáil ó thuaidh agus droch-chaighdeán na n-áiseanna a bhí á n-úsáid; an ganntanas scoileanna úra; an drochriar a dhéanann an córas ar shainriachtanais oideachais; an caighdeán teagaisc sna naíonraí; an easpa maoinithe don ghaelscolaíocht; cur chun cinn na gaelscolaíochta.

---

[1] Is é Seán Ó Coinn príomhfheidhmeannach Chomhairle na Gaelscolaíochta. Ceapadh é sa phost i Mí Feabhra 2001. Go dtí sin, bhí obair déanta aige i réimse rólanna leis an Ghaeilge mar chraoltóir, mar mhúinteoir, mar bhainisteoir agus mar aistritheoir. Bhí baint aige le bunú na gaelscolaíochta in Ard Mhacha agus le bunú agus teagasc ranganna do dhaoine fásta i roinnt áiteanna. Faoi láthair tá sé ina chathaoirleach ar choiste i ndeisceart Ard Mhacha atá ag iarraidh an Ghaeilge a chur chun cinn sa cheantar agus tá sé ina iontaobhaí le hIontaobhas Ultach / Ultach Trust.

Is fiú comparáid a dhéanamh idir na riachtanais atá san earnáil ó thuaidh faoi láthair agus na riachtanais a bhí ann nuair a socraíodh na struchtúir thuasluaite a chruthú.

Caighdeáin teagaisc v. Easpa múinteoirí

Ní droch-chaighdeán teagaisc is mó atá ag déanamh buartha d'earnáil na gaelscolaíochta faoi láthair ach ganntanas múinteoirí. Tá caighdeán an teagaisc sa chuid is mó de na gaelscoileanna an-ard agus bhí riamh. Is dóigh liom go raibh sé go hard tríocha bliain ó shin, i mblianta tosaigh na gaelscolaíochta ó thuaidh, agus atá sa lá atá inniu ann, d'ainneoin nach raibh oiliúint ar leith ann le múinteoirí a dhéanamh réidh don ghaelscolaíocht san am sin. D'ainneoin gur rud fiúntach ann féin oiliúint ar leith bheith ar fáil do mhúinteoirí ar mhian leo dul ag obair in earnáil na gaelscolaíochta, níl na struchtúir oiliúna atá ann faoi láthair inchurtha leis an deacracht is mó a bhaineann le teagasc sa gaelscolaíochta, is é sin easpa múinteoirí. Is gá an bhéim sna cúrsaí atá ar fáil i láthair na huaire a athrú agus a lúbadh le dul i ngleic leis an ghanntanas múinteoirí agus is gá sin a dhéanamh mar ábhar práinne.

Is cinnte go bhfuil easpa áiseanna ag cur isteach go mór ar an earnáil agus is dóigh liom go bhfuil sin aimsithe ag an earnáil struchtúr cuí le tabhairt fúithi ach acmhainní go leor a bheith ag Áisaonad na Gaelscolaíochta le dul i ngleic leis an obair.

Maidir le líon na scoileanna atá le bunú is fiú cuimhniú nach ionann méadú ar líon na scoileanna agus forbairt na gaelscolaíochta. Le cois líon scoileanna, baineann forbairt le caighdeáin, le soláthar acmhainní, le fáil ar an gaelscolaíochta agus le seirbhísí tacaíochta. Ní ganntanas scoileanna atá ag cur isteach ar an earnáil faoi láthair, ach na scoileanna bheith sna háiteanna cearta a bhfuil pobal ann le freastal orthu, na scoileanna atá ann faoi láthair bheith ag fás agus riar iomlán cuimsitheach bheith á chur ar fáil ó réamhscolaíocht go hiarbhunscolaíocht. Mar an gcéanna le ceist na múinteoirí, caithfidh Gaeloiliúint agus an struchtúr bunaithe scoileanna, bheith in inmhe a mhodhanna agus a mhúnlaí a lúbadh le tabhairt faoin obair.

De thairbhe sainriachtanas oideachais de, is cinnte nach bhfuil riar sásúil á chur ar fáil faoi láthair don ghaelscolaíocht. Tá na háiseanna agus na hacmhainní atá ar fáil ag earnáil na gaelscolaíochta go hiomlán easnamhach. Is maith ann GESO le tús a chur le riar ar an chuid seo den ghaelscolaíocht. I ndeireadh na dála, is iad na húdaráis oifigiúla oideachais agus sláinte a chaithfidh dul i ndeabhaidh leis an obair seo.

Tá mórán easpaí in earnáil na réamhscolaíochta ar gá tabhairt fúthu. Mar sin féin, is féidir a rá gurb é an ganntanas daoine le Gaeilge le dul ag obair sna naíonraí an bac is mó faoi láthair ar fhás na réamhscolaíochta agus, dá réir sin, ar fhorbairt na gaelscolaíochta go ginearálta. Faoi láthair, tá na struchtúir atá ann in Altram dírithe ar chaighdeáin soláthar sna naíonraí seachas ar oiliúint sa Ghaeilge.

Is beag fadhb san oideachais ná sa ghaelscolaíocht nach gcuideodh infheistíocht airgid léi. Mar sin féin, dá mbeadh earnáil na gaelscolaíochta ó thuaidh le hí féin a eagrú mar ba cheart d'fhéadfaí maoiniú reatha a aimsiú ón stát do gach scoil úr. Ní heaspa airgid atá ag cur isteach ar an earnáil ach páistí go leor a bheith ann le critéir mhaoinithe na Roinne Oideachais a shásamh. Faoi láthair, tá an Roinn Oideachais sásta maoiniú reatha a chur ar fáil do scoil ach 12 páistí a bheith ann le dul uirthi san aon bhliain amháin. Dá bhféadfaí scoileanna úra a bhunú le go mbeadh maoiniú acu ón chéad lá amach d'fhéadfaí airgead Iontaobhas na Gaelscolaíochta a chaitheamh ar iarrachtaí le líon na bpáistí a mhéadú san earnáil ina hiomláine trí fheachtais fhógraíochta agus chaidrimh phoiblí. Arís eile, ní hionann an fhadhb ar bunaíodh an struchtúr le tabhairt fúithi agus an fhadhb ar gá dul i ngleic léi faoi láthair. Is de bharr gan eolas a bheith ag cuid mhór den phobal ar an ghaelscolaíocht agus gan éileamh a bheith ann don ghaelscolaíocht nach féidir maoiniú a aimsiú ón Roinn Oideachais do scoileanna ó thús a mbunaithe.

I dtaca le Comhairle na Gaelscolaíochta de, is é seo an chomhairle a bhunaigh an Roinn Oideachais le hearnáil na gaelscolaíochta a chur chun cinn. De réir bhunreacht na Comhairle titeann dualgais go leor ar a crann: caighdeáin teagaisc sa seomra ranga; sealbhú na Gaeilge sa chóras; caighdeáin chóiríochta agus trealaimh; seirbhísí tacaíochta; líon páistí; líon scoileanna; leathadh scoileanna; an ghaelscolaíocht iar-bhunscolaíochta; éileamh don ghaelscolaíocht a spreagadh; bunú scoileanna a éascú; múinteoirí a oiliúint; taighde a dhéanamh.

Ach cén chuid den ghaelscolaíocht is mó a bhfuil cur chun cinn de dhíth air? Caighdeáin teagaisc sa seomra ranga, sealbhú na Gaeilge sa chóras, caighdeáin chóiríochta agus trealaimh, seirbhísí tacaíochta, líon na bpáistí, líon na scoileanna nó leathadh na scoileanna, an ghaelscolaíocht iar-bhunscolaíochta, éileamh don ghaelscolaíocht a spreagadh, bunú scoileanna a éascú, múinteoirí a oiliúint nó taighde a dhéanamh.

Leis an fhreagra ceart a aimsiú is gá soiléiriú a aimsiú ar na dualgais a bheidh na heagraíochtaí eile a thabhairt orthu féin. Cad é na rólanna a fheiceann Iontaobhas na Gaelscolaíochta, Gaeloiliúint agus Altram dóibh féin?

Lena chois sin, is gá soiléiriú a aimsiú ar na cúraimí a mbeidh na struchtúir úra ag plé leo – Foras na Gaeilge agus a n-oifigí oideachais i mBéal Feirste, Forbairt Naíonraí Teoranta agus An Chomhairle Um Oideachais Gaeltachta agus Gaelscolaíochta.

An bhfuil lucht eagraithe na struchtúr úr seo ag breathnú ar a bhfuil ann faoi láthair thuaidh agus theas sula ndéanfaidh siad a gcinní. Má tá, an bhfuil siad ag breathnú ar na fadhbanna cearta is gá a réiteach?

Tá earnáil na gaelscolaíochta óg go leor go fóill maidir le forbairt le go dtig na struchtúir a athrú agus mhúnlú. Ach leis na struchtúir úra a bheidh ag teacht chun cinn beidh sé ag éirí níos deacra agus is mithid anois an díospóireacht seo a bheith ann nuair a thig toradh a bheith uirthi.

Tá géarghá le hathruithe sna struchtúir atá ann faoi láthair le tabhairt faoi na riachtanais atá ag an earnáil. Ná tugaimis faoi na hathruithe go drogallach agus tábhacht na struchtúr féin á chur roimh thábhacht na hearnála ach tugaimis fúthu go fonnmhar le leas na hearnála iomláine a dhéanamh.

Summary

In this talk I examine the current structures in place to address the needs of the Irish-medium (IM) sector including teacher training in St Mary's University College, the Irish-Medium Education Resource Unit, the voluntary organisations Gaeloiliúint, Altram and GESO (Special Needs in Irish-medium) and the newly-created structures the Irish-medium Education Trust and the Council for Irish-medium Education.

I consider the issues these structures were created to address including standards of teaching, lack of and standard of resources, lack of new schools, poor provision for IM special needs, teaching standards in the IM pre-schools sector, lack of funding sources for IM education and the promotion of IM education.

I draw comparisons between these issues and the issues that are most pressing at present in the IM sector and the appropriateness of the current structures to deal with them effectively.

I argue that rather than addressing teaching standards in schools we should be addressing the lack of trained teachers and adapting the teacher-training courses to focus on this issue; that the resource unit is addressing current needs but that it needs additional resources; that Gaeloiliúint must adapt its focus from one of simply establishing schools to one of strategic placing of schools in areas of population growth, working towards an even and comprehensive spread of schools catering for the full educational range from pre-school to post-primary; that GESO is providing a badly-needed service to school but that ultimately it should fall to the official educational authorities to cater for IM special needs; that Altram needs to shift its emphasis from childcare and curriculum provision to training and support in areas specific to the IM sector, i.e. Irish-language competence and second-language acquisition; that Iontaobhas na Gaelscolaíochta, the IM Education Trust needs to encourage the IM sector to move away from the practice of setting up schools without Department of Education (DE) funding and using its resources to increase awareness of IM education in general thus ensuring that sufficient numbers exist to achieve DE funding from day one and finally, that Comhairle na Gaelscolaíochta, the IM Education Council will only be able to narrow its focus when the other organisations react to the new situation.

I argue that now is the time to address the issue of the appropriateness of the structures while the sector is still relatively young and still taking shape and that the various organisations should engage in this debate with enthusiasm and with the broader interests of the IM sector in mind rather than a narrow, sectoral or selfish focus aimed at maintaining the current structures at any cost.

Structures for Gaelic-medium Education[1]

Margaret MacIver

1. Introduction

The Prospectus for the Third Language and Politics Symposium raised the following issues with regard to Irish-medium and Gaelic-medium education. To teach through another language (e.g. Irish in Northern Ireland and the Republic of Ireland and Gaelic in Scotland), what structures do we need to have in place? Is teacher training the only structure and where does it exist? What is missing from present structures? Even if we had ideal structures in place, would they work? If not, why not? In both parts of Ireland, there are Councils for all-Irish education: can they be overlooked? Does the Government or the political system help or hinder? How is Politics an obstruction to the implementation and smooth-running of education through another medium? Why doesn't the government better support such a policy? What is Government afraid of? Why is it worth the trouble and effort?

In this paper, I will address these and other issues in the context of Gaelic-medium Education (GME) in Scotland. I will consider them through the structures that we presently have in place and that have enabled us to progress from the small tentative beginnings in 1985 to our present situation. These structures are in 6 main domains. Each domain is crucial in structural terms if GME is to develop in Scotland and gain parity with the English medium system.

2. Parents and Children and The Home

I will begin with the home – that is with parents and their children – as the basis of any language regeneration programme. There are in place the following structural groups:

1. *Taic nam Pàrant – Neart na Gàidhlig*, 'The Support of Parents – The Strength of the Language' is one of the publicity slogans used in Comunn na Gàidhlig education publicity materials to promote Gaelic. Support for parents comes in different forms.
2. Comhairle nan Sgoiltean Àraich (CNSA), The Gaelic Pre-School Council, which works with parents through Family Language Plans and which provides pre-school support at all levels. (Information available from 53 Church Street, Inverness, IV1 1DR).
3. Playgroups and Mother and Toddler Groups, which are run by leaders trained at special training courses provided by CNSA. (Information available as at 2)
4. Nursery provision for 4 year olds, which are run in the main by local authorities. (Information available as at 2)

---

[1] The version presented at the symposium was delivered in Scottish Gaelic.

5. Gaelic Language courses designed specifically for parents, which are run by parental groups and Community Education programmes.
6. *Comann nam Pàrant* (CPN), Parental groups, which are set up with constitution at local level to support the promotion of GME and lobby local authorities on its behalf.
7. *Comann nam Pàrant* (*Nàiseanta*), abbreviated as CNP(N), which was set up by Comunn na Gàidhlig in 1994 to act as a voice for parents, and which is now very active at national and political levels (cf. www.parant.org.uk).
8. Promotional materials, which are prepared and distributed for raising awareness and informing parents of the choice now open to parents in Scotland.

For each of these eight parent-based or parent-related groups, a different structure is necessary to give parents support and finance initiatives which will help them in their efforts. If parents are not supported, then lack of confidence will result.

3. Statutory Provision - Primary and Secondary Schools

Most of GME provision is given in "units" within "host" schools. One dedicated school has been set up in Glasgow – Bunsgoil Ghàidhlig Ghlaschu, and another is due to be set up in Inverness (As it has not yet been set up it doesn't have a name). Because of the growth of GME, teacher demand and supply is still not breaking even. Five disadvantages may be identified shortage of primary teachers, which is hampering progress (no new units have been set up since 1999); shortage of specialist teachers able to teach specialist subjects through the medium of Gaelic which is hampering progress at Secondary level; shortage of Supply Teachers, whereby some schools have to revert to English medium when classroom teachers are absent; shortage of qualified and trained support staff, as a result of which children especially with learning difficulties are often not given a fair deal (GME must not become an elite system of education); and shortage of educational specialists, whereby a dearth of Gaelic-speaking psychologists, speech therapists, etc., creates difficulties in assessing needs of bilingual children especially at early stages. GME desperately requires a national co-ordinated Teacher Recruitment Strategy with a training programme geared to the needs of GME at all levels. Until such a strategy is achieved, then GME provision will neither progress nor develop as quickly or as effectively as we would wish. A Teacher Recruitment Strategy is one fundamental structure which we still need to put in place with more government support if GME is to increase and develop. Local Authorities provide in-service courses for teachers in post. Scottish Executive provides financial resources to run courses for Gaelic speaking teachers who do not have the confidence to teach in GME system. Participating teachers are seconded from their posts for 5 – 6 weeks. This programme has added a considerable number of teachers to the system, especially at primary level. A National Resource Centre – STÒRLANN – was set up by the Scottish Executive with its own Board of Directors. This is a crucial new structure enabling teachers to have updated and suitable resources and materials in the classroom. Teachers are involved in the preparation of these materials which can now be produced more quickly and effectively e.g. new Gaelic reading and mathematical schemes.

4. Further and Higher Education

GME is entirely dependent on the Further and Higher Education sector for providing fully trained teaching staff, supporting professionals and undertaking necessary research. This sector must keep abreast with what is happening in GME and at other levels of education. In the Gaelic context this sector includes:

1. 3 Universities - Glasgow, Edinburgh and Aberdeen, which offer Celtic/Gaelic degrees
2. 2 Universities – Aberdeen and Strathclyde, which offer Teaching Degrees/Diplomas
3. 1 Gaelic College, Sabhal Mòr Ostaig, where instruction is through the medium of Gaelic (www.smo.uhi.ac.uk)
4. 5 Colleges which offer Full-time Gaelic Immersion Courses for learners – Inverness, Sabhal Mòr Ostaig, Lews Castle, Stowe College, Kilmarnock College.

All of these are funded through the Scottish Higher Education Funding Council.

5. The General Teaching Council for Scotland, which is the professional body that validates courses and provides teachers' registration prior to them taking up classroom duties, has already undertaken research into the needs of training in the GME system and have made recommendations which we are now looking to implement with government support. (*Teaching in Gaelic Medium Education: Recommendations for Change.* GTCS, 2000. www.gtcs.org.uk)
6. A Body of Research has been undertaken by the government in GME schools, which has highlighted the strengths of GME system. (*The Attainments of Pupils Receiving Gaelic-medium Primary Education in Scotland,* Scottish CILT, 1999). Also research undertaken by Lèirsinn Research Centre at Sabhal Mòr Ostaig in various aspects of GME.

5. Local Councils

A total of 14 Local Authorities make provision for GME through the following three measures. There is Specific Grant Funding, which was originally provided by the Government in 1986, and which has proved to be the catalyst as far as most of these Councils are concerned. Specific Grant Funding is still being continued by the Government and requires its own structures at local and national levels. Details are available from the Scottish Executive. There are dedicated Gaelic Committees, which the larger spending Councils such as Western Isles, Highland, Argyle & Bute, Glasgow City have in addition to their local Education Committees to monitor the progress of GME. In addition one or two members of staff are given a specific Gaelic remit. It is their duty to liase with parents, schools, Gaelic organisations and other Councils. And there are Inter Authority

Structures, which co-ordinate action in the use of specific grants and which are crucial for the promotion of Gaelic within education at a national level. Inter Authority co-operation in Gaelic takes place regularly and especially at the following levels: primary and secondary, community education, management and directorate level, political level (allowing member input). and finally at the national resource centre, which is supported on an inter-authority basis through a joint budget monitored by local authorities

Since Gaelic is now a National Priority, each Council has to submit a development plan for Gaelic. These plans are subject to Executive scrutiny through the Her Majesty's inspectorate. This is a new and important development.

6. Community

A strong community dimension is crucial. A language will never survive without a community of speakers. Examples of some community initiatives set up to support statutory provision for GME are:

1. SRADAGAN (Gaelic for 'sparks'), which are youth groups set up in various communities by Comunn na Gàidhlig. By 2002, 50 for Primary pupils had been established. These groups give opportunity to use Gaelic outwith the classroom. (cf. www.cnag.org.uk).
2. Fèisean, which are tuition festivals concentrating on Gaelic music and culture. By 2002, over 30 of them had been set up throughout Scotland (cf. www.feisean.com).
3. Mod, which is a competitive festival held at both local and national levels. (cf. www.the-mod.co.uk).
4. Gaelic Career Events for Secondary pupils and adults, which take economic dimension into Gaelic development, and which are important for youngsters (cf. www.bithbeo.org.uk).
5. Bilingual signage and materials, which reflect an effort to create a Gaelic ethos outwith school precincts, although there is not as much as we would wish. Throughout Scotland, street, shop, railway, b&b, etc. signage are appearing. Signage is also being undertaken by a variety of bodies and agencies.

Each of these five initiatives requires its own specific structures with dedicated committees and separate funding and workforce. Communities have their own politics which can be very different to those of the government and can vary from one community to another. The strength of Community Programmes lies in the number of indigenous and fluent Gaelic speakers who are willing and able to offer their help and support. These programms are also dependent on support of local authorities and Gaelic organisations.

The media are also very important for the community dimension, especially TV and radio programmes crucial for all age groups. This dimension also requires a well-supported and financed structure. In Gaelic, we have the Comataidh Craolaidh Gàidhlig, 'Gaelic Media Committee'.

7. Government

It is government support and structures that will ultimately underpin all that has been achieved at educational and community levels. In the Scottish Parliament, there is bilingual signage and two Gaelic Parliamentary Officers appointed (cf. www.scottish.parliament.uk). In the Scottish Executive, despite good progress especially through *A New Start for Gaelic*, the report produced by the Ministerial Advisory Group for Gaelic, the Scottish Executive is still not willing to give Secure Status through a Language Act (cf. www.scotland.gov.uk). The Scottish Parliament has formed a Cross Party Committee on Gaelic which is proving a useful tool for communicating with and lobbying government for parliamentary and legislative matters. The fact remains, however, that GME needs the security of a Gaelic Language Act to make it a credible option in the eyes of parents.

The UK Westminster Government still retains responsibility for the Media dimension and is presently not willing to give Gaelic T.V. a dedicated Gaelic channel.

8. Conclusion

Whilst I am aware that secure status on its own will not save the language, it is imperative that we achieve it. Secure status would give the overall credibility to the language thus enhancing its position in the eyes of many, especially parents. Despite all the good progress, particularly in education, there is still a lack of confidence in the system simply because the language is not protected by a Language Act. This continues to be one of our greatest weaknesses and, at the end of the day, our system will prove to be as strong as our weakest link.

Thus we must continue to strive for a Language Act whilst at the same time ensuring that all the other structures in the various sectors are not being neglected. Structures are important for all of them in whatever sector and at whatever level. Each aspect of the language has its own importance and, for this reason, it is vital that all our systems and structures are co-ordinated to form an integrated approach. If we do this then we will build a strong infrastructure and support mechanisms around the language enabling it to develop in a normal and natural way.

With our present structures, we only have the foundations of a Gaelic revitalisation programme. But it is a beginning, and all of us involved in the development of the language are very well aware that we still have a long road ahead before our desired goal is finally achieved. With co-operation and co-ordination of effort, and the right set of structures, there is no reason why we should not achieve it.

Teaching through the Target Language – Preparation of Teachers

Pádraig de Bhál

The proper and adequate training and education of teachers is an essential factor in improving any aspect of the educational system. The training of language teachers is one such vital aspect which rarely commands the attention which its central importance deserves.

Since much of language teacher preparation arises from general educational perspectives, one needs to comment, briefly, on the training and education of teachers generally. Down through the years the focus in teacher education has oscillated between various models. In an earlier period the apprenticeship, skills, craft model dominated. This was based on observation, imitation and the learning of essential skills. It is still a vital part of the exercise but its limitations are obvious. Another model advocated the development of specific competencies such as those relating to the subject and content of teaching, to performance in the classroom, the methodology, etc. A recent widespread model was that of the reflective practitioner[1] whose professional artistry is constructed through thinking and a reflective analysis on the art and science of teaching. Finally, the most complete model is that of the technical rational approach in which theoretical knowledge or the applied science of education provides a flexible developmental backdrop to the everyday art of teaching.

An admixture of these models is involved in the preparation of teachers for the various levels of the Education system. It is a long complex undertaking encompassing as it does differing personalities and talents of aspiring teachers as they prepare for a great variety of learners of varying ability. It involves a partnership with schools which is of the utmost significance.

Internationally, a variety of institutional frameworks leads to different qualifications e.g. BEd, PGCE, Higher Diploma in Education, etc. There are also many private language-training institutions which provide a range of courses varying in length and quality.

The study of applied linguistics must feed into the professional preparation, whether it be in the private or public sector. Also the findings of research in its various dimensions whether observational, action or analytical should be presented to student teachers. The quality of the student at the initial access point to training is significant. Ideally, an interview should determine adequate oral and written language competence and overall suitability of personality. After an initial training period focused on theory, suitable placements would provide experience. Final qualification could lead to further specialisation. Competent mentoring and induction are also an essential phase of the complex teacher preparation task.

The Literature on teaching through the target language points to three basic requirements:

---

[1] Schon, Donald 1995 *The Reflective Practitioner: How Professionals Think in Action*: London, Arena.

a)   A high degree of competence in the target language. This is the
        responsibility of the language departments. The student teacher also
        needs to be at ease with the classroom language of the subject and also
        the language of textbooks.
b)   A high degree of competence in classroom skills and in language
        teaching methodology. This competence comes with practice. As
        academic subjects have a much higher status, the vital area of
        methodology is sometimes undervalued and frequently does not have a
        significant research base.
c)   The teacher also needs to have a good qualification in the actual subject
        so that he/she is confident and at ease with the material.[2]

While there are in language teaching circles in Europe and the US, some
programmes, either in the pre-service or in the career development stage
dedicated to preparation for teaching through the target language, in the Republic
of Ireland these are generally modules in other courses and are not really
formalised.

There are many other significant factors which contribute to best practice in
teacher training. Careful classroom placement during pre-service with
experienced and competent teachers, who are trained to act as helpful mentors, is
of the essence. The student teacher also needs to be initiated into the area of
materials preparation and adaptation, curriculum development, selection and
adaptation of texts, etc.

A life long perspective and understanding of education needs to be developed
through the foundation disciplines of education. Topics such as motivation for
teaching, adolescent psychology and the processes of understanding and learning,
classroom organisational techniques, use of audiovisual equipment, interactive
video, internet, etc are all central and necessary.

With this generic framework pre-supposed, I will now discuss some specific
aspects of content-based language instruction or content and language integrated
learning (CLIL). The approach is also referred to as Content and Language
Integrated Classrooms (CLIC). A very useful website is www.euroclic.net.[3]

Content and Language Integrated Learning

A clear definition of what is involved is given by David March (2002).[4] He
states "Content and Language Integrated Learning refers to any **dual focused**
context in which an **additional language**, though not usually the **first** language
of the learners involved, is used as a medium of teaching and learning of **non-
language content**. It is dual focused because whereas attention may be
predominantly on either subject — specific content or language, both are always

---

[2] McDonagh, S. 2002 *Applied Linguistics in Language Education*, London,
Arnold.
[3] There is also a magazine called *The Euroclic* which provides up to date
comparative information on developments in this area.
[4] *Considering the Potential of Content and Language Integrated Education*,
Document of University of Lyvasjyla, Finland p.1 (2002).

accommodated. This approach is currently implemented in a range of ways depending on the age range and location of learners".

Many varieties of this approach exist in mainstream education in Europe and U.S. It also takes various forms in the private language-teaching sector.

Many approaches such as language across the curriculum, languages for special purposes and immersion education assume that language is learned most effectively using meaningful, interesting and relevant content. A dual focused approach means that there is significant exposure to language input without the requirement of extra time.

Given that content-based instruction is an effective way to teach language skills, a number of practical realisations of the approach have been developed. These are described by Brinton, Snow & Wesche.[5] They include **theme based language** instruction where the language class is structured around topics or themes and "the content material presented provides the basis for language analysis and practice". The **sheltered content approach** consists of content courses taught in a second language to a segregated group of learners by a content-area specialist". These are close to the traditional immersion courses. In the **adjunct model approach** "Students are enrolled currently in two linked courses – a language course and a content course. The two courses share the same content base and complement each other in terms of mutually co-ordinated assignments". (pp 14-16).

Within the Irish Context, the value of the dual focused approach has been well documented. Harris (1984) in *Spoken Irish in the Primary School*[6] points to an outcome of his survey which confirms that the achievement in spoken Irish of pupils in all-Irish schools is considerably superior to that of pupils in ordinary schools. Also pupils of all levels of academic ability have higher levels of achievement in Irish if they are in classes which are exposed to some Irish medium teaching (Harris 1993).[7] This insight led to the funding of a project which developed full courses in Science and Art for Irish medium teaching in fourth class in the primary school. This is significant, as there has been a dramatic growth in all-Irish schools and in all Irish pre-schools in recent years. Canadian, Northern Ireland, Welsh and Scots-Gaelic researchers have reached similar conclusions. Regarding the comparison of academic outcomes in Wales, Canada, Ireland and Scotland, "there is broad agreement in current research findings that point to an equivalent or favourable performance among total immersion pupils in comparison with English medium peers."[8]

Significant advantages claimed for this approach are the following. The time saving factor is attractive to policy makers. Also the students experience enhanced motivation since language and knowledge are presented in meaningful association. It is also much easier to provide authentic communication. Co-ordination and co-operation between teachers is also enhanced.

---

[5] Brinton, D., Snow, M. , Wesche, M. (1989) *Content based Second Language Instruction* New York, Newbury House

[6] Harris, J. (1984) *Spoken Irish in the Primary School* I.T.É., Dublin.

[7] Harris, J. (1993) *An Ghaeilge Labhartha sa Ghnáthscoil* (unpublished).

[8] Neil, P., Ni Uidhir, G. Clarke, F. (2000) *Native Speakers immersed in another language – A Review of the Literature* Belfast, DEN 1.

In the current sociopolitical context, where there are constant calls for the inclusion of more and more fashionable curricular additions, the value and efficacy of content-based language instruction needs to be highlighted, and better propagated and explained. In the context of European union and the accession to the EU of new countries, languages as resources, problems and rights will provide an urgency for greater efficiency in language teaching. This will raise the profile of CLIL through more publicity and awareness. Also recent immigration and migration have created a greater diversity of peoples, languages and cultures in our community.

There are many questions which arise in practice regarding this issue. The lack of adequate textbooks and the language difficulty in textbooks is a major one. Also, this approach requires significant resources and expertise. Language teacher trainers and educators need to provide more formal courses of training for teachers aspiring to use the CLIL approach. Certain modern foreign languages dominate in this area and an effort has to be made to redress this. There is need for further research in the area to ascertain levels of pupil and teacher interest in CLIL, to increase parents' support for it and to discover the degree of teacher co-operation, etc. These factors enhance learning. There is also need for closer attention to what types of classroom activity and communication in the foreign language are more likely to help pupils to learn.

Schools of education and other language institutes need to be aware of the benefits of this approach and to prepare students to implement it. Policy makers have to be convinced of its value before they will provide the resources to properly bring it about. I conclude with a quotation from Davis Marsh:

> To learn a language and content simultaneously provides an extra means of educational delivery which offers a range of benefits relating to both learning of the language and also learning of the non-language subject matter."[9]

CLIL has therefore to be evaluated in any consideration of language policy and language planning. It is, in fact, a significant issue in public policy and in the political arena.

---

[9] *Considering the Potential of Content and Language Integrated Education* (Document of University of Jyväskylä, Finland p.4).

Initial Teacher Training for Irish-medium Schools

Gabrielle Nig Uidhir

1. Introduction

In 1971, when the first Irish-medium primary school (bunscoil) in Belfast was being planned, parents travelled to Donegal and Dublin, among other places, in search of a qualified teacher for their new school. At that time (and for the following 25 years), teachers did not receive any specialist training for immersion schools in Northern Ireland.

In this paper, the introduction and development of Irish-medium Initial Teacher Education (IMTE) at St. Mary's University College is outlined. This account highlights the constraints and influences, which shape the nature and scale of present provision, and points to ways by which we can build on the very solid foundation which has been laid in recent years.

2. History

The demand for specialist training came primarily from Gaeloiliúint, the umbrella organisation for IMTE. This body was also directly involved in founding new schools and was very aware of the growing challenge of finding qualified teachers. St. Mary's College responded positively to the proposal submitted by Gaeloiliúint by appointing a researcher, in 1994, to design a model for Irish-medium provision which could be implemented within the BEd and postgraduate courses. By that time, the number of bunscoileanna in Northern Ireland had increased to 13 and had extended from urban centres into rural areas. Gaeloiliúint was founded in response to the need for co-ordinated, strategic planning within this evolving sector. Teacher training was one of many questions tackled by the new organisation. By the early 90s, this had become a more urgent issue. New teachers for the Irish-medium sector were then being drawn from the English-medium BEd courses and from postgraduate certificate courses, designed for primary or secondary teachers in the English-medium schools. Most of these were modern language students who would receive most of their specialist vocational training in post. As the schools and class sizes were small, it was possible for existing staff to assist newly qualified colleagues become familiar with immersion pedagogies and to develop necessary teaching materials. As existing schools grew in size and new schools were opened (without an experienced staff available to support the new teacher) the need for specialist training increased. This situation became critical when the shortage of qualified teachers who were competent in Irish, began to impact upon the opening of new primary schools and upon curriculum development at secondary level. The provision of Irish-medium teacher training became a priority. Negotiations were opened with various third level institutions and with the Department of Education (McKendry 1994). The outcome of this groundwork was a decision to train teachers for Irish-medium primary schools at St. Mary's College, Belfast.

3. Criteria for successful introduction of programme

3.1 Supportive infrastructure and environment

During the design phase of the course structure and content, it became apparent that certain internal factors would contribute significantly to the success of the initiative. The fact that the introduction of Irish-medium provision was strongly supported by the College Senior Management was central to the development. The College Principal had experience of teaching in an Irish-medium primary school and understood the immersion system. The Irish language was also spoken by some members of staff from non-language disciplines who were willing to deliver lectures in their subject specialism through Irish. Others demonstrated a willingness to learn the language. Other staff members simply expressed a positive attitude to the development of a bilingual environment. Staff development programmes included language classes and one residential course. This support continues. However, the recent retirement of three lecturers from the Irish-medium course team, who were competent Irish speakers and specialists in other subject areas, has impacted upon the delivery of the course.

3.2 Funding facility

Another factor that was considered crucial for the successful implementation of an Irish-medium programme, at the outset, was the commitment to ring fence the funding for this development. Potential tensions and conflicts would be avoided by having a transparent and separate budget which clearly did not influence staffing and resourcing issues in other discipline areas.

3.3 Designated areas of responsibility

St. Mary's was also an appropriate choice within the political structure of the northern academic institutions. Some rearrangement of areas of responsibility in IMTE delivery has since occurred and, presently, can be delineated as in Table 1.

Table 1: Designated areas of responsibility

St Mary's University College, Belfast	BEd Degree (English-medium and Irish-medium) *Mainly Primary* PGCE (Irish-medium) *Primary*
Stranmillis University College, Belfast	BEd Degree *Mainly Primary* PGCE in Early Years *Nursery/Primary* PGCE for Educational Psychologists *Primary*
University of Ulster, Coleraine	PGCE (English Medium) *Primary/Secondary*
Queen's University, Belfast	PGCE *Secondary*
University of Ulster, Jordanstown	PGCE *Secondary*

4. Present Provision for IMTE

The approach to Irish-medium provision at St. Mary's University College, mirrors the philosophy which guides pedagogy in the schools. The aim is an additive bilingual situation. Irish is a functional medium which students use and develop as they acquire the teaching competences relevant to their year group. Therefore, in addition to studying immersion education and to analysing and reflecting upon good teaching practices within an immersion context, they gain first hand experience of the teaching methodologies which pupils in their own as it is for most Irish-medium pupils in schools. It is valuable for students to be sensitive to this methodology from the perspective of pupil/student as well as teacher. Similar programmes at the University of Ottawa were described as 'late late immersion' initiatives by Burger, et al. (1997: 65-83).

Students who successfully complete their course are awarded a Certificate in Bilingual Education. It is important that these students have gained competences and experience relevant to teaching in an Irish-medium and English-medium environment. Both languages and both educational systems are valued and that these values are built into the course structure and content. Therefore, the aim is that students experience roughly 50 per cent of College-based and School-based work with an Irish focus and 50 per cent with an English focus. However, practical restraints such as staffing issues and the availability of suitable school

Table 2: Irish-medium courses

	Curriculum Studies	Education	Main subject	School Experience
PGCE	Literacy, numercy, science, history, geography, rel. studies – through Irish or bilingual.	Nursery/early years/KS1 bilingual I.M.E. issues through Irish	(No Main subject) Personal Language Skills in Irish	2 blocks I.M. 1 block E.M.
	Curriculum St.	Education	Main subject	School Experience.
BEd 1&2	Literacy, science and numeracy via Irish	Teaching Studies through Irish. Other aspects in English.	Main subject 'Irish'	TE block in English-med. Some visits to IM schools
BEd 3	All subjects through Irish or bilingual	Mostly English-medium. Some bilingual input.	Main subject 'Irish'	TE block in Irish-med. at KS1 / Nursery
BEd 4	All subjects through Irish or bilingual	Immersion Education and IME issues	Main subject 'Irish'	TE block in Irish-med. at KS2

placements are the predominant considerations which impact upon the linguistic profile of the course delivery.

The Irish-medium course structure from a linguistic perspective is outlined in Table 2.

The implementation of this model required a creative and innovative approach to developing teaching methodologies at third level. Burger describes the continual pedagogical adaptation that was central to the late, late immersion project in Ottawa University (1997, 74). The success of this Irish-medium initiative was dependent upon a similar openness to pedagogical development. The full-time and part-time Irish-medium staff delivered subjects like literacy and education as individual lecturers. Non-language specialists who were competent Irish speakers (science, geography, religion) gave their lectures to the Irish-medium cohort in Irish. Team teaching was introduced in other subject specialisms. This worked as part of a staff development programme, with the subject specialist taking a leading role in the first year and reducing input in the second year. By the third year, the subject specialist was time-tabled mainly for consultation and support. Initially, the input of the I.M.E. lecturer involved language support during the lecture, translation of notes, preparing and introducing Irish-medium resources and materials. In subsequent years, the Irish-medium lecturer took over the delivery of these lectures. For example, within numeracy, the numeracy lecturer introduced the subject of the lecture, in English, in appropriate detail. The students were then divided into groups for practical activities related to the lecture. During this second part of the session, the language switched quite naturally to Irish among the students. The Irish-medium lecturer interacted with the students during activities, drawing attention to key terminology in Irish and supporting the students' language needs in the context of this other discipline. Relevant notes in Irish were distributed. This approach was most dynamically developed in the multilingual context of the early PGCE lectures. Until 1999, the PGCE cohort was part of a larger group of English-medium postgraduates and Erasmus students. During the practical activities, three or four different languages were sometimes in use among students in a most natural manner. That particular team teaching situation facilitated the application of linguistic and cultural diversity in a very meaningful way . However, it was also important that the Irish-medium students could participate in lectures, workshops and other pedagogical activities, as a single group. Students need direct access to the immersion experience and they benefit from the sense of social cohesion afforded by opportunities to interact with Irish-medium peers and future colleagues. Linguistically, this interaction also encourages use of Irish as a functional medium among the students and is essential to this late, late immersion approach.

5. Projected demand and student intake

In the Report produced by St. Mary's College (Nig Uidhir 1996), projections made for numbers of Irish-medium schools and teachers in Northern Ireland, spanning the years 1996-2000, proved to be quite accurate. Predicted numbers of schools and teaching posts were recorded up to the year 2000. In this year, the first cohort of Irish-medium BEd students would graduate and take up positions. The projection can now be extended to show the existing number of Irish-medium schools in Northern Ireland as 26 at primary and a further three at secondary level. These projections were presented as the **minimum** number of schools and posts predicted.

The first Irish-medium year group of BEd students included five students whose main subject was Irish and a further two students whose main subject was history and physical education. These students chose the bilingual degree course option once they had passed general entrance requirements and had been offered a place in the College. This number of BEd students would therefore change from year to year. Applicants for the postgraduate certificate course were interviewed specifically for the Irish-medium PGCE course. The number of postgraduate students is decided by the Department of Education. Initially, five places were offered. This number has risen to sixteen places in the current year. The numbers of Irish-medium students about to enter the profession (i.e. in their final year) are shown in the following illustrations.

An initial glance might suggest that there is a fairly close match between the numbers of students and the numbers of schools and predicted posts. Why, therefore, in the year 2002, are school principals and committees still frustrated by staff shortages and the problems which arise from these shortages? What are the constraints that impact upon the number of Irish-medium students in Initial Teacher Training and how can these influences be managed?

A closer examination of the above illustrations, which also note the number of students from Northern Ireland, gives some insight into relevant issues. The pattern of employment among new graduates shows a tendency among students from the Republic of Ireland to take up teaching posts in schools in the Republic. The vast majority of all Irish-medium students stay within the Irish-medium professional sector. Nevertheless, appointments outside Northern Ireland leave the increasing number of schools involved in the projections with a reduced pool of applicants.

This fact is frayed all around its edge with political sensitivities. Furthermore, it is only one of a cluster of factors that influence this situation. Other factors include the increase of part-time staff required in schools and the growing need for a pool of substitute teachers to facilitate attendance at courses, etc.

Teachers applying for a position in an Irish-medium school are entering a growing sector with a high demand for qualified staff. The anomaly of this situation lies in the fact that so many newly qualified teachers in the English-medium primary sector are still unemployed in the school term following their graduation (NASUWT 2002). Is there a way to channel some of that talent

Figure 1: New posts Created in Irish-medium Schools (Nig Uidhir 1996)

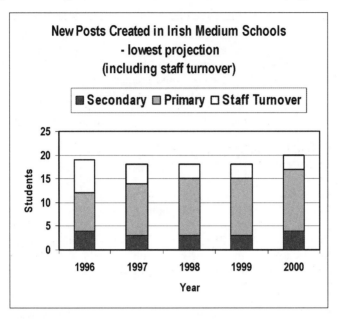

Figure 2: Irish-medium Primary Schools in Northern Ireland

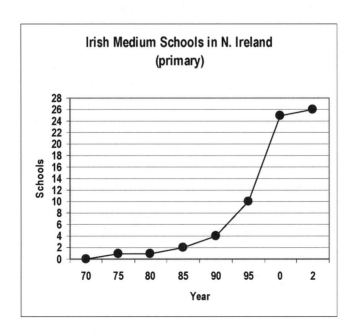

Figure 3: Irish-medium Education BEd Students

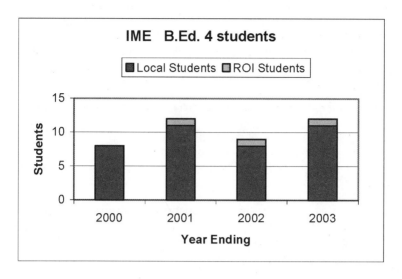

Figure 4: Irish-medium Education PGCE Intake

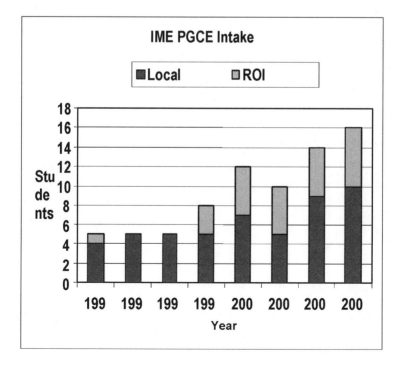

into the Irish-medium sector? Certainly, questions concerning separate quotas for Irish-medium; inducements to attract student teachers into this high demand area; resources to facilitate the transfer of teachers from the English-medium sector into Irish-medium schools open up a debate that raises further political issues. This Symposium addresses this question of how politics impact upon teacher education in Irish-medium and Gaelic-medium education. I do not attempt to unravel the entire mesh of political influences, which shape many aspects of that provision. However, some influences have already emerged during this analysis of specialist training for Irish-medium teachers. Within the context of the Good Friday Agreement and the European Charter for Regional or Minority Languages, politics should become less of an obstruction to language planning. This legislation should ease some of the tension in the handling of language issues. Although, the European Charter has been welcomed as a significant development, its limitations have been documented in the report by Pobal (2002). Clearly, the full implementation of these legislative instruments has some way to go to filter through to the levels of school committees and boards of governors trying to fill staff vacancies. Planners and practitioners within the area of Irish-medium teacher education are sensitive to this strain on schools and work in close partnership with schools on these issues.

Unsurprisingly, political factors have shadowed the development of the Irish-medium initiative at St. Mary's. Even a supportive Management could not have introduced IMTE into a third level institution if the political climate had not been favourable. During the development of the Irish-medium initiative, many political tensions have been smoothed out and worked through but these influences continue to arise.

At the macro level, political factors have affected the development of Teacher Education in a similar way to that experienced by schools. The Department's response to the growth of the Irish-medium sector has been delicately handled in parallel with negotiations involving the Integrated sector. Yet, because of this approach, different needs can be mismatched within a common policy framework.[1]

6. Constraints and Ways Forward

At the micro level, three principal constraints on student numbers repeatedly emerge during these consultations with partner schools: teaching experience placements, resourcing for Irish-medium IMTE, and the allocation of student quotas. These factors interlink and give further insight into the complexities inherent in the implementation of any legislative language policy.

---

[1] One example of different needs among the schools is class size. This is a key issue in immersion education where the class teacher may be the only linguistic model for many pupils and English is often the language of the home. In this context, low teacher–pupil ratio becomes a greater priority in the Irish-medium schools than in the English-medium schools.

6.1 School Placements

Eighteen weeks of the PGCE course is school-based and the remaining 50% of the course is College-based. These students spend three blocks of Teaching Experience in primary schools in Northern Ireland. BEd students spend eight weeks in each of their four years on Teaching Experience in primary or nursery (or secondary) schools. On average, 60 students are participating in the Irish-medium course at any point in time. This means that Irish-medium students require approximately 85 places in each year. As our graphs show, there are 26 Irish-medium primary schools in Northern Ireland at present. The availability of places for Teaching Experience is also further limited by the fact that many of these schools have a small and newly qualified staff who do not have the experience required to support a student.

As the IM provision has evolved, various initiatives have been introduced to help the College and schools, in partnership, to manage this situation. For example, postgraduate students now spend their first Teaching Experience in pairs. They collaborate in planning schemes and in team teaching activities. They are also introduced to peer evaluation. The College offers professional support to the classroom teacher as well as to the students in order to implement this model efficiently. In this way, the motivation to reduce the number of places required in schools can be complimented by educational advantages.

Further steps, which would impact favourably upon student numbers, would be the introduction of school placements in the Republic of Ireland for some students. School placements in a Gaeltacht school would carry the additional benefit of facilitating linguistic support for Irish-medium students. Both of these potential ways forward would carry certain costs.

6.2 Resourcing

Another political development, which impacts upon Irish-medium education, including teacher education, is the government's funding operative for education. Primary and secondary schools are funded via the Department of Education. Third level institutions are funded by a separate government department (DEL). Therefore, even the most positive dialogue between the Irish-medium schools the IMTE institution can be unproductive in terms of the implementation of proposals if the discussion occurs outside an inter-departmental context.

The key resource in the provision of Irish-medium teacher education (as in schools) is its staff. As Irish-medium student year groups increased, the Irish-medium budget has also increased to facilitate a second full-time lecturer's appointment. These two lecturers plan and deliver undergraduate and postgraduate courses across the curriculum. Obviously, further development requires additional staff. An expansion of the lecturing team would facilitate extending the range of subject areas with an Irish-medium input. Staffing time would also be a factor in planning for additional students; teaching experience spanning an extended geographical area; developing marketing programmes for schools; developing training programmes for teachers in the English sector; responding to requests for training provision for the Irish-medium secondary sector. All of these very logical developments require a reasonable level of staffing for the I.M.E. programme at St.Mary's.

6.3 Allocated student quotas

This question of student quotas arises each year, particularly in relation to the PGCE quota. This figure has risen from five to ten students. Further negotiations usually resulted in a limited number of additional places being allowed by the Department of Education. This year, this quota has reached 16 postgraduate places. In the case of BEd students, this administrative system requires revision. The anomaly, referred to earlier, whereby a surplus of newly qualified teachers for the English system is offset by a critical shortage in Irish-medium schools, needs to be addressed. Surely, the correspondence of teacher demand in Irish-medium schools and Irish-medium student placements could be built into the model for deciding student quotas.

7. Conclusion

The provision of Initial Teacher Education has evolved over the past six years in a way that is integrated into College structures and College life. This development is periodically reviewed and adapted to overcome constraints and not only to parallel developments in schools but also to take a lead in this field. Potential developments are held in check by a number of factors, including political influences.

On a yearly basis, groups of very competent and high calibre students graduate with specialist qualifications in bilingual education. These are highly motivated students who opted for a very rewarding but demanding course. In making this choice, they demonstrate a level of commitment that mirrors the vocational choice made by Irish-medium teachers in the schools.

Nevertheless, the numbers of newly qualified teachers are filtering through rather than surging into the Irish-medium system. The high level of excellence that is achieved by these Irish-medium student teachers could be maintained among a larger student population. However, resourcing constraints on staffing and strategic recruitment, in particular, continue to restrict further development in this area.

References

Burger, S., Wesche, M., Migneron M. 1997 Late, Late, immersion: Discipline-based second language teaching at the University of Ottawa. In eds. R. K. Johnson and M.Swain. *Immersion Education: international perspectives.* Cambridge: Cambridge University Press. 65-83

Mc Kendry, E. 1994. Gaeilge / Irish in Northern Ireland. In eds. E. Ní Dheá, M. Ní Neachtain and A. Ó Dubhghaill. *The Lesser Used Languages and Teacher Education: Towards the promotion of the European Dimension.* Limerick: Mary Immaculate College. 26-35

NASUWT. 2002. Survey of Final Year Student Members in N.I. Colleges, 2002. Belfast: NASUWT

Nig Uidhir, G. 1996. *Teacher Training for Irish-Medium Schools: Report on the introduction of a new Irish-medium pathway into St. Mary's College, June 1996.* Belfast: St. Mary's University College

POBAL. 2002. *The European charter for Regional and Minority Languages. The Implementation of the Charter with regard to the Irish language July 2001-July 2002. Submission by Pobal to the Committee of Experts on the Charter.* Prepared by Teresa Gorman.

Teacher Training in Gaelic in Scotland

A G Boyd Robertson

Initial teacher education in Scotland is provided by seven Teacher Education Institutions (TEIs). All the TEIs are now based in universities, following a series of mergers between former independent colleges of education and the universities within the last decade. The TEIs are located in the Universities of Aberdeen, Dundee, Edinburgh, Stirling, Glasgow, Strathclyde and Paisley (Ayr Campus). There is no TEI in the Highlands and Islands.

Only three of the TEIs make provision for teacher education in Gaelic. The main provider is the Faculty of Education of the University of Strathclyde, formerly Jordanhill College of Education. The others are the Faculty of Education of the University of Aberdeen, formerly Northern College of Education, and the University of Glasgow Faculty of Education, formerly St Andrew's College, Bearsden. The latter caters particularly for Roman Catholic students.

Initial teacher education for the primary school takes two forms, a four-year Bachelor of Education (Honours) course or a one-year postgraduate course leading to the award of a Postgraduate Certificate in Education (Primary) [PGCE(P)]. The first degree may be in any discipline. There are also two routes into secondary school teaching, the one-year postgraduate course leading to the Postgraduate Certificate in Education (Secondary) [PGCE(S)] and the concurrent degree route which is only available in certain subjects. Most secondary teachers enter the profession by the PGCE(S) route which confers a qualification to teach one or two school subjects. Entry to this course requires the equivalent of three years study in each specialist subject. There is also some cross-sector initial teacher education, most notably in Physical Education where a BEd degree in that specialism entitles students to teach in both primary and secondary schools.

Initial teacher education in Gaelic takes place within the context of the main BEd and PGCE courses. Contrary to some public perception and student expectation, there are, as yet, no parallel Gaelic-medium versions of these courses. Indeed, the Gaelic element within both primary courses is very limited and largely optional and does not warrant the designation, Gaelic-medium pathway, that has been conferred on it in certain institutions.

The PGCE courses are only offered by two of the universities – Strathclyde and Aberdeen – and, up until this year, Strathclyde was the only provider with full-time Gaelic staff. Gaelic is one of the subject specialisms within the PGCE (Secondary) and students training to be teachers of subjects such as History, Geography and Maths at Strathclyde can opt for a module in Gaelic-medium education.

Issues in Teacher Training in Gaelic

The highest profile issue is that of recruitment and the continuing shortage of Gaelic-medium teachers. Demand for Gaelic teachers has far exceeded supply in recent years and this has stunted and, in some cases, prevented the growth of Gaelic-medium education in certain areas. Local authorities are sometimes unable to open new Gaelic-medium units and schools experience great difficulty in locating Gaelic-speaking supply teachers.

The pool of Gaelic speakers from which students can be recruited is very small at 69,000 and the fact that only 60-70 fluent speakers per year sit Higher Examinations in Gàidhlig underlines this. While the number of candidates is increasing as a result of the development of Gaelic-medium education in the secondary sector, there is still a need to enlarge the overall pool by enabling more young people to learn the language to the advanced level required to function as Gaelic-medium teachers.

A number of marketing initiatives have been taken by Comunn na Gàidhlig, the main Gaelic development agency and these, together with the priority given to Gaelic-medium recruitment by the Scottish Higher Education Funding Council (SHEFC), on the advice of the Scottish Executive, have led to a considerable improvement in recruitment in the primary sector. As a result, it is anticipated that 20 new teachers will be added to the Gaelic-medium workforce in 2003-04. There is, nevertheless, continuing cause for concern about the nature of the career guidance being offered to Gaelic speakers in certain schools and recruitment to secondary Gaelic-medium teaching remains alarmingly low.

Linked to recruitment is the issue of access to training. The main Gaelic-speaking areas are in the islands and the West Highlands but the TEIs are situated on the opposite side of the country and in the Central Belt. This may not deter young and mobile prospective students but it does, in many instances, preclude mothers with young families from embarking on training courses. Distance-learning provision would alleviate this problem and the University of Strathclyde is currently developing an open-learning version of the PGCE(P) course in collaboration with Lews Castle College. The intention is that this course will be rolled out to other colleges within the University of the Highlands and Islands Millennium Institute (UHIMI).

The needs of the Gaelic-medium sector were largely overlooked in the selection procedures and arrangements adopted by TEIs until very recently, when steps were taken to ensure that all Gaelic-speaking applicants were interviewed and Gaelic-speaking staff and teachers were included in selection panels. For many years, TEIs resisted the notion of positive discrimination in favour of Gaelic-speaking applicants on the grounds of maintaining equal opportunities despite the fact that there was a shortage of Gaelic-medium teachers and an over-supply of English-medium teachers. Pressure from Gaelic agencies and local authorities led to a gradual softening of this line and the introduction of allocated places for Gaelic-medium students by SHEFC in the past two years further improved the prospects of Gaelic applicants.

A major issue which has still to be addressed is the fact that no specific qualification is required to enter Gaelic-medium teaching. The specialised nature of the training for Gaelic-medium education undertaken by students is not formally recognised by certification and there are no benchmarks for Gaelic-medium education to parallel those produced for English-medium education by the Scottish Executive Education Department.

Certification was one of the issues considered by a sub-group of the General Teaching Council for Scotland (GTCS) which was asked "to examine the current training and accreditation needs for Gaelic-medium education and to make recommendations to the Council and the Scottish Executive on the way ahead".

Members of the sub-group were drawn from the local authorities, the Scottish Executive Education Department, the TEIs and the GTCS itself. The Report produced by the sub-group, *Teaching in Gaelic Medium Education: Recommendations for Change*, was accepted by the General Teaching Council for Scotland and published in 2000.

The GTCS Report asserted that "the general perception in the Gaelic school community is that teachers entering Gaelic-medium are inadequately prepared" and cited probationer teacher and head teacher feedback as well as research evidence in support of this claim. A research report, *Meeting the Demand for Gaelic in Education; the availability of Gaelic-speaking teachers*, produced by the Lèirsinn Research Agency in Skye in 1998 noted three main areas of deficiency in present training arrangements highlighted by newly-qualified teachers: competence in Gaelic language, limited opportunities for placement in Gaelic-medium centres, and under-developed classroom skills, particularly in delivering a whole Gaelic-medium curriculum and handling multi-level and bilingual differentiation

The GTCS Report concluded that "there is a professional concensus that the current initial teacher education arrangements are not meeting the needs of Gaelic-medium teachers".

The GTCS Report analysed current teacher education courses and found that "preparation for the demands of the Gaelic-medium classroom is unsatisfactory". The main flaws identified were that students proposing to teach in Gaelic-medium education are under no compulsion to opt for Gaelic courses; that language development, tuition in Gaelic and the number of Gaelic-related electives are all limited; that much of the training is dependent on additional courses taken in the student's own time, for which staff may not be timetabled; that provision for Gaelic-medium education is not made in each year of the four-year BEd course; that school experience in Gaelic-medium classes is limited and unsatisfactory – it does not cover all primary school stages, it need not include the critical immersion stage; and there are few visits by Gaelic-speaking tutors, and that there is inadequate preparation for the unique professional and pedagogical demands of the Gaelic-medium classroom, for example, the philosophical dimension of bilingualism and immersion stage methodology

One point not covered in the Report is the deleterious effect the minimal amount of course delivery in Gaelic has on the linguistic development of learners of the language. An increasing number of recruits to Gaelic-medium teaching are students who have learnt the language in intensive immersion courses. Many of these students find that their language proficiency regresses during the period of training because of the restricted opportunities to hear and use the language.

There are also a number of defects in regard to professional development arrangements for serving teachers. New induction arrangements introduced in 2002 mean that entrants to the profession are allocated to local authorities rather than to schools and the system is not yet sufficiently refined to guarantee that students who have undertaken training in Gaelic are placed in Gaelic-medium schools. Nor is there any requirement on students, specifically recruited for Gaelic-medium places, to seek employment in the Gaelic-medium sector. Few, if any, students deliberately exploit this loophole but some do opt for English-medium teaching, preferring to live and work in an urban environment rather than in a rural setting.

Teachers serving in the Gaelic-medium sector often experience a sense of isolation and this is compounded by the limited opportunities for continuing professional development at regional and national level. Funding constraints and the lack of Gaelic-speaking supply teachers are among the factors at play in this regard. It is anticipated that this situation will improve as a result of a national professional development initiative resulting from a review of teachers' pay and conditions of service. The proposal to introduce a new category of Chartered Teacher might well allow the introduction of modules leading to an in-service qualification and certificate in Gaelic-medium teaching.

Staff development is further inhibited by the lack of Gaelic advisors and staff tutors in many parts of the country. This is but one of several examples of the need for a better infrastructure for Gaelic-medium training. One major drawback in the system at present is the absence of a co-ordinating mechanism. Many of the issues identified above have been recognised and discussed by the various interested parties over a period of several years but there has not been enough concerted action to tackle these problems. There is a clear need for the relevant agencies to devise a programme of action and to give one of the agencies responsibility for implementing that programme. The new Bòrd Gàidhlig na h-Alba might be an appropriate body to broker such inter-agency collaboration.

The Political Dimension

Political attention at both local authority and national level has focused largely on the issue of teacher recruitment. Education authorities which have experienced difficulty in staffing new or extended provision have come under considerable pressure from parents through the Comann nam Pàrant network and from Gaelic agencies such as Comunn na Gàidhlig and groups of activists like Fàs Dhùn Eideann. The local authorities have responded by lobbying the Scottish Executive and Members of the Scottish Parliament. Meetings have been held with education ministers and with education officials and the issue has been raised in the Scottish Parliament in question to Ministers and in debates on Gaelic and on educational matters. The Cross-Party Parliamentary Group, led by Maureen MacMillan MSP, has been active in making representations to the Executive on the need for more teachers.

The Ministerial Advisory Group on Gaelic, chaired by Professor Donald Meek, acknowledged the centrality and urgency of this issue in the development of Gaelic-medium education in its report published in 2002.

> *Educational provision is going to be the life-blood of any Gaelic revival. There is a desperate under-provision of teachers and resources at primary, secondary and tertiary levels. If Gaelic is to survive, then Gaelic-medium education must grow exponentially [...] We believe that immediate action should be taken to prepare and implement an emergency recruitment strategy for Gaelic-medium teachers at primary and secondary levels and that targets be set for the next ten years in the first instance.*

The Scottish Executive has taken a number of steps to address the issue. It has funded a number of recruitment initiatives undertaken by Comunn na Gàidhlig and has advised the Scottish Higher Education Funding Council on the need to prioritise Gaelic-medium education in the allocation of places on courses at the

TEIs. The Executive has also funded short courses for Gaelic-speaking teachers interested in transferring to the Gaelic-medium sector at both primary and secondary levels. A personal initiative by the former Minister for Gaelic led to collaboration between the University of Strathclyde and Lews Castle College designed to allow students in Lewis and Harris to undertake most of the PGCE (Primary) course in their home area. Criticism was levelled at the Minister for establishing such provision in his own constituency where the shortage of teachers was least acute.

The location of teacher education for the Gaelic-medium sector has become highly politicised. Local authorities in the Highlands and Islands perceive a need a need to establish some form of training provision in the area in order to capitalise on the currently untapped pool of recruits unable to undertake initial teacher education courses due to the urban siting of the TEIs. The local authorities foresee a potential role for the University of the Highlands and Islands Millennium Institute in the delivery of teacher education and are anxious to explore open-learning and off-site modes of delivery. Access to training in the Highlands and Islands is also seen as a means of counteracting, or at least reducing, the problem of students finding life in the cities attractive and resisting the allure of teaching in sparsely-populated areas of the North and West.

Expansion of provision of Gaelic-medium teacher training will have considerable resource implications and political intervention will be required to provide the funds required. The Scheme of Specific Grants for Gaelic education established in 1986 has played a vital part in the development of Gaelic-medium education in schools. The Scheme allows local authorities to bid for new projects and, if successful, to receive 75% of the costs of the project in its initial phase. The Scheme does not extend to tertiary and higher education but a similar mechanism is needed if the universities are to expand their Gaelic-medium provision to address current inadequacies in teacher education in Gaelic.

Teacher education is no different from other fields in which a variety of agencies and interests are involved. Each agency has its own responsibilities, priorities and interests. A considerable amount of inter-agency collaboration and partnership will be needed to effect improvements in Gaelic-medium provision and that will be best achieved within the context of a national strategic plan initiated by the Scottish Executive. The strategic planning process could be greatly facilitated by the GTCS Report. The recommendations in the Report would, if implemented, resolve many of the issues already discussed.

Internal institutional politics can also play a significant part in facilitating or obstructing development of provision. The attitude of course management teams to Gaelic and the extent to which they are familiar with the demands of Gaelic-medium education can be influential factors. Even well-disposed individuals may not understand the full implications of immersion teaching and the Gaelic-medium curriculum. It is, therefore, highly desirable that Gaelic staff have as much control as possible over the management and operation of programmes of initial teacher education in Gaelic.

Future Development

The scale of the issues and problems discussed above suggests that a concerted programme of action is required to bring about quantitative and qualitative improvements in provision. Several of the measures and actions I propose below are also recommended in the GTCS Report.

The introduction of a certificated qualification in Gaelic-medium education for both primary and secondary teaching would be a major advance. The qualification should be a requirement for teaching through the medium of Gaelic and should be open to students in initial courses and also, in modular form, to serving teachers. Preservice courses would need to be redesigned to provide fully bilingual versions that would fulfil the requirements of the certificate. These developments should be overseen by Gaelic staff who should also have managerial, administrative and operational control of the courses.

Access to training courses could be greatly extended through the provision of off-site and open-learning modes of delivery. TEI partnerships with local education authorities and Further Education colleges could ensure more local delivery of courses and assessment of school experience.

Greater availability of, and access to, adult immersion courses could significantly increase the recruitment pool for Gaelic-medium education and financial barriers to enrolment on these courses could be overcome by measures such as increased weighting for Gaelic in the funding of student places. A sustained, high profile and coordinated recruitment and marketing campaign are also needed.

These, and other actions such as the introduction of a specific funding mechanism for Gaelic-medium teacher education and the creation of a robust infrastructure for the delivery of a coherent system of initial teacher education and continuing professional development, should form part of an overall strategy for the training of teachers in Gaelic. The issues have been well rehearsed and debated over the years and modest progress has been made on some fronts. However, the key issues of recruitment, certification and course content have yet to be resolved. It is to be hoped that the new Bòrd Gàidhlig na h-Alba will accord teacher education the highest priority and that it will be given sufficient powers and resources by the Executive to produce and implement a meaningful and effective programme of action.

References

Brown, S 2002 *Teacher Education for Gaelic Medium Teaching*. Stirling: Stirling University Institute of Education

General Teaching Council for Scotland 2000 *Teaching in Gaelic Medium Education*. Edinburgh: General Teaching Council for Scotland

MacNeil, M and Stradling, R 1997, *Meeting the Demand for Gaelic-speaking Teachers*. Skye: Lèirsinn Research Centre, Sabhal Mòr Ostaig

Ministerial Advisory Group on Gaelic 2002 *A Fresh Start for Gaelic/Cothrom Ur don Ghàidhlig*. Edinburgh : Scottish Executive

Robertson, B 1999 *Gaelic Education* in eds. T Bryce and W Humes *Scottish Education*. Edinburgh: Edinburgh University Press

Robertson, B 2001 Gaelic: The *Gaelic Language in Education in the UK*. Leeuwarden : Mercator Education

Stradling, R and MacNeil, M 1995, *Teacher Training for Gaelic Medium Education*. Skye : Lèirsinn Research Centre, Sabhal Mòr Ostaig

Research, Innovation and Policy Change: Lessons from the ITÉ Evaluation of the Irish Programme at Primary Level

John Harris

In responding to the theme of this session, 'politics and assessment', I will take the broadest meaning of 'assessment', to include programme evaluation and national monitoring of standards of achievement. I will be mainly talking about my work on the evaluation of the teaching and learning of Irish at primary level in the Republic of Ireland. I will focus in particular on ordinary schools outside Gaeltacht areas. I will not be talking in any detail about routine classroom assessment of pupil progress in Irish. That kind of assessment by teachers is important but it is not the subject of my paper here today. My concern will be more with how we might use evaluation and monitoring exercises to illuminate the teaching and learning process in the case of Irish and thereby identify ways in which programmes or teaching could be made more effective.

In all of this, there is a variety of ways in which politics, broadly defined, is relevant both to the language learning process itself and to evaluation. First, there is the issue of how the world outside school impinges on the actual process of teaching and learning Irish day to day in school: such matters as the political and social status of the language, what people feel about it, how visible or present it is in the lives of pupils outside school, the extent to which parents support the enterprise of learning the language at school. Second, all school subjects have a political dimension in another sense: people in general, and therefore the government, are concerned with how well pupils are progressing in different areas of learning, because success in these areas of learning always have implications for the achievement of national political goals. Achievement in science and mathematics, for example, will determine progress towards national goals related to employment and prosperity. Success in reading in the mother tongue will be closely related to the elimination of poverty and social exclusion. And of course in the case of Irish, the success of schools and programmes is critical to the broad national aim of maintaining the language and of promoting its wider use nationally. Finally, programme evaluation can impinge on politics in so far as it reveals policy successes and failures and the need for new structures and institutions to achieve stated goals.

It is within this broad context that I would like to give an outline of some of our work on evaluating the Irish programme at primary level and to indicate a few of the important lessons we have learned from it. One of the points I would like to illustrate with our data is that to be effective, monitoring and evaluation exercises must acknowledge the full complexity of the phenomenon being studied. Evaluation must be sensitive to the full range of contextual factors outside the school, as well as to the interactional factors inside the classroom, which together determine success in developing proficiency in Irish. Otherwise, such monitoring and evaluation is unlikely to be enlightening and helpful in relation to policy, planning and action. Second, I will try to show, by referring to some of our own work in ITÉ, that innovation in language teaching, materials and programmes is likely to be most effective when motivated by the findings of research and evaluation. And third, I will try to illustrate in the case of Irish at primary level how the quality and sophistication of the policy response to the findings of evaluation studies must be equal to the scale and range of difficulties uncovered.

Overview of research on achievement in spoken Irish in the 1970s and 1980s

We begin with an overview of research on achievement in Irish at primary level. Three issues are examined: the extent to which curricular objectives in spoken Irish are attained; how standards have changed in the last few decades; and some of the social, educational and other factors which affect achievement.

Achievement of curricular objectives in Irish at primary level

National surveys conducted by ITÉ in the late 1970's and 1980's showed that an average of about one-third of pupils in ordinary schools attained mastery of each of the curricular objectives in spoken Irish at sixth, fourth and second grade. The tests were of the criterion-referenced kind and were based on the *Nuachúrsaí,* the official Department of Education conversation courses in Irish for primary schools. Another one-third of pupils, on average, made at least minimal progress in relation to each of the objectives at each grade, but did not attain mastery. And one-third of pupils, on average, failed to make even minimal progress in relation to each of the objectives at each grade (Harris, 1982, 1983, 1984, 1988; Harris and Murtagh, 1988a,b). The fact that the various proportions remained reasonably stable as the objectives become more demanding at successive grades suggests that proficiency in spoken Irish grows steadily during the primary school years. The proportions failing to attain mastery or to make even minimal progress in relation to objectives at each grade, however, indicate the existence of a substantial gap between the level of performance in spoken Irish which the curriculum implicitly aimed at that time and the actual level of performance which was attained by most pupils.

Changes in standards of attainment in Irish

The second main issue concerns changes in standards of attainment. Research conducted in the 1970's and early 1980's indicated that standards of achievement in Irish were generally holding up well in the junior grades of primary school but were declining in the senior grades and at post primary. The findings were based on data relating to teachers' perceptions, scores on standardised reading-tests and public-examination grades (Ó Domhnalláin and Ó Gliasáin, 1976; Irish National Teachers Organisation (INTO), 1976; Fontes and Kellaghan, 1977; Greaney, 1978; Ó Riagáin, 1982; Bord na Gaeilge, 1986). A comparison between the results of ITÉ national surveys of achievement in spoken Irish, again based on objective criterion-referenced tests conducted in 1978 and 1985, revealed a modest but statistically significant increase in the mean percentage of pupils attaining mastery of each of the sixth-grade objectives over the seven year period (Harris and Murtagh, 1988a).

Finally, a major new national survey of achievement in Irish at sixth-grade level carried out this year will allow us to say whether overall standards of achievement in spoken Irish at sixth-grade level have changed in the seventeen years since 1985. In order to ensure the comparability of the surveys, the ITÉ tests of speaking and listening used in the earlier surveys have been carefully revised to take account of social and other changes in the meantime while making the minimum possible changes to the language content of the tests themselves.

The new survey covers ordinary schools, all-Irish schools and Gaeltacht schools and is being jointly carried out by ITÉ and the Educational Research Centre (ERC) in St. Patrick's College, Dublin at the request of the Department of Education and Science. The survey team consists of John Harris and Siobhán Nic Fhearaile from ITÉ and Peter Archer, Patrick Forde and Deirdre Stuart from the ERC. The survey is more comprehensive than previous ones in that it includes reading in Irish, based on a new test developed by the ERC, as well as the revised speaking and listening tests developed by ITÉ. The survey also makes use of adapted forms of questionnaires for pupils and parents originally used in the *Twenty Classes Study* (Harris and Murtagh, 1999) described later, as well as new questionnaires for principals and class teachers on various aspects of Irish and the teaching and learning of the language. The survey was carried out in over 200 primary schools in April and May 2002 and is supported by a consultative committee representative of the main partners in education. Because of the interval which has elapsed since the original ITÉ surveys in the 1980's, and the range and quality of the additional contextual information now being collected, the results of this new survey are potentially interesting.

General ability, social class and achievement in Irish

The third issue is the influence of various factors on pupil achievement in Irish and attitude to Irish. We begin with general academic ability and social class and then proceed to a number of other factors, including gender, regional/urban-rural location, size of sixth-grade group in class, home language and amount of Irish-medium instruction at school.

There is substantial evidence from Ireland and elsewhere (Genesse, 1976; Carroll, 1979) of a strong link between pupils' general academic ability and second-language achievement generally. A number of studies conducted in Irish primary schools show significant positive associations between general academic ability, as measured by a test of verbal reasoning in English, and achievement in both Irish reading (Martin and Kellaghan, 1977; Fontes, Kellaghan and O Brien, 1981) and spoken Irish (Harris and Murtagh, 1988b). Verbal reasoning has also been found to correlate strongly with success in Irish in public examinations at post-primary level (Greaney and Kellaghan, 1984).

Various national and international studies have also indicated that social-class background is positively linked to general educational outcomes, including second-language achievement and attitude (Hannan, Breen *et al.*, 1983; Skehan, 1990). In interpreting such findings, it should be borne in mind that social class tends to be primarily defined, as it is in the present study, in terms of parents' occupation. It has been argued, however, that the really critical factors in determining success in school life are 'cultural capital' indices such as parental values, attitudes, tastes, beliefs and linguistic practices (Bourdieu, 1974, 1977; Lynch, 1985). The *Twenty Classes Study* described below tried to identify some of these home factors in the case of Irish. National surveys of Irish ability and use of

Irish among the adult population have also identified significant positive associations between social class and both ability to speak Irish and attitude to Irish (CLAR, 1975; Ó Riagáin, 1997).

Demographic, educational and other factors

We turn now from general academic ability and social class to the other factors which have been linked to achievement generally and to Irish in particular. First, research on gender differences in second-language achievement indicates that girls, by and large, do better than boys as far as both verbal skills generally and second-language achievement are concerned (Maccoby and Jacklin, 1974; Burstall, 1975). In the case of Irish, tests of reading confirm the superior performance of girls over boys (Martin and Kellaghan, 1977). The ITÉ surveys of spoken Irish (Harris, 1984; Harris and Murtagh, 1988a) consistently show that more girls than boys attain mastery of grade-related objectives in spoken Irish. Published examination statistics for the three years 1992-1994 also show that girls regularly outperform boys in Irish in both the junior and Leaving Certificate examinations (Department of Education, 1993, 1994, 1995). More girls than boys opt for higher level papers, more girls receive honours and fewer girls fail.

Regional/locational factors have also been found to influence achievement. In the 1978 sixth-grade survey of spoken Irish, Harris (1983) reported that classes in the Dublin region and in city locations generally had significantly lower levels of achievement in Irish than classes in other regions/locations - classes in Munster were best overall. In addition, smaller sixth-grade classes were associated with significantly higher levels of achievement in Irish.

Home use of Irish is also an important factor. A national survey on languages in Ireland in 1994 reported that Irish was never spoken in over two-thirds of Irish homes (Ó Riagáin and Ó Gliasáin, 1994). While the opportunities for children outside the Gaeltacht to use Irish at home are fairly limited, therefore, various ITÉ surveys of schools have nevertheless confirmed the positive effects of even moderate home use of Irish on pupil achievement in the language (Harris, 1984; Harris and Murtagh, 1988a,b).

Finally, there is evidence that target-language use outside the language lesson proper can positively influence proficiency. Quite aside from the high levels of achievement found in all-Irish primary schools (Harris, 1984; Harris and Murtagh, 1988a), there is also evidence that at least some Irish-medium instruction in ordinary schools leads to higher levels of achievement than is found in schools/classes where it is not used at all. In the 1978 ITÉ sixth-grade survey, Irish-medium instruction in ordinary schools emerged as a strong predictor of achievement in spoken Irish (Harris, 1983). Similar results were found in the 1985 sixth-grade replication study: the overall mean percentage attaining mastery of sixth-grade objectives was substantially different depending on the amount of Irish-medium instruction received: no Irish-medium instruction (30.4%, on average, mastered each objective); less than one-hour of Irish-medium instruction per week (36.1%, on average, mastered each objective); one hour or more such instruction (48.7%, on average, mastered each objective) (Harris and Murtagh, 1988b).

The Twenty-Classes Study

While the kind of national surveys of achievement conducted by ITÉ which we discussed above, as well as other work such as the major INTO survey of teachers' perceptions of the teaching of Irish in 1984 (INTO, 1985) were very informative, many questions about the teaching and learning of Irish had hardly been researched at all. The role of parental attitudes, pupil attitudes and interests, and many other factors in determining success and failure in learning to speak Irish, had yet to be studied. Most importantly, we had little objective information on exactly how Irish was taught - our information was limited to anecdote and individual case studies. New national surveys would not be an appropriate or effective way to obtain this kind of information, however, because they require the sampling and testing of large numbers of pupils. National studies cannot be used to collect detailed process-type information on teaching and learning because the burden that this would place on school time and resources would be unacceptable. In addition, the volume of data-analysis and interpretation involved would be prohibitive.

The *Twenty-Classes Study,* which I carried out with my ITÉ colleague, Lelia Murtagh, was designed to overcome some of these problems by confining itself to a detailed examination of a small number of contrasting schools/classes. Full details of the study can be found in Harris and Murtagh (1999) on which the present brief account is based. The field work was carried out by Primary School inspectors of the Department of Education and Science. The study had two main aims:

1. to describe the range of conditions under which spoken Irish is taught and learned at sixth-class level by studying a small number of diverse classes which were nevertheless representative nationally
2. to describe the teaching and learning of Irish in this small group of classes in more detail, and from a greater number of different perspectives than had ever been done hitherto.

Our intention was that the data collected would be a resource for anyone concerned with the range of social, educational and linguistic conditions under which Irish is taught at primary level. Thus, it might be useful, for example, to those engaged in the development of courses and syllabuses in Irish, in the assembly of information packages for parents and so on. As it turned out, I subsequently made exactly this kind of use of the data when, working with three other colleagues, Pádraig Ó Néill and Máire Uí Dhufaigh of ITÉ, and Dr. Eoghan Ó Súilleabháin of the Department of Education and Science, we carried out the *Communicative Materials Project.* This project was funded by the Department of Education and Science at the request of the National Council for Curriculum and Assessment. The *Communicative Materials Project* is described later.

Carrying out the *Twenty-Classes Study* involved the development of a number of new instruments and classroom observation procedures. One of these instruments provides a measure of different aspects of pupils' attitudes to Irish and their interest in learning Irish and foreign languages. Another questionnaire investigated parents' attitudes to Irish and the school, and parents' own practices in relation to such matters as praising their child's achievement in Irish and helping with Irish homework. In addition, we asked the class teacher to make his or her own assessment of each pupil's ability in Irish, interest in Irish, and experience of difficulty with Irish. We also, of course, tested each pupil's proficiency in Irish, listening and speaking, using the ITÉ criterion-referenced tests described earlier.

Particularly significant were two new classroom-observation instruments designed to allow primary school inspectors, with the teacher's agreement, to record the activities, materials and dynamics of typical Irish language lessons at sixth-grade. Written instructions were given to the inspectors/observers concerning the general procedure to be followed in each classroom. Two observers worked side by side, but independently, in each classroom. Observer 1 was guided in his or her observation by the *Irish Lesson Analysis System (ILAS)* (Harris and Murtagh, 1999). Central to *ILAS* is the notion of a lesson segment - 'naturalistic' teaching units or events. In *ILAS*, segments are defined in terms of five main dimensions of analysis: *Topic, Language activity, Pupil behaviour, Teacher mode of involvement* and *Classroom organisation*. For each of these five dimensions, there is a set of descriptive categories. In the case of *Language activity*, for example, there are categories such as 'Translation', 'Imitation', 'Drills', 'Real communication in Irish' and 'Simulated communication in Irish'. The inspector also systematically recorded changes in class interest and class attention as the various parts of the lesson unfolded. Observer 2 used another ITÉ classroom observation instrument to classify the general behaviour, participation and language use of three pre-selected pupils. An audio-tape recording was made of each lesson so that it could be re-examined later to obtain additional information and, if necessary, to correct some of the codings. This 'process' type information on the teaching of Irish was entirely new

Our ultimate goal in collecting all this information was to see if we could explain variations from pupil to pupil and from class to class in achievement in Irish by relating them to the range of data we had collected on teaching, pupils and parents. Information gathered by our various research instruments was also related to a number of background variables such as social class (a variable which had not previously been studied in relation to spoken Irish at primary level), pupil general academic ability, gender, the urban/rural location of the school and size of sixth-grade group. We will not discuss here the variety of correlation and regression analyses used to investigate all these questions but a full account can be found in Harris and Murtagh (1999).

In order to make the study more useful, we 'calibrated', as it were, the Irish achievement of the 20 sixth-grade classes in terms of the achievement of classes nationally (Harris and Murtagh, 1988a). Thus, when we examined data on such variables as pupil attitudes, levels of interest or teaching activities in each of the 20 classes, we were able to interpret these data in terms of how good or bad the Irish achievement of each class is compared to classes nationally. Implicitly, our goal throughout was to predict the achievement in spoken Irish of the twenty classes, by showing how variables combine to determine the level of success achieved in each class. This meant trying to show the manner in which favourable social, educational or attitudinal factors came together to produce a high level of achievement in spoken Irish in some classes, while corresponding unfavourable circumstances in others produced low levels of achievement.

Some findings of the *Twenty Classes Study*

Before we outline these findings it should be emphasised that the *Twenty Classes Study* was carried out before the revised curriculum in Irish was introduced. Indeed these findings and others from the *Communicative Materials Project* described later would have been taken into account by the Irish Curriculum Committee of the NCCA.

(a) Pupil attitude/motivation
- The study showed that pupils were reasonably well disposed towards the Irish language itself and towards the idea of integrating with the Irish-language-speaking 'group'. But motivation, or actual commitment to learning Irish, is less positive. Pupils with better motivation and attitudes are more successful in learning Irish.
- A substantial minority of pupils do not believe that they have the support and encouragement of their parents in the task of learning Irish. Where parental encouragement is present, it has a strong positive effect on pupil *achievement* in Irish and an even stronger effect on pupils *attitudes* and *motivation* to learn Irish.
- Pupils tend to have a poor estimation of their own ability in Irish compared to their self-concept in relation to other subjects. A substantial minority are anxious about speaking Irish in class.

(b) Pupils' reactions to the Irish lessons and courses in their own words
- Pupils experience the Irish lesson and materials as boring, old-fashioned and repetitious. They would like lessons and courses which are more modern, more fun and more realistic and which place a greater emphasis on conversations and games.
- Pupils and classes with low levels of achievement in Irish often complain of difficulty in understanding the lesson or the teacher and express general apathy and discouragement about learning Irish.

(c) Parents views and practices
Parents are generally positive about Irish and supportive of the notion of their children being taught the language in school. In practice, however, many parents have a lukewarm, hands-off attitude to the actual *enterprise* of their children learning Irish. For example, a majority of parents do not directly promote positive attitudes to learning Irish; they are much less likely to praise their child's achievements in Irish than they are to praise other subjects; and they are less likely to help with homework in Irish than in other subjects. A quarter of parents know nothing about how Irish is taught while another half know 'a little'. Parents generally are happy with the efforts of the local school in relation to Irish.

(d) Direct observation of the teaching of Irish by inspectors

- The study validates the general orientation to teaching Irish which is proposed in the revised curriculum - the communicative approach. It does this by showing that classes in which a greater emphasis is placed on communication do better in a variety of ways than other classes: they have higher achievement in Irish, pupils show higher levels of attention and interest during the lessons and report lower levels of anxiety about speaking individually in class. In contrast, generally negative outcomes are associated with traditional language-practice (non-communicative) activities such as 'Drills' or repetition-based activities.

- Classes in which pupils spend a lot of time on routine (language-practice type) reading aloud tend to have lower achievement in spoken Irish and less positive attitudes to Irish. In addition, where a lot of time is spent on routine reading aloud, pupils tend to higher levels of anxiety about the Irish lesson and display lower levels of attention and interest in the lesson.

(e) Pupil participation in the Irish class

Observation of *individual* pupils in each class by inspectors showed that about half of all pupil 'behaviours' during the Irish lesson consisted of the pupil speaking individually - and in Irish in 91% of cases. The results also showed that (i) pupil speech is not produced very often in the context of real communication or of meaning negotiation, (ii) pupils with lower levels of ability in Irish speak less often than other pupils, (iii) when pupils with lower levels of ability in Irish are silent they are less attentive to the lesson than those with higher levels of ability who remain silent, and (iv) pupils speak more often and for longer in classes which emphasise communicative teaching activities.

Innovation in teaching Irish based on research and evaluation

I will now turn to the second main issue set out at the beginning: that innovation and improvement in language teaching, materials and programmes is most effective when motivated by the findings of research and evaluation. I will illustrate this point by reference to two ITÉ development projects which I directed in the second half of the 1990's. Both projects grew out of, and were guided by, earlier ITÉ national monitoring surveys as well as the *Twenty Classes Study*. These are the *Communicative Materials Project* and the *Teaching through Irish Project*.

The Communicative Materials Project

The *Communicative Materials Project* was carried out by ITÉ in close cooperation with the NCCA Irish Curriculum Committee (Harris *et al.*, 1996a,b). The goal was to produce guidelines and sample materials for a primary-school programme which would adopt a broadly communicative approach. We were conscious of the need for this exploratory work, knowing that a long period of experimentation and debate had also preceded the adoption of a communicative approach to modern languages and to Irish at post-primary (e.g. ITÉ, 1980). There had been no really large-scale, systematic attempt prior to this to investigate the relevance of the new ideas about communicative teaching to Irish at primary level.

Apart from introducing a new emphasis on communication in teaching and learning Irish, the *Communicative Materials Project* also attempted to find solutions to the range of problems identified in the *Twenty-Classes Study*. Among the problems in question - though not necessarily present in all classes or schools - were low levels of class attention and class interest, pupils' difficulty in understanding the lesson, pupils' reluctance to speak in class, pupils' lack of confidence in their own ability to succeed at Irish and lack of active support from parents.

The *Communicative Materials Project* involved over 60 teachers from *Galltacht* (English speaking areas) and *Gaeltacht* schools. Galltacht and Gaeltacht teachers met separately with the ITÉ Working Group. The account here focuses only on ordinary Galltacht schools. In the initial meeting with teachers, the basic principles of the communicative approach to second-language teaching were outlined. The contrast between communication /meaning-negotiation and language practice was explained (see Harris and Murtagh, 1999, Chapter 6). The emphasis was to be on using Irish in the classroom in ways which simulated the 'naturalness' of first-language acquisition and which maximised opportunities for 'life-like' rehearsal of the language (Mitchell, 1994). Teachers were given a draft unit appropriate to their particular grade(s) and they discussed it in small groups along with one or more members of the ITÉ Working Group. A few weeks were then set aside for testing out the prepared unit in the classroom. During this time teachers completed a simple questionnaire on each lesson, recording progress and difficulties in using the materials.

Although communication and meaning negotiation were paramount, an emphasis on form was still maintained. This secondary goal was realised by first drawing pupils' attention to the relevant grammatical forms in the context of a communicative activity. This was then followed up by activities which involved more formal analysis and practice of the target structure. Language structures were not practised in a formal manner, however, until their communicative significance had already been illustrated. We made no attempt to replace the existing language-practice activities of teachers but simply asked them to integrate the new materials and ideas with their own approach as they saw fit. Neither did we dissuade teachers from using their existing reading schemes, though we did add some communicative reading tasks.

Lessons mainly consisted of communicative activities incorporating the four skills of listening, speaking, reading and writing. Where possible, authentic materials in the form of texts, street signs, notices, menus, application forms etc. were used. Authentic materials related to our cultural and literary heritage, such as songs, poems and place names, were also used. In the junior grades, the emphasis was on listening activities in which real messages in Irish had to be understood and responded to. Versions of stories at two levels of difficulty, some of them on audio tape, were made available to accommodate classes of varying ability in Irish.

A central goal was to promote a positive attitude to learning Irish and to make the learning process itself more enjoyable and interesting. Communicative games and tasks, in which the pupil must use simple Irish in a purposeful way in order to participate effectively, feature strongly in the materials. In some games, different pupils or groups of pupils have different pieces of simple information, and they have to communicate with each other in Irish in order combine the information necessary to succeed in the game. Social-interaction-based activities (e.g. role-play, sketches and drama) also play a major part, as does the acquisition of real new information or skills - e.g. learning Irish dances such as *Ballaí Luimnigh* through Irish. Everywhere in the materials, the pupils' own lives are to the fore and there is a sustained effort to ensure that the situations, characters and, as far as possible, speech and communication styles are consistent with pupils' interests and daily experience. This latter aspect of the work was the one that required the most thought. Substantial investment and research will continue to be needed in the years ahead if courses and materials in Irish which are realistic and which appeal to pupils are to be produced. The final report on the *Communicative Materials Project* makes the point that creative writers and other artists have a considerable contribution to make in this area.

Another problem was how to develop lessons and materials which would stimulate and engage those pupils with low levels of achievement in Irish, while providing some challenge for those with a better command of Irish. To ensure that this problem would be confronted head-on, teachers from a wide range of schools, including those in disadvantaged areas, were invited to participate in the project. Given the poor attitude/motivation results for pupils with low levels of ability in Irish which was revealed in the *Twenty Classes Study*, we set out to provide experiences which we hoped would allow all pupils to say 'I'm good at Irish' or 'I can speak Irish'. This aspect of the project was an unqualified success - a frequent remark made by teachers who used the materials was that even those children who were very weak at Irish were, for the first time, actually requesting that the Irish class begin.

We also encouraged teachers to find ways of defining and explicitly marking pupils' progress as they gradually develop communicative proficiency in Irish. To this end, a communicative objective was set out at the beginning of each of the lessons supplied to the teachers. Finally, we tried to provide for more able pupils and classes in a systematic way. For example, a feature of all units was the inclusion of *Dúshláin Bhreise* so called because of the added challenge which these optional activities posed.

Teachers were exhorted not to correct pupils' errors during communicative activities but to do it later. Pupils were to be encouraged in every way to use whatever Irish they had at their disposal in order to understand or transmit messages. This meant learning to tolerate uncertainty and to take risks in situations where communicative difficulties were encountered. Pupils, in other words, were to be helped to develop 'strategic competence'. More generally, the teacher was urged to cultivate a tolerant, supportive, affirmative atmosphere in class which would promote a high level of pupil participation and personal expression.

The final versions of the sample units were published in two reports (Harris *et al.*, 1996a,b). An audio tape containing material for various lessons accompanied each report. Substantial numbers of sample lessons were provided at each grade level e.g. a total of over 130 lessons are included for grades 3-6. The reports also included guidelines for implementing a communicative approach to teaching Irish as well as detailed specifications for the production and format of courses and teaching materials following the introduction of the new curriculum. They also deal with issues such as the importance of using children on audio and video tapes, and of employing native speakers of Irish - though not necessarily always from Gaeltacht areas - to record lesson material. It was never intended that these reports would constitute anything like a definitive statement on a communicative approach to Irish at primary level, but that they would serve as a contribution to ongoing debate and development. There has been a considerable demand from teachers for these reports during the period that the inservice for the revised curriculum has been in progress.

The ITÉ Teaching through Irish Project

I initiated this project with my ITÉ colleague, Seán Mac Giollabhuí, just as the *Communicative Materials Project* was being completed. Perhaps it should be made clear straight away that we did not undertake it with the expectation that anything other than a small minority of teachers in ordinary schools would initially be interested in teaching entire school subjects through Irish. We felt, however, that it was important to begin this work and we believed that it could contribute to the development of Irish-language teaching in a number of significant ways as the revised curriculum was introduced. Earlier research by ITÉ has shown that pupils in ordinary schools who are taught some aspects of the curriculum (apart from Irish) through Irish have substantially higher levels of achievement in spoken Irish than other pupils (Harris, 1983). More importantly, pupils of all levels of academic ability, as measured by an English-language verbal-reasoning test, have higher levels of achievement in Irish if they are in classes which are exposed to some Irish-medium teaching (Harris, 1993; Harris and Murtagh, 1988b). The Department of Education and Science had a policy for many years also of generally encouraging this approach. Despite this official policy, materials in Irish, specifically geared to the linguistic needs of pupils in *ordinary schools*, and to the requirements of teachers who were embarking on Irish-medium teaching for the first time, had never been made available.

The project involved us working regularly with 50 third- and fourth-grade teachers over a two-year period to develop full courses in Science and Art through the medium of Irish. The teachers came from a wide variety of ordinary schools, including those in disadvantaged areas. The vast majority of them had no previous experience in teaching through Irish. Separate groups of teachers in Dublin and Tullamore met us in workshop sessions where we explained and discussed our proposals and distributed sample lessons. Having tried out the materials in their own classrooms, the teachers returned and discussed progress and completed questionnaires concerning the lessons. The lessons were then revised on the basis of this information. The teachers found the approach both enjoyable and rewarding and the courses, 'Bain Triail As' and 'Lean den Ealaín' (Harris and Mac Giollabhuí, 1998), are now on general sale.

None of the lesson material consisted of translations or adaptations of existing courses in English. Instead, every aspect of each lesson was planned and developed with the particular needs of pupils and teachers in ordinary schools in mind. We choose Art because so many of the activities appropriate to the subject at this level involve language use which is located in a practical, concrete context. Science was chosen as the other subject in the knowledge that it would make greater demands on pupils in terms of vocabulary and perhaps use of language. In addition, while it was intended at the time that science would be introduced as a subject for the first time in the revised primary curriculum, that curriculum had not yet appeared at the time the project was carried out. Thus, we expected that pupils would have a high level of interest in this subject since they had not been taught it before. The teachers themselves also would not have taught science before – even through the medium of English. Thus, it was possible for both teachers and pupils to make an entirely fresh start on this subject through the medium of Irish.

The teacher's material for each lesson was in three parts. The first consisted of background material including (i) a statement of the objective of the lesson, (ii) materials required, (iii) a list of the main vocabulary items involved (Irish and English), and (iv) a list of informal phrases or idioms that might be useful to the teacher during the lesson. The pupil's material in the case of Science also includes a pictorial vocabulary in Irish at the beginning of each lesson.

The second part of the teacher's material consisted of an outline of the main steps in the lesson, usually illustrated, including a full script for the teacher. The aim was to anticipate some of the difficulties which would be presented by the limited linguistic ability of pupils, and to suggest possible ways around these difficulties. The availability of the prepared material had the effect of freeing teachers from some of the minute-by-minute decisions about the lesson to be taught, thus allowing them to attend more fully to classroom dynamics. In particular, they could devote more of their creative energy to responding to the individual needs of pupils who were learning through Irish for the first time. We expected and encouraged teachers to depart from the script and we know that they actually did. Nevertheless, there was general agreement that having the lesson planned in advance in this way was a major factor in the success of the project. The third part of the prepared material consisted of an optional development of the basic theme for more able classes.

The initial guidelines to teachers made it clear that the materials provided could be used in any way that the teacher saw fit, but we suggested, after some general discussion, a number of principles that might be followed. We proposed, for example, that in the beginning teachers would accept questions from pupils in English but answer them in simple Irish. In the longer term, teachers might rephrase in Irish the questions which had been posed in English by pupils. Discussions in English between pupils should also be permitted initially, but pupils should gradually be encouraged to use Irish. It was agreed that, particularly in the light of the results of the *Twenty Classes Study*, pupil understanding and enjoyment of the subject were paramount considerations.

We believe that the provision of materials which are specifically designed for teaching pupils in ordinary schools through Irish is important in a number of ways. First, it is clear from the ITÉ surveys conducted in the 1970's and 1980's, as well as from the *Twenty-Classes Study,* that a limited programme of Irish-medium instruction is an essential ingredient in the success of those classes in ordinary schools which have really high levels of achievement in Irish - in some classes stretching all the way up to the mean level of performance attained in all-

Irish schools (Harris and Murtagh, 1999). Even though the percentage of such schools nationally may be small, they make a significant contribution to the overall performance of ordinary schools in relation to Irish. Providing high-quality, specifically-designed Irish-medium materials also helps to maintain this traditional diversity in the ordinary primary schools' programme. The proven and widely acknowledged success of all-Irish schools in teaching through Irish, should not have the unintended effect over time of creating an expectation that ordinary schools are homogeneously 'Irish-as-a-subject-only' in character.

There is perhaps a slightly greater danger of that happening as we adopt a communicative approach to teaching Irish. Communicative language teaching originated in foreign languages at post-primary, where the tradition of teaching parts or all of other subjects through the target language has never become really established. Thus, while we have much to learn from that valuable foreign-language teaching experience, we must also recognise that that tradition has tended to locate communication in the target language within the core lesson. It would be ironic, of course, if the element of the primary-school programme which traditionally involved the most truly communicative use of Irish were to fall into disuse as a 'more communicative' core programme came into being.

Admittedly, content-based teaching has grown in recent years as an adjunct to, and as a development of, communicative language teaching. Content-based teaching involves working out from the core subject, incorporating elements of other subjects into the teaching of the target language. This is a very desirable strategy and indeed we adopted it to a significant extent in the *Communicative Materials Project*. But we believe that the bolder approach of attempting to teach a whole subject, such as Science or Art, through Irish has distinct advantages. The more radical approach obliges us to investigate the whole range of mechanisms by which sometimes complex information can be transmitted using relatively limited linguistic resources. It also identifies a broader range of topics suitable for integration with the core Irish lesson, topics which would almost certainly not come to light with a more piecemeal approach. In any case, one way of using the new materials would be for teachers to select certain *elements* of these Irish-medium lessons for inclusion in a conventional communicative approach - e.g. '*ag déanamh cárta na Nollag*' in the case of Art or '*ag úsáid uisce*' in the case of Science. Such elements could be readily integrated into the regular Irish lesson because the prepared materials have been specifically designed to accommodate the linguistic capabilities of pupils in ordinary schools. On the basis of that potential alone, a case can be made for repeating the *Teaching through Irish* experiment with other school subjects.

An adequate policy response to the findings of evaluation

In this final section, I would like to argue that the quality and sophistication of the policy response to the findings of evaluation studies on Irish in ordinary schools must be equal to the scale and range of difficulties which research has identified. I will be concerned with the kind of policy response needed rather than with trying to define precisely the institutions and structures which might be required to implement that policy. These matters are discussed in more detail in Harris and Murtagh (1999).

The first thing to be considered is the scale and importance of the task. From the language revival point of view, ordinary primary schools have a central role in reproducing speaking proficiency in Irish in each new generation. There are a number of reasons for this. First, there is the fact that the overwhelming majority of children learn Irish in ordinary schools (rather than in the considerably smaller number of Gaeltacht or all-Irish schools). Thus, any initiative which enhances the success of such schools has the potential to affect large numbers of pupils and, thereby, make a substantial contribution to the language-revival effort. It must be borne in mind too that a small but significant minority of ordinary schools produce levels of achievement in Irish which approach or equal the average level obtaining in all-Irish schools (Harris and Murtagh, 1999). Second, exposure to Irish at primary level is probably both more intense, and more focused on speech and conversation, than it is at post-primary level. The informal use of Irish for school and class communication, and the teaching of parts of other subjects partly or wholly through Irish, are more common at primary than at post-primary. At post-primary, the language tends to be restricted to the Irish lesson, in part because teachers at this level are subject specialists. At primary, every teacher is an Irish teacher. Thus, for the majority of pupils, primary school provides the most sustained exposure to the spoken language that they will ever have. These schools have a special importance for the language in other ways too: they lay the groundwork for further language learning at post-primary and third level and, to the extent that they provide the first introduction to Irish, they can have a considerable influence on long-term attitudes towards Irish.

A second crucial factor to be taken into account in developing a policy response to the findings of evaluation studies is the minority, second-language status of Irish. The key sociolinguistic consequence for the teaching of Irish is that pupils have little or no interactive contact with the spoken language outside school. The resulting paradox is that while pupils learn to speak Irish in school in order to use it in their own lives, they know that there are very few occasions outside (particularly involving their peers) in which there might be either a real need, or even an opportunity, to speak it. The problems which this presents for teachers and schools are set out in some detail in Harris *et al.* (1996a,b). For present purposes, we can enumerate just a few of them. First, it is more difficult for both teachers and pupils to identify a proximal goal or motivation outside school for learning to speak the language in the classroom. In addition, in teaching the language, and in developing tasks and materials for use within the classroom, it is more difficult to identify situations, contexts and even language registers which make the prospect of using Irish credible or plausible. Another result is that the range of authentic Irish-language materials and the volume of commercially-produced resources available for teaching and learning Irish at this level bears no comparison with that available in the case of the major European languages.

It must be emphasised that these are challenges, not insurmountable difficulties. It is important to acknowledge them however if structures and resources equal to the task are to be provided. The response required has both creative and research-and-development dimensions. The creative challenge is, in some respects, analogous to that confronted by Irish-programme makers in TG4 and RTÉ - and indeed by Irish dramatists and writers - who wish to use Irish to reflect and incorporate life outside Gaeltacht areas. But the creative work in the case of primary schools needs to be backed up by, and located within, a sustained research-and-development enterprise - to identify educational problems and possibilities, to set up pilot programmes, and to ensure that adequate provision is made for in-service training. Essentially, what is required is a long-term exercise in educational and language planning focused on the complex interaction between the school on the one hand and the home/community on the other. Among the tasks to be done are the following:

1. Provide a support system for the teaching and learning of Irish, taking account both of the educational aspects of the issue and the national aim of promoting bilingualism and the wider use of Irish.
2. Adopt a proactive approach towards this task - finding out what teachers, parents and pupils require in the way of materials etc.; identifying the problems and possibilities which exist in relation to teaching and learning Irish; and establishing pilot schemes and commissioning research to investigate new ways of responding to these.
3. Coordinate the production of textbooks and audio, video and IT-based teaching and learning materials.
4. Identify in-service needs generally, and to ensure, in particular, that adequate training and support is provided for teachers who are involved in new initiatives relating to Irish.
5. Establish what various agencies and institutions could contribute to developing a more supportive out-of-school environment for primary school pupils learning Irish; coordinate the work of these various bodies; and provide a forum for ideas and debate in this area.

We cannot discuss all these points in any detail, but it may be useful to mention some of the implications of the development projects already discussed for (3) and (4) above. In producing textbooks and other materials, there are advantages, as the *Communicative Materials Project* showed, in having applied linguists working side by side with a consultative groups of teachers, who try out new materials and approaches in their own classrooms and report back their experiences and the reaction of pupils. The issues which Irish-language materials development and teaching at primary level must constantly confront are discussed in some detail in Harris *et al.* (1996a,b). We can take just one of these issues, language registers, for illustrative purposes here. Because the day-to-day experiences of most children of primary-school age outside the Gaeltacht has not yet found expression in Irish, Irish-language registers appropriate to many situations of interest to them have yet to evolve. Consequently, pupils often feel ill at ease using forms of language that they associate with the formality of school rather than with 'real' life outside. It will require an ongoing effort to find innovative solutions to problems such as these. As we pointed out in the report on the *Communicative Materials Project*, a number of strategies may be needed - e.g. involving creative writers in Irish as well as those with educational expertise directly in materials development, and soliciting the opinions of pupils themselves about ways of using Irish in their own lives.

Creating opportunities for young people to influence the evolution of the language is an important enterprise in its own right, of course, since it is young people who bring vitality and change to any language. Experimentation and failure are an inevitable part of this process of innovation. The alternative is the provision of learning materials which can all too quickly acquire the dated characteristics of which pupils complained so often in the *Twenty-Classes Study*. It scarcely needs to be said that the introduction of a communicative approach to teaching Irish will not, in itself, solve the problems we have been talking about here - although their existence, and the need to respond to them, is brought more clearly into focus with a communicative approach. In structural-linguistic or language-practice based approaches, or where the emphasis is on narrative texts, the realities of using the language for real communication may never be confronted and so sociolinguistic issues can be more easily obscured or ignored.

The *Teaching through Irish Project* also has implications for how Irish at primary level must be supported. First, there is the question of why such materials were not developed earlier, and why the content-based teaching option has not been more vigorously promoted - given that a substantial minority of teachers already conduct a small amount of Irish-medium instruction, mainly in music and physical education (Harris 1983, 1993; Harris and Murtagh, 1988a; INTO, 1985). Second, because the project was a limited one, designed simply to explore possibilities in the area, Irish-medium materials suitable for other grades and subjects have not yet been developed. Third, the project illustrates how in-service workshops can be used to develop innovative approaches to the teaching of Irish. It also serves as a model for how a limited programme of instruction through Irish in ordinary schools could be promoted more widely on an entirely voluntary basis. Workshops allow teachers an opportunity to share experiences and to provide mutual support as they respond to the new professional challenges presented by teaching through Irish.

The task for the future will be to identify and exploit precisely these kinds of possibilities at the earliest possible moment. While the ITÉ project makes an initial contribution, further initiatives are needed - materials-development for other grades and subjects, and the establishment of pilot schemes and in-service. Without the support and validation provided by a comprehensive scheme, it will continue to be difficult for individual teachers, acting alone, to choose this teaching option. In that case, the potential for Irish-medium teaching in ordinary schools will almost certainly remain dormant.

Finally, it is worth bearing in mind that a carefully coordinated approach to tackling problems related to Irish at primary level may provide guidance and direction for the language-promotion and revival effort nationally. Some of the enduring problems in the two domains are the same: for example, how to energise people to actually begin using the language for real communication and how to identify and cultivate registers and contexts of use which facilitate the switch to Irish. If we can find practical solutions to some of these problems in a school context, perhaps these solutions can also be applied in the larger language-promotion domain.

References

Bord na Gaeilge: An Coiste Comhairleach Pleanála (1986) *Irish and the education system: An analysis of examination results.* Dublin: Author.

Bourdieu, P. (1974) The school as a conservative force: Scholastic and cultural inequalities. In J. Eggleston (ed) *Contemporary research in the sociology of education.* London: Methuen.

Burstall, C. (1975) Factors affecting foreign-language learning: A consideration of some relevant research findings. *Language Teaching and Linguistics Abstracts,* 8, 105-25.

Carroll, J.B. (1979) Twenty-five years of research on foreign language aptitude. In K.C. Diller (ed) *Individual differences and universals in language learning aptitude.* Rowley, Mass.: Newbury House.

Committee On Irish Language Attitudes Research (CLAR) (1975) *Report.* Dublin: Stationery Office.

Fontes, P. and Kellaghan, T. (1977) *The new primary school curriculum: Its implementation and effects.* Dublin: Educational Research Centre.

Fontes, P., Kellaghan, T. and O'Brien, M. (1981) Relationships between time spent teaching, classroom organization, and reading achievement. *Irish Journal of Education,* 15 (2), 79-91

Genesee, F. (1976) The role of intelligence in second-language learning. *Language Learning,* 26, 267-80.

Greaney, V. (1978) Trends in attainment in Irish from 1973 to 1977. *Irish Journal of Education,* 12, 22-35.

Greaney, V. and Kellaghan, T. (1984) *Equality of opportunity in Irish schools: A longitudinal study of 500 students.* Dublin: Educational Company of Ireland.

Hannan, D., Breen, R., Murray, B., Watson, D., Hardiman, N. and O' Higgins, K. (1983) *Schooling and sex roles: Sex differences in subject provision and subject choice in Irish post-primary schools.* Dublin:, ESRI General Research Series, Paper No 113.

Harris, J. (1982) Achievement in spoken Irish at the end of primary school. *Irish Journal of Education,* 16 (2), 85-116.

Harris, J. (1983) Relationships between achievement in spoken Irish and demographic, administrative and teaching factors. *Irish Journal of Education,* 17 (1), 5-34.

Harris, J. (1984) *Spoken Irish in primary schools.* Dublin: Institiúid Teangeolaíochta Éireann

Harris, J. (1988) Spoken Irish in the primary school system. *International Journal of the Sociology of Language,* 70, 69-87.

Harris, J. (1993) An Ghaeilge labhartha sa gnáthscoil: Fadhbanna is féidearthachtaí sa ré nua. *Teangeolas,* 32, 50-8

Harris, J. and Mac Giollabhuí, S. (1998a) *Lean den ealaín! Ealaín trí Ghaeilge do na gnáthscoileanna. Lámhleabhar an mhúinteora.* Dublin: Institiúid Teangeolaíochta Éireann

Harris, J. and Mac Giollabhuí, S. (1998b) *Bain triail as! Eolaíocht trí Ghaeilge do na gnáthscoileanna. Lámhleabhar an mhúinteora.* Dublin: Institiúid Teangeolaíochta Éireann

Harris, J. and Mac Giollabhuí, S. (1998c) *Bain triail as! Eolaíocht trí Ghaeilge do na gnáthscoileanna. Leabhar an dalta.* Dublin: Institiúid Teangeolaíochta Éireann.

Harris, J. and Murtagh, L. (1988a) National assessment of Irish-language speaking and listening skills in primary-school children: Research issues in the evaluation of school-based heritage-language programmes. *Language, Culture and Curriculum*, 1(2), 85-130.

Harris, J. and Murtagh, L. (1988b) Ability and communication in learning Irish. Unpublished

Harris, J. and Murtagh, L. (1999) *Teaching and learning Irish in Primary School.* Dublin: Institiúid Teangeolaíochta Éireann.

Institiúid Teangeolaíochta Éireann (1980) *Modern Languages Syllabus Project for Post-Primary Schools: Skeleton syllabus.* Dublin: Author.

Ireland: Department of Education (1993) Tuarascáil Staitistiúil (Statistical Report) 1992/93. Dublin: Stationery Office.

Ireland: Department of Education (1994) Tuarascáil Staitistiúil (Statistical Report) 1993/94. Dublin: Stationery Office.

Ireland: Department of Education (1995) Tuarascáil Staitistiúil (Statistical Report) 1994/95. Dublin: Stationery Office.

Irish National Teachers' Organisation (INTO): Education Committee. 1976. *Primary school curriculum: Curriculum questionnaire analysis.* Dublin: Author.

Irish National Teachers' Organisation (1985) *The Irish language in primary education: Summary of INTO survey of teachers' attitudes to the position of Irish in primary education.* Dublin: Author.

Lynch, K. (1985) An analysis of some presuppositions underlying the concepts of meritocracy and ability as presented in Greaney and Kellaghan's study. *Economic and Social Review,* 16 (2), 83-102.

Maccoby, E.E. and Jacklin, C.N. (1974) *The psychology of sex differences.* Stanford, Ca.: Stanford University Press.

Martin, M. and Kellaghan, T. (1977) Factors affecting reading attainment in Irish primary schools. In V. Greaney (ed) *Studies in reading.* Dublin: Educational Company of Ireland.

Ó Domhnalláin, T. and Ó Gliasáin, M. (1976) *Audio-visual methods v. A.B.C. methods in the teaching of Irish.* Dublin: Institiúid Teangeolaíochta Éireann.

Ó Riagáin, P. (1982) The influence of social factors on the teaching and learning of Irish. In W.F. Mackey *et al.* (eds) *Contemporary perspectives on the teaching of Irish.* Dublin: Bord na Gaeilge.

Ó Riagáin, P. (1997) *Language policy and social reproduction: Ireland 1893-1993.* Oxford: Clarendon Press.

Ó Riagáin, P. and Ó Gliasáin, M. (1994) *National survey on languages 1993: Preliminary report.* Dublin: Institiúid Teangeolaíochta Éireann.

Skehan, P. (1990). The relationship between native and foreign language learning ability: Educational and linguistic factors. In H. Dechert (ed) *Current trends in European second* language *acquisition research.* Clevedon: Multilingual Matters.

Irish-medium Assessment and Examinations

Seán Mac Nia

As the Principal Officer with the general responsibility for Irish-medium at the Council for the Curriculum Assessment and Examinations (CCEA) it would be expected that I should be in a position to offer some insights, views and opinions in relation to assessment and examinations in the Irish-medium (IM) sector. The following offering is obviously informed by the knowledge and experience gained at CCEA. However, some views and opinions here are not necessarily expressions of official CCEA views or policy.

To talk about assessment in such a short extract is not only a very difficult task but is unlikely to do the subject any justice at all. To try to do this within the context of Irish-medium is even more daunting given the complexities and sensitivities of the sector - not to mention the scarcity of useful information on which to base any exploration or findings. There is a temptation to avoid anything that may appear to be a criticism of Irish-medium and yet there is a need to take a step back and look objectively, if not coldly, at the present state of provision and outcomes and ask some hard questions of them. However, it must also be borne in mind that this is a very small and relatively new sector driven by largely enthusiastic, determined and well-intentioned people who have achieved much in the last 20-30 years and particularly in the last 5-10 years. The recent establishment of Comhairle na Gaelscolaíochta (The Council for Irish-medium Education) is likely to build upon and consolidate past achievements. However, success in terms of expansion and growth does not equate with success in terms of teaching and learning outcomes. This is where I believe the success of Irish-medium really counts and the only area really worth measuring. This is also where one treads carefully as this aspect can be all too easily over-looked, ignored or simply not understood, and yet this aspect is probably most crucial to the success of Irish-medium schools. One could use any aspect of assessment as the basis for a lengthy thesis. Here, it is my intention to touch upon assessment in Irish-medium in the broadest sense, highlighting some of the issues for the sector and probably raising more questions than answers. I hope that this will at least contribute to the debate on Irish-medium in a positive way and, by extension, contribute to its longer-term success. I shall address these issues by looking at the present assessment arrangements, at what is assessed and how, by looking at the outcomes for the Irish-medium sector and asking if a meaningful comparison can be made with mainstream schools and, finally, how assessment in Irish-medium may be addressed in the future.

For the purposes of this article the term 'assessment' refers to the full range of statutory assessments, selection and examinations including Key Stage 1, Key Stage 2, Key Stage 3, the Transfer Test, GCSE and GCE. These refer to the reported outcomes of summative assessment and high stakes testing and examinations rather than to the wider range of methods for evaluating pupil performance and attainment or any on-going formative assessment.

In general, the focus in terms of outcomes in Irish-medium tends to be on end of Key Stage 1 and 2 and the Transfer Test, probably as many more pupils, schools and personnel are involved at primary level than at secondary level. Conveniently, perhaps, it is difficult to discuss assessment and examinations issues and refer to outcomes at secondary level when only three schools presently exist – only one with post 16 provision, one essentially as a satellite of a mainstream secondary school with provision on a small scale up to GCSE and one recently established Irish-medium unit within a girls comprehensive school. Therefore, the focus on this paper will also be mainly on the primary level.

The statutory assessment at present in Northern Ireland arranges for pupils to be assessed at the end of Key stage 1 (approx 7 year olds) in Irish and Mathematics and at the end of Key Stage 2 (approx 11 year olds) in Irish, Mathematics and English. In mainstream schools i.e. the large majority of schools where pupils are taught through the medium of English, pupils are assessed in English and Mathematics at the end of Key Stage 1 and Key Stage 2. The assessment is carried out by teachers using a variety of tools including Assessment Units provided by CCEA in order to confirm teacher judgements. Each individual piece of pupil work is assessed using performance indicators and levels are assigned to the pupil based on level descriptors. All pupils are assessed at these stages but schools need only submit pupils' work in the form of a pupil portfolio every three years for the purposes of moderation. The rationale for this system of assessment lies mainly in the demand for accountability, comparability and consistency. This would appear not unreasonable in mainstream schools but may well be more problematic in Irish-medium. For example, while schools could be expected to be accountable in terms of learning outcomes, the teaching and learning in IM schools are very different given the nature of the immersion in a second language approach adapted by IM schools. The teaching of Irish as a subject and through Irish as a medium is a very different scenario to that in mainstream schools. Therefore, would it be reasonable to expect the same outcomes at the end of each Key Stage or in any other testing? As there are no specific targets set by the Department of Education for IM schools, accountability in terms of outcomes may not be as meaningful. Yet, IM schools are still expected to achieve. Some comparability can be made across the small number of IM schools but it would not be reasonable to compare them with performances as presented in the N. Ireland summary for each subject at each Key Stage for all schools. Given these small numbers, it is also difficult to achieve a large degree of consistency in terms of the quality expected at each Level. In other words, teachers in all mainstream schools could be expected to have the same perception of work adjudged at, for example, level 3. However, because of the small numbers involved and because of the fact that the sector is still evolving, a critical mass of experience and expertise has yet to emerge. That's not a criticism. However, this does not exonerate IM schools from being accountable, comparable and consistent, but it does make it more difficult for them do so in such a way as to be meaningful and equitable. There are many mitigating circumstances that could easily be said to skew the performances in IM schools including the high ratio of young and less experienced teachers, the high proportion of children with little or no support in terms of Irish spoken outside the school or in the home, the high proportion of composite classes, the dearth of material resources in general, the lack of focused INSET type training, a shortage of specialist subject teachers at secondary level in particular. Many of these issues are being addressed of course, but not necessarily in a coordinated and coherent strategic fashion.

Given all of that, how do IM schools perform in assessments and examinations? The following is a snapshot of the N. Ireland summary in 2002 for IM schools for Irish, English and Mathematics at each Key Stage compared with its counterpart in mainstream schools. It may be useful in ascertaining the state of play in IM schools but it needs to be issued with the rather large health warning that such bench marking may not be actually relevant. However, it is possibly the only tangible evidence available for such a purpose.

Table 1: Irish at Key Stage 1

Irish	W	1	2	3
Irish-medium	1 0.4%	8 3.2%	184 78.6%	41 17.5%

Table 1 above shows the numbers and percentages of pupil attainment from W (working towards) to Level 3 in Irish-medium schools.

Table 2: English at Key Stage 2

English	W	1	2	3
Mainstream	65 0.3%	1171 5.8%	11780 57.9%	7322 36.0%

Table 2 above shows the numbers and percentage of pupil attainment from W (working towards) to Level 3 in English in mainstream schools.

Given that the targets set by the Department of Education for Northern Ireland (DENI) are that by 2002 all pupils should be at Level 2 or better and that 35% should attain Level 3, what can be made of these figures? A statistician may not make anything of them at all, but at face value one could be reasonably satisfied an deduce, from an Irish-medium perspective, that these almost achieve the DENI target for Level 2 but then fall well short of the Level 3 target. However, these targets were not set with Irish-medium in mind but are the targets for English in mainstream schools. It must be remembered that the large majority of the IM children come to IM schools armed with whatever limited amount of Irish has been learned at preschool and enter an immersion programme meeting Irish in a real and meaningful situation for the first time. The acquisition of Irish in this programme depends heavily on the teacher and curricular content and is a major factor in the outcomes of the teaching and learning. There is an obvious challenge here not encountered by mainstream pupils or teachers. It would not be reasonable to expect a high proportion of them to reach the same levels of attainment, particularly at Level 3. At face value, it could be said that IM schools compare quite favourably with mainstream schools in this respect. However, face value is of little value here. The difference in the numbers of pupils in each sector renders the percentages almost meaningless. The circumstances under which the two subjects are taught are so different as to make them apples and pears. That said, what these figures show is that there is at least an indication that pupils do perform reasonably well in IM schools despite the early disadvantage of language acquisition and even though the assessment system is not entirely appropriate or designed for a bilingual or immersion situation. Perhaps this could be also turned around and the question asked of mainstream schools of why IM schools pupils are performing equally well despite their difficulties at Key Stage 1 in terms of these percentages.

Table 3: Mathematics in IM schools at Key Stage 1

Mathematics	W	1	2	3
Irish-medium	1 0.4%	6 2.6%	182 77.8%	45 19.2%

Table 3 above shows the numbers and percentage of pupil attainment from W (working towards) to Level 3 in Irish-medium schools.

Table 4: Mathematics in mainstream schools at Key Stage 1

Mathematics	W	1	2	3
Mainstream	86 0.4%	1077 5.3%	10624 52.2%	8580 42.1%

Table 4 above shows the numbers and percentage of pupil attainment from W (working towards) to Level 3 in mainstream schools.

Given that the same DENI targets for 2002 apply to Mathematics, how to IM schools perform? Once again IM schools are quite close to meeting the DENI target of 100% at Level 2 or better but fall well short of the Level 3 target of 35%. Mainstream schools also fall a little short of the Level 2 target but exceed the Level 3 target of 35%. A pattern seems to emerge which suggests that IM schools perform well as far as Level 2 but drop back in Level 3. There is no easy explanation for this but part of the answer probably lies in language acquisition in an immersion situation and pupils' ability to absorb mathematical concepts with limited language. This is not necessarily a weakness but in part the natural state of development in a bilingual or immersion situation in which there needs to be the recognition of the 'catch up' factor. Again, the question of the appropriateness of the assessment arises. However, other factors should also be considered here, namely if this state of development is indeed natural at all. Often, bilingualism and immersion are mentioned in the same sentence as being the same thing, when in fact they may well be entirely different. In the same way, Irish-medium children are mentioned in the same breath as bilingual Hispanics in the United States or Asian children in Britain. These are very different situations in that Hispanics, for example, come from one strong language background and enter into an educational system where the language is different, namely English, but also very strong. In the IM situation, almost all of the children come from a strong English-speaking background and enter into an education system where the language, namely Irish, is generally weak. In fact, it could be argued that IM children are not true bilinguals at all but rather artificially created bilinguals whose second language is little more than a classroom language with little relevance outside of that. The degree to how bilingual anyone is cannot be easily measured and is rarely ever 50-50. The degree to which IM children are bilingual is even more difficult to ascertain, but it obviously starts from a very low base and steadily improves. I would not hazard a guess as to how close it comes to being 50-50 at the end of Key Stage 2 or even by much later in their educational careers.

At Key Stage 2 IM pupils are assessed in both Irish and English as well as Mathematics. The following tables illustrate the attainment for Irish and English in IM schools and the attainment for English in mainstream schools.

Table 5: Irish at Key Stage 2

Irish	2	3	4	5
Irish-medium	1 1.8%	42 25%	103 61.3%	20 11.9%

Table 5 above shows the numbers and percentage of pupil attainment from Level 2 to Level 5 in Irish-medium schools.

Table 6: English at Key Stage 2

English	2	3	4	5
Irish-medium	1 0.6%	54 32.1%	100 59.5%	13 7.7%

Table 6 above shows the numbers and percentage of pupil attainment from Level 2 to Level 5 in Irish-medium schools.

Table 7: English at Key Stage 1

English	2	3	4	5
Mainstream	885 4.0%	5006 22.5%	11652 54.4%	4564 20.5%

Table 7 above shows the numbers and percentage of pupil attainment from Level 2 to Level 5 in Mainstream schools.

Given that DENI targets for 2002 are that 80% of pupils should reach Level 4 and that 35% should reach Level 5, how do IM schools perform at this Key Stage? Again, a similar pattern seems to emerge. IM schools do not quite meet the target for Level 4 (approx 73%) in Irish and fall well short of the Level 5 target (approx 12%). The percentages in English indicate that they perform less well at Level 4 (approx 67%) and fall very short of the Level 5 target (approx 8%). There are no surprises here. The attainment at Level 4 or better compares favourably with the performance in mainstream schools which is also approximately 73%. Mainstream schools also fall well short of the Level 5 target of 35%. The reasons for comparable performance at Level 4 need much more analysis than can be offered here, but in general terms at least, IM pupils have probably 'caught up' by this stage and could be expected to perform at reasonably high levels. However, as Irish is still essentially the language of the curriculum rather than the language of the street or the home, never mind the enrichment through modern popular media, Irish and English develop very differently in the Irish-medium situation. The acquisition of Irish, although impressive in value-added terms, is still lacking in terms of depth and breadth and in terms of attainment in the current assessment arrangements. The quality of pupils' language is not in any way comparable to their counterparts in mainstream, given their limited linguistic exposure. Again, that's not a criticism, merely a reality for immersion children and not uncommon in other immersion programmes in other countries. The fact that attainment in English is lower than in mainstream schools can hardly be surprising as it is, although a 'core' curriculum subject and taught through the medium of English, still just a subject. This is further complicated by the fact that English is generally the language of the street and of the home but not of the school, as stated earlier. To measure IM children by the exact same criteria may not be appropriate in the first instance.

Table 8: Mathematics in IM schools at Key Stage 2

Mathematics	2	3	4	5
Irish-medium	0	40 23.8%	93 55.4%	35 20.8%

Table 8 above shows the numbers and percentage of pupil attainment from Level 2 to Level 5 in Irish-medium schools.

Table 9: Mathematics in mainstream schools at Key Stage 2

Mathematics	2	3	4	5
Mainstream	766 3.4%	4404 19.8%	8581 38.6%	8362 37.6%

Table 9 above shows the numbers and percentage of pupil attainment from Level 2 to Level 5 in mainstream schools.

As for English, the targets for 2002 are that 80% should be attaining Level 4 or better and 35% should be at 35%. The same pattern seems to continue emerging. IM schools fall just short of the target at Level 4 (approx 76%) but fall very short at Level 5 (approx 12%). The performance at Level 4 is again quite comparable with that in mainstream schools (approx 76%) but not so at Level 5 where mainstream schools exceed the target. While the reasons for 'poorer' performance in English at Level 5 are probably more understandable and to be expected, this performance at Level 5 in Mathematics is not so easy explained. Language acquisition probably has a large part to play but is unlikely to be the only reason. The nature and appropriateness of the assessment may have a part to play also, but is unlikely to impact greatly. This is obviously an area worthy of further consideration and exploration.

The most difficult and controversial area in Irish-medium in terms of assessment and examinations is probably the Transfer Test (TT). One of the most controversial issues in our present education system is, of course, the Transfer Test which is also currently under review. The current format of the TT, in place since 1996, requires IM pupils to be tested in Irish, Mathematics and Science, while mainstream pupils are tested in English, Mathematics and Science. The Mathematics and Science elements of the TT are translated into Irish while the Irish element is generated in Irish and is not a translation of the English pieces used in mainstream schools. The TT is Graded as A, B1, B2, C1, C2 and D. Many of the arguments for and against the TT in general have often been rehearsed, not least its competitive and selective nature. What are much less rehearsed are the issues within the IM sector. The nature of the issues is quite complex and would need to be dealt with separately in another paper. The main problem in exploring the issues is that it is an extremely sensitive area and facts and figures are not readily available and therefore cannot be shared here. In general terms, IM pupils' performance varies greatly from year to year, particularly at grade A. Typically, IM pupils tend to perform better in the Irish element than their counterparts in the English element. However, their performance in the Mathematics and Science elements is also typically lower than their counterparts and has been dropping over a period of years. There would seem to be an expectation that the 'good' performance in Irish should compensate somehow for the expected 'poorer' performance in Mathematics and Science. It should be stressed that that is indeed just an expectation, not an arrangement. This has probably arisen because the Irish elements are set, according to the specification for IM schools, 'not higher than Level 4'.

Regardless of the grade A percentage performance in anyone year, the perennial concerns about the 'discriminatory' nature of the TT against IM children surface. These are usually genuine concerns and should not and are not dismissed lightly. The concerns generally challenge the level of difficulty of the Mathematics and Science (which is the same for both IM and mainstream) the standard and appropriateness of the translated elements, terminology and the fact that IM children are tested on only 75% of the 'core-curriculum' i.e. that the 'core' consists of Irish, Mathematics, Science and English, whereas the mainstream 'core' consists of only three subjects, namely English, Mathematics and Science, and the validity and reliability of the TT in general and also how IM pupils are graded.

The validity and reliability of the testing of bilinguals is a complex and hotly debated issue. In a nutshell, protagonists would argue that bilinguals should not be tested by instruments or on content essentially designed for monolinguals and also that they should not be tested in their second language which is usually the weaker of the two. What would be more desirable then would probably be a TT generated in Irish with original material in all three subjects with different test types designed specifically for bilinguals. All things being equal, that would seem reasonable and could be seen as a long-term objective. However, it is probably not practical or necessarily desirable at this point in time. There are too many difficulties involved, not least the dearth of expertise both inside and outside the classroom that could be sourced and the small numbers involved in order to ensure that it in itself would be valid, reliable and equitable. The concept of testing bilinguals in anything other than Irish is contrary to the ethos of the sector at present and is unlikely to be acceptable, though worthwhile considering and not anathema in other immersion systems. The current format of the TT is not designed with Irish-medium in mind but it has been adapted to meet, as far as is possible and practical, the needs of approximately 60-90 pupils as apposed to approximately 18,000 pupils who sit the TT in mainstream. IM schools have been developing over the years in order to offer an alternative but equally high standard of education. Intentionally or otherwise, it has tried to strike the balance between being different and alternative and at the same time conforming to and adapting to the system in general. It can indeed offer a different type of pedagogy but cannot reasonably expect an alternative education system or that the system adapts solely to meet the needs of Irish-medium. The demand for a completely different type of TT, therefore, is probably unreasonable also. If IM schools are intent on participating in this selection process then it would be more reasonable to expect IM schools to adapt and meet the demands of the TT rather than the reverse. The fact that the shelf life of the TT is likely to be limited, depending on the outcome of review underway, would also make radical change at this late stage undesirable.

In the meantime, CCEA does have the responsibility to ensure that present provision for the TT in Irish-medium is adequate. The main bone of contention has been the translated elements. One of the criticisms made is that the language used is much too difficult for IM pupils and that these pupils have to process information by essentially internally translating into English and then back to Irish before answering a question. There is a time factor which does not apply to mainstream children, but which would be extremely difficult to quantify. It is also claimed that those involved in the translations of the TT do not take cognisance of the difficulties of the IM pupils because firstly, they do not have any direct or chalk face experience of Irish-medium, and secondly, that they indulge in a kind of perfect translation exercise regardless of the target audience. How this could be known is intriguing as no one, other than those directly involved, knows what personnel are involved in the process due to its essential confidential nature. Nevertheless, nothing could be further from the truth. Over recent years, CCEA has made strenuous efforts to ensure good, appropriate and accurate translations through a number of measures including employing the services of a highly experienced specialist team of translators and revisers supervised by myself as the Officer responsible for IM at CCEA. It has been suggested that these Tests be translated using 'language' closer to that used by the children and therefore making the Tests more easily understood by them. I have yet to be convinced of what form this 'language' would take or if indeed it could be called a language at all as what is really being suggested is a type of diluted or 'dumbed down' version of Irish. The assumption here, of course, is that the language used by the children is not of a high standard. This approach would be a retrograde step indeed for the Irish language, even if it did in some way get around a difficulty in a particular test situation. This issue is a complex one in itself which asks questions of the quality of language acquired and of the degree to which children are bilingual in immersion programmes or if indeed they are bilingual or only 'semi-lingual'. It has been argued that this state of 'semi-lingualism' or 'semi-proficiency' (sometimes referred to as *idirtheanga* in Irish) is natural, normal, healthy and perfectly acceptable. Personally, I am not convinced of this and feel that there is a certain complacency and a self-limiting expectation of these children. I would much prefer to explore ways in which language acquisition and competency could be raised and improved rather than settling for something less than full bilingual competency. In regard to providing materials that reflect this 'diluted' linguistic state, this is an avenue CCEA is not prepared to go down but rather support the promotion of good language competency and good standard written Irish as demonstrated in all the materials it produces and in collaborating with other agencies and groups to promote best practice. This includes the provision of terminology lists for Mathematics and Science at Key Stage 2 and also for other subjects for Key Stage 3 and beyond in order to help ensure that schools are familiar with and use the same terminology used in tests, examinations etc. and more recently, a set of translated commercial TT practise papers which were not available before. As for how the operational TT papers are translated, CCEA has also put in place a number of important quality assurance measures to insure that cognisance is indeed taken of the issues. These include having IM revisers (with sound IM experience) participating in meetings at which the Mathematics and Science questions are selected for pre-testing and again when the final versions are selected before they are translated. These same revisers also select from a bank of materials the Irish elements for pre-testing and again select the final version. They also review and revise the work carried out by the translators and recommend and agree any necessary change required in consultation with the translators. This is also followed through by a 'Question Paper Scrutineer' who sits the Tests, in as far as possible, as a pupil might in order to ensure that the questions are indeed answerable and consistent with the mark scheme. Even with all that in place there is no absolute guarantee that all will be well. Things can slip through that may disadvantage the pupil. If that happens and it is identified in time, corrective measures are taken in order to ensure fairness.

There are quite a few issues here and whether or not the TT existed at all, some of these would still be up for debate. The TT itself is of course very contentious and probably even more so in Irish-medium. Why IM teachers should want to put themselves and their pupils through this annual competition for grammar school places is another question. If a fully developed IM sector at both primary and secondary level were in place the question may not even arise. There can be no doubt that there is strong parental pressure to have children entered, for whatever reason, despite the difficulties and 'disadvantages' perceived or otherwise. It would also be inappropriate and unfortunate if the TT were used as the success criterion for Irish-medium by parents or others.

At Key Stage 3 and beyond many of the same issues arise in one form or another. As stated earlier, there is only a small number of schools at secondary level, two of which have been involved in the Key Stage 3 assessments. IM schools pupils are assessed in Irish, English, Science and Mathematics, while their counterparts are assessed in English, Science and Mathematics. Given that there are only two schools involved it would probably not be fair to give a detailed breakdown of their combined percentage performance and compare it against mainstream schools. Nevertheless, even without presenting the detailed 'evidence' it is worth pointing out that the trends do seem to continue into Key Stage 3. The levels at Key Stage 3 range from Level 2 – Level 8 and preceded by Level Not Achieved (LNA). The DENI targets for Key Stage 3 are that 60% should be at Level 5 or better in English and 29% at Level 6 or better. In Mathematics 75% should be at Level 5 or better and 33% at Level 6 or better. There are no targets for Science. IM schools continue to perform fairly well in Irish with approximately 75% attaining Level 5 or better, which is about the same as the attainment in English in mainstream schools – both sectors performing well ahead of the target. However, there is a considerable difference between IM attainment in English and that in mainstream with only 35% attaining Level 5 or better. Again, the same explanations may be presented in that IM pupils could not be expected to attain the same high percentage performance as English is just a subject and not the medium of instruction. That explanation may be too simplistic though when one considers that English is still the pupils' first language for all intents and purposes and the language of their immediate environment. Studies in the Republic using standardised tests have shown that IM schools there have performed as well as, and sometimes better than, English-speaking schools. On the other hand, what would be a reasonable performance for this subject in IM schools has not been identified. Neither is it certain that IM pupils should be doing the exact same assessment under the same conditions as their counterparts.

The Science and Mathematics assessment are rather like the TT in that they are translated into Irish for IM pupils. Unlike the TT, pupils also have access to the English version but invariably use and answer in the translated versions. There are some associated advantages and disadvantages with having access to the English versions, not least the time factor. In Mathematics the trend tends to follow that found in the TT in which IM pupils would appear to be performing well below that of their counterparts e.g. approximately 52% attain Level 5 or more in IM while approximately 70% attain these levels in mainstream. The difference between the two sectors in terms of attainment of Level 6 or better becomes even more pronounced. The trend in Science is quite similar with approximately 43% attaining Level 5 or better in IM schools while mainstream achieve approximately 67%. Again, the difference in attainment at Level 6 or better becomes much more significant with approximately 40% of mainstream pupils attaining level 6 or better while only approximately 12% of IM pupils attaining the same. There are no easy explanations as to why there should be a considerable difference in attainment between the two sectors. It must also be remembered that the numbers and percentages here may well render comparison wholly inappropriate. There are probably many of the same difficulties at this level as exist at primary level mitigating against success here, particularly the dearth of good teaching materials, textbooks and qualified and experienced subject teachers. These problems also exist at GCSE and GCE levels which are considered much more as 'high stakes' examinations. The performances at these levels will not be examined in this paper, particularly as they involve much smaller numbers and the fact that the two schools involved have only been in existence little more than 10 years building up resources and experience during that time. The subjects taken at these levels are all translated into Irish. Pupils also have access to the English versions but mostly use the translated versions. Once again this presents its own difficulties such as the appropriateness and effectiveness of being examined in other than the first language, resources, preparation etc. CCEA has been working closely with the schools over recent years in developing and providing a range of materials including lists of consistent terminology for all subjects and in providing expert subject advice where appropriate. I think it would be fair to say that much has been achieved by the schools over recent years as they grow, develop and broaden curriculum provision despite inherent difficulties, but also that these difficulties need to be addressed in order to improve the outcomes.

As stated earlier, the issues in IM in regard to assessment and examinations are indeed quite complex. There are issues for both the IM sector and the various educational agencies to consider and address. Any claims of deliberate or institutionalised bias are completely unfounded and unfair. What is more likely to be the case is that the various agencies, including CCEA, often have to catch up with the rapid development of the IM sector and all the needs and demands created as the sector continues to evolve. Where there are problems or difficulties, solutions must be found if for no other reason than children are at the centre of all this. Solutions can be found by, firstly, recognising or admitting that a particular problem exists, identifying the nature of the problem and rectifying the problem through discussion and consultation. This requires the cooperation between the various agencies in an atmosphere of openness, realism and objectivity. It will also require much more research into good practice and effectiveness in immersion systems, particularly in assessment. The next major step for IM schools in all of this is to be found in the current review of the curriculum and assessment. This is probably the first real opportunity for the sector to have a genuine input into the development of the curriculum as a whole and to have an influence in how it should impact on the sector and not just as an 'afterthought'. This has already happened in the early stages of the review. Taking this a step further, CCEA has established an IM advisory group whose remit will be to advise on general matters and how they impact on IM, to advise on how IM pupils will be assessed and to identify areas for development in terms of materials etc. There is also an onus on the sector as a whole to respond to the curriculum review proposals and to come forward with ideas, opinions, and suggestions etc in order to inform the process as much as possible. CCEA recently has taken the step in consulting directly with IM schools through a consultation seminar specifically aimed at IM schools. This is indeed a golden opportunity for the sector to develop in a number of ways, not least in regard to how and when its pupils will be assessed but also what actually will be assessed. Many of the assessment issues raised here have been discovered as the sector has grown and developed. Now, as never before, is the time to address the issues. That is the invitation and the challenge for everyone involved.

Na toir breith gus nach toirear breith ort:
Tuilleadh 's a' chòir measaidh ann am Foghlam na h-Alba

Iain Mac Ille Chiar

Chan ann tric a bhios mi fhìn an làthair sgoilearan ionnsaichte, foghlaimte mar a tha cruinn cothrom còmhla an seo an diugh. Tha e a' cur nam chuimhne sgeulachd a tha againne ann an Alba – chan eil fhios agam a bheil e agaibh ann an Èirinn. Bha am madadh-allaidh agus am madadh-ruadh a-muigh cuairt còmhla. Bhiodh an dà ainmhidh daonnan a' feuchainn ris an car a thoirt às a-chèile agus làmh an uachdair fhaighinn air a-chèile – rud beag coltach ri sgoilearan, tha mi cinnteach. Co-dhiù bha am madadh-allaidh agus am madadh-ruadh gu math leisg agus thuirt am madadh ruadh ris a' mhadadh-allaidh "Thèid sinn dha leithid seo de bhaile agus, gheibh sinn fearann agus cuiridh sinn coirce." Rinn iad sin agus bha bàrr torach coirce aca. Aig àm foghair, dh' fhaighnich am madadh-ruadh dhen mhadadh-allaidh gu dè a b' fheàrr leis am bun no am bàrr. "Am bun "fhreagair am madadh-allaidh. Mar sin bha aran-coirce math aig a' mhadadh-ruadh fad na bliadhna agus cha robh ach connlach aig a' mhadadh-allaidh.

An ath-bhliadhna, 's e buntàta a chuir iad. Dh'fhàs am buntàta gu math agus dh' fhaighnich am madadh-ruadh dhen madadh-allaidh dè a b' fheàrr leis am bun no am bàrr. Am bàrr an turas seo, thuirt am madadh-allaidh. Mar sin, fhuair am madadh-ruadh am buntàta agus cha robh aig a'mhadadh-allaidh ach bàrr a' bhuntàta. Mar sin bhiodh am madadh-allaidh a' sìor-ghoid a' bhuntàta air a' mhadadh-ruadh fad a' gheamhraidh.

Dh' fhàs am madadh-ruadh gu math sgìth dhe seo agus dh' innis e dhan mhadadh-allaidh a dhol a-null far an robh làir ghlas na seasamh. " Leugh thusa, " ars' esan, "na tha sgrìobhte air ladhran na làireadh sin." Chaidh am madadh-allaidh a-null agus chuir e a cheann sìos a leughadh an sgrìobhaidh air ladhran na làireadh agus leig an làir aon bhreab aiste agus thug i sgleog dhan mhadadh-allaidh. Nuair a thàinig e thuige fhèin, thill e gu a charaid agus 's e a thuirt e " Chan eil mi nam sgoilear agus chan iarrainn a bhith".[1]

Mar sin, chan eil mise nam sgoilear. 'S e a tha annam ach fear a tha air a bhith a' saothrachadh ann am fìon-liosan na Gàidhlig, is uaireannan anns na mèinnean-salainn, feumaidh mi aideachadh, fad còrr is deich bliadhna thar fhichead. Nam oileanach tràth sna seachdadan, bha mi nam rùnaire de Chomann na Cànan Albannaich, buidheann a stèidhich i fhèin air prionnsabalan Cymdeitheas yr Iaith Gymraeg, Comann na Cànan Cuimrich. Bha mi a-measg an fheadhainn a chuir air chois Comhairle nan Sgoiltean-àraich, comann nan cròileagan, aig deireadh nan seachdadan. Ann an 1983, chuir mi fhìn is companach dhomh air chois Clì, Comann an Luchd-Ionnsachaidh airson inbhich a tha ag ionnsachadh na Gàidhlig mar dhàrna cànain. Goirid as dèidh sin thòisich mi a' ghluasad airson foghlam tro mheadhan na Gàidhlig ann an Inbhir Nis agus

---

[1] Campbell, J.F. 1892, ath-fhoillsichte 1984. *Popular Tales of the West Highlands, Rola 3, t.d.116-118.* Middlesex, Sasann:Wildwood House Ltd.

ann an 1985 dh' fhosgail a' cheud aonad Gàidhlig ann an Alba sa bhaile sin agus dithist dhe mo chloinn fhìn ann.

A'mhòr-chuid dhen ùine seo tha mi fhìn air a bhith ag obair an lùib foghlaim air dòigh air choreigin. Thòisich mi anns na sgoiltean agus ghluais mi dha na colaistean an ceann greis.

Mar sin, tha fiosrachadh pearsanta agam air a bhith a' teagasg aig ìre bunsgoil, àrdsgoil, ag oideachadh luchd-teagaisg ann an colaiste foghlaim, a' teagasg aig ìre foghlam adhartach ann an colaiste ionadail agus a-nis aig ìre oilthigh. Mar a chanas sinne ann an Alba, 's iomadh rud a chì an duine a bhios fada beò'. Tha fhios gur e sin pàirt dhen adhbhar nach e sgoilear a tha annam – Bha mi riamh ro thrang ann an gnìomh ann an strì na cànan airson ùine gu leòr a bhith agam airson sgoilearachd is rannsachadh. Feumaidh mi aideachadh cuideachd gu bheil mi gu math amharasach de luchd-rannsachaidh. Ro thric tha na dòighean-rannsachaidh aca bonntaichte air stataisteag agus tha brìgh a' chuspair a' dol fodha ann an àireamhan. Nuair a dh' iarr John orm an toiseach tighinn a bhruidhinn, 's e an cuspair a chuir e fam chomhair ach 'Measadh'. Nise ma tha aon rud ann a chuireas sgreamh orm, 's e measadh. Chan eil briathran agam a chuireas an cèill a' ghràin a tha agam air measadh – a bhith ga dhèanamh, a bhith ga dheasachadh, a bhith ga cheartachadh agus a bhith a' cunntas nan comharraidhean as a dhèidh! Is beag orm e, is lugha orm e, tha bith agam dha agus tha dubh-ghràin agam air. Gu dearbh chuir e nam chuimhne rannan à duanaire Dheadhain Lios Mòr. Agus tha cuid dhe na sreathan sin gu math tiamhaidh!

> *Fuath liom dobròn i dtigh n-òil*
> *Fuath liom deoch anbhfann 's ì daor*
> *Fuath liom cailleach as olc nèal*
> *Is a teanga go lèir luath;*
> *Nì fhèadaim a chur i gcèill*
> *Gach nì dà tugas fèin fuath.* [2]

Thug seo na ceòlraidh thugam agus ged nach eil mi cinnteach an e Rannaigheacht Mhòr a tha innte, seo i:

> *Fuath leam binn is breith,*
> *Fuath leam meidh nan saoi.*
> *Fuath leam measadh is teist,*
> *Fuath leam ceist gun fhaoil.*
> *Fuath leam deuchainnean fhèin,*
> *Gathan na pèin na sàil,*
> *Fuath leam measadh gun fheum,*
> *Fuath leam Dal Chè is a dàil.*

Feumaidh mi mìneachadh dhan luchd-èisteachd Èireannach gur ann ann an Dal Chè faisg air Dùn Èideann a tha prìomh-oifisean Ùghdarras Theisteanais na h-

---

[2] Watson, W.J. 1937. *Scottish Verse from the Book of the Dean of Lismore.* Edinburgh: Scottish Academic Press. 244.

Alba agus gun robh butarrais uabhasach ann o chionn dà bhliadhna nuair nach do sgaoil iad toradh nan teisteanas 'Àrd-ìre ' ann an àm airson nan oileanach a bha a' feitheamh ri àite fhaighinn anns na h-oilthighean. Carson a bha a-leithid a dhàil ann, ma-thà? Thug mi an aire o chionn seachdain no mar sin gun tuirt am ball-pàrlamaid Albannach, Mìcheal Russell, na leanas:

> *'The Byzantine complexity' of the Scottish exams system failed to deliver certificates that were clear passports containing transparent and portable information.*

Agus 's e an fhìrinn a tha aige. Nuair a thig oileanaich a-steach thugainn-ne agus a sheallas iad na fhuair iad san sgoil dhuinn, chan urrainn dhomhsa a thuigsinn, agus chanainn, mura h-urrainn dhomhsa a thuigsinn, mar fhear a tha air a bhith fad a bheatha ann am foghlam, gu bheil droch theansa ann gun tuig luchd-fastaidh no duine sam bith eile a-muigh san t-saoghal mhòr e.

'S e cnag na cùise gu bheil rian foghlaim na h-Alba, agus bha riamh, feumar aideachadh, air a bheò-ghlacadh le measadh. 'S e am bràthair mòr a tha ann, agus 's e an leabhar aig Orwell a tha mi a' ciallachadh is chan e am prògram telebhisein. Chan eil earbsa aig na riaghladairean againn annainn, agus gu seac àraidh an cuid sgalagan, na seirbhisich stàite. Ach feumar aideachadh gu bheil e a' dol nasa fhaide is nas doimhne na sin. Mar a chì sibh bhon litir seo a nochd o chionn ghoirid ann am pàirt foghlaim a' phàipeir-naidheachd, an t- Albannach, tha foghlam ann an Alba, aig gach ìre, air a luchdachadh le tuilleadh 's a chòir pàipeir.

Jargon is the Food of Education

Learning outcomes and performance indicators, grade-related criteria and (dodgy) descriptorsinstruments of assessment and unit assessment strands and levels, modules and management, work sheets and help sheets, contracts and codes, remits and business links, targets and modes, plans and league tables and Easter revision. Or what about...grades and reports and social inclusion, reviews and appraisal and computer training, budgets and fast-track learning, testing and testing (isn't it?), paper to chase...

And don't forget about...QA and SQA, SDA and SDO, SVQ and DSM, PSD, IT, PE and HE, HMI, NAB, PAT and PPP, EIL, FLG, OHP and OTT...

But whatever happened to things such as the democratic intellect, the generalist tradition, inspiration and spontaneity, originality and creativity, intellectual integrity, love of learning, responsibility for learning, general knowledge and independent thought and ...?

Don't be ridiculous. Give them that and the next thing you know they will all be demanding socialism.

Jim Aitken,
Penicuik.[3]

---

[3] *The Scotsman*. Litir thun an Deasaiche.

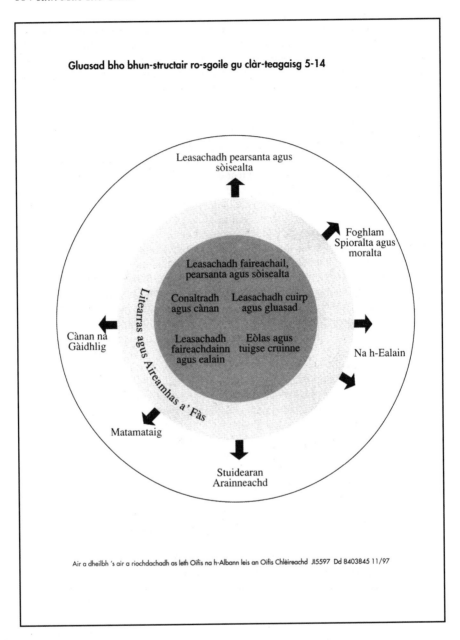

Gluasad bho bhun-structair ro-sgoile gu clàr-teagaisg 5-14

Leasachadh pearsanta agus sòisealta

Foghlam Spioralta agus moralta

Leasachadh faireachail, pearsanta agus sòisealta

Conaltradh agus cànan

Leasachadh cuirp agus gluasad

Leasachadh faireachdainn agus ealain

Eòlas agus tuigse cruinne

Cànan na Gàidhlig

Na h-Ealain

Litearras agus Àireamhas a' Fàs

Matamataig

Stuidearan Arainneachd

Air a dheilbh 's air a riochdachadh as leth Oifis na h-Albann leis an Oifis Chlèireachd JI5597 Dd 8403845 11/97

Clàr 1[4]

---

[4] Luchd-sgrùdaidh na Bànrigh airson Sgoiltean. An t-Sultain 1997. *Bun-structair Clàr-teagaisg do Chloinn nam Bliadhna Ro-sgoile, t.d. 57.* Dùn Èideann:Oifis na h-Albann. Tha mi taingeil airson cead seo ath-fhoillseachadh

ann a bhith a' cluinntinn neach-labhairt no òraidiche, agus feum air cànain bhodhaig a bhreithneachadh gus tuigse iomlan fhaighinn air a' chonaltradh anns an fharsaingeachd; no an uair a thàtar a' frithealadh dràma no a' coimhead air film no air prògram telebhisein, agus gun seachnadh air a bhith a' beachdachadh air nithean faicsinneach.

1.1

Adhbhair

Tha mothachadh air **adhbhar** 's air **luchd-amais** a' toirt barrachd smachd do luchd-labhairt agus do luchd-sgrìobhaidh air an cuid chànain agus air a buil. Tha e 'na chuideachadh do luchd-èisteachd agus do luchd-leughaidh greim fhaighinn air na h-adhbhair a tha air cùl earrann labhairt no sgrìobhaidh, gus tuigse nas fheàrr fhaighinn air a brìgh agus gus tomhas a dhèanamh air a h-èifeachd. A bhàrr air sin, tha buaidh ro mhòr aig na **suidhichidhean** anns a bheil a' Ghàidhlig air a cur an cèill 's air a gabhail a-staigh air conaltradh sam bith agus air mar a thuigear an conaltradh sin. Tha sgilean na Gàidhlig air an cur ann am feobhas le eòlas air na h-adhbhair ann am pailteas sheòrsachan shuidhichidhean, agus bheir seo cothrom do luchd-ionnsachaidh tomhas nas buadhmhoire a dhèanamh air an adhartas a rinn iad agus air na tha iad a' toirt gu buil.

Bidh na h-adhbhair a leanas aig obair na Gàidhlig anns na sgoiltean:

Èisteachd

Gus fiosrachadh fhaotainn agus gus freagairt ann an dòigh iomchaidh;
Gus dàimh a bhonntachadh agus gus co-luadar a dhèanamh ri daoine eile;
Gus a bhith a' co-fhreagairt ri faireachdainnean dhaoine eile;
Gus cnuasachadh air smaointean, fiosraichidhean agus beachdan;
Gus riarachadh agus toileachas-inntinn fhaotainn.

Labhairt

Gus fiosrachadh a thoirt seachad;
Gus dàimh a bhonntachadh agus gus co-luadar a dhèanamh ri daoine eile;
Gus faireachdainnean a chur an cèill;
Gus smaointean, fiosraichidhean agus beachdan a chur an cèill, a cho-phàirteachadh 's a shoilleireachadh, agus gus cnuasachadh orra;
Gus riarachadh agus toileachas-inntinn a thoirt seachad.

Leughadh

Gus fiosrachadh fhaotainn agus gus freagairt ann an dòigh iomchaidh;
Gus a bhith a' co-fhreagairt ri faireachdainnean dhaoine eile;
Gus cnuasachadh air smaointean, fiosraichidhean agus beachdan;
Gus riarachadh agus toileachas-inntinn fhaotainn.

Sgrìobhadh

Gus fiosrachadh a thoirt seachad;
Gus dàimh a bhonntachadh agus gus co-luadar a dhèanamh ri daoine eile;
Gus faireachdainnean a chur an cèill;
Gus smaointean, fiosraichidhean agus beachdan a chur air dòigh, a shoilleireachadh agus a chlàradh, agus gus cnuasachadh orra;
Gus riarachadh agus toileachas-inntinn a thoirt seachad.

5

Clàr 2

1.2	**FOGHLAM TRO GHAIDHLIG LEUGHADH : CUIMSEAN-COILEANAIDH**		**Anns na cuimsean-coileanaidh seo bidh a' chlann:**	
	IALLAN	**IRE A**	**IRE B**	**IRE C**
	Leughadh airson fiosrachaidh	A' lorg, le taice on neach-teagaisg pios fiosrachaidh o theacsa-fiosrachaidh.	A' lorg agus a' cleachdadh, le taice on neach-teagaisg, fiosrachaidh àraidh air a bheil feum aca, o chaochladh ghoireasan-fiosrachaidh.	A' lorg agus a' cleachdadh fiosrachaidh air a bheil feum aca o chaochladh ghoireasan-fiosrachaidh.
	Leughadh airson toileachaidh	A' leughadh airson toileachaidh, stòiridhean, dàin agus teacsaichean-fiosrachaidh a tha sìmplidh, le taice dhealbh.	A' leughadh stòiridhean, dhàn agus theacsaichean-fiosrachaidh gu cunbhalach airson toileachaidh.	A' leughadh gu cunbhalach airson toileachaidh agus a' toirt beachd air caochladh sheòrsachan theacsaichean.
	Leughadh gus cnuasachadh air bun-bheachdan agus air ceàird an ùghdair	A' leughadh agus, le taice on neach-teagaisg, a' còmhradh mu theacsa goirid sìmplidh, a' nochdadh gu bheil iad a' tuigsinn aon smuain a tha cudthromach.	A' leughadh theacsaichean simplidh agus, ann am beachdachadh 's ann an sgrìobhadh, a' nochdadh gu bheil iad a' tuigsinn nam priomh bhun-bheachdan.	A' leughadh caochladh theacsaichean sìmplidh agus, ann am beachdachadh 's ann an sgrìobhadh, a' nochdadh gu bheil iad a' tuigsinn nam priomh bhun-bheachdan agus nam bun-bheachdan a tha a' cur riutha sin, agus a' tighinn gu co-dhùnadh on teacsa ma tha sin iomchaidh.
	Mothachadh air gnè (seòrsa teacsa)	A' nochdadh gun aithnich iad aon ni follaiseach a tha a' cur o chèile dà theacsa shìmplidh de ghnè eadar-dhealaichte, mar tha stòiridh agus liosta sheòlaidhean.	A' nochdadh aithne air beagan nithean a bhuineas do chaochladh sheòrsachan de theacsaichean sìmplidh: stòiridhean, dàin, teacsaichean-dràma agus teacsaichean fiosrachaidh.	A' comharrachadh a-mach beagan de nithean follaiseach a bhuineas do chruth agus do shusbaint ann an caochladh sheòrsachan theacsaichean: stòiridhean, dàin, teacsaichean-dràma, pìosan o phàipearan-naidheachd, agus teacsaichean fiosrachaidh.
	Leughadh a-mach	A' leughadh a-mach, le taice on neach-teagaisg, earrainn no dàin air a bheil eòlas aca gus tuigse a chur an cèill.	A' leughadh, car slùbhlach, teacsa air a bheil eòlas aca.	A' leughadh, gu siùbhlach, teacsa air a bheil iad eòlach; a' sgrùdadh agus an-sin a' leughadh a-mach teacsa goirid air nach eil iad eòlach, agus a' cur tuigse an cèill.
	Eòlas air cànain		A' nochdadh gur aithne dhaibh, gun tuig iad agus gun cleachd iad air a' char as lugha na faclan a leanas: ùghdar, tiotal, caibideil, clàr-amais, clàr-innse; pearsa, ullachadh-sgeòil; dàn, faclair: comharradh-ceiste.	A' nochdadh gur aithne dhaibh, gun tuig iad agus gun cleachd iad air a' char as lugha na faclan a leanas: ficsean, fiorsgeul, briathrachan, leabhar-fiosrachaidh; plota, co-chòmhradh, priomh-phearsa, strì; rann, paragraf, ceann-naidheachd; comharraidhean-labhairt, comharradh-clisge.
			20	

Clàr 3[5]

---

[5] *ibid, t.d.18 -19.* Tha mi taingeil airson cead seo ath-fhoillseachadh

1.2

IRE D	IRE E	IALLAN
A' lorg, a' taghadh agus a' cur còmhla fiosrachaidh o chòrr is aon ghoireas.	A' cur gu feum am fiosrachadh a fhuaras o chunntas ghoireasan eadar-dhealaichte gus rannsachadh pearsanta a chur air adhart.	Leughadh airson fiosrachaidh
A' leughadh, gu cunbhalach agus airson toileachaidh, teacsaichean air caochladh sheòrsachan cuspair, agus, le taice, a' beachd-smuaineachadh air na chaidh a leughadh agus a' clàradh mar a ghabhadh ris.	A' leughadh, gu cunbhalach airson toileachaidh, teacsaichean air mòran sheòrsachan cuspair; agus a' toirt, ann an cainnt-bheòil no ann an sgrìobhadh, làn bheachd pearsanta air na teacsaichean a chaidh a leughadh, le taice o na h-uiread de dhearbhadh iomchaidh.	Leughadh airson toileachaidh
A' leughadh theacsaichean de dh'iomadh seòrsa agus a' nochdadh ann am beachdachadh 's ann an sgrìobhadh gu bheil iad a' tuigsinn màthair-adhbhair an teacsa agus nam prìomh smuaintean agus/ no nam prìomh fhaireachdainnean aige, agus gu bheil iad comasach air fiosrachadh sònraichte fhaotainn; agus a' toirt beachd air na nithean as sìmplidh a bhuineas do cheàird an sgrìobhaiche.	A' leughadh air an ceann fhèin, a' togail agus a' sgrùdadh gus prìomh phuingean ann an teacs a chomharrachadh; a' cur air mhanadh, a' comharrachadh fo-smuaintean; a' beachdachadh ann an aithghearrachd air beachdan agus rùintean an sgrìobhaiche; a' toirt iomraidh, leis na h-uiread de stiùireadh, air na nithean as sìmplidh a thaobh stoidhle agus air an luchd-amais a tha san amharc.	Leughadh gus cnuasachadh air bun-bheachdan agus air ceàird an ùghdair
A' comharrachadh, ann an eisimpleirean den aon ghnè teacsa, nithean a tha coltach agus eu-coltach ri chèile a thaobh cruth is susbaint, mar eisimpleir stòiridhean mu thaibhsean no litrichean gearain no piosan goirid de dh'eachdraidh beatha à leabhar mòr-eòlais.	A' comharrachadh, ann an eis impleirean de theacsaichean de chaochladh gnè, nithean a tha coltach agus eu-coltach ri chèile a thaobh cruth agus susbaint, agus a' toirt beachd air mar a tha iad seo a' nochdadh adhbhar nan teacsaichean.	Mothachadh air gnè (seòrsa teacsa)
		Leughadh a-mach
A' nochdadh gur aithne dhaibh, gun tuig iad agus gun cleachd iad air a' char as lugha na faclan a leanas: cuspair, pearsa, dàimh, suidheachadh, rùintean; firinn agus beachd; dreach, clò trom agus clò Eadailteach.	A' nochdadh gur aithne dhaibh, gun tuig iad agus gun cleachd iad air a' char as lugha na faclan a leanas: gnè; lide, freumh, stoc, ro-leasachan, iar-leasachan; samhla, meatafor.	Eòlas air cànain

21

Clàr 3b

	A	B	C	D
1	COMAS CONALTRAIGH 1		%	done ?
2				
3	Comhradh	5 - 10 minute taped conversation	25	
4	Measadh Eisteachd	listening activity/written response	25	
5	Measadh Leughaidh	reading activity/written or oral response	25	
6	Leabhar Labhairteach	talking book extract (taped)	25	
7				
8	COMAS CONALTRAIGH 2			
9				
10	Comhradh	10 min.conversation (taped) con. tense	25	
11	Measadh Eisteachd	listening activity /written response	25	
12	Measadh Fuaimneachaidh	pronunciation exercise (taped)	25	
13	Storas Sgriobhaidhean	folio of 5 pieces of work	25	
14				
15	EISTEACHD,BEACHADH			
16	IS FREAGAIRT			
17				
18	Measadh Fhreagairt sa Bhad	oral response to broadcast (taped)	40	
19	Leirmheas Labhairteach	oral review of play/film (taped)	20	
20	Measadh Ath-Sgriobhaidh	transcription of broadcast	40	
21				
22	CANAN FOIRMEIL IS			
23	DREUCHDAIL			
24				
25	Storas Sgriobhaidean	folio of 3 pieces of work, notice, C.V. etc.	50	
26	Taisbeanaidhean	2 oral presentations of same info. for	50	
27	Labhairteach	two different audiences		
28				
29	LITREACHAS:SGILEAN SGRU-			
30	DAIDH IS CRUTHACHAIDH			
31				
32	Storas Sgriobhaidhean	folio of 3 pieces of creative writing	50	
33	Deuchainn Deireannach	a final written examination	50	
34				
35	BUN-FHIOSRACHADH MU			
36	GHAIDHEALTACHD NA-H-ALBA			
37				
38	Ceistean Goirid	short in-class examination	30	
39	Leirmheas	written book review	20	
40	Sgrudadh Ionadail	group local study, written presentation	50	
41				
42	GREIS GNIOMHACHAIS			
43				
44	Cunntas-Beatha/Litir	a C.V. and covering letter	25	
45	Leabhar-Latha	diary of work placement	25	
46	Fein-Luachadh	self appraisal, written or oral report	25	
47	Beachd an Luchd-Fastaidh	feedback from host organisation	25	
48				
49	CANAN SA CHOIMHEARSNACHD			
50				
51	Leabhar-Latha	audio/video/written diary of field trips	50	
52	Taisbeanadh Labhairteach	5 -10 min. oral presentation and	50	
53		written report (approx 1000 words)		

Clàr 4

Thathar a' measadh clann is oileanaich bhon chreathaill chun na h-uaghach. Nis, tha foghlam tro mheadhan na Gàidhlig, mar a chanas sibh an Èirinn, ma 's math mo chuimhne, fighte, fuaighte tron rian. Gach rud a thachras ann an rian foghlam na Beurla, tachraidh e mar an ceudna taobh na Gàidhlig cuideachd. Mus tig na h-urracha beaga dhan sgoil, tha iad gam measadh.

San leabhran Bun-structair Clàr-teagaisg do Chloinn nam Bliadhna Ro-sgoile a dhèiligeas ri clann roimh aois oifigeil na sgoile, chìthear gu bheilear a' toirt tarraing air ullachadh, rud a tha reusanta gu leòr, ach cuideachd air sgrùdadh agus measadh, a' cleachdadh sgrùdadh agus measadh gus ionnsachadh agus teagasg a bhreithneachadh. An uair sin feumar seo a chlàradh agus aithris dha na pàrantan agus tha fhios iomadaidh duine eile a thig an lùib an neach-teagaisg bhochd, mar cheannardan, oifigich foghlaim, luchd-sgrùdaidh 's a leithid. Chan e sin a-mhàin ach feumar an ionnsachadh ann an dìomhaireachd cuspairean saoghal nan inbheach cuideachd; cànain, leasachadh pearsanta agus sòisealta, foghlam spioralta is moralta, na h-ealdhain, stuidearan àrainneachd agus matamataig - is bha sibhse an dùil gun robh John Stuart Mill comasach, a' dèanamh a' ghnothaich air Greugais aig trì bliadhna dh' aois.

Nis, shaoilteadh nach biodh an còrr aca ri ionnsachadh an dèidh sin....ach tha an sgeulachd a' leantainn oirre. Eadar aois 5-14, tha iad gan sìor-mheasadh. Tha pàipearan comhairleachaidh ann air na leanas: Measadh fhèin, Beurla, na h-Ealdhain, Gàidhlig, Laideann, Matamataig, Leasachadh Pearsanta is Sòisealta, Foghlam Spioralta is Moralta, Eòlas na h-Àrainneachd, Foghlam Slàinte, Teigneòlas Fiosrachaidh is Conaltraidh agus Cànainean Eòrpach. Agus airson bàrr a thoirt orra uile - Cur-ri-chèile agus Cothrom a' Churriculuim. Airson sealltainn dhuibh cho mionaideach 's a tha seo air a thomhas dhan luchd-teagaisg, seo eisimpleirean bhon leabhran Gàidhlig 5-14.[6] Tha a' cheud chlàr a' sealltainn mar a tha a' chànain air a briseadh sna ceithir earrannan àbhaisteach: èisteachd, labhairt, leughadh agus sgrìobhadh.[7]

Ach cuideachd thathar a' measadh aig gach ìre, A gu E, mar a chithear san dàrna clàr. Bu chòir dhaibh ìre A a ruighinn eadar clas 1 agus 3, B eadar clas 3 agus 4, C eadar clas 4 agus 6, D eadar clas 6 agus 7 agus E eadar am bunsgoil agus clas 2 san àrd-sgoil.

Feumar cuimhneachadh mar an ceudna nach e aon sgil a-mhàin a tha ga mheasadh, ach grunn sheòrsaichean de sgilean anns gach cuspair aig gach ìre. Agus mu dheireadh, cha do sheall mi ach aon duilleag de dh' aon fhear dhe na leabhrain an seo. Ma thillear thun na liosta dh' fhoillsicheadh gu h-àrd, bidh cuimhne aig an leughadair - nach bi? - gu bheil aig na sgoilearan ri seo a dhèanamh leis a h-uile fear dhe na cuspairean sin!

Nis ma tha an leughadair ga dhalladh is ga bhodhradh leis an fhiosrachadh seo, tha e airson dearbhadh - mar a thuirt sgrìobhadair na litreach thun an Albannaich - mar a dh' fhaoidte gach tlachd a thoirt à ionnsachadh.

Feumar a bhith taingeil nach eil mi a' dol a bhruidhinn air na tha aig sgoilearan ri dhèanamh as dèidh na h-ìre seo. Tha seo air a leantainn leis an Ìre

---

[6] Roinn an Fhoghlaim Cuairt-litir Àir. 3/93. An t-Òg-mhìos 1993. *Clàr-teagaisg agus Measadh an Albainn, Stiùireadh Nàiseanta, Gàidhlig 5-14.* Dùn Èideann:Oifis na h-Albann. Tha mi taingeil airson cead seo ath-fhoillseachadh

[7] *ibid, t.d. 5.* Tha mi taingeil airson cead seo ath-fhoillseachadh

Choitcheann air an treas agus a' cheathramh bliadhna san àrd-sgoil, air a mheasadh gu sìorraidh aig trì ìrean: Bun-ìre, Meadhan-ìre agus Sàr-ìre. Tha seo air a leantainn leis na b' abhaist a bhith na h-àrd-ire agus a tha nis cho sgapte toinnte gum fàg mi an dàrna taobh e o nach eil mi fhìn ro chinnteach às. Dè chanar ris an ablach seo? - nas àirde fhathast.

Tha seo uile a' cur nam chuimhne naidheachd a dh' innis m' athair dhomh mu dheidhinn fhèin. 'S e ceòl an rud a b' fheàrr leis-san ach thuirt athair fhèin nach robh airgead sam bith ann. Mar sin chuireadh e gu banca an là a bha seo, far an robh triùir ghillean eile ann agus bha aca ri deuchainn a' bhanca a ghabhail. 'S e a rinn am bancair ach am pàipear fhàgail aca agus dh' fhalbh e fad uair a thìde. Mar a bhiodh dùil le ceathrar chnapach de ghillean, chuir iad comhairle ri chèile air gach ceist. 'S e a' bhuil a bha ann getà, eadar an ceathrar aca agus gach feall is cuilbheirt, nach b' urrainn dhaibh bun no bàrr a dhèanamh dhen phàipear agus mar sin cha tàinig m' athair, no duine eile aca na bhancair.

Tha seo a' dearbhadh rud na dhà, saoilidh mi. Sa cheud àite, feumaidh nach robh cus earbsa aig a' bhanca ann an deuchainnean na sgoile agus na stàite ann an linn an òir, anns na tritheadan. Cuideachd, bha na deuchainnean aca fhèin cho mu làimh, nach robh feum annta. Ach bha mi riamh a' meòrachadh, saoilsibh am bithte a' fàgail ghillean leotha fhèin mar sin airson faighinn a-mach dè cho onarach 's a bha am freagairtean, is an e an obair aca fhèin a bha ann, an àite dè cho ceart 's a bha iad. Ach, tha mi cinnteach, gun robh am banca fhèin, mar a tha a' mhòr-chuid de ghnìomhachasan thun an là an diugh, a' gabhail os làimh oideachadh an luchd-obrach aca-fhèin an dèidh dhaibh am fastadh. Fiù ' s ceumnaich a' tighinn a-mach às na h-oilthighean len cuid M.A. le urram agus a tha a' dol nam manaidsearan ann an sàr-mhargaidhean, feumaidh iad an ceàird a thoirt a-mach às ùr ann an dà-rìreadh an uair sin.

Tha buaidh phearsanta aig a' mheasadh a tha seo orm fhìn cuideachd, ge-tà. Nam obair sa cholaiste sa bheil mi ann an Inbhir Nis, tha mi-fhìn agus mo chompanach, Pàdraig Moireach, a' teagasg dà chùrsa. A' cheud chùrsa, an Cùrsa Nàiseanta 's e bun-chùrsa bogaidh a tha ann, far am faod daoine gun smid Ghàidhlig, tòiseachadh agus ìre air choreigin de fhileantachd a ruighinn an ceann bliadhna. Gheibh iad ochd uairean deug dhen uaireadair san t-seachdain de theagasg fad sia seachdainean deug thar fhichead. 'S e sin uile gu lèir mu shia ceud uair gu leth dhen uaireadair ann am bliadhna na colaiste.

Tha an dàrna cùrsa air a bheil sinn a' teagasg, an Cùrsa Comais, na ciad bhliadhna de cheum B.A. Oilthigh na Gàidhealtachd 's nan Eilean. San dol seachad, feumaidh mi fios a leigeil dhuibh, nach fhaod mi an t-ainm sin a thoirt air o nach d' fhuaras cead fhathast oilthigh a chantainn ris, ged a thathar a' toirt seachad cheumannan ann.

Feumaidh mi aideachadh, ann an gach fear dhe na cùrsaichean sin, tha measadh, cha chuir e ioghnadh sam bith oirbh, na phlàigh.

Anns a' Chùrsa Comais, tha ochd modailean air leth ann, ged nach eil sin a' freagairt air feallsanachd iomlan a' chùrsa. Nuair a chaidh a dhealbhachadh, chaidh measadh a dhealbhachadh airson ochd modailean air leth, agus coltach ri iomadh cùrsa a chaidh iompachadh o bhith na chùrsa colaiste gu bhith na chùrsa oilthigh, tha a' bhuil air agus tha e a' fulang tuilleadh 's a' chòir de mheasadh . Nis, ged a chaidh a spealadh's a thanachadh an dèidh na ciad bliadhna dheth, seo na tha air fhàgail fhathast.

Gus ur sàbhaladh o bhith a' cunntas, tha fichead pìos obrach 's a trì-deug air fad ann an seo. Tha faochadh orm cur an cèill gun deach agam air toirt air a' chomataidh chubhaidh sùil eile a thoirt air an seo a-rithist am bliadhna agus tha fiughair agam ri tuilleadh sgathaidh ga dhèanamh air fhathast. Ach ma tha sin dona, chan eil ann ach ' roghainn an dà dhiùghaidh ' , mar a thuirt fear de chinn-chinnidh nan Caimbeulach, nuair a thug iad an roghainn dha eadar an ceann a thoirt dheth no a chrochadh.

'S i a' chrois as mò a tha oirnn ach an Cùrsa Nàiseanta. A chionn 's gur e cùrsa colaiste a tha ann, feumaidh, a-rèir nan riaghailtean nàiseanta, na h-oileanaich ochd modailean deug a ghabhail os làimh, a-rithist ann an cùrsa a tha ag amas air a bhith na chùrsa iomlan cànan. Faodaidh suas ri còig measaidhean a bhith anns gach modail agus math dh' fhaoidte a-dhà no trì pìosan anns gach measadh. Ma chanas sinn gu bheil san fharsaingeachd ceithir measaidhean anns gach modail, bidh còrr math is ceithir fichead ann air fad. Chan e sin a-mhàin ach coltach ris a h-uile cuspair a tha ga theagasg ann an colaistean foghlaim adhartaich ann an Albainn, tha gach measadh air a dhealbhachadh leis an neach-teagaisg fhèin, bonntaichte air, mar a thuirt sgrìobhaiche na litreach chun an Albannaich, ' dodgy descriptor'. Chaidh rannsachadh a dhèanamh air an seo le mo dheagh chompanach, Boyd MacDhonnchaidh ann an Oilthigh Shrath Chuaidh, agus chuireadh na molaidhean a leanas gu ruige Ùghdarras Theisteanais na h-Alba.[8] Tha na molaidhean, reusanta, ciallach agus mar sin, cha chualas an còrr bhon ùghdarras bho chuireadh a-steach an uiridh iad. Seo iad:

Teisteanachadh

Bu chòir Teisteanas sònraichte airson chùrsaichean bogaidh Gàidhlig a thoirt a-steach
Bu chòir gum biodh an Teisteanas sònraichte air a bhuileachadh le SQA agus gum biodh e na dhuais nàiseanta aithnichte le luchd-fastaidh, colaistean agus oilthighean
San ùine fhada, bu chòir coimhead ri frèam Eòrpach a leasachadh airson teisteanachadh chùrsaichean bogaidh

Measadh

Bu chòir na comasan a dh'fheumadh oileanaich a tha a' crìochnachadh cùrsa bogaidh a ruigheachd a bhith air an sònrachadh
Bu chòir an cuideam measaidh iomlan a bhith air a lughdachadh gu mòr
Bu chòir measadh stèidhichte air slat-thomhais a bhith air a ghleidheadh
Bhiodh measgachadh de mheasadh cunbhalach agus deireannach freagarrach agus bu chòir eileamaid de mheasadh on taobh a-muigh a bhith air a thoirt a-steach

Clàr 5

Clàr 5

'S iad na pìosan a tha cudromach an seo, teisteanas, far a bheilear a' moladh teisteanas air leth airson a' chùrsa, gum bi e nàiseanta, agus gum bi co-òrdanachadh Eòrpach ann gus gum bi an aon luach aig a leithid a theisteanas air

---

[8] Robasdan, A.G. Boyd. *Cùrsaichean Bogaidh Gàidhlig/Gaelic Immersion Courses.* An t-Iuchar 2001. Dùn Èideann: Ùghdarras Theisteanais na h-Alba.

feadh an Aonaidh Eòrpaich. Saoilidh mi-fhìn gum biodh an t-uabhas againn ri ionnsachadh bho na Basgaich ann an seo mar eisimpleir.

Am pìos eile a dh' fhaodadh a bhith tàbhachdach, 's ann air measadh a tha e. 'S e gum bi comas deireannach gach oileanaich soilleir, gum bi gu math nas lugha de mheasadh ann, gun cumar measadh a-rèir slatan-tomhais stèidhichte agus gum bu chòir tilleadh do mheasadh bhon taobh-a-muigh.

Tha e cudromach a-rèiste gun tèid na molaidhean seo a chur an gnìomh sa mhionaid uarach le U.T. na h-Alba airson inbhe a thoirt do na grad-chùrsaichean againn, teisteanas susbainteach a thoirt do na h-oileanaich a thig trompa agus airson soilleireachd slighe a thoirt dhan luchd-teagaisg.

'S fhad bho leugh mi gun robh cainnt gach duine air a roinn anns na h-earrannan a leanas:

> 45% dher n-ùine ag èisteachd
> 30% dher n-ùine a' bruidhinn
> 16% dher n-ùine a' leughadh
> 9%   dher n-ùine a' sgrìobhadh[9]

Mar sin, bu chòir do mheasadh sam bith a thachras a bhith air a roinn a-rèir seo. Nam fhiosrachadh fhèin, ma tha oileanaich idir lag, 's ann ann a bhith a' tuigsinn an fhacail air a labhairt a tha iad, gu hàraidh ma tha e air a labhairt idir coltach ris an astar nàdarrach a tha aig fileantach na chainnt làitheil. Tha seo nas fìora buileach sna cànainean Ceilteach far am feumar a' chluas a ghleusadh ri sèimheachadh is na h-atharrachaidhean eile a thachras aig toiseach fhaclan. Mar sin, ma tha molaidhean sam bith agam fhìn mu mheasadh, 's iad iad seo. Gum bu chòir dha bhith:

1. feumail - gu bheil e a' sealltainn neart is laigse an oileanaich dha fhèin is dha neach-theagaisg.
2. dèanta bhon taobh-a-muigh - airson a bhith neo-eisimileach.
3. susbainteach - a' cur cudrom air na comasan èisteachd, tuigsinn is labhairt gu h-àraidh.
4. fìrinneach - nach bu chòir dha pàtaran roimh-òrdaichte a leantainn ach a bhith na fhìor dheuchainn, a' tachairt gun rabhadh roimh làimh.
5. luachmhor - gun toir an t-oileanach brìgh às is gum bi luach san teisteanas. seo-thuigsinn dhan taobh-a-muigh - gus gum faigh an t-oileanach cosnadh às.

Bidh mòran agaibh an seo an diugh eòlach air an sgrìobhadair Albannach, Iain Crighton Maca'Ghobhainn. Sgrìobh e dealbh-chluich smaoineachail mu fhuadach ann an Cataibh, far a bheil am bàillidh, Pàdraig Sellar, a chairt cailleach a-mach às an taigh aice gu a bàs, a-nis a' nochdadh sa chùirt. Gu dearbh, sin ainm na deilbh-chluich, A' Chùirt. Nuair a nochdas Sellar air beulaibh a' bhritheimh, tha na faclan seo air an crochadh os cionn na cùirteach.

Na tugaibh breith chum nach toirear breith oirbh. Cha leig mi leas innse dhuibh ann an dùthaich cho beannaichte ri Èirinn, co às a tha sin, ach mur eil sibh

---

[9] Rivers, a-rèir Sidwell,D.M., Smith,D.G. is Payne,R. 1978. *Modern Languge Teaching (Teaching Adults, New Series).* NIAE.

cinnteach, feuchaibh an Soisgeul a-rèir Mata, Caibideal VII, Rann 1. Bu chòir na faclan sin a chrochadh os cionn doras gach aitreabh foghlaim san t-saoghal.

English Summary: Over-assessment in Scottish Education

In the above article, the author, a long-standing teacher of Scottish Gaelic at various age and ability levels, bemoans the fact that assessment is, as it ever was, the obsession of the Scottish educational establishment. He explains that the amount of continuous assessment has overloaded the system from the cradle to the grave, and is at the point where industrial action may be imminent in schools if it is not dealt with. Where the author himself toils, in the Cinderella section of further education, an independent commissioned report has recommended sensible and substantial changes to the assessment of Gaelic immersion courses, which would greatly ease the student burden of continuous minutae of assessment, free the teachers to return to more creative ways of teaching and provide the graduate with an acknowledged and comprehensible certificate. However, over a year after the appearance of this report, no action is forthcoming.

The Current State of Irish-Medium Education in Northern Ireland

Stephen Peover

Introduction

The focus of this session is on whether the realities and needs of other-medium education are met by Part III of the European Charter for Regional or Minority Languages. However, the only answer possible to this question is that beloved of Sir Humphrey Appleby, the fictional Permanent Secretary of the Department of Administrative Affairs in the BBC television series "Yes Minister" – Yes, and No. The answer is positive in the sense that the requirements of the Charter are such as to impose an obligation on states party to it to provide in the relevant language some level of pre-school education, primary education and secondary education at least to those pupils whose families so request and whose number is considered sufficient. These are substantive obligations and would require action by a government to address them for any language specified for the purposes of Part III of the Charter.

I would suggest, therefore, that it is legitimate to regard the relevant sections of the Charter as some form of safety net for minority language education and, in turbulent political circumstances, safety nets may prove to be very valuable sources of reassurance to minority communities that their rights will be protected or safeguarded and that the actions of governments will be subject to external scrutiny.

However, while to this extent the answer to the question set for this session of the conference is positive, it is clear that the safety net is slung fairly low to the ground and that it is just that – a safety net rather than a springboard for development. Looked at from this perspective, therefore, while the Charter might be a valuable resource for some minority languages, it does not provide much of a dynamic for the further development of Irish-medium education in Northern Ireland nor does it resolve for us the difficulties we are currently facing in the further expansion of that sector. Hence my "Yes and No" assessment of the value of the Charter.

Successes

Let me situate that assessment in the context of Irish-medium education here. First, the political and statutory context for Irish-medium education has changed significantly during the period in which I have been associated with the education system here. Most obviously, the Department of Education has, since 1998, had a statutory duty to encourage and facilitate the development of Irish-medium education. The relevant statutory provisions are based almost exactly on those in the 1989 Order which relate to integrated education and for all practical purposes, the Department now treats the integrated and Irish-medium sectors on the same basis.

The creation of this new duty has led to significant changes in the criteria which govern the creation of new schools in an effort to make it easier for parents to access Irish-medium education for their children. Equally important in my view, however, has been the creation of a more supportive approach within the Department in which our aim is to work actively with the sector and other education partners to help expand provision – whether in the form of freestanding schools or as units in existing, English-medium schools. There is, of course, still some way to go before parents generally have the option to access an Irish-medium school but I would be reasonably confident that no viable project to establish a school or unit would be thwarted simply because of unreasonable requirements imposed by the Department.

Having made that claim, I should perhaps immediately qualify it by stressing that I am not asserting that the establishment of new Irish-medium provision has been rendered easy or unproblematic. I am, in fact, painfully aware that, from the point of view of parents, the process even of establishing a unit under the aegis of an existing school can still be a lengthy one, fraught with difficulty and consequently daunting and discouraging and I want to comment further on this later in this paper. It is also the case that the very expansion of the sector has itself led to problems which are sufficiently acute to be a cause of considerable concern. There is, therefore, some way to go for the sector as a whole in making the transition from being a marginal (and, perhaps, marginalised) element in the education system to being a stable and full partner in that system and it is on the challenges arising form that process of transition that I particularly want to reflect today.

In reflecting on those challenges, we should not ignore the successes in the development of the sector. There are now almost 500 children in funded pre-school places in the IM sector, almost 1800 pupils in grant-aided primary schools or units, and almost 500 pupils in grant-aided second-level schools or units. There are still other children in schools which are not yet grant-aided but in most cases there are developments which, hopefully, will lead to those schools becoming grant-aided either as freestanding IM schools or as IM units within existing English-medium settings.

Relationships between the IM sector and the other partners in the education system have improved significantly and this is being demonstrated by increased practical co-operation. In particular, the establishment of Comhairle na Gaelscolaíochta has provided a vehicle for institutional co-operation by the inclusion on the Comhairle itself of representatives of the main education partners – the Education and Library Boards and the Council for Catholic Maintained Schools. Moreover, the Comhairle has produced a clear and well-argued corporate plan for the 2002-2005 period which has been agreed by all the interests represented on that council and which, therefore, provides an agenda for action.

Challenges

So far, so good. To the extent I have outlined, we have a healthy and developing sector of minority language education and certainly viewed against any perspective on the sector's history, its current healthy state is remarkable and encouraging.

However, my main purpose today is to reflect on the way ahead rather than on developments to date and thus I want now to return to the theme of this session on the needs and realities of 'other-medium' education.

Quality Provision

The first and most obvious challenge is that of the provision of high-quality education. This is the objective of the whole education system and the objective which all parents have the right to expect to have fulfilled for their children. Of course, in the pioneering stage of any new education initiative, there will be parents who are prepared to tolerate inadequate physical or other resources for their children because of their ideological commitment to a particular form of education. In Northern Ireland this happened with both integrated and Irish-medium schools and, from my early days in the Department, I can recall visiting schools located in wholly unsuitable surroundings but sustained by tremendous commitment from parents, teachers and the communities the schools served. However, such commitment is not inexhaustible either at the individual level or at the wider community level, especially when sectors such as the integrated and Irish-medium ones become more obviously part of the normal educational structures.

Few people are prepared to be pioneers and the continued vitality of Irish-medium education depends on satisfying parents that their children's interests will be safeguarded rather than jeopardised by the choice of a school outside the mainstream sectors. So far, the Irish-medium and integrated sectors have been successful in growing a community of parents who recognise the value of what is being offered to them, and who are prepared to opt to be different. But parental opinion is not necessarily stable and its fragility has something in common with investor confidence in the stock market. Just as sound companies and even sound economies can be derailed by sudden losses of investor confidence so we know from experience in the mainstream educational sectors that even well-managed and acceptably performing schools can suffer from drastic and often sudden losses of parental confidence. Moreover we know that this can happen without there being any crisis in staffing or management and despite the best endeavours of agencies such as the Boards or CCMS to support such schools. Fortunately, this does not happen often but it does occasionally happen and if the danger exists in relation to mainstream schools it is all the more acute in small sectors such as the integrated and Irish-medium ones where any dent in parental confidence could affect not simply a single school but a whole sector.

The delivery of a quality product must, therefore, be the first and central priority of minority language education particularly in a setting such as Northern Ireland where what is being attempted is not simply the stabilisation of an existing minority language community but the creation of a larger and critical mass of fluent Irish speakers as the basis for a stable bilingual society. The growth of such a critical mass simply will not happen unless the community from which it is drawn has a full measure of confidence in the quality of education on offer.

Teacher Supply and Quality

In this context, the components of quality from the point of view of parents are probably fairly straightforward. Parents expect reasonable physical surroundings for their children and they expect access to adequate levels of books, materials and ICT resources. More importantly, however, they expect a properly qualified and fully professional teaching force able to deliver and actually delivering a standard of education broadly on a par with that delivered in English-medium schools. This is easily said but in practice it represents a major challenge for a small sector where teacher supply is limited, where teachers and even senior management teams may have limited experience in depth and where the very pace of development itself results in teachers moving between schools because of competition for scarce human resources.

There is no need to labour this point since it is widely recognised and accepted by all concerned with the sector but it is an area which needs both urgent action and a clear longer-term strategy if the health of IM schools in general is to be guaranteed.

Effective Management and Governance

My reference to the experience of senior management teams leads directly on to the whole issue of management and governance in the minority language sector. In Northern Ireland we have a complex – perhaps in fact a uniquely complex – system of education and we have evolved a set of hierarchical or tiered administrative structures which serve the needs of that system. Thus now we have the Department of Education (DE), the 5 Education and Library Boards (ELBs), the Council for Catholic Maintained Schools (CCMS), the Northern Ireland Council for Integrated Education (NICIE), Comhairle na Gaelscolaíochta (CnaG), the Governing Bodies Association (GBA), not to mention bodies such as the Council for the Curriculum, Examinations and Assessment (CCEA) and the Transfer or Representatives Council (TRC). This complex structure may change in the light of the Review of Public Administration but it is worth noting that the are significant differences between the roles, functions and powers of the various bodies and consequently differences in their capacity to support the effective management and governance of schools.

In the mainstream sectors, when problems arise, schools can draw on the resources of the ELBs and/or CCMS. Alternatively, those bodies can intervene either on their own initiative or at the request of an interested party such as a parent and experience has shown that in the main they are very successful at containing problems and preventing them from escalating into crises. In the smaller sectors, the position is less satisfactory. NICIE and CnaG can and do assist schools with advice on issues of management and governance but it is difficult for them to intervene on their own initiative and a recalcitrant Board of Governors is quite within its statutory rights in refusing offers of such help. Of course most governing bodies behave reasonably but it is not unknown for conflicts to occur within schools and there have been two instances where the Department has had to become involved to resolve serious disputes in the integrated and Irish medium sectors.

It is perhaps also worth noting that one emerging area of difficulty is in the whole process of the transition of schools in the minority sectors from being parent-led organisations to being professionally managed ones. It is of course an axiom of our system of school governance that representatives of parents should play a full role in the running of schools but that is not the same as saying that schools are best run solely by groups of parents. Schools are complex organisations in their own right and their effective management demands a range of other skills and perspectives to supplement those of parents. It is of course unhealthy for school managers to attempt to sideline parents but equally it is unhealthy when parents seek constantly to second-guess school managers on the basis that they created the school so they know best! Partnership is perhaps less satisfying than dictatorship but in the long run it is much more effective.

Of course we are not alone in facing problems in the governance of schools. The recent controversy in the South at Dunboyne has shown that the stability of even a thriving school can be seriously threatened by disputes arising amongst the parties to the governance of schools. No comparable dispute has yet arisen here (though there have been analogous tensions in the integrated sector) but as a result of the growing complexity of the responsibilities of governing bodies and of the emergence of anomalies in the support structures, the Department has identified the whole area of governance as one which requires fundamental review. The Department will therefore be initiating a consultation exercise on this topic in the near future.

Strategy, Planning and Co-ordination

The transition from pioneering status to becoming a settled component of the wider education structure inevitably makes life somewhat more complex for all concerned. In Northern Ireland the Irish-medium scene now involves not only the voluntary sector bodies originally responsible for the establishment of the schools but also all the main statutory bodies and a range of new bodies such as CnaG, the trust fund Iontaobhas na Gaelscolaíochta and the cross-border Irish language body Foras na Gaeilge. As a result, resourcing has improved, the range of professional skills available is greatly increasing and the sector has benefitted significantly. However, the growth in the range of agencies involved has exacerbated the problems of agreeing priorities and co-ordinating activity and it would be a great pity if scarce resources were wasted in duplicated efforts or in confusion about roles and responsibilities.

The Department of course looks to CnaG as the mechanism for ensuring co-ordination. It is the forum which brings together most (if not quite all) of the key interests and it therefore provides the ideal vehicle for ensuring clear planning and effective co-ordination. However, the price of co-ordination is eternal vigilance and it would be wrong to underestimate the scale or the difficulty of the task facing CnaG in achieving and maintaining consensus on the way forward for the sector.

In this context and in case all this emphasis on co-ordination sounds like an attempt on the part of the Department to 'domesticate' the IM sector, I should just like to say that we do take seriously our statutory duty to encourage and facilitate the development of Irish-medium education. In particular we are concerned to maintain as much momentum as possible in the development of the sector consistent only with ensuring that the pace of that development does not outstrip the capacity of the system to meet the needs of schools. We want to maintain a healthy level of voluntarism in the sector which will ensure that the pressure for new school projects is kept up and that any risk of complacency is minimised. Of course there is no point in creating schools which cannot be adequately staffed but without ambition and some sense of idealism, there is a real risk of stagnation and that is most decidedly not an outcome which we in the Department desire.

Diversity

Since the early 1980s there have been two strands to the development of the Irish medium sector – the creation of free-standing schools and the establishment of units in existing schools. I have always believed this to be a healthy form of diversity and indeed to be the only practical approach to ensuring that access to this form of education was possible for many parents outside the urban centres of Belfast and Derry and the larger towns.

Over time we have seen the balance in these two approaches changing with increasing emphasis on the use of units to meet demand and there has in consequence been a growing level of co-operation between the IM sectoral interests and CCMS which has greatly facilitated the growth of units in maintained schools. This will, I hope, develop still further but at the same time it is important to continue to make available the option of Irish medium education for those who either do not come from the Catholic community or who do not wish, for whatever reason, to have their children educated in a school with the Catholic ethos. In minority language education in Wales and Scotland, this issue does not really arise but it is important in the particular context of Northern Ireland (and also, as the Dunboyne example has shown, in the South) and we need to ensure that our strategy for the future offers access to the language to those of all religions and none and fundamentally that the strategy keeps options open rather than closes them down.

Outcomes

My final reflection on these issues relates to the purpose of Irish medium education which I take to be not simply the perpetual re-creation of separate cohorts of fluent Irish speakers but rather the creation of an ultimately self-sustaining (though still expanding) Irish language community here in Northern Ireland. The real vision therefore is not of a school sector which creates Irish speakers but of a society in which Irish-speaking families have their need for education through the medium of their children's mother tongue met by our school system. For this to happen requires that the language be transmitted naturally between the generations – something which has to date only happened to a very limited extent outside the traditional Gaeltacht areas and which has indeed been increasingly under threat even there.

It is of course still too early to assess the success of our local IM sector in creating or contributing to the creation of a group of stable bilinguals who use Irish as their first language in the home and in a range of other significant domains in their lives but sooner or later that will have to be the measure of its success. At some point it may be useful to carry out some research into the effectiveness of schools in assisting in the formation of new communities of Irish speakers but for the moment perhaps I can finish with a quote from a recent book by James McCloskey, Professor of Linguistics at the University of California, Santa Cruz. The book is presented in bilingual format with two titles *Voices Silenced* / *Guthanna in Éag* but the Irish text is not simply a translation of the English and in this concluding quote from the final section of the book (McCloskey, 2001: 51) I prefer the Irish version, which reads as follows :

> Táthar a rá liom ó bhí mé bliain déag go bhfuil an Ghaeilge agus pobal na Gaeilge marbh. Ritheann sé liom gur bríomhar fuinniúil an marbhán í. Nuair a smaoiním ar theangacha eile atá gafa leis an choimhlint chéanna, ritheann sé liom fosta i gcomparáid leo sin go bhfuil sé seo uilig sórt míorúilteach.[1]

McCloskey is of course referring to the wide range of areas of vitality which the Irish language is currently displaying not simply its growth in the school system but his comments are not at all out of place or inappropriate as a parting comment on the extraordinary flowering of IM schools in the Gaeltacht across the island as a whole. Such diversity enriches us all.

---

[1] McCloskey, J. 2001 *Voices Silenced / Guthanna in Éag*. Dublin: Cois Life Teoranta

An bhFreastalaíonn Cuid III den Chairt Eorpach ar Réalaíochtaí agus Oideachais Mheán Eile?

Janet Muller

Aithnítear go hidirnáisiúnta gur ceann de na heochairmhodhanna i gcur chun cinn aon teanga ar leith é, an t-oideachas. Cruthaíodh an córas bisiúil Gaeloideachais i dtuaisceart na hÉireann a bheag ná a mhór gan tacaíocht shuntasach stáit. Gaeilgeoirí iad féin a d'aithin an riachtanas agus ba iad féin a thug faoin ghluaiseacht Ghaelodeachais atá againn sa lá inniu, dá laghad í, a chruthú. Le dó nó trí de bhlianta anuas, d'athraigh an cás fad áirithe sa mhéid gur cuireadh ar leataobh, fad áirithe, mar gheall ar fhorbairtí polaitiúla Chomhaontú Aoine an Chéasta agus ar lean de, an comhthéacs doicheallach polasaí inar mhair an t-oideachas trí mheán na Gaeilge. Ach Comhaontú Aoine an Chéasta agus Cairt na hEorpa do Theangacha Réigiúnda nó Mionlaigh, chomh fada is a bhaineann sí le hOideachas, tharla siad mar phróiseas i gcomhthreo le tionscnamh pobail nárbh fhéidir a chur ó dhoras. Is suntasach a thabhairt faoi deara nach tríd an Chairt a tháinig na céimeanna ba thábhachtaí i bpríomhsruthú an Ghaeloideachais, ach trí achtú reachtaíochta 'intíre', reachtaíocht Westminster, Acht Oideachais 1998 faoinar bunaíodh Comhairle na Gaelscolaíochta. An tAire Oideachais, Máirtín Mag Aonasa, a thóg an mhórchéim eile nuair a d'ísligh sé na critéir inmharthanachta do Ghaelscoileanna a fhad le glacadh isteach sé dhalta dhéag i gceantair uirbeacha agus dáréag i gceantair thuaithe, gníomh a d'oscail doras an aitheantais agus an mhaoinithe do roinnt Gaelscoileanna a coinníodh roimhe sin taobh amuigh den lúb.

Tá againn faoi láthair, mar sin, córas Gaeloideachais ina bhfuil 36 naíscoil, 25 bunscoil agus dá mheánscoil ar fud an tuaiscirt. Tá an earnáil ag fás agus i mbunús na gcásanna, tá na scoileanna atá ann ag forbairt. Ach ní mar sin atá i roinnt cásanna. I mbliana, don chéad uair ó bunaíodh í, níor oscail Gaelscoil Dhún Lathaí a cuid doirse. I gceantair eile, tá deacrachtaí nár sáraíodh go fóill roimh scoileanna; áiteanna inar theip ar iarrachtaí le scoileanna úra a bhunú ar chúis amháin nó ar roinnt cúiseanna - ganntanas acmhainní, ganntanas tionscnóirí le scileanna oiriúnacha agus an taithí, easaontú; áiteanna a gcaithfidh scoileanna fanacht taobh amuigh den chóras príomhshrutha maoinithe cionn is go bhfuil siad gan aitheantas.

Ní leor ar chor ar bith líon na múinteoirí agus na n-áiteanna oiliúna fud fad an Ghaeloideachais. Ní leor an oiliúint inseirbhíse. Ní leor acmhainní agus ábhair teagaisc.

Ní miste a lua, sna forálacha ar an oideachas i gCuid III, go bhfuil sé míshoiléir cad é go díreach a d'aontaigh rialtas na Breataine a dhéanamh. Ba é an fhoirmle a ghabh siad chucu i roinnt de na forálacha, a rá go bhfeidhmeodh siad ceann de na roghanna a liostaíodh cheana féin, a shíneann mar shampla, ó "cur ar fáil bunoideachais trí mheán na Gaeilge", nó "cur ar fáil méid suntasach den bhunoideachas tríd an Ghaeilge" a fhad le "soláthar theagasc na Gaeilge ar an bhunleibhéal". Is suntasach an difear idir na roghanna seo. Go dtí seo, níorbh fhéidir a shoiléiriú cé acu de na roghanna atá siad ag brath a fheidhmiú. Is de laigí na Cairte go bhfuil sí scríofa ar dhóigh inar féidir a leithéid de dhoiléire bheith ann.

I dtéarmaí bhuncheart daonna na bpáistí atá á dteagasc i nGaelscoileanna, tá tromshárú ann i gcás Sholáthar Sainriachtanas. Níl aon chóras i bhfearas, ná leoga aon iarracht fhorásach chomhordaithe déanta le córas a bhunú ina mbeadh Soláthar Sainriachtanas le fáil sa Ghaeilge. Níl uirlisí fáthmheasa ann do mheasúnú dheacrachtaí urlabhra i bpáistí dátheangacha, ná aon teiripe ar fáil i nGaeilge. Is cosúil gur beag a thuigtear gur féidir go bhforbródh páistí dátheangacha ar bhealach seachas bealach páistí aonteangacha. Níl Cláir Thaca Léitheoireachta nó Uimhearthachta ann i nGaeilge diomaite den tacaíocht a chuirfeadh an Ghaelscoil féin ar fáil. Agus an Roinn Oideachais i mbun oibre faoi láthair ar mhórthionscadal faoin disléicse agus faoin uathachas, ní léir go fóill cén dóigh a gcuirfear na tionscnaimh seo i bhfeidhm san earnáil trí mheán na Gaeilge. Ceisteanna tábhachtacha iad seo maidir le hacmhainn an earnála trí mheán na Gaeilge córas oideachasúil a sholáthar a bheadh ar bhonn cothrom leis an earnáil trí mheán an Bhéarla. Ceann de na réimsí is mó ábhar imní a mbíonn POBAL, mar scátheagras, ag plé leis, baineann sé le ganntanas Soláthar Sainriachtanas. Taighde a rinne Kieran O Hagan (2001)[1], oibrí sóisialta agus taighdeoir a bhíodh le hOllscoil na Banríona, léirigh sé roinnt samplaí den dea-chleachtas ach fosta, ar an drochuair, leibhéil uafásacha aineolais agus leatroim in éadan páistí Gaeilge. Ní hannamh a tharlaíonn go gcleanglaíonn teiripigh urlabhra deacrachtaí urlabhra leis an dátheangachas féin agus go lochtaíonn siad tuismitheoirí, a bhíonn go minic ar lagchuidiú, as bheith ag iarraidh a gcuid páistí a choinneáil sa Ghaeloideachas.

Tá POBAL ag obair ar na ceisteanna seo le gairmiúlaigh shláinte agus oideachais, agus ní miste liom a lua anseo gur léirigh an taithí a fuair muid ar leibhéal feidhmitheach le réimse soláthraithe go mbíonn intinn oscailte ag a lán acu don phlé agus iad i bhfách lena seirbhísí d'iomlán an phobail a fheabhsú. Ach an Chairt í féin, ní chuireann sí ar fáil aon chreatlach tacaíochta leis an obair seo a fhiosrú agus a chothú, fiú is dá mbeadh an dea-thoil ann ar leibhéal rialtais le forálacha a dhaingniú a bhaineann le soláthar seirbhísí. Seo ceist thábhachtach, nó cé go b'fhéidir gur athraigh an comhthéacs polasaí i leith an Ghaeloideachais le blianta beaga anuas, táthar go fóill ag doicheall roimh phobal na Gaeilge. Iarrachtaí a dhéantar le seirbhísí a fheabhsú agus le tuiscint do riachtanais Ghaeilgeoirí a mhéadú, go fóill féin tarraingíonn siad freagraí atá mí-oiriúnach agus go minic seicteach. B'fhachtóirí tábhachtacha san fhorbairt iad ceangaltais láidre Chairte. Ar an drochuair, níl siad ann.

I dtús báire, dúirt mé gur aithníodh an t-oideachas bheith ar na heochair-réimsí i gcaomhnú agus i gcothú teanga. Ar aon chéim tábhachta tá an tuiscint atá againn nach uirlis éifeachtach in athbheochan teanga é an t-oideachas leis féin agus nach bhféadfadh sé bheith mar sin. Tá flúirse taighde agus barúlacha ann a dheimhníonn an cheist seo go hidirnáisiúnta. Tá againn fosta sampla athbheochan na Gaeilge i ndeisceart na hÉireann. Sa chás sin, d'éirigh le hiarrachtaí an stáit i réimse an oideachais breis a chur le líon na ndaoine sa mhórphobal a fuair ardleibhéal líofachta. Ach creidim go n-aontódh mo chomhghleacaithe sa

---

[1] O'Hagan, K. 2001. *Cultural Competence in the Caring Professions*. London: Jessica Kingsley

deisceart liom gur theip ar iarrachtai an stáit sochaí a chruthú ina dtiocfadh le Gaeilgeoirí úsáid éasca ó lá go lá a dhéanamh den líofacht sin. Féadaimid a rá, dar liom, gur ceann de riachtanais earnáil an Ghaeloideachais go mbeadh pobal labhartha Gaeilge cruinn thart timpeall uirthi agus lánréimse deiseanna leis an teanga Ghaeilge a úsáid. Tá siad ann ar ndóigh a d'áiteodh go gcaithfeadh deiseanna bheith á dtacú ag an riachtanas le níos mó ná aon teanga amháin a úsáid i ngnó oifigiúil an stáit. Ba é a mhol William Mackey, Ceanadach agus bunaitheoir an Ionaid Idirnáisiúnta don Taighde ar an Dátheangachas, tamall de bhlianta ó shin, go gcaithfí a chruthú, in Éirinn,'staideanna détheangacha', (nó 'diglossic situations') is é sin le rá, "staideanna ina dtiocfadh an Ghaeilge a úsáid d'fheidhmeanna áirithe agus Béarla d'fheidhmeanna eile."[2] Sa mhéid go dtugann an Chairt aghaidh ar a leithéid seo de cheisteanna i dTearmaí Riarachán an Stáit, ní chuireann sí tionscnaimh den chineál sin as an áireamh.

Ach, forálacha na Cairte a daingníodh sa mhír seo, ní léiríonn siad ach polasaí fulaingte foighní i leith na Gaeilge. Na páistí a bhain tairbhe as an Ghaeloideachas, na daoine fásta sin a bhunaigh scoileanna, a theagasc iontu, a thiomsaigh airgead, a thairg ábhair, a cheap agus a d'fhorbair cúrsaí oiliúna - tá cead anois ag na daoine ardghnóthachtála seo comhfhreagras Gaeilge a dhéanamh le ranna rialtais - rud a bhí Gaeilgeoirí a dhéanamh le blianta fada. Chomh maith leis sin, ní thugann forálacha daingnithe na Cairte ceart dúinn freagra i nGaeilge a fháil. Fuair POBAL amach go bhfuil ceithre Roinn ann a sháraíonn dá ndeoin féin éilimh na Cairte agus a thugann freagraí Gaeilge. Mar a dhéanann Oifig an Chéadaire agus an leas-Chéadaire. Ach an Roinn Cultúir, Ealaíon agus Fóillíochta, atá freagrach as feidhmiú na Cairte, ní dhéanann.

Ba cheann de na heochair-réimsí in athbheochan teanga, dar le duine, fostaíocht trí mheán na Gaeilge a chothú don mhuintir sin a fhágann an Gaeloideachas ina ndaoine óga atá lán-dátheangach. Faoi Alt 13 na Cairte is féidir réimse deiseanna i gcúrsaí Sóisialta agus Geilleagracha a dhaingniú. Féadfaidh rialtais, mar shampla, úsáid teangacha réigiúnacha a chothú i gcáipéisí a bhaineann le fostaíocht, nó b'fhéidir go gcoiscfeadh siad ar chomhlachtaí úsáid teangacha réigiúnacha a shrianadh san ionad oibre, nó d'fhéadfadh siad cur in aghaidh cleachtaí a ceapadh le cur in aghaidh úsáid teangacha réigiúnacha, agus dá réir sin. I gcás na Gaeilge, sheachain rialtas na Breataine gach rogha acu seo agus dhaingnigh siad an clásal a dhearbhaíonn go ndéanfaidh siad rud éigin seachas na roghanna a liostaíodh. Cén rud? Glacaimid leis go ndéanfaidh Coiste Saineolaithe na Cairte fiosrúchán ar an cheist áirithe seo. Rud nach léir, cén dóigh a dtomhaisfidh siad an freagra - má fhaigheann siad freagra.

Eochair-réimse eile i gcur chun cinn teangacha is ea an chraoltóireacht. Tá páirt lárnach aici i ngríosú úsáid na Gaeilge i suímh nach mbeadh chomh foirmiúil; sa bhaile, agus i gcásanna eile sóisialta. Na clásail Chairte a daingníodh leagann siad dualgas ar chraoltóirí leorchlárú i nGaeilge a sholáthar, ach ní thugtar sainmhíniú ar cad é a chiallaíonn sé sin. Scéal cinnte, go nuige seo, go nglacann Tessa Jowell, Aire Briotanach Ealaíon, Cultúir agus Spóirt, leis an

---

[2] Quoted in O Riagain, P. 'Bilingualism in Ireland 1973-83: an overview of national sociolinguistic surveys'. *International Journal of the Sociology of Language*, 70: 29-52

dearcadh go gcomhlíonann leibhéil reatha na craoltóireachta Gaeilge an dualgas sin.[3] Dearbhú gan dealramh, is cosúil. Níor mhéadaigh leibhéal na craoltóireachta trí mheán na Gaeilge ó i bhfad roimh shiniú Chomhaontú Aoine an Chéasta, gan trácht ar dhaingniú na Cairte. Agus sa bhreis air sin, ní luaitear an teanga Ghaeilge ar chor ar bith i ndréacht-Pháipéar Bán rialtas na Breataine ar an chraoltóireacht, ainneoin go luaitear ann an Bhreatnais agus Gaeilge na hAlban. Aithnítear an dá theanga seo faoi Chuid III den Chairt, chomh maith leis an Ghaeilge.

Cá fhad, mar sin de, a thig le Cuid III den Chairt an speictream leathan tionscnamh a sholáthar a thacódh le hearnáil fholláin oideachais trí mheán na Gaeilge? Gan amhras, léiríonn dearadh na Cairte, gona cuid Alt idirnasctha a chlúdaíonn réimse ceisteanna gach lae agus bealaí ina mbíonn an duine aonair ag idirghníomhú leis an tsochaí, le daoine eile agus leis an stát, an anailís go dteastaíonn gníomh i roinnt de réimsí na beatha má tá teanga le cur chun cinn ar bhealach fuaimintiúil. Fosta, tá roinnt gníomhartha suntasacha fuaimintiúla a dtig le rialtais ceangal leo taobh istigh de Chuid III na Cairte.

Tá Cuid I na Cairte daingean ina treoracha ar an dóigh ar chóir an Chairt, i gCodanna II agus III, a fheidhmiú. Iarracht ionraic thomhaiste atá ann le cur ar chumas na rialtas iad féin a ligean isteach sa phróiseas le déileáil le ceist na gceart teangeolaíoch. Ach, tionscadal faireacháin POBAL, ó daingníodh an Chairt don Ghaeilge, léiríonn sé i gcás na Gaeilge, gur baineadh an chiall chontráilte as an Chairt féin; roghnú íosmhéid clásal (36 don Ghaeilge); daingniú na roghanna is laige (tugann Cuid I rabhadh go háirithe ina éadan seo[4]); agus sna céimeanna iardhaingnithe, nár tugadh ar chor ar bith treorú straitéiseach, spreagadh nó fiú comhordú leathan iarrachtaí don fheidhmiú éifeachtach.

Mar a léirigh mé cheana féin, ba é pobal na Gaeilge féin sa chéad áit le tamall de bhlianta ba chúis leis na céimeanna is suntasaí sa Ghaeloideachas, agus ina dhiaidh sin trí thionscnamh sainreachtaíochta. Gníomhaíocht chéillí ar leibhéal Aireachta agus na feachtais choiteanna agus tionscnaimh pháirtíochta, chuir siad cúl méid áirithe ar na teorainneacha. Páirt atá rud beag imeallach a d'imir an Chairt sna forbairtí seo.

Tá sé i bhfad róluath go fóill le tuairimíocht chinnte a dhéanamh faoi éifeacht na Cairte ar chur chun cinn na Gaeilge i réimsí eile de shaol an tuaiscirt. Tar éis an tsaoil, níor imigh ach bliain amháin thart ó rinneadh an daingniú. Ní miste a rá, áfach, gur bhliain í nach dtabharfadh aon spreagadh maidir le gníomhaíocht an rialtais. Tharraing sí aird ar roinnt ceisteanna éagsúla a bhaineann leis an Chairt agus ar a cumas le hathrú a thabhairt ann.

---

[3] Litir ó Tessa Jowell, Aire, do POBAL, "The arrangements for broadcasting in Northern Irealnd were considered at the time of ratification of the Charter to be sufficient to enable the Government to fulfil the obligations which it undertook in relation to Irish under the Charter, and I am satisfied that the arrangements remain sufficient."

[4] An Chairt Eorpach do Theangacha Réigiúnda nó Mionlaigh, Cuid I, "The role of the states will be, not to choose arbitrarily between these alternatives, but to seek for each regional or minority language the wording which best fits the characteristics and state of development of that language".

Is é an chéad cheann acu go dteastaíonn reachtaíocht Westminster, leis an mheon a shamhláitear i gClásail na Cairte a achtú. Aithnítear an méid sin i gCuid I na Cairte nuair a luaitear go gcaithfidh tíortha a shínigh í aghaidh a thabhairt ar theipeanna roimhe seo le teanga ar leith a chur chun cinn ar dhóigh shásúil trí réimsí éagsúla, an réimse reachtúil san áireamh. Ní mhaítear in áit ar bith i réamhrá na Cairte gur leor daingniú na Cairte nó méid áirithe clásal. Is eol dúinn, áfach, go mbíonn cuid de na rialtais níos faide chun tosaigh sa ghníomhaíocht ar na ceisteanna seo ná rialtais eile agus leoga, d'fhéadfadh an Chairt bheith níos beaichte arís faoin dualgas atá ar rialtais sainreachtaíocht ar leith a achtú faoi réir na gceangaltas a chuir siad orthu féin tríd an Chairt.

Is é an dara ceist maidir le mír Oideachais na Cairte go bhfuil contúirt ann, mar gheall ar éachtaí phobal na Gaeilge, nach bhfeicfidh rialtas na Breataine daingniú na gclásal taobh istigh den Chairt ach mar sheicliosta. Bheadh sé seo déistineach ó tharla gur beag ar fad a rinne siad le hearnáil mheán na Gaeilge a thabhairt ar an saol. Rud ba mheasa, gurbh fhéidir go síltí nach bhfuil aon dualgas faoin Chairt an méid atá ann cheana féin a ghníomhú, a fheabhsú, a mhéadú nó a fhorbairt ar aon bhealach suntasach. Caithfear seo a shoiléiriú. Má úsáidtear an Chairt ar an dóigh is ísle nó fiú is diúltaí, gan de chuspóir aici ach an rialtas agus na hearnálacha poiblí a shaoradh ar dhualgas an 'gníomh diongbháilte' atá an Chairt ag iarraidh a chur chun cinn, ní bheidh inti ach bac ar an fhorbairt seachas gléas chun athraithe.

Is léir coimhlint bheith idir an fhís atá ar chúl chlásal Chuid III na Cairte agus an riachtanas is cosúil atá ann le rialtais a mhealladh isteach sa pháirteachas. Beidh le feiceáil a éifeachtaí a bheadh meicníochtaí na Cairte. Is iomaí tuairim eile a thiocfaí a nochtadh faoin dóigh a bhfuil Cuid III na Cairte á léirmhíniú i dtuaisceart na hÉireann. Leoga, tá roinnt míonna caite ag POBAL ag déanamh faireacháin ar sin díreach, agus tá na torthaí le léamh sa tuarascáil uainn a ullmhaíodh do Choiste na Saineolaithe[5].

Ní fios go fóill cad é an breithiúnas a thabharfaidh Coiste na Saineolaithe ar chéad bhliain fheidhmiú na Cairte i dtuaisceart na hÉireann. Tuigimid, i gcás tíorthaí eile, go ndearna an Coiste cáineadh a bhí géar go minic. An cheist, creidim, do Ghaeilgeoirí, nach leor an cáineadh ach sa chás go mbíonn fíorthoil ann don athrú dearfach. Ní féidir go mbeadh sa Chairt féin ach gléas trína léireofaí toil an rialtais maidir le teanga ar leith. Roghnaigh rialtas na Breataine an Chairt mar lárchuid i gcomhlíonadh na gceangaltas a rinne siad le tógáil sochaí úire i dtuaisceart na hÉireann a éascú. Mura mbíonn a n-iarrachtaí le 'gníomh diongbháilte' a dhéanamh i gcosaint agus i gcothú na Gaeilge faoi mheon na Cairte inchurtha le sin, is féidir gur sin an rud a spreagfadh éilimh i gcomhair athraithe ba mhó i bhfad.

---

[5] Gorman, T. 2002. *An Chairt Eorpach do Theangacha Réigiúnda nó Mionlaigh: Feidhmiú na Cairte i leith na Gaeilge, Iúil 2001 – Iúil 2002 – The European Charter for Regional or Minority Languages: The Implementation of the Charter with regard to the Irish language, July 2001 – July 2002.* Béal Feirste: POBAL

Irish and Curriculum Review in Northern Ireland

Eugene McKendry

It is gratifying to be placed in the 'Realities' section of the symposium, since Irish speakers are often accused of being out of touch with current realities. But then the word 'realities' can be a misnomer for orthodoxies. The orthodoxies surrounding the Northern Ireland Curriculum (NIC), language teaching methodology over the last 15 years or so, and the 'realistic' or orthodox view of Irish, all display severe limitations. Is there moreover an emerging reality or orthodoxy surrounding Irish and the Good Friday Agreement? The emphasis in the Agreement is on Irish-medium Education (IME), as is most of the content of this symposium, but is the position of Irish in English-medium schools being neglected? For example, in October 2000 the author wrote to the Minister of Education expressing concern about the position of Irish in English-medium schools, particularly with regard to curricular legislation and resources. The reply from the Minister's office sidestepped the issue by pointing out what was being done in the area of IME. Comhar na Múinteoirí Gaeilge have more recently reported a similar outcome to a meeting with the minister. But in a period of curriculum review there is also a need for Irish language interests to take account of wider language and curriculum issues.

Curriculum Review in England: The Green Paper

Curriculum review is on the agenda in Northern Ireland and in Britain. The Green Paper *14-19: Extending Opportunities, Raising Standards* was published for England in February 2002 by DfES and calls for a rethink of aspects of post-primary education. The intentions of the Green Paper are to allow choice and flexibility, and to encourage greater participation in Education post-16. These are fine aspirations but, to achieve them, the proposals for languages are radical. In Key Stage 4 (14-16) a modern language would become optional but, on the other hand, positive sentiments are expressed in favour of developing languages in the Primary School. The core subjects English pupils will have to study between the ages of 14 and 16 are:

English	ICT	Sex and Health Education
Maths	Citizenship	Physical Education
Science	Religious Education	Work-related Learning

If they wish, pupils would also be entitled to study a foreign language, design and technology, an arts subject, or a humanities subject (DfES 2002c:5).

The DfES Green Paper merits mention because the Department took the unusual step of publishing a separate paper entitled *Language Learning* (DfES 2002d) to underline the Government's professed commitment to modern languages in the wider context of reform. There is clearly a conflict here between the desire to change and the consequences for the current provision of such change. In introducing worthy new elements into a crammed curriculum, one is left with the dilemma of what to exclude or reduce in order to make time available. In the English Green Paper the circle has been squared by allowing an 'entitlement' to a language in Key Stage 4, but languages will no longer be compulsory. It is appropriate that Northern Ireland developments be seen in the wider context of these proposals in England, and also to realise that the local proposals are even more revolutionary.

Northern Ireland Key Stage 3 Cohort Study
Since the introduction of the current Northern Ireland Curriculum in 1996, CCEA has undertaken a programme of 'monitoring and research'. A major research project was carried out by the National Foundation for Educational Research between 1996 and 2000. (Harland et al.; CCEA 2002b). It was designed to discover the views of Key Stage 3 pupils and their teachers on the curriculum. The report of this Key Stage 3 Cohort Study underpins CCEA's approach to curriculum review and provides the evidence and research basis that justifies the proposed changes. Languages were reported as being prone to the greatest variation and in general come out badly in the study. Modern Languages and the creative arts were consistently seen as the subjects least useful for the future, just as they were perceived as the least important for pupils' current needs. The lack of relevance associated with languages was noteworthy, given that a third of the schools afforded this area the most teaching time. Music, RE, Irish, drama and art were found to be the least vocationally relevant subjects, becoming gradually less important over the three years. Generally, pupils felt over-worked in modern languages and maths. Pupils perceived modern languages to be the most difficult area of the curriculum.

In a discussion of Breadth and Balance in the curriculum, six main models of curriculum delivery are identified. They are defined in terms of the time schools devote to religion and languages in their curriculum provision and by management category (cf. Harland et al.:30, CCEA 2002a:1):

1. *Languages light* with a practical - active curriculum, in the Protestant-managed secondary
2. *Languages and RE light with* a practical - active curriculum, with reduced RE in the Protestant-managed secondary
3. *Languages light / RE heavy* with the humanities curriculum, in the Catholic-managed secondary
4. *Languages heavy / RE light* with the linguistic-scientific curriculum, in the Protestant-managed grammar
5. *Languages heavy* with the academic-oriented curriculum, in the Catholic-managed secondary or Grammar
6. *Languages heavy / RE heavy* with the academic curriculum and with RE emphasis, in the Catholic-managed grammar

More time is spent on Languages in Catholic secondary and grammar schools than in their Protestant counterparts. This can only be due to the provision for Irish, although the differences in provision across schools are not analysed.

The current Northern Ireland Curriculum requires schools at post-primary level to offer one of French, German, Italian or Spanish; only then may they offer Irish as a choice. This has given rise to the current pattern of language provision.

The models of language provision in Northern Ireland represent the main models in existence in other parts of the UK (Neil et al., 1998:18), and are defined as follows:

1. *Sole modern language* – only one modern language is offered to pupils in Year 8.
2. *Split provision* – two or more languages are offered in Year 8. All pupils learn one language, for instance 50 per cent take French and 50 per cent take Irish.
3. *Modular provision* – pupils are given experience of several languages in Year 8 before having to choose one to continue with at Key Stage 3.
4. *Dual provision* - all pupils in Year 8 learn two modern languages.

The greatest difference found between provision in Northern Ireland and elsewhere in the UK was the popularity of model d), Dual Provision, under which schools offer two languages for all pupils, usually French and Irish. The difference between split provision and dual provision is that pupils in the dual model have experience of two languages during Year 8. Over 30 per cent of schools in Northern Ireland followed this dual model, as against 10 per cent elsewhere in the UK. Although the Neil et al. study did not analyse distinctions between the two school sectors in Northern Ireland – the Controlled/Protestant and the Maintained/Catholic – the dual language provision deserves some closer attention. The advantages and disadvantages of this model are, on the positive side, that pupils do not equate modern languages with learning French and that they gain awareness of expressing themselves in more than one language. The negative is that they have less exposure to each language, confusion is possible, and it can be a burden for less able pupils. It is notable that all instances of dual provision accommodate Irish since by the requirements of the NIC, schools are not allowed to offer Irish alone. The position of Irish in current curricular legislation is discriminatory. If a change in curriculum is envisaged, this is the time for Irish to lobby for a fairer recognition. There is some urgency to this since the proposed curriculum changes threaten dual language provision.

Consultations and proposals
Phase One of the Northern Ireland consultation took place in Spring / early Summer 2000. The Phase One consultation document felt that there was imbalance in the Key Stage 3 curriculum and made timetabling proposals which allocated 5 per cent of teaching time to the first modern language, and 5 per cent to the second (CCEA 2000:33). Suggested time allocations for subjects were dropped in later consultation documents. The emphasis was on skills, and "each subject should identify its contribution to the generic skills framework" (ibid. 34)

The next document *Their future in our Hands* February 2001 set out the proposals for Key Stage 4, 'Giving Schools greater flexibility on what they teach 14-16 year olds'. Key skills are emphasised across the curriculum, while primary languages and disapplication at Key Stage 4 are the main subject issues:

CCEA intends, by placing the key skills at the core of the entitlement for all pupils, to signal strongly that the curriculum is changing from one that is principally content-led to one that is even more concerned with skills and competences. (CCEA 2001:5)

CCEA attaches great importance to the development of modern language competence among our young people not only in the interests of their cultural and international awareness but also to take account of the potential demands of the labour market of the future. The curriculum proposals at Key stage 3 make the study of a modern language compulsory. Pilot work is also planned in language teaching and learning in primary schools.

A positive approach to language learning in the earlier key stages is likely to create greater enthusiasm for modern language study beyond fourteen. Indeed, it is expected that all 14-16 year olds will continue to study and obtain certification in an accredited modern language course. The certification may be through GCSE or an accredited vocational alternative. CCEA recognises, however, that for a minority of pupils, it will be helpful if they have the flexibility to pursue other studies rather than to continue what, for them, is perceived by some as the unproductive study of a modern language. (ibid. 6)

CCEA reports that the proposals for a statutory core at Key Stage 4 based largely on key transferable skills and personal development were well received "with some reservations on the omission of a modern language requirement" (CCEA 2002b §1.11) "There was some comment about the dropping of ... a modern foreign (sic) language" (ibid. §4.4). Neither of these comments suggest that the concerns expressed by the language lobby were strong enough to achieve a change of course.

As a result of these two years of consultation and research, CCEA in April 2002 presented a major set of proposals, which mark, "the beginning of the biggest ever consultation carried out by CCEA". The proposals contained in this 11-16 Consultation document are revolutionary. It is proposed that "The statutory curriculum at Key Stage 3 should be specified in terms of curriculum areas and not individual subjects" (CCEA 2002b §3.5). At Key Stage 4, it is proposed that:

The core does not contain any academic subjects ... It is expected that the great majority ... will continue to follow a balanced science course, to study their own and a second language, etc. No pupil should be deprived of the opportunity to do so (CCEA 2002b §4.9).

A second language is included in the 'Language and Literacy' Curriculum Area (CCEA 2002b:§8.8), but it is not clear if it will be studied by all pupils, even at Key Stage 3. The statutory curriculum should be set out in just four components:

key transferable skills, personal, social and health education, citizenship, and education for employability (CCEA 2002b §4.5). Paragraph 4.10 of the consultation paper is particularly important for language learning:

> On the question of the second language, CCEA believes that language learning is too important to be left to age 11 ... The inclusion of some language learning in primary schools should be encouraged as soon as it is feasible to do so. .... CCEA believes that alternative strategies (including a different approach to timetabling) for language learning in post-primary schools should be explored as a matter of urgency. Improvement in these areas would be likely to in crease the number of pupils achieving the sort of success that is taken for granted in many other European countries (CCEA 2002a §4.10).

It should be noted that primary languages do not feature in the Key Stages 1 and 2 proposals and that the developments suggested above are on top of statutory primary requirements. It is doubtful whether second language learning will be a priority in our primary schools and 'feasible' is not an encouraging word. But Irish should at the same time be positive about the new proposals. For example the 1974 DENI handbook for primary schools considered the cross-curricular potential of Irish and concluded that no other language could offer the same advantages (DENI 1974:106). The Cross-Curricular theme of Cultural Heritage under NIC also promised much, but unfortunately did not come to fruition and was subsumed into Education for Mutual Education (EMU). St Mary's College (now University College) in Belfast has devoted its attention to IME at the expense of Irish in English-medium primary schools. It is certain that the continental languages will make a strong play for their place in the primary school, and one can only hope that Irish will be in a position to compete.

'A different approach to timetabling' probably presages a decrease in time devoted to languages. 'Alternative strategies for language learning in post-primary schools' could be welcome as much of the dissatisfaction among teachers and pupils with languages should be laid at the door of the CCEA Programme of Study.

One of the ironies of being English speakers is that one is unsure which language to offer. In non-English speaking countries diversification is not an issue any more. English is available in the schools of every one of our European partners, and in most school systems throughout the world. This is perhaps not appreciated in the last sentence of §4.10. The 'success taken for granted' abroad is in learning English, which has advantages for social and career motivation which do not feature so strongly in second language learning in our schools.

In the UK, there has been a policy of diversification for some years, meaning teaching languages other than French. What has happened, however, is fragmentation. Italian has practically disappeared, German is decreasing and Spanish is growing. Spanish may provide a model of how to effectively market a language in our schools, through participating in and sponsorship of all possible language and school-based projects and activities, often at minimal cost to the Spanish authorities, and by the placement of Spanish education officers in all areas of the UK and the Republic. So we have a Spanish education officer based in the British Council offices in Belfast. Irish needs at least one education officer to support the work of Gael-Linn and the re-emerging Comhar na Múinteoirí Gaeilge. One can imagine that Foras na Gaeilge has a role to play here in supporting such appointments, but An Foras has yet to establish itself in the North and make a senior appointment with responsibility for education.

State Examinations

The figures for GCSE and post-16 examinations entries are useful markers of language health and outcomes. The figures for the five years 1996-2000 are presented in Table 1.:

Table 1: GSCE Entries for Modern Languages 1996-2000

	French	Irish	Spanish	German	Italian
1996	13838	2021	1561	1496	156
1997	13275	2171	1737	1371	128
1998	13213	2180	1801	1380	93
1999	13195	2350	2105	1390	109
2000	13318	2484	1987	1489	199

One notes how strong French is, but most particularly how Irish, despite being available only in maintained schools and a few integrated schools, retained second place overall, and indeed has increased. If one goes back to 1993 there were 1589 GCSE entries in Irish, a weaker position arising from the uncertainty and controversy that surrounded Irish at the time of Education Review. The increase since the early 1990s may also be a reflection of the Government's policy of 'Languages for All' and the introduction in the Northern Ireland Curriculum of a compulsory language at Key stages 3 & 4, leading to an increase in entries from non-grammar schools in particular.

The trend is moving away from Irish, however, which has now fallen behind Spanish in GCSE entries. The Modern Languages figures for 2002 in Northern Ireland were: French 13219; Spanish 2814; Irish 2771; German 1327. Irish in 2001 shows two more candidates (1233) from non-grammar schools than from grammar schools (1231), with a small number entering from further education and other sources. This 50 per cent of candidates from non-grammar schools is much higher than for the other languages. As it is likely that curriculum review will cause a marked decrease in numbers taking languages through to GCSE in this non-grammar sector, it would be surprising if Irish could maintain its relative numerical position without developing a strategy.

This high ratio of non-grammar to grammar is reflected in post-16 figures. In 2002, the first year of the Advanced Subsidiary (A/S) examination, there were 333 A/S entries from the 2595 who sat GCSE in 2001. These 333 are mostly from the 1231 grammar pupils. The A-level total for Irish in 2002 was 253, from a year 2000 GCSE figure of over 2609. Rounded off, some 10 per cent carry Irish through to A-level from GCSE, compared with ca. 15 per cent in German and 20 per cent in Spanish.

The figures for Irish could indicate a worrying prognosis in the light of the current CCEA curriculum review proposals discussed above. As we have seen, the proposals challenge many accepted views of education. The move from knowledge and content to a skills-led curriculum is a paradigm shift in the fundamentals of curricular philosophy, and we have noted the particular challenge to language learning in general, both in the English proposals and here in Northern Ireland. There is a particular threat to Irish in the demographics presented above and in the competitive environment of schools where languages are often in competition - even more so in a curriculum where the opportunities for developing dual linguists will decrease.

But there are also opportunities to achieve positive outcomes from the review and current developments:

1. *Primary Languages*
   The cross-curricular potential highlighted in the 1974 Primary Teachers' Guide still applies "These factors are of considerable help in the teaching of Irish and confer certain advantages no other second language can claim to the same extent in Ireland" (DENI 1974:106).
2. *Globalisation*
   Reconsideration of the relevance of economic 'realities' in a global world. The hegemony of English diminishes the economic imperative often argued against Irish.
3. *Skills and Attitudes*
   The emphasis upon developing positive attitudes and the transferability of skills from primary onwards is welcome. The skills of language learning can be transferred from one language to another. Positive experience and attitudes towards languages and language learning (preferably from Irish in the Primary School) will stand children in good stead when, in later life, they embark upon the learning of other languages for specific purposes and requirements.
4. *Citizenship and Inclusivity*
   Citizenship and the emphasis upon inclusivity move from the local, through the national to the international. Recent reports and projects in languages, such as the Nuffield report and the European Year of Languages, emphasise the value of community and indigenous languages in education as well as the traditional mainland European languages.

The reasons previously presented to justify keeping Irish at a lower level of recognition should now be challenged. It is clear that languages are not now seen in the light originally intended at the time of education reform in the late 1980s. For example, the economic imperative is not so convincing now that the hegemony of English has been established. In a curriculum which places the emphasis upon transferable skills the case for Irish can be reargued. But are Irish language interests in Northern Ireland able for the challenge?

References
CCEA (Northern Ireland Council for the Curriculum, Examinations and Assessment) 2000. *Northern Ireland Curriculum Review. Phase 1 Consultation.* Belfast: CCEA.
CCEA. 2001. *Their Future in our Hands* Belfast: CCEA.
CCEA. 2002a. *Is the curriculum working? A summary of the Key Stage 3 Phase of the Northern Ireland Curriculum Cohort Study* Belfast: CCEA.
CCEA. 2002b. *Curriculum Review: A new approach to Curriculum and Assessment 11-16* Belfast: CCEA.
DENI (Department of Education for Northern Ireland). 1974. *Primary Education: Teachers' Guide* Belfast: HMSO
DfES (Department for Education and Skills). 2002a. *Green Paper. 14-19: Extending opportunities, raising standards. Consultation Document* HMSO
DfES. 2002b. *14-19: Extending opportunities, raising standards: Summary* HMSO.
DfES. 2002c. *14-19: Extending opportunities, raising standards: Young People's Summary* HMSO.
DfES. 2002d. 14-19: *Extending opportunities, raising standards: Language Learning* HMSO.
Fergusson, J. 2002 "Entitlement to languages: a Scottish perspective". *Community Languages Bulletin,* issue10:12. CILT, London
Government of the United Kingdom and the Government of Ireland. 1998. *The Agreement reached in their multi-party negotiations* ('The Good Friday Agreement').
Great Britain and Northern Ireland 1989 *Education Reform (Northern Ireland) Order, 1989.* Belfast: HMSO.
Harland, J., Moor, H., Kinder, K. and M. Ashworth. 2002. *Is the Curriculum Working? The Key Stage 3 Phase of the Northern Ireland Curriculum Cohort Study.* Slough: NFER
McKendry, E. 2001. "Modern Languages Education Policies and Irish in Northern Ireland". In eds. J.M. Kirk and D.P. Ó Baoill. *Language Links. The Languages of Scotland and Ireland* 211-222. Belfast: Cló Ollscoil na Banríona, Queen's University Belfast. Belfast studies in Language, Culture and Politics 2.
Neil, P.S., Phipps, W. and R. Mallon. 1998. *Diversification of the First foreign Language in Northern Ireland.* Belfast: NICILT/Queen's University Belfast.
Nuffield Foundation. 1998. *Where are we going with Languages? Consultative Report of the Nuffield Languages Inquiry.* Nuffield Foundation: London
Nuffield Foundation. 2000. *Languages: the next generation. The final report and recommendations of the Nuffield Languages Inquiry.* Nuffield Foundation: London

Language Policy in the Republic of Ireland

T.P. Dolan[1]

My theme is connectedness. The island of Ireland has several languages and many dialects, all connected, some remotely, some more closely. Some of the languages, particularly Irish and English, are seen to be in competition. The rivalry between the two is regarded as unfair, not least because the ubiquity of English can be wrong-headedly presented as yet another example of England's ongoing dominance of Ireland. It would be more sensible to acknowledge the success of the English Language in Ireland, and to celebrate it, without in any way diminishing the status and usefulness of the other languages which work with it, either separately, as Irish, or in tandem, as the plethora of varieties of English. It should be always be acknowledged that so-called Standard English does not have much of a role in spoken communication in Ireland. Some native speakers from England use it here, but in general the English used in Ireland, North and South, is acculturated to either the Irish Language, in the majority of cases, or to some version of Scots, in some parts of the Northern counties, or is a mixture of influences.

In this part of the conference we are concentrating on the fortunes of Ulster-Scots, within an Irish context, and in particular on its cultural role, which has been enhanced by the terms of the Good Friday Agreement. It has been granted 'parity of esteem', within what has been felicitously called the cultural corridor between Ireland and Scotland. In both countries there are a number of languages in use.

I want first of all to talk in general terms about Hiberno-English, which is used throughout this island. My *Dictionary of Hiberno-English* (DHE), which was first published in 1998, has attracted correspondence from all parts of the country and the perception shown in these letters is one of acceptance that the residents of this country, North and South, use English in a distinctively 'island of Ireland' way.

The correspondents mainly suggested additional words, or discussed alternative meanings. For instance, the word *pass-remarkable* was omitted, and will be put into the next edition. A very helpful letter came from Belfast asking me to revise my definition of the term *left-footer*, which I had entered as meaning 'a Catholic', whereas my correspondent pointed out that a *left-footer* is 'a Protestant' – a crucial difference. Similarly, this excellent correspondent also points out that the word *Protestant* itself should be used very carefully, even though it is generally thought to cover Anglican, Presbyterian, Methodist, Baptist, Brethren, and many others. Hence, to define *souper* as a Catholic who adopted the Protestant Faith in return for food during the Great Famine is wrong, not least because, as is rightly pointed out in the letter, during the Famine Presbyterians fared little better than Catholics

---

[1] I am deeply indebted to John Kirk, Karen Corrigan, Edward Kelly, Jeff Kallen, John Loftus, Hildegard Tristram, and James McCabe for their advice in preparing this paper. The views expressed are my own.

– indeed Presbyterians had been called *black-mouths* in some quarters. Thanks to this letter, we have amended the entries on *left-footer* and *souper*.

Other correspondents also joined in the discussion of what is going to happen to Irish English, which, to a noticeable extent among the younger speakers, is now losing some of its distinctiveness, especially in the Gaelic component of its lexicon, in the face of global English. But up till very recently, the relationship between the two languages, Irish and English, was much closer, especially in those parts of the country which had most recently been Irish speaking, not forgetting the present areas designated as Gaeltachts, in which the number of Irish speakers is being revised downwards. It is, of course, a matter of generation. Many of the contributors to DHE use a mixture of English and Irish. To this day this macaronic idiom is alive and well in many parts of Ireland in the usage of older people. Recently, one of our most valuable contributors, a linguistically meticulous lady from County Kerry, sent me a new list of expressions used in her locality, which included the expression *he gave her a watery smáchail* (*smaw-kawl*) *of a kiss*. She always re-spells words in this way, to indicate the local pronunciation, before providing the meaning – in this case, *smáchail* refers to 'the kind of kiss', she says, 'which requires a passionate, drooling smacking of the lips'.

This correspondent and others like her contributed so many Irish words to the Dictionary that, when I handed over the manuscript to the publishers, Gill and Macmillan, they were understandably puzzled. Is it possible that so many Gaelic words were still in use, they asked? And indeed, it was the case. Other Dictionaries, dedicated to specific localities, also prove it to be so, as, for instance, Séamas Moylan's work on Kilkenny English (1996), or Loreto Todd's *Words Apart, A Dictionary of Northern Ireland English* (1990).

But not all varieties of Hiberno-English have retained this high proportion of words from the Irish. Take, for example, the fascinating dialect of two baronies, Forth and Bargy, in County Wexford. We are fortunate in having a glossary of the words used in that area compiled by a Quaker farmer called Jacob Poole who was born in Growtown, Co. Wexford in February 1774 and died in 1827. The Manuscript [Y M Historical Collection 4.N.2] is in the Quaker Library in Dublin – on its first leaf Jacob Poole entitled his work 'Vocabulary of the Language of the Baronies of Forth and Bargie'. So far as he was concerned, it was a language used just in those two Baronies, near Forth Mountain. But, of course, in no way may it be classified as a language – it is not an independent linguistic system. It is a sub-dialect of Hiberno-English, a variety of English. It is significant that the Irish content is very small, and such words as there are can still be found in Hiberno-English from other parts of the country: For example, the word *arnauneen*[2], meaning 'working at night' (from Irish *áirneáin*), is still in use in County Kerry, with the comparable meaning of 'work done late into the night', and by extension, 'visiting at night', 'card-playing', 'story-telling late at night': 'We had a great night *áirneáning* at Begley's last night' says a correspondent from the Slieve Luachra area. A cognate form, to be found in Traynor's *Glossary of the English*

---

[2] Cf. *The Dialect of Forth and Bargy, Co. Wexford, Ireland.* ed. T.P. Dolan and Diarmaid Ó Muirithe. Dublin: Four Courts Press, 1996: 37.

Dialect of Donegal, is *airneal* ('We would have *airneals* every night, dancing, singing, and story-telling').[3]

In our search for more Irish words in the Wexford dialect, we made the mistake of giving Irish *snaoisín* for the Forth and Bargy word *sneesheen*, but it is simply a version of English *sneezing*. The vast majority of the words in the glossary are English. One of the reasons I draw attention to this dialect is that it is from a definite location in Ireland, and in a state of rapid decline, if not near to extinction, although Jeff Kallen, in a private communication, tells me that he has a student conducting research on the dialect of the baronies. With Ulster-Scots in mind, mischievously, I am tempted to ask the question: Should the Dialect of Forth and Bargy be revived, and given 'parity of esteem' with other more notable varieties of the English Language as spoken in Ireland? After all, from communications and comments I have had from Diarmaid Ó Muirithe and Jeff Kallen, as I mentioned, there is evidence that the dialect is still modestly distinctive and in some use. And it has a very long history.

No small part of its present fame concerns what happened before the Famine in the early nineteenth century, when the Reverend William Eastwood, Rector of Tacumshane, in the Barony of Forth, fancied that some of the words his workers were using resembled those in the volume of Chaucer's writings which he happened to be holding. He called them round and read them 'a page or two of old Geoffrey' aloud which, according to legend, they understood, even 'the most obscure expressions'.

Many features of the language of Forth and Bargy (an area which is only about 32,000 hectares, to the South of Wexford town) show its history as a conservative variety of English. In the glossary (see footnote 1), I noted comparable forms in Middle English, for instance, *attercop*, 'spider', from *Handlyng Synne*, *poustee*, 'power', from Chaucer and Langland, and also *yclept* and *eeclept*, 'called'. *The Dialect of Forth and Bargy, Co. Wexford, Ireland* includes the old 'n plural', as in *been*, 'bees'. Diarmaid Ó Muirithe notes that, in the 1970s, even young people were still using the old plural form in the word *ashen*, 'ashes'. Songs and poetry have also been preserved in the dialect, thanks to the work of General Vallancey; in *A Yola Song* (p. 76) we find, for instance, the use of the plural pronoun *hi*, meaning 'they':

> *Mot w'all aar boust, hi soon was ee-teight*
> 'But with all their bravado they were soon taught'

The spellings given by Poole, and retained in the first edition of his Glossary by William Barnes, in 1867, and in our recent edition, indicate the pronunciation. Although most of the vocabulary is English, as noted above, the spelling of the consonants in particular indicate the influence of Irish: for instance *h* added to show Irish aspiration, for example, *sthit* (cf. OE *stott*, ME *stot*), 'an inferior kind of horse'. Other distinctive features of the phonology are identified by Hogan (1927: 46).

I mention the Dialect of Forth and Bargy to establish parallels with Ulster-Scots, in the context of the varieties of Celtic English which are to be found

---

[3] Cf. *The English Dialect of Donegal*. Michael Traynor. Dublin: The Royal Irish Academy. 1953: 4.

throughout Ireland, North and South. To privilege one variety, though a potentially prestigious one, may impair the fortunes of other varieties, such as this famous Wexford dialect. I would argue that all varieties of English in Ireland, from general Hiberno-English to local sub-dialects, such as South Armagh (Corrigan, 1990:91-119), should be funded, not least because of the similarities which exist between these varieties. The stronger should help the weaker, in terms of scholarly support.

Thanks to the brilliant work of Michael Montgomery (1999), Philip Robinson and James Fenton we are now in a position to see what Ulster-Scots is, to identify where it fits into the assembly of Celtic Englishes (Tristram, 1997, 2000) and of Irish English in particular (Hickey, 2002), and to assess what it can do as a medium of communication. Returning for a moment to the survival of the dialect of Forth and Bargy and to the question of whether or not it merits support, there is in the Quaker library in Dublin a copy of William Barnes's 1867 edition of Poole's Glossary, which I came across some time ago. This is an important copy, because it had been borrowed in 1952 by a man called N. A. Hudlestone from Swinton in Yorkshire who visited the area of Forth and Bargy with the book and made pencil notes on it. He confirmed that the local people still pronounced *ache, face, fade,* and *glade,* with a long *a,* as entered by Poole. He also ticked off a list of words as having been heard in Wexford in 1952. The list included *bawn,* 'enclosure', *boagher,* 'road', *boorann* 'drum', *boouchelawn,* 'ragwort', *brogue,* 'shoe', *granogue,* 'hedgehog', and *hames,* 'wooden frame on a horse collar', among others. All of these words are to be found in general Hiberno-English. *Bawn* (< Irish *bábhún*), for example, is included in Traynor and in Macafee, and also appears in Seamus Heaney's translation of *Beowulf*:

> (Breca) sure of his ground / in strong room and bawn
> (p. 15, lines 522-3).

Heaney also uses words derived from Scots and Northern English, which are part of the lexicon of Ulster, such as in:

> So they duly arrived / in their grim war-graith' (p. 11, lines 323-4)

in which *graith* is derived from Scots and Northern English forms, ultimately Old Norse *greithi,* arrangement. W. F. Marshall, 'The Bard of Tyrone', also employs it in 'The Drumnakilly Divil':

> I could hear the bleats of Lily as the graith came off the ass (p. 111)

In Fenton's *The Hamely Tongue, graith* is defined as 'a working horse's harness'. Such a word symbolises the connectedness of Hiberno-English – Ulster-Scots, Scots, and Northern English – a compelling instance of the 'cultural corridor' at work.

We should try and treat all the varieties of English in Ireland with similar, if not equal, attention, and to banish linguistic separatism. The agenda should be to give prominence and prestige to an inclusive all-Ireland identity of speech, with due recognition of the Celtic and English components, which should be presented as acting together. The lexicon demonstrates country-wide connections. My colleague Diarmaid Ó Muirithe lists the word *sned,* meaning 'the handle of scythe', in the collection he made in the baronies of Forth and Bargy in 1978 (p. 28). The word appears, with the same meaning, in *The Concise Ulster Dictionary,* where it is described as 'Scots and Northern

English *sned*, Scots, also *snid*; from Old English *snaedan*' (p. 316). It is also entered in *The Hamely Tongue* (p. 191), in *The Language of Kilkenny* (p. 253), and in DHE (p. 250), with a citation from a speaker in County Meath. The ubiquitous use of such a word helps to demonstrate the inclusiveness of the pan-Celtic lexicon. It exemplifies 'the sense of kinship', on a local, national, and supra-national level, which Tom Paulin notes in the use of words such as *geg*, 'trick', 'hoax' or *gulder*, 'noisy shouting', at a micro-cosmic level (Paulin, 1983: 18). The same words are very often to be found in different locations. I have citations for the Scots and Northern English verb *redd*, 'to clear', *redd up*, 'tidy up' from Kildare and Meath in DHE (p. 215). It also occurs in *The Hamely Tongue* (p. 164), and in *The Concise Ulster Dictionary* (p. 273). Michael Longley uses it with telling effect in his magnificent, linguistic tour-de-force 'Phemios and Medon' (1998: 119).

> Go out
> And sit in the haggard away from this massacre
> You and the well-spoken poet, while I redd the house.

The similarities between Hiberno-English and Ulster-Scots are also confirmed in the syntax. Common features include: the separation of *have* and the past participle (*I have the door painted*), clefting (*It's John saw Mary yesterday*), fronting (*Three operations I stood in Blanchardstown*), omission of the relative pronoun (*It was John bought the new car*), use of *and* to head clauses in place of standard adverbial clauses (*She came in and I writing a letter*; *He took the paper, and me not having it read*), use of *till* to express purpose (*Come here, Mickey, till I comb your hair*), use of habitual *be* (*I do be here every Thursday*), use of the verb *be* in place of standard construction with *have* (*How long are you here? I'm here three years*), retention of inversion in indirect questions (*He asked was she here*). These are all general features of Hiberno-English grammar (see Filppula, 1999). Obviously, some structures in Hiberno-English seem to be local, such as the use of *but* at the end of sentences, as in Tom Paulin's *Seize the Fire* (p. 31):

> Prometheus: So I'd a big head?
> And who wouldn't?
> I'm trapped, but

This is very common in the Northern Counties. A Cavan man would say 'It's a grand day, *but*', to express emphatic response to an earlier remark about the weather. It is not exclusively Northern. Roddy Doyle uses it to great effect in *The Van* (e.g., pp. 123 and 216: 'Make it a Guinness, *but*, will ye?', 'What abou' the sweet *but*?'). We also find this feature entered in Philip Robinson's Ulster-Scots Grammar: A'm for toon thenicht, scho's no cumin *but*. (p. 178). Other features of general Hiberno-English included in Robinson's grammar include the verb placed in final position (*A hae a lettèr writ*, p. 183), and reversed word-order (*awa til Inglann scho went*, p. 184; *The this fairm a laun hè bocht*; *The these oul schune A hae* (p. 186, with the old 'n plural' for *shoes*, as noted in another example for Forth and Bargy). We also find separation of *have* and the past participle (*James haes thà hoose paintit*, p. 191); retention of verb-subject word-order in indirect questions (*Asked was it deen?*), and many other shared features.

Such examples of the Ulster-Scots vocabulary and syntax show a number of similarities with Hiberno-English and help to show that, like the English of Forth and Bargy, it has distinctive forms which link it to the prevailing use of English in the island, while at the same time displaying a connection with a Celtic language in another country, Scotland, through the cultural corridor of Ulster.

With respect to the vocabulary of Ulster-Scots, we find many words listed by Fenton which are used in general Hiberno-English. Here are a few examples, selected from many to be found in the common word-stock of Hiberno-English – *creel*, from Irish *críol*, 'a wicker basket for transporting turf'; *creepie*, 'a low stool'; *get yer death*, 'be mortally wounded' (cf. Irish *fuair sé bás*, lit. 'he got death', 'he died'), *sonsie*, 'full of life', 'perky and pretty' (with reference to a girl), a Scottish and Northern word from Scots Gaelic (cf. Irish *sonasach*).

Ulster-Scots and Hiberno-English are part of a pan-Celtic family of Celtic Englishes. In the present state of cross-border political connections between Northern Ireland and the Republic, it seems unlikely that Ulster-Scots could be encouraged to infiltrate southwards. The process, if there is to be one, should start with recognition of its qualities. Prominent members of Northern Irish Society should use Ulster-Scots in public throughout the island. At present, usage of Ulster-Scots seems, in the ROI, to be restricted to areas of Donegal contiguous to the border. The immigrant *tattie howkers*, who used to travel from Donegal to Scotland, have facilitated the spread of Ulster-Scots in the North West of the island. But, as noted above, there is an appreciable number of examples Scots-derived words to be found in Hiberno-English, not just in the Northern counties. Even so, in the ROI, Ulster-Scots seems to have attracted no more official support or interest than Hiberno-English itself.

Happily, the important scholarly work of Karen Corrigan, Martin Croghan, Markku Filppula, Manfred Görlach, John Harris, Raymond Hickey, Jeff Kallen, John Kirk, Caroline Macafee, Kevin McCafferty, Séamus Moylan, Diarmaid Ó Muirithe, Philip Tilling, Hildegard Tristram, Loreto Todd, and Richard Wall, among others, has given prominence to the study of the Irish use of English. But, there is still a reluctance to acknowledge its status, or, indeed, its very existence. After a recent radio series, which I wrote and presented on RTÉ on the Irish use of English, I received a very thoughtful letter from a Cork listener who said that Hiberno-English 'doesn't exist at all apart from a few threadbare words. The whole Hiberno-English thing may be an illusion, another pathetic attempt to fit the cultural vacancy left by the abandonment of the Irish language. An Anglo-American slum is our final destiny'. To give another example, the title of a lecture I was giving at a university in the United States was 'Hiberno-English: The Irish Use of English', but the organisers added, as a sub-title on the poster, 'Why the Irish Talk Funny'.

Hiberno-English is not taught in the ROI. Indeed, teachers are careful to point out that sentences such as *Shakespeare was after finishing* Hamlet *by 1601* would be marked wrong, in the unlikely event of such an expression being written down by a pupil, but that same student would be quite likely to use such a construction in open classroom discussion. It can be claimed that

ROI school-children are all to an extent bi-lingual, using 'Standard' English in written assignments, but Hiberno-English in oral communications with fellow-pupils and teachers in class. Obviously, the Hiberno-English idiom will abound, as elsewhere, outside the monitored environs of the classroom. I have been teaching courses on Irish English in the English Department at UCD for the past twenty years, at both postgraduate and undergraduate level, and have amassed a considerable archive of words, sayings, and constructions from our students, who have generously supplied me with information, country-wide, North and South. Many of them had not realised the linguistic wealth they had been exposed to, while they had been growing up.

One of the most important sections of the community for us to concentrate on is the educational system, at primary and secondary level. The practice of alerting younger students to the power and cultural significance of the language they use in their community, at school, at home, and with their friends, is crucial to the survival of dialectal varieties in Ireland. Some years ago an inspired School-Principal, Mrs Rae McIntyre, at Ballyrashane Primary School, in County Londonderry, encouraged her pupils to collect words that they used, and she subsequently produced their contributions in a book entitled *Some Handlin': The Dialect Heritage of North Ulster*, the first edition of which came out in 1986, with a Foreword by John Braidwood, and a second in 1990. Mrs McIntyre notes this important point in the Introduction to the second edition: "Since the first edition of this book was compiled in 1984 there has been a perceptible change in attitudes towards non-standard dialect. Six years ago it was considered quite unacceptable in many quarters, but now it is regarded as a distinct aspect of our cultural heritage." (p. 7) She also makes the point that "the first edition generated far more interest in dialect than we ever believed possible, and it was this interest that enabled us to supplement what the late Professor Braidwood referred to as our "local word hoard" with words from other parts of the province."

The Ballyrashane Collection, which is included in the Bibliography of *The Concise Ulster Dictionary* (p. 405), is a valuable contribution to lexicographical study, not least because it demonstrates, in microcosm, the connections which exist throughout the country. Some of the entries are local, such as *black neb*, meaning 'Presbyterian' (p. 13), some are Scots, such as *leggered* ('thick with mud', p. 38), some international, such as *nerd*, for 'a silly, stupid person' (p. 42), some common in other parts of Ulster, such as *forbye* ('besides', p. 25), but words such as *evening*, for 'afternoon' (p. 24), or *lock*, meaning 'a quantity of something' (p. 38), *messages*, meaning 'shopping', usually 'groceries' (p. 40), may be found throughout the island of Ireland. By encouraging pupils to become aware of their own community-speech, we are able to help give them a civic sense, an attachment to where they belong, and also to see how their individual identities fit into those of the whole island. To help facilitate such a process, in Dublin, a group of colleagues, including an expert in recording Hiberno-English technologically, two secondary-level teachers, and myself have devised a module for use in the Transition Year in ROI schools. We have been greatly encouraged by officials from the Department of Education, and by a Minister, and have conducted trials with the module, and given classes on Hiberno-English in selected schools. The results have been very promising. Such a programme could also include a module on Ulster-Scots.

For the wider public in the ROI, I have written and presented a series of programmes on RTÉ which include interviews with a range of speakers and writers who use Hiberno-English (for example, Tom Paulin and Roddy Doyle), or have views on it (such as Senator David Norris), or are involved in Irish language scholarship (for example, Dáithí Ó Hogáin and Clíona de Bhaldraithe Marsh). I was also joined on the programme by the sports commentator Jimmy Magee and the broadcaster Joe Duffy. Excellent contributions were also made by prominent scholars working in the field of Hiberno-English, including Karen Corrigan and Ray Hickey, and Tony Crowley discussed Hiberno-English in the context of his book, *The Politics of Language in Ireland, 1366-1922* (2000). These programmes generated a considerable amount of correspondence arising from the widespread interest in the topic from all over the island, North and South. A similar series could be broadcast to promote Ulster-Scots. I shall devote a programme to it in a future series.

The attention which is now being paid to Ulster-Scots is most welcome. I have a concern, though, that the frequent analysis of the linguistic repercussions of the seventeenth-century plantations may lead us to forget that the links between the two islands are much older. We should acknowledge the significance and achievements of the people such as John de Courcy, so-called 'prince of Ulster', who invaded the Kingdom of Ulaid in 1177 and established many connections, especially religious ones, between Ulster and the North of England. Links with the North West of England have always been strong. In the nineteenth century, as is well attested, workers from that area, and also from Scotland, migrated to Ulster, for employment, in Harland and Wolff (founded in 1861), among other companies. Thus, in focusing on the Scottish contribution to the culture of Northern Ireland, as represented by the constituent parts of Ulster-Scots, we should not underplay the English dimension in Ireland, from the medieval period onwards (Dolan, 1999: 208-228; Dolan, 1990: 141-170) Dolan: Lucas, 1995; Hogan, 1927; Heuser, 1904), nor should we allow the fact that both Scots and Ulster-Scots have been recognised as languages by the European Bureau for Lesser-Used Languages to segregate their influence on Hiberno-English as a whole. Northern Hiberno-English, as we have seen in the Ballyrashane Primary School Collection and in the lexicon published in *The Concise Ulster Dictionary*, is a Celtic variety of English which is connected to the whole island: it has a core of currently and widely used words, enhanced by a changing range of local vocabulary. Brendan Adams stressed the importance of Northern English influence, not only on Ulster dialects:

> On a long-term historical view the northern region of England is the basic starting-point for comparative work on Anglo-Irish dialectology; the northern character of Anglo-Irish in general was noted many years ago by Professor J.J. Hogan, while Lowland Scots, which has influenced Ulster English so considerably, is an off-shoot of northern English in the more limited sense of that term. (Adams, 1967/1986: 33)

As we have pointed out, the recent publications of *The Hamely Tongue: A Personal Record of Ulster-Scots in County Antrim*, by James Fenton (Revised and Expanded Edition, 2000), and *Ulster-Scots, A Grammar of the Traditional Written and Spoken Language*, by Philip Robinson (1997) have drawn attention to the distinctness of the Ulster-Scots. It is certainly distinct, but it shares many lexical, grammatical, and syntactical features with general Hiberno-English, and also with its sub-varieties, as I have demonstrated with reference to shared features in the Dialect of Forth and Bargy, County Wexford (Dolan and Ó Muirithe, 1996; Ó Muirithe, 1990).

Support for Ulster-Scots is understandable, given that it has long suffered from neglect. It has rarely been acknowledged as a literary medium. The Weaver Poets, for instance, have never been given their due status, even in *The Field Day Anthology*. Scots itself seems to have been neglected in Scotland, let alone in Britain as a whole. Given that Ulster-Scots may be seen as an identifiable variety of English, used by a distinct community in Northern Ireland, with a long history of currency, one may be forgiven for wondering what the Stormont Government did for Ulster-Scots in its fifty-year rule. That would have been an ideal period to encourage and foster Ulster-Scots, and its writers, enjoying the prestige and support of the Government itself, could have produced material of the highest quality, since it had the potential to be one of the main voices of the Ulster British Community. Perhaps the chance of creating a Golden Age of Ulster-Scots Literature has been lost? But not just in Literature. It could have been taught in the schools, courses could have been given at university level, and an administrative idiom could have been inaugurated and developed, gradually, without the risk of attracting unwelcome humorous reactions through seemingly hasty creations such as *Eeksie-Peeksie Skame Heid-Yin*, for 'Equal Opportunities Manager' (Görlach, 2000: 26). The will to do something for, with, and in Ulster-Scots seems to have been lacking until very recently, and one wonders to what extent there is genuine scholarly interest in it. One cannot help thinking of the newspaper report of a group of citizens taking down a street-name, written in Ulster-Scots, because they mistakenly thought it was in Irish. By contrast, the Nationalist Community has put a great deal of effort into promoting the Irish Language.

The importance and function of the Irish Language in Northern Ireland have been discussed in a series of essays edited by Aodán Mac Póilin. Thanks to the Good Friday Agreement, the status of Irish in the educational system in the North has greatly increased since the time after 1923 when 'the teaching of Irish as an optional subject had been reduced to 90 minutes a week in public elementary schools; and recognition and funding had been withdrawn from independent Irish language colleges.' (Andrews: 65). By allowing the teaching of some Irish in schools, funded from the Exchequer, without actually prohibiting it, Northern politicians in the nineteen twenties were canny enough to recognise that outright repression of the language would have been regarded as further evidence of anti-Irish sentiment on the part of the authorities and thus encouraged more support for the Nationalist cause. This was an astute use of linguistic politics, a practice which has a long, and often discreditable history in Ireland, from the time of the Statute of

Kilkenny onwards (Dolan, 1999: 213-214) and before (Ó Fiach, 1969: 101-102).

Politics has taken yet another channel of influence in the matter of Ulster-Scots. That treacherous mantra 'parity of esteem' has become useful in all discussions about language. The esteem in which the Irish Language is held in Northern Ireland is a moot point, and so the question of 'parity' seems rather puzzling. The actual terms used in the Good Friday Agreement itself (p. 22, para. 3) supply clarification:

> *All participants recognise the importance of respect, understanding and tolerance in relation to linguistic diversity, including in Northern Ireland, the Irish language, Ulster-Scots and the languages of the various ethnic communities, all of which are part of the cultural wealth of the island of Ireland.*

Whether such pious sentiments will help to preserve Northern Ireland's dialectal 'richness and variety of expression unparalleled in any area of comparable size' (Braidwood, 1986: 6) is debatable. John Braidwood himself provided practical advice on how a variety of language should be preserved, not by political means:

> *If our distinctive speech – the mark of distinctive people with much to be proud of – is to survive, it must become more than a matter of sentimental recall and reminiscence among the old; it must be handed on by them in good health to the young as their inalienable birth-right, side by side with and enriching their standard speech*
> (Braidwood, 1986: 6)

The key point is that a variety of language must be passed around and on from the family unit, from generation to generation. Hence the book of words and expression compiled by the pupils of Ballyrashane Primary School, Co. Derry, in the Foreword of which John Braidwood wrote the words cited above, provides encouraging information about the dialectal usage of the younger generation. Such information is essential to gauge the strength of the language of a given community. It is evidence which does not have to be manipulated to prove a point. This is true of all varieties of language in current usage in Ireland. The number of Irish speakers in the Gaeltacht areas is declining, in spite of the Irish Government's continuous support for the Irish language there and elsewhere, through many channels.

In Northern Ireland, 'Because the state pursues both a revivalist and a conservationist programme, there can be unresolved tensions on a policy level between the needs of the minority Gaeltacht communities and the perceived needs of the far larger – and far more influential – minority of non-Gaeltacht speakers (MacPóilin, 1997: 182). Whether or not the 'parity of esteem' accorded to the Irish Language in Northern Ireland results in greater use of the language remains to be seen. In some quarters, after the foundation of the Irish State, some idealists thought that the teaching of Irish may result in the disappearance of English. This was not to be, not least because of the prestige, portability, lexical range, and artillery of grammars and dictionaries which put English far ahead of any of its competitors.

The level of speakers of Irish in the Republic does not reflect the aspirations of the Government, though there is a widespread belief that the

Irish Language is not doing too badly, and that the position will improve with careful planning (*Pleanáil don Ghaeilge* 1995-2000). Understandably, people of an optimistic disposition point to such cultural emblems as bi-lingual signposts, notices in Irish, the success of Irish-only schools, and so forth. Their optimism is supported by the success of broadcasting in Irish on radio and television, especially with the continuing achievements of the Gaelic Television Station, TG4.

Recent successes in promoting Ulster-Scots have produced a rivalry between this 'language' and the Irish Language, with English almost being ignored. This gives a false picture, not least because of the arguments over whether or not Ulster-Scots can claim to be a language, despite legislation (Longley, 2001: 39-40; Kirk, 2000: 44). The links between the two islands are much older, much richer and much more complex than some supporters of Ulster-Scots have unintentionally suggested. These links long pre-date the seventeenth-century plantations, which constituted merely one of many different episodes of acculturation. Certainly, the British role in the formation of Ulster culture is acknowledged in the title of the 'Ulster British Society', which was founded to highlight the role of British culture in Ulster generally, but this may undervalue the importance of the English dimension in the development of the whole island, North and South. We should never pass over the achievements of Medieval Hiberno-English, which provide a rich source of evidence of the complex links which were in place from long before these plantations. The so-called 'Kildare Poems', which were written in English and survive in a Manuscript dated in the 1330s (British Library MS Harley 913), testify to this (Dolan, 1991: 152-159; Dolan, 1999: 215-220; Lucas, 1995; Benskin, 1990: 163-4). There is even a Hiberno-English version of William Langland's *Piers Plowman*. The significance of these early writings should not be ignored in the context of Irish-English relations.

Conclusion

In the Republic, the Government supports the Irish Language exclusively (*Plécháipéis, Towards a Language Act, A Discussion Document,* 1998). If it were also to support Ulster-Scots, in the spirit of the Good Friday Agreement, that would be an excellent policy, but not before the introduction of Government support for the main language of the country, Hiberno-English. Both Governments, North and South, should offer financial assistance for the study of Hiberno-English. It is used throughout the island; its lexicon and syntax harness Celtic and English strands, which provide cross-country connections, from Slieve Luachra to Ballyrashane, from Forth and Bargy to Coleraine; its pedigree symbolises the aspirations of the Good Friday Agreement (in that it links three Governments – Ireland, Northern Ireland, and Scotland). The richness of the linguistic varieties in the island should be publicly celebrated. As already mentioned, I have recently completed a series on Hiberno-English on RTE Radio and, to ensure that all ages in the community are kept informed of Hiberno-English, my colleagues and I have been developing a module for schools for students to take at Transition Year Level. A number of trials have been successfully completed. A Hiberno-

English Website, based on my dictionary and aimed at promoting the discussion of and contributions to the lexicon of Irish English among academics and the community at large, was launched in November 2002 (www.hiberno-english.com). Ulster-Scots, as a variety of Irish English, will be included in these projects. Its own level of 'languageness', to cite Manfred Görlach's vivid term (2000: 14-17), will provide a useful point for discussion. But it is Hiberno-English which expresses the ideas of the nation – its idioms confirm the underlying coherence, if not cohesion, of the inhabitants of Ireland and Scotland.

References

Andrews, Liam. 1997. '*The very dogs in Belfast will bark in Irish*: The Unionist Government and the Irish Language 1921-43'. In Mac Póilin, ed. *The Irish Language in Northern Ireland*, 49-94.

Barry, Michael and Philip Tilling. eds. 1986. *The English Dialects of Ulster, An Anthology of Articles on Ulster Speech by G. B. Adams*. Cultra: Ulster Folk and Transport Museum

Beowulf, A Verse Translation. 2002. Translated by Seamus Heaney, edited by Daniel Donoghue. New York and London: Norton

Corrigan, Karen P. 1990. 'Northern Hiberno-English: The State of the Art'. *Irish University Review* 20: 91-119

Crowley, Tony. 2000. *The Politics of Language in Ireland 1366-1922*. London and New York: Routledge

Deane, Seamus. ed. 1991. *The Field Day Anthology of Irish Writing*. 3 Vols. Derry: Field Day Publications

Dolan, T. P. 1991. 'The Literature of Norman Ireland'. In Deane, ed., *The Field Day Anthology of Irish Writing*, vol. 1, 141-170

Dolan, T. P. 1999. 'Writing in Ireland'. In *The Cambridge History of Medieval English Literature*, edited by David Wallace. Cambridge: Cambridge University Press pp. 208-228

Dolan, T. P., and Diarmaid Ó Muirithe. 1996. *The Dialect of Forth and Bargy*, Co. Wexford, Ireland. Dublin: Four Courts Press

Dolan, Terence Patrick. 1998. *A Dictionary of Hiberno-English: The Irish Use of English*. Dublin: Gill and Macmillan

Fenton, James. 2000. *The Hamely Tongue: A Personal Record of Ulster Scots in County Antrim*. Belfast: Ullans Press [for The Ulster-Scots Language Society], New Revised Edition

Filppula, Markku, 1999. *The Grammar of Irish English: Language in Hibernian Style*. London and New York: Routledge

Görlach, Manfred, 2000. 'Ulster Scots; A Language?'. In *Language and Politics, Northern Ireland, the Republic of Ireland, and Scotland*, edited by John M. Kirk and Dónall P. Ó. Baoill , 13-31 Belfast: Cló Ollscoil na Banríona

Hickey, Raymond. 2002. *A Source Book for Irish English*. Amsterdam and Philadelphia: John Benjamins

Hogan, Jeremiah J. 1927. *The English Language in Ireland.* Dublin: Educational Company

Kirk, John, M., 'Two Ullans Texts', in Kirk and Ó Baoill. 33-44

Kirk, John M., and Donall P. Ó Baoill, eds. 2000. *Language and Politics: Northern Ireland, the Republic of Ireland, and Scotland.* Belfast: Cló Ollscoil na Banríona

Longley, Edna. 2001. 'Multi-Culturalism and Northern Ireland: Making Differences Fruitful'. In Longley, Edna and Declan Kiberd. *Multi-Culturalism: The View from the Two Irelands.* Cork: Cork University Press, in association with The Centre for Cross Border Studies, Armagh, pp. 1-44

Longley, Michael. 1998. *Selected Poems.* London: Cape Poetry

Lucas. Angela M. ed. 1995. *Anglo-Irish Poems of the Middle Ages.* Dublin: Columba Press

Mac Póilin, Aodán. ed. 1997. *The Irish Language in Northern Ireland.* Belfast: Ultach

Macafee, Caroline. ed. 1996. *Concise Ulster Dictionary.* Oxford: University Press

Marshall, W. F. 1996. *Livin' in Drumlister: The Collected Ballads and Verses.* Belfast: Blackstaff Press

Montgomery, Michael B. 1999. 'The position of Ulster-Scots'. *Ulster Folklife,* 45: 86-107

Moylan, Séamas, 1996. *The Language of Kilkenny, Lexicon, Semantics. Structures.* Dublin: Geography Publications

Ó Fiaich, Tomás. 1969. 'The Language and Political History'. In Brian Ó Cuív ed., *A View of the Irish Language.* Dublin: Stationery Office, pp. 100-111

Ó Muirithe, Diarmaid. 1990. 'A Modern Glossary of the Dialect of Forth and Bargy', Irish University Review 20, 149-162

Paulin, Tom. 1983 *A New Look at the Language Question.* Derry: Field Day Publications

Pleanáil don Ghaeilge 1995-2000, *An Ghaeilge Feasta, The Irish Language – Towards the Future.* 1995. Baile Atha Cliath: Comhdháil Náisunta na Gaeilge

Plécháipéis, Towards a Language Act, A Discussion Document. 1998. Baile Atha Cliath: Comhdháil Náisúnta na Gaeilge

Robinson, Philip, 1997. *Ulster-Scots, A Grammar of the Traditional Written and Spoken Language.* Belfast: Ullans Press

Some Handlin', The Dialect Heritage of North Ulster, Collected by Pupils and Friends of Ballyrashane Primary School. 1990. Limavady: North-West Books, Second Edition

Todd, Loreto. 1990. *Words Apart, A Dictionary of Northern Ireland English.* Gerrards Cross: Colin Smythe

Traynor, Michael. 1953. *The English Dialect of Donegal,* A Glossary. Dublin: Royal Irish Academy

Tristram, Hildegard L.C. 1997. Ed. *The Celtic Englishes.* Heidelberg: Universitätsverlag C. Winter

Tristram, Hildegard L.C. 2000. Ed. *The Celtic Englishes II.* Heidelberg: Universitätsverlag C. Winter

The Executive o Scotland's Langage Apairtheid

Dauvit Horsbroch

Scots speakers alane - oot o aw the hamelt leids o the curn in the isles o Britain an Irland - tholes the brunt o discriminaition aff o officialdom. The Executive o Scotland an its pairlament haes biggit a langage apairtheid in Scotland the day whaur the richts o the Inglis-speakin communitie, an - til a faur lesser extent - the Gaelic ane, is upheld, but at the same tyme latsna the Scots speaker get a shot at onie richts. In fact, thrid cless ceitizens is whit Scots speakers is; oor leid isna seen in the pairlament, it isna quotit as a subjeck in the cless, an isna heard amang the meidia. Deed, the meidia thinks naethin o rubbagin the leid at ilka turn. We hae politeicians in Scotland pure condemns the ethnic ill will fund in the Balkans an ither airts, but at the same tyme dounhauds the richts o ethnic Lawlan fowk, nae bother at aw. In ma *ain* opeinion, the deif lugged fowk that rules ower us in Scotland is cless-ridden, narra-nebbit, an Inglified ayont aw.[1]

The fowk that speaks a parteiclar leid identifies thairsels wi common values, an adheres tae parteiclar weys an tradeitions, is, bi defineition, a kenspeckle kinred. The Lawlan Scots-speakin fowk haes existit as a sic an ethnic curn fae the Middle Ages an yet the Executive an Pairlament treats this identitie wi contemption, jalousin that daein a wee tait for Gaelic *alane* sees tae Scotland's ethnic wants. The *Cooncil o Europe Chairter For Leids O The Curn* sets furth a screid o airticles sayin whit proveisions speakers o sindrie leids haes a richt tae, an the govrenment o the Unitit Kinrik haes approven an ratified it, unner Pairt II, on behauf o Scots. Houanever, it is weil seen, in licht o the Report tae the Secretar General o the Cooncil o Europe, that the Executive o Scotland gies a deif lug tae Scots yet, an whit it in fact daes, is tae mark oot ane communitie in Scotland, an habble it. A sma, Inglified crowd is nae-sayin Scots speakers the exerceize o thair human richts.[2]

---

[1] Whyles a weil kent Scot stauns up an maks uiss o leid o the Lawlans whan politics touches on langage or identitie. In September 2002 the UK Hame Secretar, David Blunkett, pit forrit his braith that Asien fowk bydin in the UK shuid speak Inglis. As a come back tae this Bill Speirs, heid o the Tred Union Congress o Scotland, sayed, "I hope that the Home Secretary understands when I tell him, in my native tongue, that he's bin bletherin' a heap o keech." Patentlie the uiss o Scots in this instance caws hame the fact that whit's sayed in Ingland daesna necessar staun for whit Scots fowk think. See report in Aiberdeen *Evening Express*, September 21, 2002.

[2] For ma ain accoont o the the last five year or sae see Dauvit Horsbroch, 'Mair As A Sheuch Atween Scotland An Ulster: Twa Policie For The Scots

Threapin On oor Human Richts

Let me tell y'se whit Scots steerars *isna* efter - conter tae whit the Inglified press aye maks on. We'r no wantin awbodie in Scotland tae speak Scots. We'r no wantin tae gar aw weans in aw the scuils aw ower Scotland learn Scots. We'r no wantin ilka public sign in Scotland pitten intae Scots. We'r no wantin aw public documents owerset fae Inglis intae Scots.We'r no wantin awbodie in the Executive or pairlament tae hae tae speak Scots or tae cairrie oot aw thair haunlin throu the leid. We'r no wantin richts abuin ither ceitizens o Scotland, or Ulster. An we'r no efter hunners o millions o poun bein flung at the leid aether. Whit we *div* want, is tae see oor leid as pairt an paircel o the ordnar public haunlin o Scotland an Ulster sae we can get on wi leivin oor lifes an no hae tae threap on. A haud this tae be richt-myndit an reasonable.

The *Cooncil o Europe Chairter* wes ratified bi the Unitit Kinrik in Mairch an cam intil effect in Julie 2001, an nou, ower a twalmonth efter, the Secretar General o the Cooncil o Europe haes speirt at sindrie states whit thay'r daein for the leids comprehendit in the Chairter. This Simmer, as we aw ken, the UK haed tae mak an *Antrin Report* tae the Secretar General an leit whit *hit* haed duin. The burden for Scots fell on the Executive o Scotland steidit in Embro. In answerin nummer 2, Airticle 7, Pairt II, the Executive claims the'r nae practice or rule in the admeinistraition o Scotland that ettles at dingin doun, or habblin, a leid o the curn, or at pittin fowk aff speakin a leid. A wad a thocht for a stairt that no haein signs in the pairlament - whaur the ither leids daes - an refusin tae hae antrin leitratur in Scots - whaur the ither leids daes - is twa guid ensamples whaur Scots *is* marked oot for discriminaition.

It's byordnar tae think that Scots speakers is the waur for hame raign in Scotland. Whit's gauin on is the UK govrenment is signin up tae Chairters ettlin at proveison for Scots (an ither leids) whyle the Executive an pairlament in Scotland is *de facto* nae-sayin thir obligaitions tae fowk on the grun. Regairdless o thair ain narra-nebbit opeinions politeicians maun tak tent o the UK govrenment's official ratificaition o the Chairter. Sae faur ceivil servans haes made licht o Scots; but it's no a licht maiter ava becis it taks tae dae wi aw leids, wi democracie an human richts.

Afore onie remeid can be haed for Scots speakers, a puckle heids wants addressin. A made mention o thir heids fernyear but wad lyke tae gae throu thaim in a bittie mair detail this tyme roun. In general terms three things is wantit for tae gie a lift tae the leid: a wirkin govrenment policie, an agencie or buird anent the Scots Leid, an o course, siller.

Leid?', *Language and Politics Northern Ireland, the Republic of Ireland, and Scotland*, (Belfast, 2000: 133-141), an 'A Twalmonth An A Wee Tait Forder', *Linguistic Politics Language Policies for Northern Ireland, the Republic of Ireland, and Scotland*, (Belfast, 2001: 123-133), baith editit bi John M Kirk an Dónall P Ó Baoill.

Cooncil O Europe Chairter for Leids O The Curn

Whaur daes a bodie stairt wi the European Chairter? It wad be taiglesome for me tae gae throu the hail document but twa-three heids is wantin airtit oot. Wi twintie quaistions unner Pairts I an II, an twa no tae dae wi Scots, the Executive o Scotland haed echteen quaistions tae gie an answer tae. Weil, the Executive gied answers tae juist *three* quaistions anent Scots, it plenished answers til anither sax that haed naethin tae dae wi whit wes askit, an chose tae act tung-tackit wi a forder nyne.

Efter intimaitin that the'r nae legal acts tae dae wi Scots, the Executive wes askit whither the'r onie bodie or comatee that exists in the state, for tae bigg an gie beild tae the leid, an whither the Executive haed speirt at onie curns in the makin o the report; the Executive wheisht wes weil hauden wi guid reason. The'r nae agencie for Scots, an thay didna speir at nae cheil aboot the leid.

Whan askit in Airticle 7 1 d, f an g, o Pairt II, whit haed been duin for tae fleitch an forder the uiss o the leid in speech, wrytin, in public an private lyfe, or tae mak proveision for teachin the leid at aw stages - or gien a lift tae fowk wantin tae learn at aw - thare wesna a cheep oot thaim. Again, thay haena duin naethin thir gaits for speakers o Scots.

It maun be patent tae maist fowk bi nou that the Chairter isna onie uiss tae Scots sae lang as the leid is comprehendit unner the peelie-wallie proveisions o Pairt II. It haes tae be a heid ettle fae nou on that Scots is marked up tae Pairt III staunin an fowk shuid tak it for grantit that the hail fowk o Scotland shuid hae the self an same richts anent thair leids; nane o us shuid thole this langage apairtheid. Sae ma threap here is that the Executive wants tae forgaither wi representars o the Scots-speakin communitie, tae leuk at the Chairter, an the weys Pairt III can be made patent tae Scots ower marked tyme.

Scots as a Scuils Subjeck in Its Ain Richt

In 2000 an 2001 A threapit that sae lang as Scots is traetit in the curriculum unner proveision for Inglis, fowk will regaird it as nae mair as an *adjunct* o Suddron. Nae maiter hou glib teachers an oratars micht bum the chat o the Scots leid, it's no warth a preen unless it's a self-staunin subjeck. Efter aw, naebodie in Scotland learns the bairns Gaelic as a pendicle o Earse.

In August this year the war a *Warld Congress Anent Readin*, hauden at the univairsitie o Embro, an it comprehendit a hantle o fowk fae baith the warlds o Scots an scuilin. Janet Gillespie fae the Parent Teacher Cooncil o Scotland - a cooncil that haes never airtit oot the braith o Scots-speakin parents - commentit: "We would be denying our children success by allowing them to only use their local dialect". Ance again, a (feart) speaker o Inglis that daesna listen. Nae Scots steerar is ettlin tae thirl bairns tae Scots alane. *Watch oor mous*: we'r wantin Scots as a subjeck in its ain richt, offered alangsyde Inglis, as an option for thaim that wants it. Nae mair, nae less.

At this same Congress, Janet Paisley, umqhile teacher, an nou poyet, threapit that Scots-speakin bairns is traetit as saecon cless ceitizens in the clessroom an that "Scots boys feel like Jessies when they have to speak in English".[3] Whan ane teacher at the Congress speirt whit oor Scots pairlament wes daein for tae shaw Scots bairns that thair leid is respectit tae, alang wi Inglis an Gaelic-speakin bairns, she wes tell that the'r no even sae muckle as a Scots sign gauin up, an the hail Congress wes scunnert.[4] Whan the Executive wes askit anent Airticle 7 o the *Antrin Report* tae the Secretar General, whit policies is haes tae recognise the leid as a "...an expression of cultural wealth...", it quotit the Naitional Guidal anent eddication for 5-14 year aulds, an sayed that the SCCC makks teachin stuffrie for uiss in the clessroom forby. O course, the Naitional Guidal for scuils says nae mair as it *advocates* Scots leitratur; *advocate* daesna mean it daes mak uiss o Scots leitratur. The term Scots leitratur is an affa doutsome phrase tae. Leitratur in the Scots leid, ay, but Scots leitratur affen comprehends oniethin wrutten in Scotland.[5] Whit is mair important is that the Naitional Guidal in Scotland isna compulsor ava.

Sae again, ma threap anent eddication is this; oor bairns canna respeck Scots tae it's a subjeck kenspeckle in its ain richt an wi the teachers skeilie in it. We canna expeck teachers o Inglis, that's no at hame wi Scots, an affen haes views agin it, tae teach it. We maun hae teachers reared up in it an this means offerin Scots in the trainin colleges.

A Meinister for Scots

Juist as Mike Watson haes the burden as meinister for Gaelic - sae faur as the'r an official policie for hit - sae thare shuid be anither bodie that taks tae dae wi Scots. No as a subjeck happt unner peelie-wallie terms lik airt or cultur, *creative writing*, or as a deid airt furm burried unner the remit o the Airts Cooncil, but as the Scots leid in itsel. Hou ither can govrenment howp tae mak sense oot o onie policies for the leid athoot some bodie takin the burden for it, official-lyke. O course, it suits a pucklie fowk in govrenment the nou for Scots tae be weil-yirdit awa oot o sicht. Airticle 7 o Pairt II o the *Antrin Report* askit whit measurs haed been taen anent "[...] the need for

---

[3] See, for ensample, the sma report in the *Daily Record* 'Schools Tell Kids Scots Is Nae Guid', August 3 2002.
[4] For a report anent this see *Scots Tung Wittins*, nummer 106, September 2002.
[5] The doutsome term affen uised in screivins in Inglis is *Scottish literature*.

action to promote regional or minority languages in order to safugaurd them".
This is whit the answer fae the Executive wes conform tae Scots:

> *The Sport, the Arts and Culture Division of the Scottish*
> *Executive Education Department is responsible for providing*
> *policy advice, support and guidance to Ministers, colleagues*
> *and others on issues relating to Scottish Gaelic and Scots.*[6]

Richt, sae we ken wha gies advice, but this haesna answered the quaistion
that wes askit; it jouks it awthegither. The Executive isna lattin on whit firm
action it haes or haesna taen. Truth be kent, is haes duin hee-haw tae gie
Scots even a bittie beild. As wi Gaelic, the ane wey tae mak shair that the
Scots communitie haes onie kin o vyce in the daeins o govrenment that hae
ocht adae wi the leid, is tae hae a meinister that can tak tent o thaim, an tak
a bit burden for makin policies. An haein a meinister daes eik tae the staunin
o a leid in the een o the warld. This is whit wey a meinister for Scots is gey
important: for helpin dae awa wi the warst discriminaition.

The Pairlament: a Haunbuik, Leitratur an Signs

Scots steerars for a nummer o years, an no lang syne, the Aw Pairtie Curn in
the Pairlament for the leid, haes threapit on the maiter o signs. Dauvit Steel,
preses o the pairlament, haes made nae secret that he daesna gree wi onie
policie ettlin at the furderance o aw three leids - Inglis, Gaelic an Scots - an
that he, in fact, daesna regaird Scots as a leid ava. It seems that Scotland is
ower sma for sae monie leids; he shuid veisit toatie Lusinburg an tell thaim
the same.

In August this year, efter the maiter o signs in Scots wes brocht up for the
fift year gauin, the Corporate Bodie o the pairlament intimaitit "[...] signage
in the public areas in the new buildings will be in English, Gaelic and
Braille, and will also include symbols where appropriate". It comes as nae
surprise that the convener o the Corporate Bodie is nane ither nor Dauvit
Steel. His threap is that maist signs in ither pairlaments cairrie juist the twa
leids; tho Braille, in course, maks it three. But fowk ken fyne weil bi nou,
that ethnic discriminaition is whit's ahin this. It can be airgied that he haes
abused his staunin as preses o the Scots pairlament tae see that the Scots
communitie daesna get a shout, becis he hisel isna at hame wi the leid, lat
alane versant in it. The 'deceision' no tae hae Scots signs up alang wi Inglis
an Gaelic anes begunks UK ratificaition. But Scots steerars, bein a threapin
fowk, winna lat this rest, A'm siccar.

Ane ither maiter tae dae wi Scots in the pairlament is the makkin o a
dictionar, haunbuik - whitever it's tae be cryed - for the forderment o the
Scots leid in the warld o politics. Sic a haunbuik isna ettled at politeicians or

---

[6] The Unitit Kinrik *Antrin Report* tae the Secretar General o the Cooncil o
Europe conform tae airticle 15 o the Chairter.

commissionars, becis maist o thaim is Inglis-speakin, an naebodie's leukin for the pairties contrair tae aw stairt flytin in the pairlament chaumer in Scots. Na. But the buik wad be thair for thae politeicians that's wantin it. The ettle is tae plenish the Scots-speakin communitie wi the vocabular that's wantit for uisin in political discoorse an for wrytin anent politics an maiters o cultur, an mibbies for uiss in the meidia, gin programs in the leid *is* ever pitten oot. The vocabular's maistlie aw thare; it juist wants pit thegither in a wirkable wey. The haunbuik wad be recognised bi the Executive an wad be uised bi thae ceivil servans that wad tak tae dae wi Scots whenever dealin wi onie haunlin in the leid, an bi this gait Scots an politics gets taen for grantit.

Bringin the leid intae uiss in the pairlament, an giein its speakers veesible recognition, can, an shuid, mak aw oor fowk mair at hame wi ane anither's weys, an tak awa the murnin an girnin that's thare the nou. An thon girnin isna healthie ava.

Braidkestin throu Scots

Somethin maun be duin anent Scots in the meidia an in braidkestin in parteiclar. As ilka year gaes by younkers lift mair an mair o Suddron, Austrailien an Yankie speech, an it drouks oor kintra as a hail. Nou, the'r naethin wrang wi a bit influence fae ither weys o speakin - naethin at aw - but whan the'r naethin tae balance wi it, an naethin tae haud up yer ain hamelt leid, ye'r in tribble. The meidia in Scotland is for the maist pairt tuim-heidit whan it comes tae sic quaistions, pairtlie follaein on fae the cauldrif ensample o the Executive. Ane ensample o the muckle ignorance amang the meidia wes the *Newsnight Scotland* report anent the mellin o the SNDA an DOST as SLD fae 1st Mey this year. The report stairtit aff wi speirin, is Scots no thon leid that MacDiarmid makkit up? Muckle the same want o ken wes shawn wi the Census stoushie at the stairt o 2000.

The'r haurdlie a week gaes by aether athoot the papers reportin the'r Scots speakers gettin pullt up, punished or dung doun some wey, an the papers thairsels affen haud furth wi the same auld creenge an ethnic hatrent. For ensample, in Mey an Juin this year it wes reportit sindrie weys that the Scots-made pictur, *Sweet Sixteen,* that wes shawin at the Cannes Pictur Fest, wad hae tae be in sub teetles becis o the tuins o the actors; its heid actor, Mairtin Compston, wes speakin Scots.[7] It wes weil seen that reporters haedna the first notion o whit the differ is atween tuin, dialeck an leid, an in thair wryte-ups

---

[7] Reportit in the *Scotsman*, Mey 22, 2002. Ane screivar in the *Daily Record* wrut the follaein anent Compston: 'The film will probably have to be subtitled for the English and definitely for the Yanks, but if Martin can speak as posh as the other movie stars, at the end of the day he'll be over the moon [...]', August 5, 2002. Ance again here the queer norie that whyle Inglis is aye warldlie Scots canna be.

clessed awthin fae Lawlan Scotland as slang or a 'thick 'tuin; as aye, Scots wes regairdit as 'law cless 'alane.[8]

The Executive cuid, an shuid, be ettlin tae set up a comatee tae tak tent o the concerns o the Scots speakin communitie an tae leuk at weys an means o forderin the uiss o Scots in braidkestin an the papers. O course, we ken that braidkestin itsel is reservit tae Westmaister, but the Scots pairlament can redd the gait for an ammenment tae the braidkestin act that wad gie tae Scots programs a richt tae sae monie heurs in the year, as wes duin for Gaelic in 1990. It is oor richt tae hear oor leid uised, conseistent lyke on the TV an raidio, no juist tae be lauched at, but for mair douce maiters tae.[9] Scots speakers pey TV stents lik the lave o fowk in Scotland an the Executive shuid be responsible an redd the gait for a bit proveision. A meinister for Scots, a Buird anent Scots, an the Executive atween thaim, cuid makk a policie wi a wee tait will.

Buird Anent The Scots Leid

Whit Scots speakers is in sair want o is a Buird Anent The Scots Leid. No a buird tae mak mair dictionars, but a buird that will traet the Scots-speakin communitie no as an airt furm, but a leivin leid wi aw the sindrie wants its speakers haes. A buird tae pit forrit policie, wirk wi govrenment taewards wycelyke measurs, an tae see that speirin oot brings furth richt informaition. Abuin awthin, a buird tae gie a lift tae a positive eimage o the Scots leid in a modren warld. A dout sic a buird wad hae fowk drawn fae aw the airts an fae amang baith academics an steerars gin it wes tae speak for the hail communitie. Ae haun wad aye keep the ither richt, A jalouse.

A buird Anent Scots wad be gey an important ane ither gait; makin shair the leid isna sindert bi onie shed that's mair nor the sheuch. Whan askit in Airticle 7 o Pairt II o the Report tae the Secretar General whither the geographic area o speakers is respectit, an whither or no auld or new admeinistrativ diveisions is habblin the forderment o the leid, the Executive sayed naethin. As is weil kent, twa 'policies 'wirkin the nou, the ane in Ulster, an nane ava in Scotland, is makkin a fause shed in the leid, in whit is meant tae be the ane state. The Executive is tung-tackit awthegither anent

---

[8] The meidia is affen backweys-thrawin tae; ane program, *Jamie and the Angel*, made for Channel 4, an set in the days o Jamie VI, haes aw the great fowk speakin pan loaf, an the ordnar fowk speakin Scots. An instance o the modren creenge gettin in the road o the richt historie.

[9] In 1996 the war a bit campain speirin at the BBC for Scots programs; A haed tae wryte tae Lunnon tae get Lunnon tae wryte tae Glesca, afore Glesca wad fash itsel tae answer ma speir, an ither fowk fund muckle the same. Tae thaim at the BBC, the maiter o Scots wesna rael, an thay didna think thay haed tae tak tent til us.

whit it haes duin tae forder exchynges atween speakers o the leid in twa or mair states, an here Scotland, Norlan Irland an the Republic is aw relevant. A buird for Scots in Scotland cuid dae muckle tae uphaud the hailness o the leid an oxter wi sister buirds.

Pirlicue

The Executive haes the remeid in its ain hauns tae stap aw the slaps in the European Chairter. Left in the hauns o junior ceivil servans that kensna muckle, an cares faur less, aboot Scots, we gang roun in circles. The representars o the Scots communitie is seik scunnert at stottin back an forrit atween aw kin kyn o narra-nebbit bodies an depairtments speirin for the meanest o proveisons that ither leids in the UK an Irland taks sae muckle for grantit. On the morn o Fryday 20 September meinister Mike Watson gied an oraition tae this symposium anent baith the Gaelic an Scots leids. A puckle fowk gaithered haed howped for his intimaition o a policie for Scots. Whit fowk heard wes scrimp, but he did gang tae the Aw Pairtie Curn hauden in the pairlament o Scotland, an did *seem* tae preen back his lugs. At this symposium he haes cawed for academics an steerars tae pit forrit ideas an concerns tae him, an he leads us aw tae think that the Executive is awa tae makk a policie a bittie doun the gait. It micht be that he's at it, but A div howp the comin months will shaw A'm wrang aboot the Executive, an that thon fowk'll nou dae somethin aboot dingin doun the apairtheid that thay'v gane an biggit in oor kintra.

Appendix: The Wey The Apairtheid Stauns The Nou

Heids	INGLIS	SCOTS GAELIC	SCOTS
Nummer o Speakers	5 million (Jaloused)	c.60,000 (Census)	**c.1.5 million (GRO)**
Public siller bi year	£ billions (2002-3)	£13 million (2002-3)	**£200,000 (2002-3)**
Signs in pairlament	Ay	Ay	**Na**
Official Leitratur	Ay	Ay	**Na**
Scuils subjeck	Ay	Ay	**Na**
Braidkestin	Ay	Ay	**Na**
Richts afore the law	Ay	Ay	**Na**
Meinister for Leid	Ay (Eddication)	Ay (Cultur & Gaelic)	**Na**
Legislation anent leid	Ay	Ay	**Na**
Census speir	Ay (in Ingland)	Ay (in Scotland)	**Na**

'Auld Plain Scottis' and the Pre-emptive Staunardisation o Inglis

Caroline Macafee

Abstract
By default, Standard Scots has adopted a formal register similar to that of Standard English, inheriting the latinate style that emerged victorious from the 'inkhorn controversy' in Early Modern English. The anglicisation of Scots at this period drew it closer to English and eventually Standard English was accepted as the current coin of literacy in Scotland. However, 'anglicisation' covers a variety of processes that have not been sufficiently differentiated. Some, including the convergence of BOTH Scots and English on Romance models, would probably have happened anyway. In elaborating Modern Scots over again, as a project of language revival, we need not accept the latinate style uncritically as a model of good writing. Some suggestions are offered for avoiding unnecessary latinity in Scots prose.

The mair Latinate, the mair liker Inglis

As Scots and Inglis gat mair similar tae French an Laitin through the process o elaboration – borraein vocabular, syntactic structures an eidiomatic constructions – Scots ay drew closer tae Inglis (aften taiglin a wee ahint). The latinate element, an the registers whaur it is maist dominant, therefore presents a parteicular problem for Staunart Scots, namely ane o differentiation frae Inglis.

When we warsle Scots intae academic contexts, ane o the recurrent deifficulties is the latinate vocabular we fin oorsels uisin, baith in general acause o the formal register, an in parteicular acause o the specialised terminology o the topic unner discussion. Maist o this latinate vocabular is the same in Scots as in Inglis – an, for the maitter o that, in mony anither European leid forbye. There was some disteinctive forms in Aulder Scots an a few o thon has been kittlit up, bit whit tens tae happen is that we hear oorsels gaun on, for clause efter clause, athout uisin onythin at cud really be cried Scots, an we stert tae feel a need tae justify the claim at we are, efter aw, spickin Scots raither nor Inglis.[1]

In this screive, Ah wint tae leuk at the processes o staunardisation at was gaun on at the hinneren o the Aulder Scots period; an Ah wint tae ask whither the chyces at was made than has sneckit us up, aw unbekent, intae ae kyne o staunardisation, at micht no hae been the ae single possibeility lang syne.

The consait o the staunardisation process at Ah'm follaein here is that o Joseph (1987). Tae his wey o thinkin, staunardisation isna an internal process at cud happen spontaneously in ony leid gien the richt condeitions; it's a historical process mair like – ane at has spreid oot-the-wey frae Laitin, an ay keeps on

---

1 It was noticeable at the previous conference in this series at some spickers unner this pressure was gien tae arbitrarily chyngin the vowels o latinate wirds (in weys at micht or micht no bear some relationship tae the spellin).

spreidin tae affeck mair an mair leids as pairt o the muckler process o modrenisation/wastrenisation.

As is weel-kent, there a strang saur o latinity in Staunart Inglis, baith in vocabular an in grammar. The Laitin influence aften comes be wey o French, whilk was drookit be the spreidin watters o staunardisation suiner nor Inglis. Taen thegither, Laitin an French – jintly cried 'Romance' – gies Inglis mair nor 50 per cent o the lexical items i the OED (including, it sud be sayed, some daimen ickers) (Finkenstaedt and Wolff, 1973). The same hauds for Aulder Scots (Macafee and Anderson, 1997), though it likely wadna for Modren Scots, gien the loss o registers efter the Aulder Scots period.

Joseph's wark wad suggest that this latinity o Staunart Inglis cud haurdly hae been joukit, though the oreiginal staunardisers didna ay accep this, an it has a wheen misfortunate upcomes, as muckle for a latinate Staunart Scots as for a latinate Staunart Inglis. There a guid case, made for instance be Mason (1986), that the steevest boolders i the wey o wirking-cless bairns wunnin tae Staunart Inglis leiteracy isna the deifferences frae their ain dialecks, but the muckle wirds frae Laitin an Greek. Sic wirds ten tae be lang, acause o their semantic complexity, an the morphological complexity at follaes frae thon – they aften wap thegither mair nor the ae ruit, an gin there juist the ae ruit, than they're like tae hae an affix or twa. They're aften daurkly metaphorical forbye. The wecht o deid metaphor hings havy on Inglis style: a writer canna mak a play on siccan a metaphor aless he or she can lippen tae the reader's knawledge o Laitin – or leastweys Laitin (an Greek) etymological ruits.

Stages o staunardisation

Scots seems ay tae hae shaddaed the development o Inglis. We can fin an interestin parallel i the monetary relationship atween the twa kintras. Up tae the late 14th century, Scotlan an Englan was pairt o a single 'Sterling Trading Area' (Mayhew 1977: 90). Frae the evidence o coin hoards, the producks o various mints i the twa kintras was rinnin ootower the twa. Up tae 95 per cent o the cunyies, or pieces o money, discovert in Scotlan frae this period is Inglis, an conversely three tae fower per cent o the cunyies discovert in Englan is Scottish. The designs o the Scottish cunyies is derivative frae the Inglis anes. In 1367 there was a deleiberate cryin doun, or debasement, o the Scottish siller coinage, an frae aboot twinty year later the term 'the usual money o Scotlan' begoud tae be uised. Inglis cunyies awmaist disappears frae the hoards (though they are fun again later). In the 15th an 16th centuries, there was progressive debasements o the coinage (aften tae meet the losses o weir wi Englan, bit as the affcome o a lang-term European trade recession forbye). Thir debasements includit a disastrous attemp tae introduce 'black money' o only nominal value. Be the time o the Union o the Crouns in 1603, Scottish denominations was nae worth but ae twalfth o their Inglis feirs (Mayhew 1977; Nicholson 1977; Gilbert 1977; Murray 1977). The Scottish coinage was cawed in efter the Union o the Parliaments. At this pynt, continental siller cunyies ootnummert Inglis anes be three tae ane in Scottish circulation (Metcalf ed. 1977: iv). Efter the 1707 Union, o coorse, the coinage was unified.

It wadna dae for tae push the analogy ower faur, bit the seimilarities is strikin: at first a back-an-forrit flowe an mellin o currency, in unequal proportions, grantit; later an independent fiscal policy in Scotlan, bit ane at made its currency unacceptable in Englan, while Inglis money bade guid an in the coorse o time again infiltratit the Scottish money supply; the laich status o Scottish money, confirmt by the rejection o the 'black money' e'en athin the kintra; the loss o a sindry coinage; an the muckle continental element meltit doun at the Union o the Pairliaments.

As wi coinage, sae wi langage: Scots an Inglis has never been isolatit frae ither; they hae ay formt a geographical continuum o dialecks, an linguistic chynges has diffused an spreid awweys athin that. Baith at the time an in retrospeck, the sibness o Aulder Scots an contemporary Inglis has been viewed in different weys. A wheen o the seemin contradeictions are redd when we realise that at different periods the relationship was dominatit be different processes, an some o thon involvit a flowe o influences at wad hae gaed on onywey, independent o staunardisation. Ah hae propont the follaein chronological schame (Macafee and †Aitken 2002):

Stage 1: up tae aboot 1450, we fin a paitren at is ordinar, Joseph (1987) tells us, afore the introduction o staunardisation tae a vernacular: chynges flowein freely athin a group o langage varieties. Norther Middle Inglis, jooglt be langage contack wi Auld Norse, was, hooiver, the main source;

Stage 2: the spreid o Staunart Inglis (frae aboot 1450 on) didna faze on Scots at the ootset. Scots gaed richt on divergin frae its suddron neibour an its ain staunart kythed i the fore-en o the Middle Scots period. Bit it ay sharet in ongauns sic as the Great Vowel Shift and the northart spreid o *i*-digraph spellins frae Norther Middle Inglis.[2] Scots did borrae antrin bitties frae Staunart Inglis in thae days, maistly in poetic diction;

Stage 3: i the transeition tae Airly Modren Inglis / late Middle Scots, Staunart Inglis, biggin on Laitin an French, unnerwent a period o gallopin elaboration, wi Scots wallopin efter, an deil tak the hinmaist.[3] Scots noo seems tae loss ony initiative. Time an again, an innovation is shawn tae hae appeart first in Inglis.[4]

---

2 The deifferent phases owerlaps. For instance, the uise o *that* as a demonstrative adverb, meanin 'sae' (e.g. *that mekyll*), appears only at the en o the 16th century. It is first attestit (mid-15th century) in the precursor o Staunart Inglis (OED s.v. *that* dem. pron., adj. and adv. III), bit Inglis ensamples efter the 17th century is aw colloquial, an it is noo conseidered non-staunart (an is vera widespread in Inglis dialecks as weel's bein the usual Modren Scots form: see EDD s.v. *that* 11). This is the sociolinguistic profile o a feature at diffused tae Scots as a spoken form, no a leiterary anglicism.

3 E.g. the development o *quh-* relative pronouns, periphrastic *do*, the perfect infinitive, an the pluperfect progressive (see Görlach 2002).

4 A possible counter-ensample is providit be Jumpertz-Schwab (1998: 141), wha pynts oot at the available evidence is insuffeicient tae say whither the addeition o

Ah fin a uisfu analogy for this i the concep o 'pre-emptive domestication'. Thon is a term uised in anthropology, meanin that whan a species has aince been domesticatit, there nae need tae domesticate it again aless there some geographical barrier at lets it frae spreidin. In Eurasia, the kenspeckle craps an baists at are noo economically important has generally only been domesticatit the aince, an the domesticates has been sawn or keppit the width o the continent (Diamond 1998: 178ff.).[5]

Englan an the Lawlans o Scotlan is aither en o an easily traivellt space on the ae sma islan. The muckler bouk o Englan, thrang o fowk, an the walth and stabeility o its economy, is explanations eneuch for the creative vitality o Inglis in thae days (though the feck o its elaboration had awreadies been pre-emptit be French, itsel follaein Laitin). Sae be the saicont hauf o the saxteenth century we fin the northart flowe o innovation frae Lunnon in spate.[6]

The effeck was whit Joseph cries 'involuntary langage shift', a gradual-like dilution o ae langage variety through mellin wi anither. The period o mellin set up a continuum atween Scots an Staunart Inglis. As it affecks speech, the process conteenas tae spreid and is ay gaun on;

Stage 4: the neist stage, anglicisation proper, owerlappit wi the previous ane, allooin different attitudes tae coexist for a lang time (arguably up tae the present-day). I the phase o anglicisation proper, Staunart Inglis was adoptit be voluntary langage shift, involin the replacement o entire genres. The muckler micht o Englan – economic an military-poeleitical – made this langage shift gey near inevitable wintin a determint Scottish wull tae the contrar.

Aw o thir processes, at Ah've cried 'stages' acause they set in at different pynts, conteenas tae some extent: owerlappin, reinforcin ither, an makkin it deiffiicult tae grup the cause o indiveidual chynges. Ah hae screivit itherwhaur (Macafee 2002) aboot the deiffiiculty o tellin apairt chynges in Scots brocht aboot be ordinar geographical diffusion (1. abuin), be dialeck contack (3. an 4. abuin), an e'en be independent developments;

Stage 5: the hinneren is the involuntary langage shift (as abuin) o the lave o the spickers, maistly at the bottom o the social scale. At the time o writin, this is whaur we've gotten til ower wide streetches o Central Scotlan (see Máté 1996; Macafee 2000). At this pynt we begin tae spick o langage daith.

---

beand/being tae the absolute participle construction developed first in Scots or in Inglis.

5 E.g., it was recently reportit at European kye is descendit frae Near Eastern aurochs, no frae local anes (*New Scientist* 28 April 2001: 27). Be contrar, i the Americas, wi the lines o communication airtit mair north-sooth an cuttin through different climate zones, species the like o cotton has been domesticatit independently north an sooth o the Equator.

6 There was a sma counter-current flowein soothwart: see Jacobsson (1962).

The inkhorn controversy

In retrospeck, the deleiberate chyce at Stage 4 atween mither-tongue Scots an pitten-on Inglis seems tae us tae hae been the decisive ane for the future o the vernacular, an be late Middle Scots a hantle fowk was evidently awaur o this issue. Bit for a guid while afore that, it seems at an 'involuntary langage shift' gaed on quate-like. The maist conscious chyce for the feck o screivers was atween Laitin an the vernacular, an haein made the chyce o the vernacular, atween a Latinate an a 'plain' style.

Laitin was aften descreivit as 'copious'. As functions was transferrt tae the vernacular, screivers ettlit tae achieve the same 'facund eloquence' as in Laitin – whit Gavin Douglas cried 'fowth o langage'. In Englan in the late 16th an 17th centuries, the wey tae elaborate the vernacular was explicitly discussed amang three main factions:

1. the anes in favour o extensive borraein, especially frae Laitin. This was the camp at was tae bear the gree. Borraein was, arguably, the easy gate tae tak whan translatin frae Laitin (or French). It allood deifficult wirds simply tae be cairried ower frae the oreiginal. Bit it wasna juist a practick o owersetters. Educatit men o the period was snodly bilingual in Laitin an Inglis an aften trilingual wi French forbye. They aften introduced latinate vocabular athout the warrant o an oreiginal;
2. purists in favour o augmentin Inglis frae its ain resources;
3. addeitionally, in verse, archaisers follaein Spenser (see Barber 1976, 1997: ch.11). Gavin Douglas is a kenspeckle Scottish memmer o the archaising camp, though he is eclectic, an wad "sum bastard Latyn, Franch or Inglys oys, Quhar scant was Scottis" (*Aeneid* I, Prologue 117).
4.

There daesna seem tae hae been in Scotlan the same level o debate aboot thir alternatives – maybe, as Görlach (2002: 108) suggests, acause Scots writers didnae tak the latinate style tae the excessive lengths at some Inglis writers did. Twa-three o the makars is eloquent in their praises o the latinate style o Lydgate an Chaucer, an maist Scots screivers an owersetters o the late Middle Scots period seems tae faw as if naiturally intae the latinate tendency. Its creitics in Englan complaint o 'inkhorn terms'; the anes in Scotlan o *minȝard* ('mincin, affectit') terms. Bit this disna seem tae hae dreven the Scottish creitics intae the neologisin or archaisin camps, bit simply tae a less latinate style – ane at is latinate whaurever necessar raither nor whaurever possible. Douglas is notable for his aspiration tae elaborate Scots – an Scots speceifically. Bit the lave o Middle Scots screivers i the borraein or latinate camp seems tae hae seen the elaboration o the vernacular as a jynt enterprise wi Inglis screivers. Aiblins mair nor we realise noo they felt an awnership o the Staunart Inglis at resultit – they simply read it alood as gin it was Scots (Robinson 1983), an whiles they cried it 'Scottis' (Bald 1928), an gey aften 'Scottis or Inglis' (see DOST s.v. *Scottis* B.2).

The wird o praise amang the purist or anti-latinate camp is *plain*. In baith kintras, a 'plain' style o screivin conteena'd as weel. It is fun in Scots, for instance, in John Gau (translatin frae the Danish), an in orra survivals o pre-Reformation genres likes o a formal cursing o border reivers (see below) an a devout exercise.[7] In Inglis the *locus classicus* o this style is, o coorse, the Authorised Version o the Bible.

The 'plain' style as guid practick

Ah wad suggest that in screivin Modren Scots prose, we cud learn frae the plain style o Aulder Scots. There an ensample in Text 1.

Text 1

Herefore throuch the auctorite of Almychty God the fadere of hevin, his sone our salvatour Jhesu Christ and of the Haly Geyst, and throuch the auctorite of the Blissit Virgyne Sancte Marye his modere, Sanct Michael, Sanct Gabriell, Sanct Raphaell and al the Angellis, Sanct Jhone the baptist and al the haly patriarchis and prophetis, Sanct Petir, Sanct Paule, Sanct Androw, Sanct James, Sanct Jhon the ewangelist and all haly apostolis, Sanct Stevyn, Sanct Laurence, Sanct Sebastiane and all haly marthiris, Sanct Mongw, Sanct Geile, Sanct Niniane, Sanct Martyne and al haly confessouris, Sancte Tan, Sancte Katheryne, Sancte Margarete, Sanct Bryde and all haly virginis and matronis and of all the sainctis and haly cumpany of hevin, be the auctorite of our maist haly fadere the paipe and his cardinalis and of my said lord archbischop of Glasgou, be the avise and assistance of my lordis archbischop bischoppis abbotis priouris and utheris prelatis and ministeris of haly kirk, I denunce proclemis and declaris all and syndry the committaris of the saidis saikles murthuris slauchteris byrnyngis heirschippis reiffis thyftis and spulyeis oppinlie apon day lycht and under silence of the nycht alsweile within temporale landis as kirklandis, togydder with thare parttakkaris assistaris supplearis wittandlye ressettaris of thare personis the gudis reft stollin and spulyeit be thame art or part thereof and thare counsalouris and defendouris of thare evill dedis alanerlye, cursit uareyt aggregit and reaggregit with the grete cursing.
I curse thare heid and all the haris of ther heid, I curse thare face, thare ene, thare mouth, thare neyse, thare tounge, thare teith, thare cragis, thare schulderis, thare breystis, thare hartis, thare stomokis, thare bakis, thare waymes, thare armys, thare leggis, thare handis, thare feyt, and everilk part of thare bodys fra the top of ther heides to the sole of ther feyt, before and behynde, within and without; I curse thame gangand, I curse thaim rydand, I curse thame standand, I curse thame sittand, I curse thaim eittand, I curse thaim drynkand, I curse thaim walkand, I curse thaim slepand, I curse thaim rysand,

---

7 "Ane Dewoit Exercicioun ... in the honour of the Croune of Thorne" in J.A.W. Bennett ed., *Devotional Pieces in Verse and Prose* Edinburgh: Scottish Text Society, 1955.

> *I curse thaim lyand, I curse thaim at hame, I curse thaim fra hayme,*
> *I curse thaim within the houssis, I curse tham without the houssis, I*
> *curse thare wyiffis, thare bayrnis and ther servandis participant*
> *with thame in thare evil and myscheiffus deidis; I uayry thare*
> *cornis, thare catall, thare woll, thare scheip, thare horsis, thare*
> *swyne, thare geyse, thare hennis, thare cokkis and all ther quyk*
> *gudis, I wayry thare hallis, thare chalmeris, thare beddis, thare*
> *kechynis, thare stabillis, thare bernys, thare byris, thare*
> *berneyardis, thare cailyardis, thare pleuchis, thare harrouis and all*
> *the gudis and houssis that ar necessar far thare sustentatioun and*
> *uelefare.* (frae "Excommunication, in the vernacular, of Border
> reivers, 1525 (f.204)" in Donaldson and Macrae eds. (1942:
> 268–71))

John Knox descreivit this kyne o malediction as, "words of devilish spite and malice [...] cruel and abominable words."[8] But it's haurdly 'plain'. *Soi disant* 'plain' texts the like o this is 'plain' only i the sense at they're easily intelligible. An this ane caws the nail tae the heid, certes. Bit in fack this 'plain' style is buskit in mony weys, parteicularly be rhythm an be syntactic parallelism (whilk aften produces rhythm), be cheens o synonyms, an be alliteration. Gin this style, an its marra, Biblical Inglis, had lestit in the twa leids, an been cultivatit be moderate an influential screivers as the model o guid prose, we'd been spared mony eddicational problems the day.

Ah feenish wi twa-three thochts for an anti-latinate manifesto:

1. We canna expeck to get rid o mair nor a proportion o latinate terms frae oor texts. Bit whaur it's no technical terminology (the whilk we're thirlt tae acause o the subjeck maitter), we sud conseider whither we can replace it be an alternative, mair vernacular, wirdin. Aften there winna be ae single hamelt wird tae replace a latinate ane – that's forwhy the latinate vocabular was borraed i the first place. Bit gaun back a step i the writin process tae the pynt whaur we're ettlin tae turn conceps intae wirdins, we whiles fin that, if there nae single vernacular wird, there micht juist the same be an eidiomatic, proverbial or metaphorical wey o expressin the idea. An than we hae an inlat for vocabular at wadna seem, at first blenk, tae belang the academic context;

2. Whitever oor lealty tae Scots, intelligibeility cannae be awthegither pit tae the horn. Vocabular at's like tae be deifficult for the reader (or hearer) sud be introduced intae transparent contexts, i.e. the surroondin text sud render the deifficult wird guessable. Gin it's drappit in for its ain sake an no made clear, naethin that follaes sud depend on the reader kennin whit that ferlie was. (The reader canna be dependit on tae uise a dictionar or glossary.) Ane wey o gainin the necessar transparency is tae gie the problem wird a marra as ane o a pair o synonyms, the ither bein a mair fameiliar – e'en an Inglis – wird.[9] Similes are

---

8 Quotit be Donaldson an Macrae (1942: vii) frae *The History of the Reformation in Scotland.*

9 This was a favourite ploy in Aulder Scots, whaur the problem wirds was new-come lends. Thir was jynt wi hamelt synonyms, e.g. *acoutrementis and clething.*

anither wey o slippin in Scots wirds – e.g., there mony variations on the theme o 'no worth a X', whaur it haurdly maitters whither X is a weel-kent wird lik *docken* or an obsolete ane lik *doit*;

3. The tradeitional walth o the leid offers mony weys tae embellish Scots writin, sae that it can be heezit abuin the everyday athoot needin tae be latinate. Mony items – an hale areas – o vocabular has been owercome be chynges in material culture, an are kistit i the dictionars, bit they keep on desertin the kirkyaird. Whiles they bide on in eidioms an feigurative senses at can ay be drawn on. Fowk aften has a passive knawledge o vocabular weel ayont their ain uisage – frae the likes o bairn-rhymes, tradeitional sangs, an o coorse the wark o Burns. Likewise dounricht quotation an allusion can be uised.[10] Gin the wirdin is fameiliar eneuch, it can be chynged an played wi, an still be recognisable. The effeck o sic deleiberate misquotation can be witty or ironic, or juist add an interesting dimension be linkin the blaud tae an iconic text as pairt o a shared an continuin tradeition. (Mis)quotation allooes moribund wirds an eidioms tae be importit intae a text alang wi a bittie helpfu context. Ane o the things at eddication can, an sud, dae *vis-à-vis* the Scots leid is tae provide us wi shared cultural reference pynts o this kyne – especially Burns an the muckle sangs (the Child ballads).

Awbody at ettles tae screive in Scots – or lats theirsel be fleecht intil't – kens hoo important it is tae wyle Scots wirds (lexical items) an no juist wird forms (items wi Inglis cognates). Naebody wints tae draw doun Lewis Grassic Gibbon's creiticism o a Scots that is nocht but a 'spray o apostrophes' (an leain oot the actual apostrophes disna mak nae differ). Bit we sud ay hae in myne the reason whit wey the wirds maitter: they gie us disteinctive weys o pinnin doun our thochts. The affcome micht be profoun, or it micht juist saut the text in a wey at maks it mair tuithsome tae the reader, bit as MacDiarmid famously pit it, Scots offers: "a vast unutilised mass of lapsed observation made by minds whose attitude to experience and whose speculative and imaginative tendencies were quite different from any possible to Englishmen and anglicised Scots today" (1923: 210).

Sir Walter Scott uised this trick anaw, yokin Scots wi Inglis, e.g. *tacksman or lessee*.

10 A recent study o archaisms in Inglis newspapers (Minugh 1999) discovered that some supposedly obsolete features o Staunart Inglis, sic as the saicont person singular pronoun (*thou, thee, thy*) occurs at a surprisinly heich level in everyday newspaper langage, usually in quotation or misquotation (accidental or deleiberate) frae Shakespeare or the Bible. In the same wey, Douglas (2000) fun that (mis)quotation is an important inlat for the Scots leid intae Scottish journalism.

References an abbreviations

Aitken, A.J. 1971. "Variation and variety in written Middle Scots". In eds Aitken *et al. Edinburgh Studies in English and Scots*. London: Longman. 177–209

Bald, Marjory. 1928. "Contemporary references to the Scottish speech of the sixteenth century". *Scottish Historical Review* 25: 163–179

Barber, Charles. 1976, 1997. *Early Modern English*. London: Deutsch. Second edn, Edinburgh University Press

Diamond, Jared. 1998. *Guns, Germs and Steel. A Short History of Everybody for the last 13,000 Years*. London: Vintage

Donaldson, George and C. Macrae eds. 1942. *St. Andrews Formulare 1514–1546*. vol. 1. Edinburgh: The Stair Society

DOST: *A Dictionary of the Older Scottish Tongue*. 1937–2002. Eds William Craigie *et al*. 12 vols. Oxford University Press

Douglas, Fiona. 2000. "The Role of Lexis in Scottish Newspapers". Unpublished PhD thesis, University of Glasgow

EDD: *The English Dialect Dictionary*. 1898–1905. Ed. Joseph Wright. 6 vols. Oxford University Press

Finkenstaedt, T. and D. Wolff. 1973. *Ordered Profusion: Studies in Dictionaries and the English Lexicon*. Heidelberg: Carl Winter

Gilbert, John. 1977. "The usual money of Scotland and exchange rates against foreign coin". In ed. Metcalf. 131–54.

Görlach, Manfred. 2002. *A Textual History of Scots*. Heidelberg: C. Winter

Jacobsson, Ulf. 1962. *Phonological Dialect Constituents in the Vocabulary of Standard English*. Copenhagen: Lund Studies in English 31

Joseph, John. 1987. *Eloquence and Power. The Rise of Language Standards and Standard Languages*. London: Pinter

Jumpertz-Schwab, Cornelia. 1998. *The Development of the Scots Lexicon and Syntax in the 16th Century under the Influence of Translations from Latin*. Frankfurt: Peter Lang

Macafee, Caroline. 2000. "The demography of Scots: the lessons of the Census campaign". *Scottish Language* 19: 1–44

Macafee, Caroline. 2002. "The impact of anglicisation on the phonology of Scots: a keethin sicht". In eds Katja Lenz and Ruth Möhlig. *Of Dyuersitie & Chaunge of Langage: Essays Presented to Manfred Görlach on the Occasion of his 65th Birthday*. Heidelberg: C. Winter. 240–256

Macafee, Caroline, incorporating material by the late A.J. Aitken. 2002. "A history of Scots to 1700". In DOST vol.12. xxi–clvi

Macafee, Caroline and Alan Anderson. 1997. "A random sample of Older Scots lexis". *Transactions of the Philological Society* 95: 247–278

MacDiarmid, Hugh [pseud.]. 1923. "A theory of Scots letters II". *The Scottish Chapbook* 1 (March): 210–13

Mason, Mary. 1986. "The Deficit Hypothesis revisited". *Educational Studies* 12

[Máté, Iain]. 1996. *Scots Language. A Report on the Scots Language Research carried out by the General Register Office for Scotland in 1996*. Edinburgh: General Register Office (Scotland)

Mayhew, N.J. 1977. "Money in Scotland in the thirteenth century". In ed. Metcalf. 85–102

Metcalf, D.M. ed. 1977. *Coinage in Medieval Scotland 1100–1600. The Second Oxford Symposium on Coinage and Monetary History*. Oxford: British Archaeological Reports 45

Minugh, David. 1999. "What aileth thee, to print so curiously? Archaic forms and contemporary newspaper language". In eds Irma Taavitsainen *et al. Writing in Nonstandard English*. Amsterdam/Philadelphia: Benjamins. 285–304

Murray, Joan. 1977. "The black money of James III". In ed. Metcalf. 115–130

Nicholson, Ranald. 1977. "Scottish monetary problems in the fourteenth and fifteenth centuries". In ed. Metcalf. 103–114

OED: *The Oxford English Dictionary*. 1st edn 1884–1928. Eds J.A.H. Murray *et al.* 12 volumes. 2nd edn. 1989. Eds John Simpson and Edmund Weiner. 20 volumes. Oxford University Press

Robinson, Mairi. 1983. "Language choice in the Reformation: The Scots Confession of 1560". In ed. J. Derrick McClure. *Scotland and the Lowland Tongue: Studies in the Language and Literature of Lowland Scotland in Honour of David D. Murison*. Aberdeen University Press. 59–78

Ulster-Scots Language and Culture

John Edmund

Introduction and Background

This paper provides some perspectives on background, demand, and the future development of Ulster-Scots culture and language. There can be no doubt that Ulster-Scots is the traditional means of expression for a significant part of the population of Northern Ireland and of Donegal. The migration of tens of thousands of people from Lowland Scotland to Ulster in the early part of the seventeenth Century created a 'stable community of speakers'[1] spreading out from the coastal fringe to take up residence across Down, Antrim, Londonderry and in east Donegal. Scots has now been spoken in Ulster for 400 hundred years and across its geographic heartland it is today, alongside English, the medium of communications in daily life.

The historical dimensions of this Ulster-Scots territory have been known for over a century from the work of Hume and Hill. W.F. Marshall in the 1930s and G.B. Adams in the mid–late 1950s provided further delineation with Gregg's work in the early 1960s concluding that the Ulster-Scots speech areas closely approximated those of the Scottish settlement (primarily of the seventeenth century)[2]. Pulling together research from many sources Montgomery and Gregg were able to prove that the Ulster-Scots speaking areas were essentially stable over time from the seventeenth century to the modern day. G.B. Adams[3] defined the rural population resident in these areas (and therefore likely to speak, but not necessarily speaking Ulster-Scots) at that time (1960s) as 170,000 people.

The revival in interest in Ulster-Scots / Formation of the Ulster-Scots Language Society

The public face of Ulster-Scots 'revivalist' activity through the mid 1990s was most clearly seen in the Ulster-Scots Language Society (USLS) (established 1992) and the debate that developed (largely irrelevant to the mass of the Ulster-Scots population) as to whether Ulster-Scots was a language in its own right or a dialect of English.

The Language Society joined with the pre-existing lead organisations for pipebands, Scottish country dance, the Burns Clubs and the Presbyterian Historical Society in 1995 to found the Ulster-Scots Heritage Council (USHC) as a sectoral development lead body with a remit to promote awareness of Ulster-Scots language and culture, lobby for recognition of the Ulster-Scots cultural community from the public sector, support the formation and development of

---

[1] Michael B. Montgomery and Robert J. Gregg, "The Scots Language in Ulster". In *The Edinburgh History of the Scots Language*, ed. C. Jones, Edinburgh: Edinburgh University Press, 1997: 569-622.

[2] Montgomery and Gregg, op. cit.

[3] Quoted in Montgomery and Gregg, op. cit.

Ulster-Scots groups at a community level, develop projects, provide information, establish a resource 'library', and instigate research into Ulster-Scots culture and heritage.

Belfast Agreement (and associated actions by Government)

The USHC and its work was finally acknowledged when all parties to the Belfast Agreement in the section on 'Rights, Safeguards and Equality of Opportunity' affirmed their recognition of *"the importance of respect, understanding and tolerance in relation to linguistic diversity, including in Northern Ireland, the Irish language, Ulster-Scots and the languages of the various ethnic communities, all of which are part of the cultural wealth of the island of Ireland"*.
Subsequently the 'Treaty Establishing the Implementation Bodies' specified the creation of one 'Language Body' with 2 separate parts the remit for the Ulster-Scots part being defined as "the promotion of greater awareness and use of Ullans and of Ulster Scots cultural issues, both within Northern Ireland and throughout the island". In June 1999 Paul Murphy, then Political Development Minister, announced that government had "decided that Ulster-Scots in Northern Ireland will be recognised as a regional or minority language for the purposes of Part II of the *Council of Europe Charter for Regional or Minority Languages*" thus bringing it into line with the treatment of the Scots language in Scotland. Part II of the Charter sets out general principles of recognition and support for indigenous minority languages and the removal of discrimination against them.

Public Opinion / Demand

A survey commissioned on aspects of identity by McCann Erickson (an advertising agency based in Belfast) and carried out by Ulster Marketing Surveys in February 2000 confirmed, if that were needed, the appropriateness of this recognition. The survey reported that:

1. 22% of the sample saw Ulster-Scots identity as very/fairly important to them, and 21% of the sample surveyed rated Ulster-Scots language and culture as an important aspect of their identity;
2. Ulster-Scots identity was seen as inoffensive by 54% of the sample, and 51% saw Ulster-Scots language and culture as an inoffensive aspect of identity;
3. 31% of Protestants and 10% of Catholics saw Ulster-Scots identity as very or fairly important;
4. 23% of Protestants and 19% of Catholics saw Ulster-Scots language and culture as very/fairly important.

Community Engagement with Ulster-Scots Culture

The extent of community engagement with Ulster-Scots, as measured by participation in Ulster-Scots cultural activities, provides further proof of community demand. Since its formation USHC has presided over a development process with two strands – 'community'-based and 'interest'-based.

Community-Based
Some 32 geographically delineated (community) and specifically Ulster-Scots focused groups have been established in Northern Ireland with a further three groups operating in the border counties of the Republic of Ireland (principally Cavan, Donegal and Monaghan). 19 other pre-existing community development groups have affiliated to the USHC and/or have expressed a particular interest in Ulster-Scots.

Interest-Based
Chief among the interest-based groups coming together to establish the USHC were the Royal Scottish Pipe Bands Association (NI Branch) and the Northern Ireland Piping and Drumming School, the Royal Scottish Country Dance Society, the Presbyterian Historical Society, The Ulster-Scots Language Society and the Burns Clubs. To this group must now be added a variety of organisations: seven dance groups (mainly Highland dancing), two fife and drum bands, three Lambeg drumming groups, three re-enactment / amateur drama groups, one creative writing group, two festival organising groups, one independent piping society, one local history group (also many of the community groups have local history as part of their activities programme), two bands and the performance groups emanating from them (not pipe) and the Ulster Bands Association on behalf of part of the flute bands movement.

Royal Scottish Pipe Bands Association (RSPBA) has a current membership of 99 bands with active membership in excess of 3000. In addition there are an estimated 30-40 other pipe bands that do not compete and are not members of the Association. The Association's competitions circuit attracts a very large audience (95% from Northern Ireland); around 59% are 'regular' attenders. No statistics exist to quantify attendance, but best estimates would suggest that the major events attract an audience of around 1000 people.

Royal Scottish Country Dance Society (RSCDS) has three full branches in NI and three affiliated groups; total membership stands at 282. However this ignores membership of the affiliated groups and all those who attend but never join. Mid-Armagh Community Network has also developed a country dancing class, which has an additional 60 members.

Highland Dance in Northern Ireland is a very recent development; currently total participation stands at around 131 mainly girls of primary school age or in their early teens.

Ulster-Scots Language Society (USLS) has in excess of 200 members and an active committee of 16.

Survey Findings

A recent survey of Ulster-Scots groups (54 groups representing a response rate of 33%) established total group membership at 3853 – extrapolating that for non-reporters and weighting the results to balance out anomalies would suggest that there are in excess of 6000 people regularly involved in Ulster-Scots cultural activities.

Socio-demographic analysis of the statistics on membership pointed out that 41% of members are under 18 years, 59% under 30, and only 9% are over retirement age; 20% are unemployed, 15% are students, 40% are manual workers, 10% are office workers, and only 10% are senior managers/professionals; 70% are male, and the majority of females involved (53%) are under 18 years

Language Used

Of the top 10 *activities* provided by the groups reporting engagement with Ulster-Scots Language Arts was rated second most regularly provided activity (10 groups – 56%) and in the list of development priorities language classes were rated sixth – largely, it would seem, because of the difficulty of delivering language learning because of a lack of teaching materials and tutors. Only one of the groups uses Ulster-Scots as its sole medium of communications. The majority of groups (56%) use English only and 39% are bi-lingual (English and Ulster-Scots).

Government Response to this Demand

Recognising this demand, it is perhaps surprising that Government's response has been summarised in a comment from Professor Michael Montgomery, President of the USLS, as follows:

> The occasion of the United Kingdom government's initial periodical report or minority and regional languages is an important one. The report acknowledges the responsibilities of the government, as a signatory to the Good Friday Agreement and the European Charter for Regional or Minority Languages, to support and promote awareness and development of the Ulster-Scots language.
>
> However, the government has supported few measures to fulfil these responsibilities and it has failed even to begin to implement the recommendations of its own commissioned report (published in 2000) advising how to meet its commitments. This report fails completely to give any evidence of this. It therefore represents a major disappointment for all within the Ulster-Scots community and indeed within the wider community who expect the government to honour its stated obligations.

Ulster-Scots and Part III

The initial brief for this session was to consider how education policy should be developed to enable Scots to be delivered so as to satisfy Part 3 of the European Charter. Given the quote from Professor Montgomery as to the USLS's perspective on the way Government has gone about fulfilling its obligations under Part II, Part III is an aspiration that has been put well out of reach.

My colleague John McIntyre, who, unfortunately, was unable to attend the symposium, has considered this issue at length. It is his view that the minimum provision required for Ulster-Scots to meet the requirements of the Charter (Part II) is that Ulster-Scots should be taught in schools in the same as any other modern language. No attempt at all has been made to deliver this.

At this time there is no agreed position within the Ulster-Scots cultural movement as to how conformance with Part III should be met. What follows are some ideas on what might be done but again, they have no endorsement from any public or voluntary body.

Examples from Europe

In Europe, many of the minority language communities are moving towards tri-lingualism in both primary and secondary education. In primary education, they are teaching both the minority and the majority language over the P1 – P3/4 years. Then in P4/5 they introduce another European language – in most cases this is English. In Friesland children are taught only Frisian and Dutch from P1 – P4 and then English   is introduced as the foreign language. Similarly in the Basque country teaching focuses on Basque and Spanish with English as the third language.

The Alternative Option Taken by Irish

In Northern Ireland, the total immersion model adopted for Irish medium education presents another option for consideration. However given the importance of English both as our lingua franca and as a world language, minority language medium education is not an attractive model for many. The advantage of speaking another modern European language in a multi-lingual Europe also has compelling reason behind it. The European model of tri-lingual education seems a good one for Ulster-Scots. English and Ulster-Scots should be taught in P1 – P4 with a third modern European language (French, Spanish, Italian or German) being introduced in P5. Spanish is an attractive option. Spanish is relative easy to learn, it is a world language, it is the second most spoken language in the US (the world's biggest economy), and it is likely to be more useful if only because more people go to Spain for their holidays.

With this model, tri-lingual schools will work to affirm children in their traditional language of Ulster-Scots while preparing them for a world where English is the lingua franca and they will also have a third modern European language. The image of the monoglot English speaker is not a desirable one. Tri-lingual education should appeal to both those parents who want their children to learn Ulster-Scots and to parents who want early access for their children to modern language teaching. Many parents see the benefit of their children learning languages early in their school careers with a view to learning more languages as they progress through education and young adult life. Tri-lingual education will bring Ulster-Scots language teaching into line with European practice.

Ulster-Scots Language Development Strategy

Ulster-Scots language development will not happen if the movement waits for Ulster-Scots to reach the curriculum. Professor Montgomery referred to the development plan for Ulster-Scots commissioned by the Department of Culture Arts and Leisure and published in 2000. I would like to reflect on this plan.

Aims and Objectives

Aim
The aim of the strategy is to promote awareness, understanding and respect for the Ulster-Scots language as a central and integral part of the Ulster-Scots identity and to support its use and development.

Objectives
Its objectives are the preservation, maintenance and regeneration of Ulster-Scots in native speech and writing, the transmission of Ulster-Scots as a language of daily life to the next generation of 'native speakers'; and the encouragement of the use and development of Ulster-Scots as a language of modern life, in both formal and informal registers. Its final objective is to ensure that the contribution that Ulster-Scots has made to the richness of the way we speak in Ulster is recognised by non-native speakers and to encourage them to knowingly use Ulster-Scots day to day.

Target 'audiences' (prioritised) for Ulster-Scots development
The target audiences to whom Ulster-Scots should be promoted are prioritised as native Ulster-Scots speakers still actively using the language, lapsed Ulster-Scots speakers, members of the Ulster-Scots community who have never used the language, academics actively involved in researching language, literature and history, and others in the community who are actively involved in pursuing personal interests in the cultural and heritage sectors e.g. members of local history societies, those taking Irish classes, etc., as well as anyone else who is interested in Ulster-Scots and from the perspective of USLS whose interest can be accommodated efficiently and effectively by their activities.

Strategy Defined

The research on which the development plan was based defined need for a compound strategy, which would build credibility for Ulster-Scots and on that basis, awareness and recognition of the language, seek, as a matter of urgency, to establish the extent to which Ulster-Scots is currently spoken and to record (in order to preserve) as much of the language in use today as possible, codify and standardise Ulster-Scots in order to facilitate its use, develop learning materials, programmes and teaching competence to enable those who wish to learn the language to engage profitably with it, provide opportunities for individuals on their own and in groups to speak and write in Ulster-Scots, and engage with the whole community in Ulster.

Tactical Implementation

The tactical implementation of the strategy is defined as having three 'core' interlocking elements – the need to develop academic credibility to underpin use (for this structures and resources are required), to create formal and informal opportunities to use Ulster-Scots (this is the 'community' strand), and to develop a strong media 'communications' programme to raise awareness. Successful implementation was, however, seen to have two basic underpinning conditions. First, language activity is recognised as being more likely to attract an audience if it is delivered as part of a larger cultural programme. Second, it is recognised that, if native speakers do not recognise Ulster-Scots as it is taught and used, they are unlikely to become committed to its expansion. Within these 'core' development platforms the following key activity strands were defined as prime requirements:

Structural (including Language Planning) Programme
The structural programme recognises the need to research and record the use of the language and the 'culture' of the Ulster-Scots community today, make accessible history resources, standardise spelling and grammar, collect materials that help define the community and support the re-engagement with traditional cultural pursuits, develop language learning and teaching materials, prepare Ulster-Scots for the curriculum, tackle the status issues that Ulster-Scots culture and language faces, and learn from others what systems and support structures work best for developing language up-take and cultural re-engagement.

Community Programme
Generating maximum community involvement in preservation and development is seen to require the involvement of the community in researching today's use of the language, the provision of more opportunities to speak and write in Ulster-Scots, efforts to be made to encourage the involvement of non-native speakers in Ulster-Scots cultural activities, the provision of language classes for anyone who wants to learn, and the adoption of best-practice in developing community involvement with the language movement.

Communications Programme
The basic theme of this programme was defined as, tackling the image, awareness and understanding deficit through media relations and communications programmes that explain and contextualise Ulster-Scots for the whole community, promote the contribution to society of Ulster-Scots and its cultural wealth, promote involvement by everyone in Ulster-Scots events and activities, raise the profile of Ulster-Scots cultural activities so as to attract funders, and promote and strengthen Ulster-Scots as a cultural and community identity.

Structural
The establishment of a Dictionary and Grammar Programme, the implementation of a Tape-recorded Survey of Ulster-Scots use today, The establishment of a Text Base, the development of language and cultural programmes for schools, and the development of language, cultural and historical materials for use outside of school for both adults and children.

Community

The establishment of a community and special interest level 'branch' structure and a networking activity programme, the provision of pre-planned and resources branch programmes to facilitate early development, the establishment of a series of community level Ulster-Scots Festivals, and the establishment of a national festival – the *Ulster-Scots Gaitherin.*

Communications (Status Building)

An active publicity programme of media contact at national and local level; the development of media opportunities such as radio programming in Ulster-Scots and the negotiation of a TV documentary series with a historic and cultural focus; a generic advertising campaign followed up with an involvement generating campaign and supported by enquiry packs and events and activities on-the-ground; an Ulster-Scots Website; and the development of partnerships with cultural organisations and institutions in Scotland and in Europe (primarily minority language/cultural organisations).

Progress to date

As outlined above, community engagement with Ulster-Scots has grown significantly. Formal progress with language development has been poor. The more the community engages with Ulster-Scots cultural things the more the absence of available resources becomes an issue and the more urgent the demand for action. The Ulster-Scots community appears to many to have 'reached the end of its tether'; the taking to task of the Department of Culture Arts and Leisure and its Minister by the Ulster-Scots Language Society has been, perhaps, the most public expression of the community's dissatisfaction but it has been by no means the only one. It remains to be seen if the message will get through this side of the forthcoming elections in Spring 2003; elections are of course the battlefield on which cultural communities extract the price for their support.

Twa Ulster Scotses – Authentic versus Synthetic

Ian J. Parsley

A taakit here fernyeir about the differ atween whit A cryd 'acceptable' Scots an whit wisna acceptable, whit A'm nou for cryan the differ atween 'authentic Scots' – the real thing at reflects the wey fowk taaks an kens the differ atween Scots an Inglis – an 'synthetic Scots'. A'm juist for eikan twathree wirds tae thon wee discourse.

A wheen fowk haes argied at it's mebbe easier definean Scots frae whit it's *no*. 'Synthetic' Scots is aathing frae Inglis screeds wi twathree weird wirdies taen frae Burns cloddit in, richt throu tae pure invention. 'Authentic' Scots is sumwhar atween the baith, richtlie identifeeable as Scots (aften frae a cleek tae literar screeds), but yet near eneuch tae fowks richt wey o taakin – richtlie separit frae Inglis, but no gan tae ridiculous lenths for tae evyte onie sign ava o Inglis influence.

Thaim as haes Scots for thair hamelie tongue taaks a leid ats neardest relation is Inglis, bides in a state ats leid o administration is Inglis, an wirks in a warld whar the leid o the economie is Inglis. It's gey sweir for onie Scots taakar ein tae say an aefauld sentence wi nae wirds taen direct frae the Inglis, an thar nae dout about the influence o Inglis on Scots idiom an gremmar. For aa that, thar a differ atween Scots an Inglis. Thar a wheen aspects o idiom, gremmar or vocabular whar Scots taakars bes lyke ilkither but differs frae Inglis – uiss o *dinna* no *don't*, uiss o *bricht* no *bright* an siclyke. Research is a-wantan yet, but thar uisses thar as wad be 'authentic Scots', an ithers as wad be Inglis. An thar nae dout, pairticular furth o the Doric-taakan airts, at the maist fek Scots taakars mixes Scots an Inglis in the ae sentence. But thar nae dout aither at thar sicna thing as Scots, Scots can be defined (ein frae whit it's no), an ye can tak a keek at onie screed an wirk out gif it be 'authentic' or 'synthetic'.

It wad be heich pretension for me tae allou at fowk as disna taak Scots sudna tak a pairt in the forder an oncum o the leid. A haena Scots as ma ain mither tongue masel! Fowk is needan tyme for learnan, an A'm learnan yet. Aabodie wi a genuine interest for the fen o the tongue sud be aible for takan pairt. But sic fowk maun recognise at thay dinna richtlie taak Scots, an whyles thay canna richtlie separit guid Scots frae Scottifeed Inglis or ocht at's juist airtificial. For thair attempts at writean Scots aften gies thaim as richtlie taaks it forordinar the scunner, an juist daes skaith tae the leid in the public ee.

For ensample, A cudna say but thar a wheen screeds made in Scotlan in whit the makars *crys* Scots, but is richtlie *Inglis*, ein gif thay'r a wee bit 'Scottifeed'. Ye canna juist pit *wee* an *anent* in a screed an set it furth cryan it 'Scots' – it's no. Nor can ye tak the argiement at sic screeds reflects fowks wey o taakin. That cud be richt, pairticular in the Scots mairches an sic airts, but that disna mak the screeds 'Scots'. This bean sae, fowks 'wey o taakin' is richtlie a mixter maxter o Scots an Inglis, an thar sud be nae dout that's whit hit is – no braid Scots, but a mixter maxter – whyles 'Inglifeed Scots' (an lyke A sayed afore, near aa Scots is a wee bit 'Inglifeed'), whyles 'Scottifeed Inglis'. But fowk sud ken whit maks a screed or a bit banter 'Inglis', an whit maks it 'Scots', ein gif bits o the baith kythes in the ae bit o discourse.

Thar a wheen fowk as maks sic texts, ein haill beuks fou o thaim, at knaws whit thay'r writean besna richtlie Scots. But whar thay cud juist accept that an lea official letters an beuks tae thaim as kens (an A'm no allouan tae be ane o the latter masel), whit thay'r daean is settan screeds furth in 'Scottifeed Inglis' an cryan thaim 'Accessible Scots'. The argiement wad be at the mair fowk can unnerstannd the discourse, the mair will tak pairt in the Scots leid muivement. Mair fowk wad aiblans be for takan pairt, but sicna muivement wad hae nocht a-dae wi the braid Scots leid. Sicna muivement wad aiblans forder 'Scottifeed Inglis', but the Scots leid wad dree its weird acause o it. Mairatowre, the mair fowk can unnerstannd the discourse (acause it's richtlie Inglis), the mair fowk (an that comprehends thaim in heich govrenment positions) faas tae thinkan the haill muivement's juist daft, for hit leuks tae be forderan 'ill Inglis'. It wad be a pitie lossan the auld Scots leid o Burns an Lorimer – an mair sae gif siclyke cam off for a want o richt Scots kythean in letters tae the government anent its loss, an for a want o beuks in an about Scots made frae Scots taakars thairsels!

Nou, wha wad this bodie be thinkan he is, an Ulster steerar criticisean the Scots? An a wheen fowk in Scotlan makan sae-cryd 'Scots' at's owre near Inglis (an sud richtlie be cryd 'Inglis'), a wheen fowk in Airlan gaes owre far in the tither airt! Thar screeds sat furth in Airlan as besna Scots an besna Inglis – thay'r nocht ava! Sic wirds lyke *langbletherer* an *billiehood* juist daesna exist, nae maitter whit leid ye'r taakan!

For thay'r no ein richtlie inventit. Fowk daesna aye *blether* on the telephone – no whar hit's an importin business caa! An whit wad thay blether *lang* for? In traditional Scots thay wad aiblans *speak furth*, but *bletheran lang* is, weel, juist blether! *Billiehood* wad be waur yet – no monie Scots taakars wad caa *billie* appropriat for a formal screed, an nane ava wad ken the suffix *-hood* as Scots, whar wi nae dout ava the richt *Scots* suffix wad be *-heid*. Sic screeds bes airtificial, wi ill-inventit wirds, an near aye comprehends a want o consistencie o spellin an gremmar, the lyke o thaim illustrate fernyeir.

Nou, fowk aften caas sic screeds an attempt at a 'formal register'. Deed, thar sicna thing in maist wastren leids, but no sae as fowk as taaks thaim forordinar disna ken thair ain tongue whar it's prentit! Here twa difficulties: first, wirds lyke *langbletherer* or *billiehood* cudna cum pairt o onie 'formal register', ein gif ye war for inventan twathree wirds – an that's anither argiement – ye wadna invent thaim in sicna mainer; saicond, thar a better argiement at says sicna 'register' exists aareddies. For Scots haes baith a literar tradition an a spoken form, an a formal register can cum frae the former, an unformal frae the latter. Gif Scots wantit a formal register, A cudna be stanndan here nou uisean it!

Mairatowre, conter tae popular misconception, Scotlan an Airlan isna fou o dafties! Fowk in Scotlan kens an Inglis screed whan thay sees ane – ein gif hit be a wee bit 'Scottifeed'. Fowk in Ulster kens an airtificial screed, ein gif thar a wee element o thair ain dialect comprehendit athin it. Fowk in Scotlan says 'Thon's nae leid, sure hit's juist Inglis wi a bit dialect in it' – an wi a wheen sae-cryd 'Scots' screeds thay'r juist richt! Fowk in Norlin Airlan an Donegal says 'Whar hae thay gat this leid frae, sure the fek o it is juist made up an thon wey a taakin's aucht naebodie' – an wi a wheen sae-cryd 'Ulster Scots' screeds thay'r juist richt!

Fowk as taaks o 'Rab C. Nesbitt Inglis' haes a pynt – but thay'r no taakan about the 'Authentic Braid Scots' o Burns or contemporar fowk leevean in the kintra airts o Aiberdeenshire. Fowk as taaks o *'a DIY language for Orangemen'* haes a pynt – but thay'r no taakan about the 'Authentic Braid Ulster Scots' o Orr or contemporar fowk leevean in the kintra airts o Antrim. For thon 'Authentic Scots' disna kythe in sic screeds.

Tae the ministers an officials A wad say: tak tent whit ane o thir twa leids ye'r taakan about! Ane is authentic, kythes in literatur, an is uisean deyandeilie, an the tither isna! Tae the steerars A wad say: thar nae caa for thrawan the heid up! Mebbe ministers an officials haes whyles been awfu langsum, but gie thaim a strategie for the authentic leid an hae nae dout thay'l heir tae ye. Tae thaim as stannds agin the leid A says: tak tent whit ye'r stanndan agin! Ye'r mebbe dingan doun a precious pairt o our cultur in Scotlan an Airlan ein gif ye daena ken it! Aabodie sud tak tyme for tae cum acquaint wi the *authentic* Scots tongue – it's an unco byordinar thing!

Developing Scots: *How Far Have We Still To Go?*

J. Derrick McClure

My starting point for this talk is a review by Manfred Görlach (2002) of a book entitled *Teaching Scottish Literature: Curriculum and Classroom Applications*, edited by Alan MacGillivray (1997). The book's editor and its reviewer are well known scholars. With his usual forthrightness, Görlach comments: "The quality of the individual contributions is, I am afraid, uneven and the total impression not convincing. Much of the argumentation is vague and the terminology unclear, and sociolinguistic realities are not discussed in any helpful way." I propose to offer a brief examination of what I take to be the grounds of his objections, and raise the question of what they reveal about the situation of Scots which we are trying to improve.

The first article on Scots is "Language in Scotland Today" by George Sutherland (1997). A sentence from near the beginning, clearly intended to encapsulate a first principle on which discussion must be based, is "It has first to be stated firmly that, in objective linguistic terms, Scots is a language like any other, with its own structure, its own literature, and its own set of varieties." (p. 57) Most readers, presumably, are sympathetic to this view and many would heartily endorse it. Yet it is symptomatic of an over-simple approach which, while it has certainly led to some success in the promotion of Scots, is unlikely to bring the movement to the desired conclusion. Does "a language like any other" mean a language like Japanese, one like Luxembourgish, or one like Navaho? Socially and culturally, these languages are very unlike each other; and Scots is like none of them; yet they are all languages by any definition. Scots certainly has "its own structure, its own literature, and its own set of varieties"; but the question of how to classify a given speech form is never simple; and each case is unique. Scots is *not* "a language like any other": nothing is. I do not, of course, intend to insult George Sutherland by suggesting that he could not express his position more completely if he wished to; but merely to point out that supporters of Scots do not further their cause by laying themselves open to easy criticism in this way.

Again and again in the book, we do indeed find statements of this kind which, though interesting as discussion points, are wholly inadequate if taken (as they were not necessarily intended to be taken) as academically respectable summaries of a case. As a few more examples from Sutherland's essay, one could cite "It is conversely argued, with some passion, that the use of English is an inhibiting factor in situations of social class mingling and educational development". (p. 59) This is certainly not *in principle* true: in bilingual or diglossic societies with accepted "high" and "low" speech forms, conversations in which one speaker makes consistent use of the "high" form and the other of the "low," without either being inhibited thereby, are perfectly commonplace in some societies. It is not always true in Scotland: the situation frequently depicted in Sir Walter Scott's novels, of an Edgar Ravenswood talking English and being answered by a Caleb Balderstone in Scots, is readily recognisable in the sociolinguistic reality even of today. The social context with which the book is concerned, namely school teaching, can indubitably furnish instances of a speaker of Scots being inhibited in the presence of a speaker of English; but there, in the asymmetry of the power relation between pupil and teacher, another and a wholly independent factor is operative. "Passion" is not helpful in identifying, much less in responding to, these aspects of the Scottish sociolinguistic context. Furthermore, to the extent that English *is* an inhibiting factor, it is not self-evident that a greater amount of attention paid to the study of Scots texts in the schools would counter it: what if we found ourselves putting our pupils in the position that many of my generation were in with respect to their French or German – able to read the language easily and write it with a high degree of grammatical and orthographic accuracy, but hopelessly tongue-tied when trying to converse in it? Again, "Middle-class objections to much of current Scots prose fiction usage seem to be more on grounds of social taste than of linguistic appropriateness." (p. 60) Perhaps, but what follows? If English teachers declines to take a lower secondary class through *Trainspotting* or *How Late it was, how Late* because of their language and content, they are hardly being unreasonable; and the argument, which they might well accept, that the language is a brilliant literary representation of the actual speech of the kind of people depicted in the novels is not in the slightest degree relevant to the position they are taking. This issue is raised again and discussed in more detail in Anne Donovan's paper "Contemporary Scottish Fiction in the Upper School." Donovan does not raise the issue of Scots and does not therefore fall into the trap of suggesting an association between Scots language and bad language; but she certainly suggests that part of the *Scottishness* of writers like Kelman and Welsh inheres in their breaching of sociolinguistic taboos. As an attempt to further the cause of Scottish literature or Scots vernacular speech, such an argument is at best, and on the kindest possible interpretation, a calculated risk.

I trust I do not need to assure anybody that I am not arguing *against* the promotion of Scots, nor denigrating the efforts or demeaning the achievements of those who are working in the field. I am merely suggesting that a number of different questions are being conflated, or at least confused, in a manner which impedes progress by over-simplifying the very complex issues.

John Hodgart, in a more substantial article entitled "The Scots Language in the Scuil", after a clear and vigorously-expressed summary of much that has been wrong with social and educational attitudes to Scots in the past, makes the rash statement "We need in fact tae accept that the 'best' Scots is whit the local weans bring tae their ain scuil in aw its varieties". (p. 86) But how can we accept anything of this kind? The statement occurs in the context of an argument against the well-established notion that the traditional rural dialects represent "good" Scots and the urban demotic forms "bad" Scots (or just bad English). Certainly this standpoint must be challenged: sociolinguistically, the emergence of low-prestige urban basilects is a common and well-attested development in industrial and post-industrial societies; structurally, such speech forms, in Scotland as elsewhere, are just as consistent and cohesive as traditional dialects; in terms of "Scottishness", Glasgow demotic as described, on different levels of scholarship, by Caroline Macafee and Michael Munro is no more like standard English than a dialect of the Doon valley. But a child's speech, whether he comes from Marchmont or Maggieknockater, is *not* "the best": children, in the nature of things, do not speak "the best" of anything. Children's use of language is immature and unpractised; and one of the central functions of education is to help them to improve it. Which at once raises the question: how do we improve the speech of a child who comes to school speaking fluent Castlemilk? The thrust of the entire book, and the orthodoxy of Scots activists and sympathisers, is that the old assumption that we improve it by making the child speak English instead is to be rejected out of hand. But then, what? Make him speak something more like a dialect of rural Ayrshire or Lanarkshire? Make him speak a richer and more sophisticated version of Castlemilk demotic? If the latter, where are our models? (To mention Billy Connolly in this context would be all too obviously a reductio ad absurdum — or *would* it?) I know of no evidence, in the book or elsewhere, that this question has even been examined, never mind answered.

Shortly afterwards, Hodgart argues: "If we only gie oor weans readin material in standard English an ask them tae dae aw their writin in it, we are no only failin tae teach them a sufficient range o linguistic skills an registers, but staun guilty o linguistic neglect bi makkin Scots weans illiterate in their native culture." (p. 88) Countless Scots from the eighteenth or even the seventeenth century to the present day acquired an excellent command of written English, retained Scots as their normal language of conversation, and were not in the slightest degree handicapped in either respect. Of course, Hodgart is arguing for a cause which we all support, that children should be taught to read and write Scots *as well as* English. But the fact that this is a desideratum does not entail the corollary that a knowledge of English is an inadequate provision for life's activities. It is certainly a valid point that monolingualism in standard literary English is a limitation to anyone's intellectual development: the intellectual and cultural advantages of bilingualism and multilingualism have been eloquently expounded by other speakers at this symposium. But is this the best argument for giving a greater degree of attention to Scots? Those who are not already committed to the Scots cause would surely maintain that a language like French or German — or one like Arabic or Chinese — would not only have greater market value but (a more academically respectable argument) would more effectively stimulate the development of the child's linguistic skills by confronting him with the structures of languages much more unlike English than Scots is. The reference to "makkin weans illiterate in their native culture" is even more assailable. It presupposes that they could and should be literate in Scots as they can be in English. But can this be sustained? In English there is a well-established culture of literacy; in Scots there is not. There are several steps to be covered, in the development of a language, between having a literature, even an extensive and splendid one, and being a language at the level of English or French. It may be said that we are trying to raise Scots to this stage; but we will not do this by simply talking as if it had already been done. A quarter of a century ago, I wrote: "We only have to imagine a national daily newspaper like *The Scotsman*, with its news articles, features, sports pages, editorials, financial and business sections and cartoons, written entirely in Scots, to see how far we are from the state of full literacy." Much has been achieved since then, but the statement is still true.

Later in the article, the same point recurs: "We need tae mak siccar that aw weans lea the scuil literate in the native tungs o Scotland as weel as oor ain distinctive form o standard English." (p. 89) *How?* If what is envisaged here is that children by the time they leave school will be able to write letters, job applications, insurance claims and the like in Scots as easily and naturally as in English, this is simply not realistic: it may become so in the future, but short of a revolution it will not occur in the school careers of today's pupils. For it to happen we will need an agreed set of canonical rules for the spelling and grammar of Scots (or one for each of the different forms of Scots); a full knowledge of these rules, and an ability to impart them over the years of children's elementary and primary education, among all teachers; a ready supply of teaching materials — text books, exercise books, audio-visual aids — and, equally important, a social context in which the teaching of Scots is accepted as a matter of course. How close are we to that? Our grandchildren may be able to ensure that their school pupils become literate in Scots as in English, but there is no point in talking as if *we* could.

In the same article, the question is asked: "Is it really no aboot time that we woke up tae this tremendous linguistic potential inherent in Scottish culture, insteid o continuin tae be obsessed wi 'correctness' an repressive monolingual policies o the past?" Certainly it is; but what if old naïve assumptions of social and linguistic correctness are merely replaced by new but equally naïve assumptions about political correctness? For that, assuredly, is an ally that Scots does not need. I have argued elsewhere that what we do *not* want for Scots is a degree of basic tolerance given on the pathetic and ridiculous ground that one speech form is just as good as another. The point has often been made that we must emancipate ourselves from the notion of "bad" Scots, just as most people (it is to be hoped) have by now emancipated themselves from the notion that Scots itself is bad English. But a simplistic "anything goes" attitude will help nothing and no-one. What we require is a far greater degree of understanding, at all levels of society, of the principles of sociolinguistics and historical linguistics, and of the Scottish language situation as exemplifying our own particular ways in which these principles are demonstrated.

An internationally-renowned language scholar like Görlach would predictably take a dim view of the over-simplifications in the present book; and the obvious counter to his criticisms is that the purpose for which the essays were written was not to provide an in-depth analysis of the past, present and potential future status of Scots. The writers are skilled, experienced and dedicated professionals in the fields of secondary and tertiary education, and their specific intention, that of providing encouragement and assistance to teachers introducing their charges to Scottish literature, is certainly fulfilled in the book. But the thought with which I want to leave you is this. Much has been achieved in the last few decades: and to counter what may have seemed an excessively negative tone to much of my talk, allow me to digress momentarily on the very real progress that has been made. The amount of published and ongoing research on Scots has increased considerably, and as it is conducted in the context of developing approaches to the general fields of sociolinguistics and historical linguistics, understanding of Scots not only in itself but as exemplifying general tendencies and principles in language behaviour is at a far more advanced level, if only among scholars. As a result of this, classroom material for teachers wishing to include Scots in the curriculum is more abundant and readily available. Scots is no longer studied in isolation: one of the outstanding achievements of the Language Committee of the Association for Scottish Literary Studies was to bring together Scots and Gaelic studies by the founding of the triennial International Conferences on the Languages of Scotland. This expansion — a combination of academic collaboration and political forging of links in the common cause — was subsequently extended to include Ulster, the words *and Ulster* being added to the title of the Forum for Research in the Languages of Scotland; and then the whole of Ireland: the fact that at this symposium we are discussing Scots as used in both the homeland and Ulster, Scottish and Irish Gaelic, and English, not to mention immigrant languages, is on any showing a sign of progress. Another is the fact that the language issue is no longer simply the province of language scholars and men of letters: the study of Scots has come out of its ivory tower into the workaday world of politics, education and social work. And the Good Friday Agreement, the advent of home rule, and in a wider context the work of the European Bureau of Lesser Used Languages, have changed irrevocably the political context of the debates: we now have an enormous advantage denied to activists of the seventies and eighties in that the legal and political rights of the Scots tongue no longer need to be argued.

And yet ... The establishment of a Scottish Parliament has not solved Scotland's problems: it has shown with daunting clarity just how grave and how deep-rooted they are, and how far we have still to go before a solution is in sight. And one of the main obstacles in our way is the abysmal level of political awareness and political sophistication in a Scotland deprived for three hundred years of a context in which these could be developed. In precisely the same way, the progress that has been made in the cause of restoring Scots to its rightful status is now forcing us to a growing realisation that the complexities and ramifications are much deeper, more far-reaching and more daunting than we may have anticipated. Scots has come out of its ivory tower, as I said a minute ago, to find that the world beyond is thick beset with thorns and briars. At this symposium we have heard several experts pointing out the defects and inadequacies of the institutional structures that exist for the teaching of Irish and Gaelic. For Scots, such institutional structures do not exist at all. Who is going to bring them into being? There are those who have made substantial and valuable contributions to the study of Scots as an academic discipline, but who have less expertise in the fields of practical sociolinguistics and sociology, less still in educational theories and methodologies, and none whatsoever in practical politics. And among the people who *are* experts in those fields, detailed knowledge of Scots and understanding of its nature and linguistic status, and commitment to he cause of developing and encouraging it, are not as common as we would like them to be.

In the domain of literature, the achievements of Hugh MacDiarmid, Sydney Goodsir Smith, Robert Garioch, Tom Scott, Alex Scott, Alasdair Mackie and their contemporaries and successors were collectively nothing short of staggering; but the negative side is this: their very magnitude proved conclusively that the desired restoration of Scots to the status of a fully-developed functioning national language was not within the power of poets alone. In the same way, the mighty works of Sir James Murray, William Craigie, Jack Aitken, David Murison, Angus McIntosh, Eugen Dieth, Jim Mather, Hans Speitel and *their* contemporaries and successors have likewise proved that it was not within the power of scholars. We need the support of those whose actions affect people's lives on a daily basis: politicians and educationists. We will not raise Scots to a position comparable to that of English, or of Gaelic, by continuing to augment the magnificent corpus of literary and scholarly work done on, in and for Scots in the last hundred years — though it goes without saying that we *will* continue to do so. These endeavours, vital as they are, can achieve no more than limited success if conducted in a context where the most elementary facts regarding language in its social, political and historical contexts — language in general and ours in particular — are as unknown as the far side of the moon to the general populace. The facts are there for all to see. Those who are unwilling to look must be made to do so. That is the task facing Scots language activists today.

References

Donovan Anne. 1997. "Contemporary Scottish Fiction in the Upper School", in MacGillivray 1997, 108-10.

Görlach, Manfred. 2002. Review of MacGillivray (1997). *Scottish Language* 21: 72-3.

Hodgart John. 1997. "The Scots Language in the Scuil" in MacGillivray 1997, 84-90.

MacGillivray, Alan. ed. 1997. *Teaching Scottish Literature: Curriculum and Classroom Applications* Edinburgh: Edinburgh University Press

Sutherland George. 1997. "Language in Scotland Today", in MacGillivray 1997, 57-63

Unblocking the Right Nostril

Sheila Douglas

William Soutar, poet o Perth, wrote in his diary on Tuesday 6th July 1943, the year o his daith, "My right nostril is Scottish, but my left is English" as a wey o expressin the orra wey Scots writers feel, no juist bilingual, but buchtin twa leids. The umquhile David Buchan distinguished professor o Scots ethnology, spak o the "Scots schizophrenia"[1] that gien the Scots o the achteenth century a feelin o dichotomy that debilitated Scottish culture an precipitatit a decline intae the vernacular o the Scots language. William McIlvanney descrieved it as "inhabiting the paradoxes of the cultural milieu. Billy Kay sees this dichotomy as no producin a clean divide atween pro-Scots and pro-English factions, but existin "within individuals who were now heir to both the Scots and the imported English tradition."[2] Een Robert Burns wis awar in his ain time that there wis a slap atween the Scots that he spak an the English he yaised for his letter tae Mr George Thomson, wha askit for English words tae Scots airs. "I have sprinkled it with the Scottish dialect,"[3] he wrote of one song, "but it may easily be turned into *correct English.*" Ithergates, he murns, "What pleases me, as simple and naïve, disgusts you as ludicrous and low."[4] At lang an last he maun girn, "These English songs gravel me to death. I have not that command of the language that I have of my native tongue."[5] But he was weel able tae yaise baith leids, juist as Willie Soutar wis, and they were baith birsit tae think ane o them the better.

Like mony Scots, I can verra weel unnerstaun thon feelin, haein graduatit in English at Glesca University in 1954, then cam tae re-discover ma Scottishness in the Fowk Sang Revival o the 1960s. Syne, I read the Medieval Makars, and the 20th century Scots Renaissance poets, as weel as discoverin the poetry o William Soutar, when I cam tae bide and teach in Perth. I can mind hou angert I wis that, in spite o bein weel schuiled in Scotland, I hadnae heard onythin o him afore. Forby that, I sang ballads and sangs and wrote baith poetry and sangs in Scots, as weel as continuin tae write in English. Someb'dy had unblockit ma richt nostril. I cuid noo breath in the air o ma ain culture and fin a vyce in whit I kent tae be ma ain leid. This hasnae stappit me fae yaisin English, but it has enlairged ma linguistic foun: I hae twa leids. There are mony ither Scots in the same set. But hoo dae we luik on it as a kinch and a cummer, a deeficulty tae fash aboot?

Raicently I wis at an international conference in Belgium whaur mony leids were spak. I haed collogues wi French an German speakin friens an forby fun that Flemish haed a wheen o Scots words intil't. English an German were the twa offeecial languages o the conference an papers were gien in baith. But the

---

[1] David Buchan, *The Ballad and the Folk*. London: Routledge and Kegan Paul, 1972; reprinted Edinburgh: Tuckwell Press, 1997.

[2] Billy Kay, *Scots: The Mither Tongue*. Edinburgh: Mainstream, 1986.

[3] Robert Burns, Letters to Mr. Thomson, quoted in James Currie, *Life of Robert Burns*, 1838, 105

[4] ibid., 106

[5] ibid. 110

"world English" o some o them wis gey queer. It wis weel descreivit by ballad scholar Tom McKean as "putting the emph*a*sis on the wrong syll*ables.*" That an ither fauts o yaisage made it a bit o an orra messen. But een in the toon o Leuven, whaur the conference wis haudit, fowk in the streets didnae juist speak different leids, but switchit fae ane til the ither athoot ony fash. In some wyes we dae that in Scotland tae, but aither we dinnae ken we're daein it or we nyte it aathegither. We maun tak tent o the fack that maist o the kintraes o Europe hiv mair nor ae leid. Scotland haesnae iver in its history been monoglot aither.

Unfortunately, many Scots people are still half-stifled by a social environment that frowns on the use of Scots for anything more important than casual conversation. Even though, as Paul Scott pointed out in *Towards Independence* in 1991 "good Scots words and the distinctive rhythms and flavour of Scots speech can still be heard every day on our streets," our schools still "correct" our speech, when we use it in the classroom.[6] There is a built-in prejudice against Scots that strangely can accept old songs, stage comedians and even old poetry, but cannot abide it when it is used in a present day context. Even among school pupils, there can be confusion, as recognised by Alan Keay of Portobello High School, whose work in getting his pupils to read, write and speak in Scots is legendary. He quotes what he describes as an "Anglophile Scotophobe" as saying, "I dinnae ken how he disnae juist gie us ordinary poems."

I had an interesting experience a few years ago when I was invited as a storyteller to evening sessions for Aberdeen primary school pupils who had come to Glenshee for ski instruction. I arrived early on the first evening and heard the pupils chattering in good Aberdeen Doric all around me. Then came the storytelling after which they were packed off to bed. I sat talking to their teachers, one of whom said, "It was so good to hear the Scots stories", adding, "Unfortunately none of our pupils speak Scots at all." When I told her that they did and I'd enjoyed listening to them before the storytelling session began, she looked puzzled. Then I suggested that they might not speak Scots to her. She agreed that that was true. When I asked her if she would mind if they did, she *said* that she wouldn't. I asked he if she had ever told them that, but she had never thought of it. She said she would do so and I would like to have believed that, but I had my doubts. Many teachers who say they have no objections to Scots being used either do nothing in practice or do the opposite. This is because of the prevailing ethos of the school environment. There is a role here for the training colleges, and, while most of them have the material that is on the market, they make little use of it. Several student teachers have contacted me for help, because, although their training colleges have the materials, they have done nothing with them.

There is also the constant repetition of the dire warning that those who use Scots are isolating themselves, but in fact in practice it is found that using Scots is a liberating experience for all concerned, the writers, the readers and the speakers. It leads to an interest in language skills and communication and increases both. It is true that resources are needed to help bring this about. We have Scots dictionaries, even one on CD ROM, and anthologies like The Kist,

---

[6] Paul Scott, *Towards Independence*, Edinburgh: Polygon, 1991, 133.

the Merlin Press material,[7] and a growing number of books and recordings specially tailored for the classroom, and most recently the Lottery-funded products of the Itchy Coo project, and Colin Wilson's excellent book and CD, *Luath Scots Language Learner*. But there seems to be an invisible brick wall that holds back their dissemination. News of the fact that there is now teaching material available to help pupils develop and build on their use of Scots has not reached a large proportion of our class teachers.

Publicity about the availability of dictionaries and teaching material has been sent to all schools but in many cases, it goes straight from the headmaster's mail in-tray to the waste paper basket. It is given no priority at all in education, but regarded at best as an optional extra. Although it is official educational policy to accept Scots in the classroom, teachers are so intimidated at the thought of re-acquiring what was beaten out of them in school, that they chicken out of trying to do it, in the absence of any form of in-service training to support it. The idea of Scottish Studies as a school subject hasn't been taken up, as the idea of ghettoising Scots doesn't appeal to anyone. What would be more acceptable would be to give all subjects a Scottish dimension, so that the whole ethos of learning would be more related to the world the children inhabit. But it needs money to do that in terms of resources and training, and that is not forthcoming. Just recently, the new Chairman of the Scottish Arts Council, James Boyle, made a strong point that the SAC should concern itself more with education and not treat the arts as an optional extra. This might signal a change in SAC policy, because at the moment they don't fund educational projects.

The situation of lack of funding, of course, exists only with regard to Scots, not to Gaelic, which has received millions of pounds, though only 2% of the population speak it. As Mike Russell MSP told the Saltire Society Conference in Edinburgh on 11 September 2002, all that funding has not increased the number of Gaelic speakers, which sadly is still falling. A Scots Executive that refuses to recognise the existence of Scots as a language does not help the situation. This negative attitude persists, although it is spoken or understood by the majority of the population, including many MSPs. The Executive continually reiterates the same old hoary excuses for not being able to define it, instead of engaging in a serious debate on the subject. There is a cross-party group in the Scots Parliament that is meant to put pressure on the Executive but so far it has not made as much progress as it would like, even though the truth is that most MSPs' constituents speak or understand Scots to varying degrees.

The language has a clearly documented origin and history, has been used for six centuries of literature, right down to the present day, so to suggest that it does not exist is absurd. This point of view takes no account of the fact that to condemn a person's language is to belittle them, brand them as inferior and cut them off from their own culture. This is what has been done to generations of Scots for three hundred years, and the scandal is it, that it has been done by Scots themselves. Thus it a hard process to reverse: the right nostril is in many cases immovably blocked and the brains of these Scots, starved of oxygen, so to speak, have lost a sense of identity, a pride in being who they are and any

---

[7] Merlin Press website is at www.sol.co.uk/m/merlinpress .

incentive to express themselves in what few of them recognise as their mother tongue..

Sae hou are we tae see Scots gien its proper place, an oor bairns their ain heritage? The answer is no haurd tae jalouse: it cuid be dune gey aisily, gin the pooers-that-be wad gie their support tae this. The problem is no tae learn oor bairns hou tae speak Scots but tae forder respeck for the leid an aa that gies it birr, sic as oor leeterature, baith fiction an non-fiction, oor theatre, oor film compnies, oor poetrie an oor sangs. Mair fowk wad accep Scots gin they saw it bein gien a heicher profile in government, education an cultur. But an aefauld request tae hae nems an witters in the Scots Parliament *in Scots* haes faan on deif lugs. Gin ye luik at the televised proceedins o the Scots Pairliament, ye'll hear Scots pronunciation, Scots vocabulary and Scots idioms bein yaised on a daily basis. Ye wadnae think ye were onywhaur else but amang Scots, yet they dinnae seem tae be awar o it. Hoo thae fowk wha are agin Scots can ken o a thae kythins o oor cultur athoot takkin tent o the fack that they are tae the fore because Scots is rael an no a feegur o fantise, is mair nor I can unnerstaun.

Or maybe I can. The haill thing is a maitter o politics. Gin they acceptit that Scots is aye leevin, they wad *hae tae* mak a draucht tae gie it a prap an a haud an they wad hae tae pit siller intil't. This cuid chynge mony things that haud back the leid. Mair o a heize cuid be gien tae Scots in oor media an Scots publishin cuid be helpit tae bide solvendie an no gae bust or get taen owre by bigger anes fae sooth o the Border. In maist o oor schuils, no jist the bairns but the teachers aaready spick Scots, een gin they dinna aa awn up til it. But they dinnae aa yaise it in the schuil, bar at Burns Suppers. Yince a year they hae leave tae yaise Scots, but the Scots o Burns poetry an sang is no the same as the Scots they spick nooadays, sae it's sauf tae thole it as a pawkie ferlie o lang syne. There are a fyowe schuils that apen their yetts no jist tae screivers an makars but tae shennachies, an I can tell ye fae haein dune it masel that the spreit o the bairns is strangly kinnlet up by the auld tales fu o the mense an smeddum o aulder generations. Whan I wrocht as an English teacher, I gied my classes a guid sairin o Scots leeterature an learned them tae scrieve in Scots. Whyles, I yaised stories tae cuddeich an bribe bairns wha were sweirt tae dae their darg. Apairt fae aa that, we maun nourrice the imaigination an the ingyne o oor bairns, the hert an the harns, in ony wey we can.

For the last five years, I have been the Scots Language Tutor on the Scottish Music Course (BASM) at the Royal Scottish Academy of Music and Drama in Glasgow.[8] From this experience, I have learned many things. The Academy felt itself obliged to appoint tutors in Scots and Gaelic, because without these languages, they would be missing out a basic element of Scots culture, that is not only in the background to the music, but is the basis of it. The "distinctive rhythms" which Paul Scott recognises in Scots speech, are what we hear in the music, as well as the vocabulary and usage to make sense of the songs. My class each year has been a unique combination of Scots from different parts of the country, as well as from English, Irish and American sources. This presents a teaching challenge greater than any other one I have faced in schools, although the classes are much smaller. As you might expect it is the non-Scots who have

---

[8] RSAMD has the same standing as a university in the awarding of degrees.

the least difficulty in accepting Scots as a language, because they can see it is both akin to but different from English. They are less surprised than the Scots to find that Danish, Norwegian, Dutch, Flemish, German and French are also related to Scots. Most of the Lowland Scots are bi-lingual, but the Highland ones, who very often have no Gaelic, have only Highland English. Some of the Lowland Scots have been to private schools which means, although they may have elected to study piping or fiddle playing, they cannot sing in Scots. Their tongues are frozen by inhibition. In my experience, this is remedied by giving them the historical facts about Scots. This makes all the difference. The different forms of Scots present no problem as most of them see that the common ground between them, the amount of vocabulary and usage that they share, is much greater than the differences of pronunciation and vocabulary, which exist in all languages anyway.

In my time at the RSAMD, I have succeeded in getting students to write songs, take part in Scots presentations and record Scottish traditional stories told in Scots. The CD is called *Aince Upon a Time*, and comes with an accompanying book. They feel they are extending themselves by doing this, acquiring skill that is relevant to their course, not exploring a blind alley or wallowing in nostalgia. Recorded material that I have given to the Music School's archive is now being used on computer within the Academy through its teaching/learning department called HOTBED, which stands for "handing on tradition through electronic dissemination." My work is in the Music School, but from the outset I have been in touch with the voice coach in the Drama School, to whom I have given tapes of different Scots dialect speakers. I have to emphasise here, that when you are dealing with the training of actors in speaking parts that require different pronunciation, books are of limited use: they need to hear the voice. That is not my opinion, but that of the voice coach. Most of the best known Scottish actors, such as Robert Carlyle, are former students of the RSAMD, so I feel I am making a small contribution to a very important course.

Maybe we are gaein forder than we think. Edwin Morgan, the Glesca Poet Laureate said in 1983, "The acceptable emergence of Glasgow speech, both as an object of linguistic study and as a medium for serious writing, is recent and still has much headway to make, but one can say today with some confidence that the long-ingrained attitudes – linguistic, social, aesthetic – which hindered that emergence have lost the almost automatic respectability they once enjoyed."[9] This is due no jist tae the poetry o Morgan hissel but tae the wark o ither Glesca poets and writers sic as Tom Leonard, Alan Spence, James Kelman, Tom McGrath an Bill Bryden. I hae aye thocht o Glesca Scots as the maist poetic an succinct o aa forms o the leid. Sae I hae fun it hard tae thole the sough o mony Scots activists agin the pith an virr o the speak o the pairt o the kintrae whaur maist Scots bide. Alang wi the vieveness o it gaes a gift for flytin, a black humour an a love o word play that maks ilka Glaswegian a scancer on the social scene. The meltin pat o the city is like the modren warld an haes the same effeck on language an cultur, sae we can dae waur nor tak tent o the wye Glesca haes

[9] Edwin Morgan, 'Glasgow Speech in Recent Scottish Literature', in *Scotland and the Lowland Tongue*, ed. J. Derrick McClure Aberdeen: Aberdeen University Press, 1983. 195-208.

haunlet this. The reconvenin o the Scots Pairliament haes brocht in a stranger sense o identity an it is great tae walk alang Sauchiehaa Street an fin Donald Dewar staunin at the heid o Buchanan Street, een tho I wadnae hae votit for his pairty. The last time I wis there, someb'dy had left a sheaf o lilies at his feet. Whither that's a wittin o the unblockin o the richt nostril, I wadnae like tae say, but I'm shair that whit Edwin Morgan said is richt: there's no the same nerra-nebbit view o Glesca Scots noo that's it's borne the gree amang the leeterary prizes.

To sum up, I think it is clear that the freeing of Scots from the inhibition against using their own tongue, while it may not be making as much progress as it should, it must inevitably take place. The fact that despite all the wailing and gnashing of teeth that has gone on for three centuries about Scots disappearing and dying, it has not happened. It's no deid yet! In the words of Paul Scott, "Scots would not have survived against all the massive pressures against it, unless it served some purpose or was seen to have some value." Poetry and prose, song and story, continue to be written and performed, and people in the community still speak it. Even in ethnic communities you will hear councillors, lawyers and business men, as well as shopkeepers and householders, who are second and third generation immigrants, speaking Scots, as well as their own native languages. Their right nostrils have been unblocked and they breath in the air of two cultures, and can speak as part of both of them. This is the way forward. As eminent writer Carl MacDougall wrote in the fifth chapter of his fascinating book *Painting the Forth Bridge* "[...] if identity is to become a recognisable part of our national life, it will have to be educated into our consciousness, and into the consciousness of successive generations, as surely as it has been educated out."[10]

---

[10] Carl MacDougall, *Painting the Forth Bridge: a Search for Scottish Identity*. London: Aurum Press, 2001, 196.

Nae Chiels: Scots Language in Scotland

Liz Niven

I was in the Netherlands in February 2001 where Mercator, the Education base for the European Network for Regional or Minority Languages, is located. Dossiers are produced for minority languages in Europe and each dossier *"gathers, stores and distributes information about the educational provision for minority languages"*. Until then, there was no Dossier for Scots and Alie van der Schaaf, the coordinator, asked if I would compile one. My first reaction was to say, "Sorry, I can't do this." In fact I did briefly attempt to say that. Why? Having read many of the other dossiers such as Frisian in the Netherlands, Basque and Catalan in Spain, Slovenia in Austria, I knew it would be an impossible task. We do not have sufficient statistics. That is why the title of this paper is "Nae Chiels". This comes from the phrases *facts are chiels that winna ding* – 'facts don't lie'.

The Minority Language Dossiers

The Dossiers follow a strict format which is the same for every minority language: foreword, introduction, pre-school education, primary education, secondary education, vocational education, higher education, adult education, educational research, prospects, and summary statistics. At a glance, it was clear there would be major gaps in statistics for Scots provision. Alie's response was that the lack of statistics would speak volumes about the treatment of Scots in Scotland. It was this perceptive comment that convinced me to attempt to compile a dossier. Hopefully, when the next edition is compiled, there will be more additions and progress will be very visible. As we go through the dossier, noting the areas which require more facts and figures, a clear picture emerges of the areas where research into Scots might be targeted. This in itself seems valuable information for the Scottish Executive, academics and students seeking research topics. In fact, as the foreword to the document states, the target group is policy makers, researchers, teachers, students and journalists and they will use the dossiers to assess developments in European minority language schooling. Most of my points will begin therefore with a *no* or a *nae* in an attempt to list areas which would provide fruitful research for Scots language.

The foreword defines regional or minority languages as:

> *languages which differ from the official language of the state where they are spoken and which are traditionally used within a given territory by nationals of the state who form a group numerically smaller than the rest of the population.*

In the case of Scots in Scotland, it might be argued that, if we consider Scots of all densities, and accept one research body's statistics, then the language is not actually spoken by a minority at all. Three million speakers in a population of six million is not a minority. Bit fir obvious reasons, we'll no go doon that road the now. The Dossier's Introduction sets out to describe the language its history, characteristics and contemporary situation. For Scots, then, its history and development from the early centuries to present day dialect variations are outlined and, importantly, its present existence on a continuum from broad Scots to Standard Scottish English. Recognition is given to the enormous barriers to Scots acceptance in society and education due to its close proximity to English and thus its frequent denigration as merely "inferior English".

The aim of the Cross Party Group on the Scots language in the Scottish Parliament is quoted, *"to promote the cause of Scots, inform Members of the culture and heritage of the language and highlight the need for action to support it."* In the autumn 2002, the group will launch a Declaration of Linguistic Rights for Scots, modelled on the Barcelona Declaration.

The controversial issue of standardisation of the language is noted in this introductory section. In general, for the reader with no knowledge or preconceptions about the Scots language, a realistic and neutral picture must be presented. It is this latter requirement that presented the greatest difficulties for me – remaining neutral. As you might imagine, after each section, where gloomy i.e. no substantial facts emerged, the desire to lament and girn was a force difficult to overcome. I achieved it but have to admit that one or two sentences were rewritten at Alie's request as being "too political". I can safely share this with you at a conference with such a title as this. It is probably unnecessary to make subjective comments anyway. As stated earlier, *nae facts are chiels that winna ding.*

All the regional dossiers present statistics about the population's language competence. The Scots dossier informs readers that the General Register Office rejected the inclusion of a Census question in 2001 and agreed to a trial question. The resultant estimate of 1.5 million speakers of Scots was followed by a research study by Aberdeen University Scots Leid Quorum which provided a figure of 2.7 million speakers. In conclusion, this section states, "According to the GRO there is not yet sufficient linguistic self-awareness amongst the Scottish populace to record statistics accurately." For many, a figure of 1.5 million, one quarter of the Scottish population, might be considered a rather healthy self-awareness – and that without any public awareness-raising campaign.

This section provides a statement about the status of the language, that Scots was given Part II recognition through the European Charter for Minority Languages, and that this, in reality, has had little effect on the treatment of the language or in its educational arrangements. I was allowed to retain this in the dossier. It's not a biased opinion. It's fact.

The official status of Scots language education, an important fact supplied in all the Dossiers, is recorded as being non-existent at the present time.

After completing a picture of the structure of the general education system in Scotland – compulsory from the ages of five to sixteen, and 95 per cent of pupils are educated in the public sector – the administration of the system is briefly presented. It is administered at two levels, at a State level through the Scottish Executive Education Department (SEED) and at local authority level with 32 local authorities providing in-service teacher training. It is pointed out that, in recent years, several functions have been devolved to parents through School Boards.

The role of Her Majesty's Inspectors of Education is described in that they are responsible for inspecting schools, assessing quality and advising on issues relating to standards. In a 1992 report on English the HMI said, "it should be the aim of English teaching throughout the secondary school to develop the capacity of every pupil to use, understand and appreciate the native language in its Scots and English forms", However, evidence suggests that rarely, if at all, do the Inspectorate enquire of schools if any Scots is being taught or studied.

The dossier then moves on to consider curriculum and assessment, beginning with the impact of the Scottish Executive's 1993 English Language 5-14 Document which aims to, "foster a sense of personal and national identity through pupils' experience and study of Scots writing and Scots song and through their conscious awareness and use of Scots language".

The reminder appears here that, in Scotland, there are National Guidelines, rather than a compulsory curriculum as in England and Wales and, presumably, Northern Ireland. Thus, although 5-14 is in theory supportive of Scots, teachers are not obliged to include it.

The Scottish Executive's *Scots Language Factsheet*, referred to in this section of the dossier reinforces the point that the curriculum is, "not prescribed by statute...responsibility rests with individual education authorities and headteachers."

Finally, reference is made to the support structure known as Learning and Teaching Scotland. This body was formed from the Scottish Consultative Council on the Curriculum and the Scottish Council for Educational Technology, and gives advice to the Scottish Executive Education Department.

So, to sum up thus far: we have *nae* single version of spoken Scots language, *nae* standardization, *nae* Census statistics, *nae* Linguistic self-awareness, *nae* Implementation of Part II recognition, *nae* Official status in the education system, *nae* Questions asked (by HMI), and *nae* Compulsion (to teach Scots). The dossier next considers provision for the language in Pre-school, Primary and Secondary education.

I will now refer to some of the significant points made in these sections.

Pre-School

In 1997 a consultation document for *Education in the Early Years* from SOEID, stated, "Discussion of educational priorities would be incomplete without special reference to Gaelic-medium pre-school education".. Despite lobbying from activists, the Early Intervention scheme launched in 1999, makes no reference to Scots. There are no qualifications for nursery teachers or assistants to train in Scots language.

Primary Education

In official documents, support exists. 5-14 English Language recognises that the language of a pupil *"will sometimes be a dialect and that pupils should be allowed to use their mother tongue throughout the school"*. There has been no formal assessment carried out to establish how widespread the teaching of Scots is in Scottish primary schools. In this writer's experience it would seem to vary greatly across the country with interested individuals teaching pupils about Scots and non-interested teachers omitting it entirely from the curriculum.

Secondary Education

The similar situation which exists in secondary education is outlined here. Subjects are not compulsory, Scots language and literature are subsumed into English teaching, if they are included at all. It is possible for an English teacher to avoid teaching anything about Scots although there is a compulsory requirement to include a Scottish text. This need not be a Scots language text. Writing in Scots is encouraged *'where appropriate'*. No pupil has yet been presented for the optional Scots Language component of Advanced Higher, an exam created three years ago.

Teaching Material

The reluctance of commercial publishers to produce Scots language materials for a relatively small market is referred to. Excellent projects such as the Kist, Channel 4's *Haud Yer Tongue* remain only partially available, the Teacher/Pupil Workbooks being out-of-print in both. The publication of *'Turnstones'* incorporating Scots and English together is a relatively new and welcome development as is the Itchy Coo Project, funded by an Arts Council Lottery award, and producing four richly illustrated books about Scottish history, Scots alphabet and retelling of Greek and Roman legends.[1] Many other small publishers are referred to but generally, the lack of support for Scots resources is highlighted here as well as in later sections.

Vocational Education

No policies or provision exists at this level.

Higher Education

Undergraduate teaching of Scots is in English Language Department at Edinburgh and Glasgow Universities. Glasgow and Aberdeen include an optional module in a Master's degree for teachers re-training for Higher and Advanced Higher curriculum.

There are no courses or certificates available for trainee teachers and any reference to the language exists through English Departments. One compulsory course exists. It is at Strathclyde University and is a two hour session on promoting Scots in the classroom. At all the institutions content is optional through students choice of Extended Study or dissertation.

There is no regular provision of Scots in-service training for teachers .

There is no Scottish Executive Education Department funding specifically for Scots.

Adult Education

There are occasional courses run through Universities but no regular provision. Many courses are more focused on cultural and historical aspects of creative writing rather than proficient Scots speaking or improving literacy. There is no establishment in the country dedicated to continuous teaching of Scots language, *nae* Pre-school Scots Policy, *nae* Qualifications in Scots for Teachers. (optional module in a Master's degree), *nae* Formal Assessment as to how widespread is Scots teaching, *nae* systematic approach to teaching Scots in Primary or Secondary, *nae* discrete Scots teaching, *nae* Examination in Scots or about Scots – except Advanced Higher Option and *naebody* has sat it – *nae* Management level discussion about language, *nae* School Policies, *nae* Resources that stay in

---

[1] The Itchy Coo imprint currently comprises the following four titles: Susan Rennie, *Animal ABC* and *Kat an Doug on Planet Fankle,* Matthew Fitt et al. *The Hoose o Haivers*, and James Robertson, *The Scottish Parliament* – see www.itchy-coo.com.

print, *nae* Regular In-service provision for teachers , *nae* seed funding for Scots, and *naewhere* to learn Scots.

Research

Although excellent post-graduate research takes place around the world, it is patchy and not systematic. There are no specific Scots departments in Scottish universities. Several bodies in Scotland focus on sociology, ethnology, Scots corpus, dictionaries both electronic and in traditional forms. There is no central bank where Scots related material can be studied or research topics discussed. There is a Scots Language Resource Centre funded by the Scottish Arts Council which is currently being restructured. It is uncertain as to how this will be organized in future but many people regard it as requiring radical change to enable it to fulfill its function as a Resource Centre for teacher use.

Prospects

It is difficult to predict the prospects for the language. It might seem that the formation of a Cross Party Group for Scots would herald a more optimistic time, but it does depend on the backing given by MSPs and by the Parliament as to how successful the Group can be.

The following statements from the Executive do not instill great confidence.

> *[The Executive] does not consider that any action is necessary to comply with the European Charter for Regional or Minority Languages [...] has not formulated any policy on the numbers of speakers of Scots [...] has not set any targets to increase the numbers of Scots speakers.*

In spite of this, the current Scots Language *Factsheet* continues to state:

> *There is therefore, continuing support on the part of the Scottish Executive, the Scottish Consultative Council on the Curriculum, and the Scottish Qualifications Authority which is designed to assist schools in making their pupils aware of the richness and diversity of language, including Scots, in introducing them to a range of Scottish literature, and in encouraging them to develop ability to understand and to communicate effectively in forms of Scots.*

Section 10 of the dossier is called "Summary Statistics". The entry under this reads, "There are no statistics available on the Scots language in education." There are *nae* plans from the Executive, *nae* Money from the Executive, and *nae* Statistics on Scots in education.

In summary, my compiling of the dossier led me to believe that we require statistics, planning and maintenance for the Scots language. Anything less would be in breach of Part II recognition by the UK government.

The Language Components of the 'Higher Still' Examinations in 'English': Confessions of an Item-Writer for a Token Exam

John Corbett

The early summer of 2000 saw the introduction of new 'Language' components into the Scottish 'Higher Still' series of examinations in 'English and Communication'. Their inclusion was the result of years of lobbying, and the initiative happened partly as a result of the controversial merger of the two examinations bodies: the more 'academic' Scottish Examination Board (SEB) and the more 'vocational' SCOTVEC, which was more popular in Further Education colleges. The SEB's examinations in English were externally assessed, and SCOTVEC's courses in 'Communication' were internally assessed but externally moderated.

When the two bodies merged to form an all-purpose exams board, the Scottish Qualifications Authority (SQA), the new 'Higher Still' series of exams in 'English and Communication' was developed in three stages, increasing in difficulty from 'Intermediate' to 'Higher' to 'Advanced Higher'. These exams are partly internally and partly externally assessed. That is, some aspects of the curriculum are assessed by teachers on a pass/fail basis in a range of formats, with external moderation, and other aspects are externally. The forms of assessment were originally broadened to include portfolios of coursework as well as traditional essay-based assessment. The transition to the new format allowed some curricular innovations, and the inclusion of specific 'Language' and 'Scottish Language' components in the curriculum as options was a considerable breakthrough. Unfortunately, recent revisions to the 'Intermediate' and 'Higher' exams have had the side-effect of pushing these topics far into the background again.[1]

To glance at current Scottish exams in English you would be forgiven for thinking that 'Language' plays a considerable part at all three levels. 'Language Study' figures largely in the assessment from 'Intermediate' to 'Advanced Higher' – however, 'Language Study' means 'Close Reading' and 'Writing'; it does not necessarily mean 'knowledge about language' in the sense of linguistic analysis and description of a systematic type. In other words, 'Language Study' aims to promote development in the key language skills, which can easily be done without explicit attention being paid to linguistic knowledge, just as driving can be taught without reference to anything that lies under a car bonnet.

Systematic linguistic study remains marginalised, but for a moment it was there, even at 'Intermediate' and 'Higher' levels. At these levels there was briefly an option to do an externally assessed 'Specialist Study' project, worth a fraction of the overall grade. Although this could be on a literary topic, there was also the

---

[1] The changes, which were prompted less by an antipathy towards language study and more by the real need to simplify the assessment burden on teachers, have not been universally welcomed by teachers: see Beth Dickson, 'Lower Yet: The Writing on the Wall' in *ScotLit*, No. 26, (Association for Scottish Literary Studies, 2002), pp. 4-5.

chance of focusing on language in this part of the course. There was indeed explicit encouragement to focus on language use locally, implicitly some aspect of Scots:

Higher Still Specialist Study: Language[2]

The candidate will identify, investigate and analyse an aspect of language use (written and/or spoken) such as:

- *personal*
- *local*
- *vocational.*

Outcome
Investigate critically a chosen aspect of language use.
The candidate will produce an extended piece of writing of between 1200 and 1800 words in which he or she reports on an investigation into a chosen aspect of language use. [...]

The extended response (hereafter referred to as the Investigation) will take the form of a detailed independent study of an aspect of language use. The material for study must be the choice of the candidate, but obviously guidance can and should be given. Ideally, candidates should feel free to choose from a range of topics or issues for language study. They should be encouraged to focus on material which they regard as stimulating. [...]

Candidates should be advised to aim for full exploration of (an) aspect(s) of the language topic. The Investigation of a specific area - such as an Investigation which examines local variations of regional dialect - could be more successful than the portmanteau piece which attempts, within the word limit, to cover sketchily the historical development of dialect.

Clearly, without the support of resources and detailed exemplars, this was asking a lot of teachers and pupils. However, it had its attractions to a significant minority, and I know of one lecturer in Further Education in a Glasgow college who successfully ran modules in language-based 'Specialist Study' as part of a 'Higher' programme in 'English and Communication' and 'Media Studies'.[3] However, recent revisions to 'Higher English' (the 'and Communication' has been dropped) mean that this promising child has been effectively strangled at

---

[2] Except where noted, all quotations about the SQA exams are taken from documents produced by the Scottish Qualifications Authority. Current documents – e.g. Arrangements documents, Specimen Papers and Specimen Answers – are available on their Website: <www.sqa.org.uk>
[3] See Lydia Rohmer's contribution to this volume.

birth: 'Specialist Study' has this year been ditched and replaced by an internally-examined 'Personal Study' component. It is still possible to choose a language-based topic for this component but the credit awarded for what amounts to a considerable amount of work is even smaller than it was before the recent revisions.

But – the dewy-eyed optimists argue – the language option at 'Intermediate' and 'Higher' levels is still there, so we must ask what it leads to. The answer is the still-substantial language options at 'Advanced Higher' level (though watch this space: we are warned that 'The Arrangements for Advanced Higher are to be updated to provide a new edition for the start of session 2003-4'). From the 2000 examination onwards, candidates have had the opportunity of not just doing 'Specialist Study' on 'Language' and 'Scottish Language' – they have had the choice of answering questions on these two topics from a menu of six in the 'Advanced Higher' examination in 'English and Communication' (the other four topics are: 'Literature', 'Scottish Literature', 'Textual Analysis', and 'Reading the Media'). Candidates normally choose one question from each topic area and spend 45 minutes on each answer. The areas covered by 'Scottish Language' and 'Language' are as follows:

Scottish Language
The use of Scots in a particular geographical area, the linguistic characteristics of Scots in informal conversation, variations in the use of Scots among older and younger people, uses of Scots in the media, and uses of Scots in contemporary literature.

Language
The use of English in a particular geographical area, variations in the use of English related to social class, variations in the use of English related to gender, the linguistic characteristics of informal conversation, and the linguistic characteristics of political communication

It is possible to write on Scottish topics for the 'Language' examination – in fact, one of the questions in the 2002 paper on political communication was an analysis of a speech made by the leader of the SNP, John Swinney, and the authentic texts chosen for the 'social class' question were transcripts of middle class and working class Ayrshire speakers.

The 'Scottish Language' questions for 2002 included the following:

> *Give an account of the influences of other languages on the development of Scots. You should base your answer on your research into the development of Scots in ONE or MORE THAN ONE geographical area.*

> *With reference to your own study of informal conversation in Scots, describe how speakers draw upon a range of linguistic resources when recounting personal narratives.*

> *Based upon your own research into variations in the use of Scots*
> *among older and younger people, discuss to what extent Scots is*
> *spoken, understood and valued in Scotland today.*

> *'There can only be limited use for Scots in the media.' Discuss*
> *this statement with reference to the use of Scots in any media*
> *text(s) you have studied.*

> *Select TWO or THREE specialised areas of Scottish life where*
> *elements of Scots language have been significantly retained. From*
> *your own research, identify those elements, account for their*
> *retention and illustrate how they are used today.*

There were also text-based questions: more transcripts of informal conversation to analyse, and contemporary literary uses of Scots to describe and comment on.

It is useful here to consider what kinds of things the item-writers had in mind when setting the questions. I set questions for the 'Language' sections, which also in principle could be answered with reference to Scottish data. The first question on the 2002 Advanced Higher examination is the following:

> *Describe in detail the distinctive features of a particular regional*
> *or overseas or 'new' variety of English you have studied. You may*
> *wish to consider features such as: vocabulary, grammar,*
> *pronunciation, context of use.*

Clearly, candidates who are looking at language variety are expected to know what the 'new' Englishes are (i.e. the relatively recent post-colonial national varieties found in India, Africa and such countries as Singapore or Malaysia), and to distinguish them from more established 'overseas' varieties as North American or Australasian national varieties. Equally, they are expected to know that within these national boundaries there are more localised 'regional' varieties, such as Yorkshire, Liverpudlian or the several varieties of Scots (as legitimate examples of 'World English'). Candidates have to know at least enough to choose what they wish to talk about – some might be hooked on *Neighbours* or the American idiom; in multicultural Scotland, some might be interested in the 'new English' of a classmate or relative; some others might be interested in exploring a local variety. Once the choice is made, the candidates are expected to be equipped to explore the different levels of language *systematically*, by looking at vocabulary, grammar, pronunciation and discourse issues (e.g. contexts of use) separately.

For example, a candidate would be expected first of all to choose a variety of Scots that he or she has been studying, such as Border Scots. An obvious way into a regional variety would be an exploration of its vocabulary. Here there are various reference books available, most obviously the *Concise Scots Dictionary,* and local guides such as Elliot Cowan Smith's *Braad Haaick* (1927), which would be available in public libraries (*The Patter* would serve a similar function for Glasgow, *Buchan Claik* for around Aberdeen, and *The Hamely Tongue* or the *Concise Ulster Dictionary* for Northern Ireland). Such reference materials could be trawled for a sample of 'local' vocabulary, such as the following items from *Braad Haaick:*

Term	Example of usage	Meaning
Eppie Suitie	*as black as Eppie Suitie*	'very black'
happenin	*a happenin yin or twae*	'occasional', 'odd'
jaappertie-jee	*it's aa ti jaappertie-jee*	'wrack and ruin'
ti pit eet on	*She can aye pit eet on*	'exaggerate'; 'talk posh'
randan	*on the randan*	'on a spree'
ratten's rest	*It's duist ratten's rest i this hoose*	'continual movement'
ti sort	*The sklater cam ti sort thi ruif.*	'mend'; 'fix'
waister	*it's thon waister o a son o his*	'worthless person'

Obviously, simply listing a set of definitions is not sufficient. The candidate would be expected to consider a number of deeper issues, such as the currency and the breadth of usage of these expressions. Interviews with different members of the local community, old and young, can give data about the currency of such expressions. Reference to other informants, to word-lists and to the *Concise Scots Dictionary* can give insights into the breadth of usage, both within Scotland and possibly elsewhere. *Waister*, however it is spelled, is only one of the items above that is used far beyond the Border dialect area.

Similar explorations can take place with reference to Scots grammar. The dictionaries can again be exploited for the grammatical information they contain. Moreover, there are an increasing number of descriptions and prescriptions, such as David Purves' *A Scots Grammar.*[4] While Purves' grammar is based on literary usages, it is still a useful starting-point for explorations of Scots morphology and syntax. It gives information, for example, on the formal elements that make up the verb in Scots:

-it (preterite/past participle)	*sortit*
-in/an (present participle)	*is/was sortin/sortan*
-ing (verbal noun)	*the sorting o the mail*

It also has an extensive section on idioms, showing how different words combine in Scots phrases, for example:

> *I'm away tae my bed.*
> *See thon Mr Frazer, he's that doitit gettin.*

As with the exploration of vocabulary, it would not be enough simply to list such features of Scots. Evidence of data-gathering and analysis are essential – and so the candidate would be expected to have identified a set of such features and done some systematic fieldwork to establish whether they were still current, and how widely they were used.

Questions of pronunciation are amongst the most difficult, perhaps, for teachers and pupils at secondary level to address, since they demand a certain amount of phonetic awareness. In brief, candidates should ask questions such as:

---

[4] David Purves, *A Scots Grammar: Scots Grammar and Usage* 2nd edition (Edinburgh: Saltire Society, 2002)

> *(a) What distinctive features of regional pronunciation are there?*

Reference material on phonetics can be found once more in the dictionaries, and in new teaching materials, such as *Scotspeak,* a guide to the pronunciation of modern urban Scots.[5]

> *(b) How are these features represented in local 'dialect literature'?*

A legitimate question to pursue is how regional and social pronunciation features are represented in local writing. For example, the larger number of diphthongs used in Borders accents is evident in such spellings as *yowes* ('ewes') in 'Ca' the yowes tae the knowes'.

Finally, the candidate would be expected to ask whether the variety of Scots under investigation was used mostly in certain contexts, e.g. by particular age groups, in speech or writing, in literary or discursive writing, in formal/informal social settings, by males more than females or vice versa, in certain types of workplace but not others, etc.

A discussion of these contexts of use could lead naturally to a discussion of the prospects for survival of the variety under consideration – is it used mainly by older generations, for example; or mainly in the types of traditional industries that are disappearing? Or is the variety associated with growing or popular aspects of community life? Is it represented in the media (in local radio, in the local press, or on websites)?

Ideally, then, the candidate's answer should be a mixture of reading and fieldwork. He or she should display accurate knowledge of appropriate linguistic terminology and the ability to apply it to observation and investigation of his or her social world. Crucially, the candidate should not just be memorising out-of-date linguistic 'facts' but rather becoming, in effect, a trainee researcher.

Much of the material collected for this question in 'Language' could also be used in the corresponding 'Scottish Language' question on varieties of Scots (although the 2002 paper required candidates choosing this topic to address the specific issue of the relationship of a 'local' Scots to Scots in general).[6]

These two questions focus on the familiar methods and issues of old-fashioned dialect study. Not all the 'Language' and 'Scottish Language' questions do this. In both the 'Language' and 'Scottish Language' sections of the Advanced Higher paper, there also transcriptions of recorded speech for discussion. This year the 'Scottish Language' paper had interviews with Scottish punks at a rock concert, while the 'Language' paper had interviews with middle and working-class Ayrshire speakers. The 'Scottish Language' paper asked candidates to focus on linguistic characteristics of informal conversation, whilst the 'Language' paper

---

[5] Christine Robinson and Carol Ann Crawford, *Scotspeak* (Perth: SLRC, 2001)

[6] There is obvious overlap between the 'Language' and 'Scottish Language' topics. The grapevine suggests that the promised revision to the Arrangements in 2003-4 will merge the two sections into a single paper on 'Language'. The grapevine suggests that 'Literature' and 'Scottish Literature' will be similarly merged, which, if it happens, will undo another few decades of lobbying.

asked candidates to focus on issues of class. These questions refer more to techniques and issues in conversation analysis and sociolinguistics. One legitimate question is whether teachers have enough background in language studies to be able to prepare candidates adequately for these kinds of question.

All examinations are fallible human constructions, of course, and the 'Advanced Higher' language components are no different. They are the usual compromise between different individuals with differing agendas. Given the lack of models in Scotland for language curricula, the original blueprint was drafted by tertiary-level scholars in the field, and based loosely on their respective universities' first-year courses. It was then taken, humanised and made slightly more teachable at secondary level by task groups of interested lecturers, teachers and educational consultants. I joined the team of item-writers for the 'Language' components late in the day, in 2001, and I've contributed questions to the 2002 and 2003 papers. Four of us get together three or four times a year, contribute our questions and critique the others, until we come to what we think are acceptable sections for the overall exam. These then go through a further 'editing' process by person or persons unknown and the exam eventually appears. Marking is made much easier by the fact that to date not a single candidate has been entered for the 'Advanced Higher' language options.

At first glance, the level is probably too high – the questions still would not be out of place in university examinations. In fact, some of them are not unlike questions I've set on university courses I teach. However, the level of response expected from upper-level schoolchildren is slightly less sophisticated than you would hope for from an experienced undergraduate. The questions allow the topic of 'Scots' to be approached from a number of directions:

1. Pupils can use their background reading in conjunction with their observation to give a characterisation of the language of their local community.
2. Pupils can think about and talk about issues pertaining to social class and language – they can reflect, indeed, on what education is *doing* to their use of language.
3. Pupils can explore cross-generational speech within their own family or community, and become better acquainted with the speech of their immediate ancestors.
4. Pupils can reflect on the use of Scots in the media and ask why it might be deemed appropriate to comedy and drama but not, say, current affairs reporting.
5. Pupils can explore the different varieties of literary Scots.
6. Pupils can explore those areas of life (traditional industries, the law, the kirk, schooling) where Scots is still used today.

None of these topics is beyond the capacity of a bright and motivated teenager; however, both pupil and teacher need to be supported by accessible materials[7]

---

[7] Learning and Teaching Scotland (LTS) has produced some Staff Notes for the 'English and Communication' exams: however, Charles Jones, *English and Communication: Language: Staff Notes and Annotated Bibliography* [*Advanced*

and confident that their hard work is going to be given credit by a system that keeps changing its mind about what is going to be assessed and how. They also need to have been trained to think in a clear and systematic way about levels of language use: pronunciation, vocabulary, grammar and discourse. They need to have spent time developing analytical skills at lower levels of the school – even in the 5-14 curriculum.

In principle, pupils also have the right to explore language topics using Scots as a medium of written academic communication. How that would be dealt with I do not know – the one candidate I heard of who wished to write answers for the 'Advanced Higher' paper in Scots was apparently dissuaded by his Head of English, a man who is a kenspeckle supporter of Scottish literature and who actively encourages writing in Scots at all levels in his school. The teacher's concern, as I understand it, was that in order to deal with sophisticated linguistic topics, the pupil was busy devising an idiosyncratic extended Scots whose external validity he was unsure of. The possibility of marking this candidate's submissions caused some debate but since the candidate did not in fact sit the exam, the issues are still unresolved. Indeed, like many aspects of the curriculum they sound progressive, but they have hardly begun to be thought through. We desperately need the awkward experience of dealing with real, live candidates.

In short, then, the transition to Higher Still opened up possibilities, but the downside is that the period of transition has also been marked by prolonged agonising and abrupt changes, so new (and possibly short-lived) innovations are rightly regarded with suspicion by an educational workforce whose conservatism can be understood as a means of safeguarding their pupils' best interests as well as their own sanity.

I am disappointed but I am not entirely surprised at the examination's total lack of take-up so far. Still, I have a fondness for this unloved exam. The madly optimistic idea was that, eventually, interested teachers and pupils would gradually develop pupils' skills of linguistic description and analysis as they progressed through the 5-14 curriculum to the Intermediate and Higher curricula. Pupils would look at how they construct, negotiate, maintain and evolve their personal, regional and national identity in and through language, and they would consider the role of language in our social and working life. They would develop a basic set of descriptive skills and a technical vocabulary that would be ready, come Advanced Higher, to address the challenge of confronting some more sophisticated texts and linguistic concepts. As supporting materials slowly come on-line (and some are beginning to, such as the 'Language into Languages Learning' cd-rom that aims to support English and Modern Languages teachers and pupils by giving them a common descriptive vocabulary for linguistic concepts[8]), then the language options should become more attractive, particularly

---

Higher] (Glasgow: LTS, 2001) is probably pitched at too high a level for secondary schools. Unfortunately, misprints also render it confusing. William Hershaw has produced for LTS a useful guide to Scottish language resources, but his guide also serves to highlight the scarcity of suitable materials. A whole series of specifically-targeted language titles is urgently required.

[8] University of Glasgow, *Language into Languages Teaching: A Staff Resource for Scottish Primary and Secondary Schools*, (Scottish Executive, 2001).

for those pupils who are less interested in the traditional canons of literature (or even 'Backstage with Boyzone', one of the current suggested texts for Close Reading at Intermediate level) but who might be interested in exploring the way language is used across different generations in their own family, or by different members of their local community, or by the different nations making up their state. I am still an optimist enough to hope that this ideal will come to pass. But I am realistic enough to know that it will not come to pass without a number of factors being in place: support materials, clearer guidelines, teachers trained specifically to deliver the curriculum and a curriculum that is stable enough to be relied upon for more than a couple of years.

I suspect – possibly pessimistically – that the writing is on the wall for the Advanced Higher. Even token exams disappear if no-one loves them. I hope, however, that its very existence has established a precedent that will allow it to be replaced by something more rather than less ambitious. Ironically, we may be forced to look south of the border, to England, to show us the way. As a minor contributor to the recent 'great educational debate' in Scotland, I wrote to the Scottish Education Minister, asking for consideration to be given to a new, separate 'Language Studies' qualification. This could indeed allow for the progressive development of linguistic production, understanding, description and analysis right through the 5-14 and Higher Still curriculum. It could focus on language as it is used in Scotland – Scots, Gaelic, English, Sign, Community Languages, and it could support the acquisition of other modern languages by teaching the kind of cross-linguistic knowledge they do not have the time or space or inclination to include. It could even give space to writing in Scots for the minority of teachers and pupils interested and motivated enough to explore this area. I received a polite note to the effect that a new National Qualification would need substantial evidence of parental demand and of expertise amongst the professionals who would teach and assess it. Still, looking towards England, it is remarkable that in the period between 1994-2000 numbers taking 'A Level English Language' increased while numbers taking 'English Literature' decreased:

> While numbers taking English Literature fell by around 10,000 over the period, from 64,000 to 54,000, those taking the other two subjects [i.e. English Language or joint English Language and Literature] rose from 24,500 to 33,000, a rise of 8,000.[9]

About 14,000 pupils were taking 'English Language' as a separate 'A Level' by 2000, the year that the nod towards language study in the Scottish 'Advanced Higher' came on line. Partly this seems to be because Language Studies is seen as a better 'fit' than Literary Studies with popular newer topics such as Media Studies. So, I remain hopeful that if we can convince the Scottish Executive and the SQA that there *is* parental demand and expertise in Scotland to match that of our English cousins, then I will in future no longer be – guiltily – writing items for what amounts to a token examination.

---

[9] Sadie Williams, *Admission Trends in Undergraduate English: statistics and attitudes.* English Subject Centre Report No.1 (April 2002), p. 14. See also the discussion in 'The Common English Forum' in *The English Association*, No. 169 (Spring 2002), pp. 3-4.

Specialist Study of Language within the English Higher Curriculum: Approaches to Practice

Lydia Rohmer[1]

Aim

The aim of this paper is to provide a case study exemplifying an approach to Specialist Study: Language (*SSLa*) within the Scottish New National Qualifications (NQ) English and Communication curriculum at 'Higher' level[2]. Firstly, I would like to delineate the scope of this study, clarifying the context in which SSL takes place and outline the assessment requirements attached to this study as part of the English Higher. Furthermore, I am going to expound approaches to 'delivery' or facilitation of *SSLa* within the curriculum and briefly discuss some student exemplars of *SSLa*. I shall conclude with a summary of approaches which have proved worthwhile in the classroom and those which have not, as well as suggestions how these approaches to *SSLa* can be adopted within the recently revised English Higher[3] curriculum through the unit 'Personal Study'[4].

Disclaimer

I have to begin this paper with a disclaimer: I offer these thoughts on integrating *SSLa* into the English Higher curriculum not as an 'expert' in the sense of having any specialist knowledge on the basis of which I may be able to offer a valid and reliable theoretical framework for language study in the classroom *per se*, but as a 'practitioner' who has been involved in the facilitation of *SSLa* projects for the last few years as part of preparing students for the English and Communication Higher course assessments. A further disclaimer is necessary: until June 2002, *SSLa* has formed part of the English and Communication Higher course. Whilst the subject of this paper is based on the approaches to a unit which no longer

---

[1] This paper was originally presented at the Association of Scottish Literary Studies Conference on *Language in the Scottish School Curriculum* at University of Glasgow on 4 October 2002. I am most grateful to John Kirk for the invitation to publish the paper here. On that occasion, the other papers presented were by John Corbett, who presented a version of the paper in the present volume, Matthew Fitt, who introduced the Itchy Coo series of readers (see www.itch-coo.com), and Jim McGonigal, who discussed the need for teachers to have a knowledge about language in order to teach it.

[2] Scottish Qualifications Authority. 1999. *National Course Specification and Arrangements for C039 12 English and Communication Higher*, version 04. Glasgow/Dalkeith: Scottish Qualifications Authority. 66-72

[3] Scottish Qualifications Authority. 2002. *National Course Specifications and Arrangements for C115 12 English Higher*. Glasgow/Dalkeith: Scottish Qualifications Authority

[4] ibid. 36-48

forms part of the revised NQ English Higher course, it nevertheless may be of interest to those who may wish to adopt these approaches for their facilitation of the new 'Personal Studies' unit. Hence, this paper stakes a claim to currency. More thoughts on this are offered at the end of this paper.

Why 'Specialist Study: Language'?

With the overwhelming majority of Scottish centres successfully offering 'Specialist Study: Literature' as part of the English and Communication Higher course, the question arises as to the rationale of the choice of the *SSLa* option instead.

Candidates undertaking the English and Communication Higher course at a Further Education College usually present with a rather diverse entry profile in terms of prior academic achievement, age, social and cultural background, and expectations for career progression. In general, language skills are in need of improvement, and a contextualised approach which bridges the gap between the academic and vocational promises to be more successful. Furthermore, improvement of language skills through an extended investigative individual project was seen to support the vocational direction of the wider programme of study the candidates were undertaking at the same time as studying for English and Communication Higher, as well as helping candidates move closer towards their stated career aim, namely entry of the communication and media industries.

Context

The context of the study for English and Communication Higher was set against the wider context of study for the programme of Scottish Group Award: Communication and Media (Higher), a one year, full time National Qualification. Approaching the English and Communication Higher course as part of this programme suggested the exploration of curricular links to the other two courses studied at Higher level, namely *Media Studies* and *Advertising, Marketing and Public Relations*.

To enlarge further on the curricular context, candidates were expected to enter the English and Communication Higher course with a skill level at or equivalent to Standard Grade English at Credit level ('1' or '2'), as well as draw on skills gained in individual SGA programme units, particularly from the units 'Research Skills', 'Internet' and 'Information Technology'[5]. Having achieved these units prior to commencing the *SSLa*, candidates would be assumed to have skills at Higher and Intermediate 2 levels for identification of information sources, retrieval of information from information sources; evaluation of information and

---

[5] Scottish Qualifications Authority. 1998. *National Unit Specification for D669 12 Research Skills (Higher)*, Glasgow/Dalkeith: Scottish Qualifications Authority; Scottish Qualifications Authority. 1998. *National Unit Specification for D01D 11 Information Technology (Intermediate 2)*, Glasgow/Dalkeith: Scottish Qualifications Authority; Scottish Qualifications Authority. 1999. *National Unit Specification for D096 11 The Internet (Intermediate 2)*, version: 03. Glasgow/Dalkeith: Scottish Qualifications Authority;

information sources; essay and report writing; competent use of online information systems and baseline word-processing, database and graphic communication. Given the range of these skills and the time which has to be allocated for their development, the timing of the *SSLa* within the curricular year is of special importance. There is little sense in commencing the project too early in the academic year if the skills required have not yet been attained by the candidate; On the other hand, the project must not be started too late, allowing not enough time for the candidate's data gathering, analysis, reflection and writing-up, given the deadline for inclusion in the externally assessed Personal Studies Folio at the end of April in the academic session.

The *SSLa* is designed with a nominal unit length of 20 hours. Given a holistic approach to the unit as part of the English and Communication Higher course, the scheduling of the project does not lend itself to 'block'-delivery. Enough time needs to be allowed for project planning, research, drafting and re-drafting of the project in the lead up to the final submission. A timeline for schedule may look like Figure 1.

English and Communication Higher course elements across academic year	Sep	Oct	Nov	Dec	Jan	Feb	Mar	Apr	May
Language Study									
Literary Study									
Specialist Study: Language									
Individual Oral Presentation									
Personal Studies Folio									
External Assessment (Exam)									

Figure 1: Scheduling of *SSLa* within Academic Year

Assessment Requirements

The *SSLa* has a single unit outcome, namely a 'critical investigation into an aspect of language use' which is not otherwise taught in class. The investigation must be presented in essay or report format of 1200-1800 words in length. The investigation must be carried out independently by the candidate under limited tutor supervision. The supervision may take the form of guidance, but not direction.

The standards to which candidates need to carry out the investigation are similar to all other units which form the mandatory parts of the English and Communication Higher curriculum, namely 'understanding' (of "key elements characteristic features and significant details of language use"[6]); 'analysis' (of the "ways in which key elements and characteristic features of the nominated aspect(s) of language use contribute to meaning/effect/impact"[7]); 'evaluation' (in terms of "clear engagement with the nominated aspects of language use, substantiated with detailed and relevant evidence"[8]); and, finally, 'expression' ("structure, style and language, including use of appropriate critical terminology, are deployed to communicate meaning clearly and develop a line of thought which is consistently relevant to purpose [...]"[9]).

Induction

As *SSLa* is not a 'taught' unit, the main function of the tutor is in the role of facilitator of a successful project. A key element is the proper delivery of induction to this unit. Candidates need to be reminded of their familiarity with the performance criteria, the reading and analysis activities from other units of the English and Communication curriculum, as well as skills and concepts acquired from the other two Higher courses in 'Media Studies' and 'Advertising, Marketing and Public Relations'[10].

Commencing the *SSLa*, candidates already have acquired project planning and evaluation skills from units such as 'Research Skills' studied earlier in their programme; writing skills for report and essay writing required in the mandatory units Language and Literary Study in the English and Communication Higher course. From 'close reading' activities and 'textual analysis' undertaken in these units, candidates have also acquired tools for critical evaluation of points of view and have learned to develop a stance in engaging with 'text'. The use of these tools is concomitant with the acquisition of critical concepts within the 'Language Study' and 'Literary Study' units, as well as the 'Media Analysis' unit within the Media Studies Higher course.

The next step of induction needs to be a facilitation of the selection of a suitable topic. Here it is important to stimulate candidates sufficiently by building up an awareness of the language(s) they themselves find themselves immersed in everyday contexts and by looking at aspects of language use which may be relevant to themselves. These may be personal, local or vocational language use, to name but a few examples.

---

[6] Scottish Qualifications Authority. 1999. *National Course Specification and Arrangements for C039 12 English and Communication Higher*, version 04. Glasgow/Dalkeith: Scottish Qualifications Authority. 68
[7] ibid.
[8] ibid.
[9] ibid.
[10] Scottish Qualifications Authority. 1999. *National Course Specification and Arrangements for C058 12 Media Studies Higher*, version 03. Glasgow/Dalkeith: Scottish Qualifications Authority; Scottish Qualifications Authority. 2000. *National Course Specification and Arrangements for C01H 12 Advertising, Marketing and Public Relations*. Glasgow/Dalkeith: Scottish Qualifications Authority

Personal Aspects of Language Use

Candidates are encouraged to look at their very own use of 'slang' or 'informal register'; language use associated with clubbing, a particular hobby or leisure pursuit, a particular 'sub-culture' they know of or belong to; their own language behaviour when using the internet communication tools, such as email, instant messaging and chat rooms; their own language use of SMS text messaging when using their mobile phones.

Local Use of Language

Candidates could think about the use of accent, dialect or language use in their family; e.g. analysing family conversations where several generations take part; the language used by children, adolescents, parents and grandparents; what are the differences in lexical choice, speech patterns, speech acts, accents, dialects, etc.). Beyond the family, candidates could investigate language use in a particular part of their local or regional area, investigating, for example, occasions when people use formal register or standard language and when they slip into semiformal or informal registers. A similar investigation could be undertaken in bi- or multilingual communities: when do members of these communities use their native language and in which situations do they use their second language?

Suggestions for areas of study

Please note:
The following are general suggestions for possible areas of study. They are NOT fully worked topics for your specialist study. As the specialist study is an independent project with limited tutor support, YOU will need to decide on the details of your topic. Your tutor will give you guidance on how to present your chosen topic and outline in class.

1. *The language of 'gender' in advertising (media: print; TV; Radio; cinema; internet).*
2. *The language of party politics (individual political parties or individual politicians within parties).*
3. *The language of newspaper headlines (compare broadsheets and tabloids).*
4. *The language of sports commentary (any sport; media: Radio; TV; print; internet).*
5. *The language of news commentary: comparison of comment on one chosen event in different publication of the same medium or different media (media: print; TV; Radio; internet).*
6. *The language of subcultures (local; global; internet).*
7. *The language used in the labeling of beauty products (any advertising medium).*
8. *The language of medical soaps (medium: TV).*

9. The language of science fiction *(medium: print; TV; film; Radio; internet).*

10. The language in a *novel/poem/short story/play/screen* – or *radio script known to you. (This must be a piece of writing NOT studied elsewhere as part of the English and Communication course).*

Vocational Use of Language

Candidates could look at the use of language in a particular aspect of their course of study, for instance the use of technical language or jargon within the field of Media Studies or in a particular vocational area, such as Advertising, Marketing and Public Relations or Journalism, Law, Medicine or Politics. This exploration and exemplification of what might constitute a suitable topic for language investigation is rather important for most candidates in order to break through the barrier question of the 'legitimacy' of a particular topic for the *SSLa*. The purpose of this approach is to give candidates a cognitive framework within which they can understand the investigation of language use as a possible tool to explore their own social and cultural identity. Hence, candidates were asked to choose their area of language investigation on the basis of language use familiar to them and in the context of their own interests. Furthermore, they were asked to ensure that the language 'data' used for their *SSLa* was suitably accessible and that their topic allowed them to build on their own strengths, both in terms of analysis as well as composition.

Completing the induction stage of their *SSLa*, candidates were given examples of available from Scottish Qualification Authority's (SQA) National Assessment Bank[11], as well as projects from previous successful candidates. Candidates were then ready to be moved on to the Project Planning stage of their *SSLa*.

The Planning Stage

In the first instance, candidates were required to produce two planning documents: a topic and project outline, emphasising the area of investigation and methods of data collection; and a full project plan, following agreement of the topic and project outline with the tutor.

Some tutor-led support was required in thinking through concepts such as 'data' and 'data collection' at this stage. It was important that candidates understood that 'data' could be either spoken language accessed through, for example, interviews/transcripts, questionnaires or taped recordings of both radio and TV programmes, or songs; or that 'data' could be derived from any source of written language; or, that 'data' could be derived from a combination of both spoken and written language sources.

At the planning stage, particularly when formulating a detailed project plan, candidates were encouraged to ask critical questions of their data. The ability to

---

[11] Scottish Qualifications Authority. 1999. *National Assessment Bank D214 12/001 Intermediate 2 and Higher English and Communication: Specialist Study: Language.* Glasgow/Dalkeith: Scottish Qualifications Authority

think through possible questions before settling for a final topic helps candidates to both 'visualize' the investigation process and formulate effective research questions. Small group activities such as 'Brainstorming' and 'Mind-mapping' were particularly useful in this context, not least in engendering a shared 'investigation' experience amongst the candidates.

The kind of critical questions candidates were encouraged to ask of their data were those typically associated with any kind of investigative reportage: 'what', 'where', 'why', 'when', 'who' and 'how'? *What* is the purpose of the 'text' or 'data' investigated? *Where*, in what situations or context does this language use occur? *Why* is this particular language used? *When* or on what occasions does this language use occur? *Who* uses this language and who or what audience is it aimed at? *How* or in what style or register is the language used to achieve a particular purpose and reach a particular audience?

In this context, candidates were asked to apply critical concepts for language analysis, such as 'phonology', 'graphology', 'syntax', 'semantics' and 'pragmatics'. In general, candidates responded much better to an inductive, rather than a deductive approach in dealing with these concepts in a way which can be expected of them at this stage and level of study. Formulating critical questions by themselves, candidates went a considerable way towards a competent use of the related critical concepts. An investigation of the sound of spoken data in terms of patterns and rhythms, stresses, etc. would introduce the concept of 'phonology'; an investigation of how the written data appears on the page, poster or screen would introduce 'graphology'; analysis of a particular use of structure, lexical choice, punctuation and sentence types may introduce 'syntax'; an analysis of why particular words were chosen, of their intended connotative or denotative meaning, may introduce 'semantics'; and finally, following questions like 'who is using this language?', 'in what situation(s)?', and 'for what purpose(s)?', may help to introduce 'pragmatics'.

In completing their planning stage, candidates needed to have a clear vision of the scope of their language investigation, how and when they were going to access their data, the methods they would deploy for their analysis and an action plan with time lines for each research task, including draft and final submission dates.

Implementing the *SSLa* Project

Moving on to the implementation of the *SSLa*, candidates were encouraged to create databanks of primary, secondary and tertiary data (again, skills acquired earlier in the programme for the unit 'Research Skills') and to apply their critical questions to this data, making notes of their findings at all stages. Candidates had access to College resources, such as minidisk recorders, video recorders, use of the College Radio Station and IT-facilities and were encouraged to use these.

Writing up a draft version of the *SSLa*, candidates needed to think about the best way of presenting their data, either in report or essay formats. A draft in their chosen format needed to be presented at the time agreed in the candidate's project plan. The draft should, like the final version, include a statement of intent, methods used, the analysis of the data, a conclusion and reference to sources used. Following tutor feedback, candidates have an opportunity to re-draft, taking tutor comments on board and submit the piece for internal or unit assessment. Candidates are given time to prepare the piece for inclusion in the externally assessed 'Personal Studies Folio'.

Looking over *SSLa* projects submitted over the last few years, it is noteworthy that some candidates have excelled here despite only moderate achievements in the mandatory parts of the English and Communication course, not least because they experienced 'ownership' of their project. At best, the projects reflect considerable richness of critical engagement with 'language'. *SSLa* project titles included:

> *"Phonesthesia and its application in brand names"*
> *"An investigation into the language used by contemporary female songwriters in their lyrics in order to define the term 'psychobabble', focusing on the lyrics of Alanis Morissette"*
> *"The Language of Profits - an investigation into how the term 'free trade' is used by both sides of the economic divide in the context of 'globalisation'"*
> *"Tabloid Hysteria versus Broadsheet Rationale - an analysis of the language used by tabloid and broadsheet press in the coverage of the events on 11/9/01"*
> *"The Slang used in "Goodfellas" (screenplay by Martin Scorsese and Nicholas Pialeggi) - an analysis of use, effect and impact"*
> *"The evolution of a racist slur - an examination of the modern usage of the racist slur 'nigger' "*

The diversity of approaches and topics reflects the diverse identities of the candidates, their different experiences of language, culture and society.

Conclusion

Summarising the approach to practice for the facilitation of the *SSLa*, I would like to offer the following thoughts: what has worked for candidates is a cross-curricular, holistic approach which links up skills and concept-acquisition both within the English and Communication curriculum as well as other relevant subjects studied with the programme; tutor focus on individual learners needs, knowledge and interests and making the *SSLa* topic directly relevant to the candidate's linguistic experience of their own social and cultural identity; tutor facilitation of the candidate's 'ownership' experience of the *SSLa* project; tutor guidance through thorough project planning and candidate's application of project management skills; and, finally, the timing of the project at the appropriate juncture in the curricular programme.

In terms of 'bad practice', *SSLa* projects, not unlike other types of projects, have become problematic in the past when candidates chose too wide or vague a subject area for investigation; they have not developed a detailed enough project plan, not having asked sufficient critical questions of their data; and, consequently, when candidates 'describe' their data instead of engaging in analysis and evaluation. Major problems also occur when candidates do not have the ready access to data they originally had intended or stated in their project plan; when they do not log, store and manage their data sources appropriately; when they do not follow agreed timelines of their project plan; and, finally, when a candidate does not produce a project draft, but a final submission instead. The latter presents difficulties for assessment, as the project cannot be properly authenticated as being the work of the candidate; and, more gravely, any serious omissions or deficiencies cannot be properly rectified at this stage through timely guidance.

Outlook

As indicated at the beginning of this paper, the English and Communication National Qualifications have been subject to recent revision, resulting in the replacement of all options within the course (Specialist Studies (Language as well as Literature) and oral/aural communication elements) with the new unit 'Personal Study'. The revision has resulted, as has been argued, in a distinct lack of emphasis on language study and communication elements, which not least has manifested itself in a change of course title from 'English and Communication' to 'English'. However, I would argue that the 'Personal Study' unit offers a place for language investigation for those who wish to integrate this into their approach to the revised NQ English Higher course. Like the *SSLa*, 'Personal Study', both in its written[12] or spoken response[13] versions, is a project based on an agreed topic. As it was designed to replace both specialist studies as well as oral/aural communication options, it has a notional design length of 40 hours (instead of the 20 hours allocated to each of the previous options). In terms of content and context, it allows considerable freedom for a candidate to chose a project topic, drawing on a merged set of parameters stemming from the arrangements of both specialist studies, as well as the oral/aural units of the original course. Language investigations are explicitly referred to as a legitimate topic choice. The assessment outcome of Personal Study is either a one hour assessment in which the project findings are written up in form of a critical essay (for the 'written response') or a 10 minute oral presentation of the project outcomes (for the 'spoken response') with an option to deliver in Scots. Whilst the assessment outcome has been modified, the project activities I have exemplified for *SSLa* above can be adopted for either version of the unit 'Personal Study'.

---

[12] Scottish Qualifications Authority. 2002. *National Course Specifications and Arrangements for C115 12   English Higher.* Glasgow/Dalkeith: Scottish Qualifications Authority. 36-41
[13] Scottish Qualifications Authority. 2002. *National Course Specifications and Arrangements for C115 12   English Higher.* Glasgow/Dalkeith: Scottish Qualifications Authority. 42-48

Irelands, Scotland, Education and Linguistic Human Rights: Some International Comparisons[1]

Tove Skutnabb-Kangas

> Some people have described Kaurna language as a dead language. But Kaurna people don't believe this. We believe that our language is a living language and that it has only been sleeping, and that the time to wake it up is now and this is what we're doing (Cherie Watkins in *Warranna Purruna – Pa:mpi Tunganar – Living Languages* video, DECS, 1997, quoted in Amery 1998: 1).

1. Introduction: Mother tongue medium education - the most important linguistic human right for the survival of a language

Some of the basic linguistic human rights of individuals in education have, in my view, to do with the following rights: the right to identify with one's mother tongue(s) and have this identification accepted and respected by others, to learn one's mother tongue properly, both orally (if that is physiologically possible) and in writing, the right to use one's mother tongue in most official situations, including as a medium of education in at least primary education, the right to become bilingual, i.e. to learn an official language in addition to the mother tongue, the right not to change one's mother tongue except voluntarily, and the right to profit from education, regardless of what one's mother tongue is (see Table 1, from Skutnabb-Kangas 2000: 502). Linguistic human rights in education, especially the right to mother tongue medium education, are needed for several reasons. I shall now list six of them.

Reason 1. Counteracting "illiteracy"

The first reason is to counteract so called illiteracy. The most important PEDAGOGICAL reason for "illiteracy" is the wrong medium of teaching. Indigenous and minority children and children from dominated groups are taught subtractively. **Subtractive teaching** means that indigenous or minority children (or dominated majority children, for instance in many African and Asian countries) are taught through the medium of a dominant language which replaces their mother tongue. They learn the dominant language at the cost of the mother tongue. Instead, they should be taught additively.

It takes many years to become profoundly literate. If one only needs the technical skill to decode text, that can be achieved in 1 – 2 years of formal

---

[1] Some parts of this article draw on my recent books and articles, especially Skutnabb-Kangas 2000, but also others listed in the bibliography.

Table 1. Linguistic human rights of individuals in education

> ## A UNIVERSAL COVENANT OF LINGUISTIC HUMAN RIGHTS SHOULD GUARANTEE AT AN *INDIVIDUAL* LEVEL, IN RELATION TO
>
> ### THE MOTHER TONGUE(S)
>
> that everybody has the right to:
> • identify with their mother tongue(s) and have this identification accepted and respected by others;
> • learn the mother tongue(s) fully, orally (when physiologically possible) and in writing[2]. This presupposes that minorities are educated mainly through the medium of their mother tongue(s), and within the state-financed educational system;
> • use the mother tongue in most official situations (including schools).
>
> ### OTHER LANGUAGES
>
> • that everybody whose mother tongue is not an official language in the country where s/he is resident, has the right to become bilingual (or trilingual, if s/he has 2 mother tongues) in the mother tongue(s) and (one of) the official language(s) (according to her own choice).
>
> ### THE RELATIONSHIP BETWEEN LANGUAGES
>
> • that any change of mother tongue is voluntary (includes knowledge of long-term consequences), not imposed.
>
> ### PROFIT FROM EDUCATION
>
> • that everybody has the right to profit from education, regardless of what her mother tongue is.

[2.] An alternative formulation (instead of referring to sign languages through the 'orally (when physiologically possible)' was suggested by Timothy Reagan (personal communication, December 1998): '... learn the mother tongue(s) in natural, communicative settings, and in writing'. But even this may be misused: some people might claim that a signing community (which might necessitate boarding school education at least for those 90% of deaf children who have hearing parents) is not a 'natural' communicative setting. A task for the reader: find an inclusive formulation which cannot be misused!

formal education. More lasting technical literacy seems to take some 4–6 years. Being able to use basic literacy for further education and as a member of civil society takes minimally some 9 years of formal education, and, finally, using literacy (including computer literacy – see Naz Rassool's excellent treatment of changes in literacy requirements, 1999) for full participation on labour market and in society takes the time we usually reckon people use before entering university, meaning some 12 years of formal education.

But all these assessments of the number of years presuppose that children get their education through the medium of their own language, or a language that they understand, in an additive learning situation. If the school situation is subtractive, we need to add at least 2 years to the basic decoding skills assessment, and some 4–7 years to the others - this is the time it takes for children who are taught in a dominant foreign language to catch up with native speakers of that language so that they can use the dominant language as a medium of education in decontextualised cognitively demanding problem-solving situations (see, e.g. Cummins, and Thomas and Collier in the bibliography). This means, that since most of the world's indigenous and minority children are taught subtractively, through the medium of a dominant language, not their mother tongue, most of them do not stay in school long enough to become fully literate.

What does subtractive teaching do? Firstly, it prevents profound literacy. Secondly, it prevents students from gaining the knowledge and skills that would correspond to their innate capacities and would be needed for socio-economic mobility and democratic participation. Thirdly, it is genocidal, according to UN Genocide Convention's definitions of genocide. Fourthly, it replaces mother tongues and kills languages. Fifthly, it wastes resources, and finally, it prevents (sustainable) development. Instead, it would be perfectly possible to teach ALL children additively. In **additive teaching**, children are taught through the medium of the mother tongue, with good teaching of the dominant language as a second language. Additive teaching makes them high level bilingual or multilingual. they learn both their own languages AND other languages well. Thus linguistic human rights are necessary for global literacy for all.

Reason 2. Counteracting linguistic genocide

The second reason for mother tongue medium education and linguistic human rights is that they can be used as tools to counteract linguistic genocide. There are two basic paradigms explaining why languages die. The first one describes the disappearance as ("natural") death. A few people applaud it ("What the world needs most is about 1000 more dead languages – and one more alive" – C.K. Ogden 1934 – and guess which one he meant...); many are indifferent, and some regret it but see it as inevitable. The other paradigm (which I represent) sees the disappearance of languages in most cases as a result of "murder". This paradigm asserts, as opposed to the death paradigm, that languages do NOT just disappear naturally. "Languages" do NOT "commit suicide", i.e. in most cases, speakers do NOT leave them voluntarily, for instrumental reasons, and for their own good. Instead, languages are "murdered". Most disappearing languages are victims of linguistic genocide.

When people hear the term "genocide", many ask: Is the term not too strong? Is it not watering down the concept to use it about languages and culture, rather than about physical atrocities. I don't think so. I use the definitions of genocide from the *UN International Convention on the Prevention and Punishment of the Crime of Genocide* (E793, 1948). The Genocide convention has six definitions of genocide. Two of them fit what happens in today's indigenous and minority education.

Article II(e): 'forcibly transferring children of the group to another group'; and Article II(b): 'causing serious bodily *or mental* harm to members of the group'; (italicised emphasis added).

I shall present a few examples of this genocide in education. As becomes clear, all of them involve subtractive teaching through the medium of a foreign language, and lack of linguistic human rights. I would like you to compare the examples with what has happened historically in the part of the world that the conference is about: why is there now a need to revive minority languages? Why are they not healthy and unthreatened?

The first example is a longitudinal study from Europe by Pirjo Janulf (1998). She studied Finnish immigrant minority children in Sweden who had Swedish-medium education. She also went back to many of them after 15 years. Of those Finnish immigrant minority members in Sweden who had had Swedish-medium education, NOT ONE SPOKE ANY FINNISH TO THEIR OWN CHILDREN. Even if they themselves might not have forgotten their Finnish completely, their children were certainly forcibly transferred to the majority group, at least linguistically. Assimilationist subtractive education is genocidal (see, e.g., Kouritzin 1999 and Wong Fillmore 1991 for other examples).

The second example comes from Africa. It is Edward Williams' 1995 study from Zambia and Malawi, with some1,500 students in grades 1-7. The results state that large numbers of Zambian pupils (all education in English) 'have very weak or zero reading competence in two languages'. The Malawi children (taught in local languages during the first 4 years, English as a subject) had slightly better test results in the English language than the Zambian students. Williams' conclusion was that 'there is a clear risk that the policy of using English as a vehicular language may contribute to stunting, rather than promoting, academic and cognitive growth'. This fits the UN genocide definition of "causing mental harm" (see also the conclusions in Lowell and Devlin 1999).

The next two examples are from South Africa. Zubeida Desai's 2001 study shows similar results to Williams' study. Xhosa-speaking grade 4 and 7 learners in South Africa were given a set of pictures which they had to put in the right order and then describe, in both Xhosa and English. In Desai's words, it showed 'the rich vocabulary children have when they express themselves in Xhosa and the poor vocabulary they have when they express themselves in English' (ibid., 321). The Pan South African Language Board (where Desai was since 1996 a member and has also served as the Chair and the Deputy Chair) argued in March 1999, criticising the Government, that 'African learners are not likely to receive quality education if they are not able to access knowledge equitably. The board further argued that a more pedagogically sound approach would be to enable all learners to write their examinations in their primary languages' (ibid., 337-338; see also other references to Desai in the bibliography).

Kathleen Heugh showed in a study (2000a; see also other references to her in the bibliography; likewise references to Alexander and Desai) that the percentage of Black students who passed their exams went down every time the number of years spent through the medium of the mother tongues decreased.

The following example comes from the USA. In an article called 'Educational Malpractice and the Miseducation of Language Minority Students' (2000), John Baugh draws a parallel between how physicians may maltreat patients and how minority students (including students who do not have mainstream US English as their first language, for instance speakers of Ebonics/Black English), are often treated in education in the USA. The harm caused to them by this maltreatment and miseducation also fits the UN definition of "causing serious bodily *or mental* harm to members of the group".

The last examples come from Canada. Katherine Zozula and Simon Ford tell in their 1985 report *Keewatin Perspective on Bilingual Education* about Canadian Inuit 'students who are neither fluent nor literate in either language' and present schooling statistics showing that the students 'end up at only Grade 4 level of achievement after 9 years of schooling' (quoted in I. Martin 2000a: 3; see also I. Martin 2000b). The same type of results are presented in the *Canadian Royal Commission on Aboriginal Peoples 1996 Report*. They note that 'submersion strategies which neither respect the child's first language nor help them gain fluency in the second language may result in impaired fluency in both languages' (quoted in I. Martin 2000a:15). The Nunavut Language Policy Conference in March 1998 echoes this in claiming that 'in some individuals, neither language is firmly anchored' (quoted in I. Martin 2000a: 23). This statement is partially based on the empirical study by two experienced Arctic College educators, Mick Mallon and Alexina Kublu, in a 1998 Discussion Paper for the conference which states that 'a significant number of young people are not fully fluent in their languages', and that many students 'remain apathetic, often with minimal skills in both languages' (quoted in I. Martin 2000a (9: 27). A 1998 report (*Kitikmeot struggles to prevent death of Inuktitut*) notes that 'teenagers cannot converse fluently with their grandparents' (quoted in I. Martin 2000a: 31).

I could take literally thousands of similar examples (see Skutnabb-Kangas 2000a for many more), also from Deaf education (see, e.g. Branson and Miller 1998, 2000, Grosjean 2001, Jokinen 2000, Lane 1998, D.S. Martin 2001). My conclusion is that most indigenous and minority education in the world participates in committing linguistic and cultural genocide, according to the genocide definitions in the UN Genocide Convention.

In addition to the definitions I have used, we could also refer to the specific definition on *linguistic* genocide. When the United Nations did preparatory work for what later became the *International Convention for the Prevention and Punishment of the Crime of Genocide* (E 793, 1948), linguistic and cultural genocide were in fact discussed alongside physical genocide. All three were seen as serious crimes against humanity (see Capotorti 1979: 37). The Ad Hoc Committee which prepared the Convention had specified the following acts as examples constituting cultural genocide in Article III: 'Any deliberate act committed with intent to destroy the language, religion or culture of a national, racial or religious group on grounds of national or racial origin or religious belief, such as:

1. Prohibiting the use of the language of the group in daily intercourse or in schools, or the printing and circulation of publications in the language of the group.

2. Destroying or preventing the use of libraries, museums, schools, historical monuments, places of worship or other cultural institutions and objects of the group' (emphasis added).

When the Convention was finally accepted by the General Assembly, Article III, which covered linguistic and cultural genocide, was not adopted (see *Official Records of the General Assembly, Third Session, Part I, Sixth Committee*, 83rd meeting). It is thus *not included* in the final Convention of 1948. What remains, however, is a definition of linguistic genocide, which most states then in the UN were prepared to accept. All our examples above also fit this definition of linguistic genocide.

On the other hand, it is perfectly possibly to educate minorities so that their linguistic human rights are respected. Arlene Stairs has shown that 'in schools which support initial learning of Inuttitut, and whose grade 3 and Grade 4 pupils are strong writers in Inuttitut, the results in written English are also the highest.' (1994, quoted in I. Martin 2000a: 60; see also Stairs 1988).

The same experience is echoed all over the world, with the Navajo (Lee and McLaughlin 2001), with the Saami (see Aikio-Puoskari 2001, Aikio-Puoskari and Pentikäinen 2001), with all those 'national' minorities who have mother tongue medium education, like the Swedish-speakers in Finland, the Welsh in UK, the Frisians in the Netherlands, the results in dual language programmes in the USA and so on.

In Alaska, just to mention a few examples, the Yu'piq teacher Nancy Sharp (1994, quoted in I. Martin 2000a: 62), compares, partly on the basis of her own experience: when Yu'piq children are taught through the medium of English, they are treated by 'White' teachers as handicapped, and they do not achieve; when they are taught through the medium of Yu'piq, they are 'excellent writers, smart happy students' (quoted in I. Martin 2000a: 62; see also Lipka et al. 1998).

Sustainable education leads to profound literacy, creativity, and high levels of multilingualism for the student, and maintenance of the world's languages. But when confronted with the facts, most politicians counter with the question: is it possible, and economically viable? My answer is yes, and I shall present only one example.

Papua New Guinea has a population of around 5 million, and the number of languages is over 850. A study by David Klaus, who has just retired from the World Bank, sums up results from a large-scale educational experiment as follows. As of 2002, 470 languages are used as the media of education in preschool and the first two grades. What can be seen already is that children *become literate* more quickly and easily in their mother tongues than they did in English, *learn English* more quickly and easily than their older brothers and sisters did under the old system; the results of the Grade 6 examination in the three provinces which were the first to begin the reform in 1993 were much higher than the results of students from provinces where students were immersed in English from Day One of Grade One. Access is increasing because many parents now appear more willing to send their children to school and to make the sacrifices necessary to keep them in school. Dropout has decreased. In particular, a higher proportion of girls are in school than was previously the case. Children are more excited, pro-active, self-confident, and inquisitive about learning, and ask more questions (Klaus, in press; Nagai and Lister, in press, Skutnabb-Kangas, in press c).

Educational LHRs which guarantee additive language learning are one of the necessary (but not sufficient) prerequisites needed for preventing linguistic genocide and for linguistic diversity to be maintained on earth. And the knowledge about how to organise education that respects LHRs certainly exists (see, e.g., Fishman 1991, Fishman and Fishman Schweid 2000, Fishman (ed.) 2001, Hinton and Hale (eds) 2001, Huss 1999, Huss et al., in press, I. Martin 2000a and b, May (ed.) 1999, Skutnabb-Kangas (ed.) 1995, Skutnabb-Kangas and Cummins (eds) 1988, and references to Alexander, Annamalai, Cummins, Desai, Heugh, Kamwangamalu, and Collier and Thomas, in the bibliography, just to mention a few).

Reason 3: Maintenance of the world's linguistic diversity

The third reason for the importance of linguistic human rights, especially in education, has to do with the maintenance of linguistic diversity on earth, and partially through this, also maintaining the prerequisites for the survival of the planet. This is how the argument goes:

Most of the world's languages are very small indeed. The median number of speakers of a language in the world is 5.000-6.000 (Posey 1997). Some 5.000 of the world's almost 7.000 spoken languages and 99% of the Sign languages have fewer than 100.000 users. What is happening today to the world's languages? Are they being maintained? NO, they are not. Languages are today being killed faster than ever before in human history. Optimistic estimates assess that 50% of today's spoken languages may be extinct or critically endangered[3] in 2100 (e.g. Wurm, ed., 2001). Pessimistic but still realistic estimates (e.g. Krauss 1992, 1995) say that 90-95% may be extinct or critically endangered in 2100.

Educational systems and mass media are (the most) important direct agents in linguistic and cultural genocide. Behind them are the world's economic, techno-military and political systems. When children got most of their education informally, in their families and communities, their languages were maintained: they were transmitted from the older generations to the next. Formal education can kill languages in a couple of generations, languages that had survived for hundreds or even thousands of years with informal education.

In the context of this symposium, it is important to state that English is today the world's most important killer language. There are of course others too – any dominant language can become a killer language[4]. What does the term mean?

---

[3] The terms often used have been "dead" or "moribund"; many people, including myself, have not liked these terms (see Skutnabb-Kangas 2000: 47-48 for the reasons). The terms recommended by a UNESCO Ad Hoc Expert Group on Endangered Languages (2002) are "extinct" and "critically endangered".

[4] The term was used by Glanville Price in 1984.

When "big" languages are learned subtractively (at the cost of the mother tongues) rather than additively (in addition to mother tongues), they become KILLER LANGUAGES. Killer languages pose serious threats towards the linguistic diversity of the world.

But are there other reasons for maintaining the world's linguistic diversity? Are there other reasons for not only teaching indigenous and minority children through the medium of their own languages and teaching them dominant languages up to a high level as well? And might there even be reasons to try to make linguistic majority populations like native English speakers in Britain and in all the regions and countries that today's conference is about, high level multilinguals? I shall point out three additional reasons for maintaining all the world's languages.

Reason 4: English is not enough

The Financial Times, 3.12.2001 reports that inability to speak client's language can lead to failure. A survey undertaken for the Community of European Management Schools, an alliance of academia and multinational corporations, concludes that a company's inability to speak a client's language can lead to failure to win business because it indicates lack of effort. If you have "foreign" language skills, you earn more, reports the British newspaper *The Independent* 31.5.2001). According to it, graduates with foreign language skills earn more than those who only know English. Likewise, the Nuffield Languages Enquiry (2000) concludes that English is not enough: They say: "We are fortunate to speak a global language but, in a smart and competitive world, exclusive reliance on English leaves the UK vulnerable and dependent on the linguistic competence and the goodwill of others ... young people from the UK are at a growing disadvantage in the recruitment market". Tariq Rahman from Pakistan states (email March 2002; see also references in the bibliography): "English-medium schools tend to produce snobs completely alienated from their culture and languages". He also asserts: "We are mentally colonialized and alienated from our cultures if all we know is in English".

'Good' English will be like literacy yesterday or computer skills today: employers see it as self-evident and necessary BUT NOT SUFFICIENT for good jobs. Supply and demand theories predict the following: When many people possess what earlier was a scarce commodity (near-native English), the price goes down. According to François Grin (2000; see also other references to Grin, and see Skutnabb-Kangas 1999), the value of 'perfect' English skills as a financial incentive decreases substantially when a high proportion of a country's or a region's or the world's population know English well (see also Graddol 1997 for some prognoses about the future of English and Phillipson 1992 and other references to Phillipson and Skutnabb-Kangas for the spread of English).

Reason 5: Creativity and new ideas are the main assets (cultural capital) in a knowledge society and a prerequisite for humankind to adapt to change and to find solutions to the catastrophes of our own making. Multilingualism enhances creativity, monolingualism and homogenisation kill it.

In industrial societies, where the main products are/were commodities, those who control access to raw materials and own the other prerequisites and means of production, do well. In contrast, in a knowledge society or information society, the main products are knowledge and ideas. In a knowledge society, those who have access to diverse knowledges, diverse information, diverse ideas: creativity, do well. In knowledge societies uniformity is a handicap. Some uniformity might have promoted certain aspects of industrialisation, but in post-industrial knowledge societies uniformity will be a definite handicap. We know now that creativity, innovation, investment are related, and can be results of additive teaching and multilingualism. This is, because:

1. Creativity precedes innovation, also in commodity production.
2. Investment follows creativity.
3. Multilingualism enhances creativity.
4. High-level multilinguals as a group do better than corresponding monolinguals on tests measuring several aspects of 'intelligence', creativity, divergent thinking, cognitive flexibility, etc., and
5. Additive teaching leads to high-level multilingualism.

Therefore, again, additive teaching, through the medium of indigenous and minority children's mother tongues (or though minority languages, i.e. second languages, for linguistic dominant group children, in immersion or two-way-immersion programmes – see Skutnabb-Kangas 1996a, ed. 1995, Skutnabb-Kangas and García 1995, for comparisons of these), is necessary.

Despite the importance of the five reasons listed so far, reason 6 is in my view probably the most important one from a futures point of view.

Reason 6: Linguistic diversity and biodiversity are correlationally and causally related. Knowledge about how to maintain biodiversity is encoded in small languages. Through killing them we kill the prerequisites for maintaining biodiversity

If we do a simplified calculation, according to optimistic estimates, 2% of biological species but 50% of languages may be extinct (or critically endangered) in a 100 years' time. Pessimistic estimates are that 20% of biological species but 90% of languages may be extinct (or critically endangered) in a 100 years' time (Table 2). Linguistic diversity disappears much faster than biodiversity.

Table 2. Prognoses for 'extinct' or 'critically endangered' species and languages

Percentage estimated to be extinct or critically endangered around the year 2100	PROGNOSES	Biological species	Languages
	'Optimistic realistic'	2%	50%
	'Pessimistic realistic'	20%	90%

But what is the relevance of this information? Firstly, linguistic and cultural diversity on the one hand and biodiversity on the other hand are correlated - where one type is high, often the other one is too, and vice versa. Secondly, some of the main causes for the disappearance of biodiversity that have been identified

Table 3. Endemism in languages and higher vertebrates: a comparison of the top 25 countries

Endemic languages	Number	Endemic higher vertebrates	Number
1. PAPUA NEW GUINEA	847	**1. AUSTRALIA**	1.346
2. INDONESIA	655	**2. MEXICO**	761
3. Nigeria	376	**3. BRAZIL**	725
4. INDIA	309	**4. INDONESIA**	673
5. AUSTRALIA	261	5. Madagascar	537
6. MEXICO	230	**6. PHILIPPINES**	437
7. CAMEROON	201	**7. INDIA**	373
8. BRAZIL	185	**8. PERU**	332
9. ZAIRE	158	**9. COLOMBIA**	330
10. PHILIPPINES	153	10. Ecuador	294
11. USA	143	**11. USA**	284
12. Vanuatu	105	**12. CHINA**	256
13. TANZANIA	101	**13. PAPUA NEW GUINEA**	203
14. Sudan	97	14. Venezuela	186
15. Malaysia	92	15. Argentina	168
16. ETHIOPIA	90	16. Cuba	152
17. CHINA	77	17. South Africa	146
18. PERU	75	**18. ZAIRE**	134
19. Chad	74	19. Sri Lanka	126
20. Russia	71	20. New Zealand	120
21. SOLOMON ISLANDS	69	**21. TANZANIA**	113
22. Nepal	68	22. Japan	112
23. COLOMBIA	55	**23. CAMEROON**	105
24. Côte d'Ivoire	51	**24. SOLOMON ISLANDS**	101
25. Canada	47	**25. ETHIOPIA**	88
		26. Somalia	88

are habitat destruction, for instance through logging, spread of agriculture, use of pesticides, and the poor economic and political situation of the people who live in the world's most diverse ecoregions. What most people do not know is that disappearance of languages may also be or become a very important causal factor in the destruction of biodiversity.

One of the organisations investigating the relationship above is Terralingua (http://www.terralingua.org/). 'Terralingua is a non-profit international organisation devoted to preserving the world's linguistic diversity and to investigating links between biological and cultural diversity.' Conservationist

Table 4. Endemism in Languages Compared with Rankings of Biodiversity

Country	Rank Order and Total Numbers						On mega-diversity list?
	Endemic Languages		Endemic Vertebrates		Flower-ing Plants	EBAs	
	rank	no.	rank	no.			
PAPUA NEW GUINEA	1	847	13	203	18^t	6	yes
INDONESIA	2	655	4	673	7^t	1	yes
Nigeria	3	376					
INDIA	4	309	7	373	12	11	yes
AUSTRALIA	5	261	1	1,346	11	9	yes
MEXICO	6	230	2	761	4	2	yes
CAMEROON	7	201	23	105	24		
BRAZIL	8	185	3	725	1	4	yes
DEM REP OF CONGO	9	158	18	134	17		yes
PHILIPPINES	10	153	6	437	25	11	yes
USA	11	143	11	284	9	15	yes
Vanuatu	12	105					
TANZANIA	13	101	21	113	19	14	
Sudan	14	97					
Malaysia	15	92			14		yes
ETHIOPIA	16	90	25	88			
CHINA	17	77	12	256	3	6	yes
PERU	18	75	8	332	13	3	yes
Chad	19	74					
Russia	20	71			6		
SOLOMON ISLANDS	21	69	24	101			
Nepal	22	68			22		
COLOMBIA	23	55	9	330	2	5	yes
Côte d'Ivoire	24	51					
Canada	25	47					

(source: Skutnabb-Kangas, Maffi and Harmon, 2002).

David Harmon of Terralingua has investigated correlations between biological and linguistic diversity, using several indicators of biodiversity. Harmon has compared endemism of languages and higher vertebrates (mammals, birds, reptiles and amphibians), with the top 25 countries for each type (1995: 14) (Table 3). I have **bolded** and CAPITALISED those countries which are on both lists. 16 of the 25 countries are on both lists, a coincidence of 64%. According to Harmon (1995: 6) 'it is very unlikely that this would only be accidental.'

Harmon gets the same results with flowering plants and languages, birds and languages, etc. - a high correlation between countries with biological and linguistic megadiversity (see also Harmon, 2002, Skutnabb-Kangas and Harmon 2002, Skutnabb-Kangas, Maffi and Harmon, 2002). I have just counted some of the correlations between butterflies[5] and languages, and the correlations are similarly high.

Table 4 shows more of the correlations. The figures for languages are derived by Harmon from the Ethnologue, 12th edition, and for vertebrates from Groombridge 1992; the countries which are on the top lists for endemism for both vertebrates and languages are still bolded and capitalized. The list ranks countries not in terms of all languages but according to the number of endemic languages. Remember that endemic languages represent the vast majority (some 83-84 percent) of the world's languages. As can be seen, Papua New Guinea, which ranks first in terms of endemic languages, is country number 13 in terms of endemic vertebrates. The USA is number 11 on both the languages and the vertebrates list. On the other hand, Nigeria is number 3 on the languages list but is not among the 25 top countries for any of the biological species diversity indicators used here. Still, the correlations are very high indeed.

Recent research shows mounting evidence for the hypothesis that it might not only be a correlational relationship. It may also be causal: the two types of diversities seem to mutually enforce and support each other (see Maffi 2000a). UNEP (United Nations Environmental Program), one of the organisers of the world summit on biodiversity in Rio de Janeiro in 1992 (see its summary of our knowledge on biodiversity, Heywood, ed., 1995), published in December 1999 a mega-volume called *Cultural and Spiritual Values of Biodiversity. A Complementary Contribution to the Global Biodiversity Assessment*, edited by Darrell Posey (1999) summarising some of this evidence of causality. Likewise, Luisa Maffi's (2001) edited volume *On Biocultural Diversity. Linking Language, Knowledge and the Environment* illustrates it (see also Maffi 2000a, b, 2001). The strong correlation need not indicate a direct causal relationship, in the sense that neither type of diversity should probably be seen directly as an independent variable in relation to the other. But linguistic and cultural diversity may be decisive mediating variables in sustaining biodiversity itself, and vice versa, as long as humans are on the earth. As soon as humans came into existence, they started to influence the rest of nature. Today it is safe to say that there is no 'pristine nature' left - all landscapes have been and are influenced by human action, even those where untrained observers might not notice it immediately. All landscapes are cultural landscapes. Likewise, local nature and people's detailed knowledge about it and use of it have influenced the cultures, languages and cosmo-visions of the people who have been dependent on it for their sustenance. This relationship between all kinds of diversities is of course what most indigenous peoples have always known, and they describe their knowledge in several articles in the UNEP volume. At the Johannesburg World Summit on Sustainable Development (August - September 2002) there seemed to be a breakthrough in the sense that "orthodox" Western scientists now also acknowledge the relationship between traditional indigenous knowledge and science in a way which suggests that science has learned and should learn from traditional knowledge; they should be equal partners. The International Council for Science (ICSU) also acknowledges

---

[5] I used Tables 17-20 in Mittermeier and Goettsch Mittermeier 1997: 28-29, as a basis; these give the top 12 countries in the world for butterfly and swallowtail butterfly diversity and endemism.

that formal education plays a part in the disappearance of languages and cultures (ICSU 2002):

> Universal education programs provide important tools for human development, but they may also compromise the transmission of indigenous language and knowledge. Inadvertently, they may contribute to the erosion of cultural diversity, a loss of social cohesion and the alienation and disorientation of youth. [...] In short, when indigenous children are taught in science class that the natural world is ordered as scientists believe it functions, then the validity and authority of their parents' and grandparents' knowledge is denied. While their parents may posses an extensive and sophisticated understanding of the local environment, classroom instruction implicitly informs that science is the ultimate authority for interpreting "reality" and by extension local indigenous knowledge is second rate and obsolete. [...] Actions are urgently needed to enhance the intergenerational transmission of local and indigenous knowledge. [...] Traditional knowledge conservation therefore must pass through the pathways of conserving language (as language is an essential tool for culturally-appropriate encoding of knowledge)...

We in Terralingua[6] suggest that if the long-lasting co-evolution which people have had with their environments from time immemorial is abruptly disrupted, without nature (and people) getting enough time to adjust and adapt (see Mühlhäusler, 1996), we can expect a catastrophe. The adjustment needed takes hundreds of years, not only decades (ibid.). Two examples from different parts of the world: nuances in the knowledge about medicinal plants and their use disappear when indigenous youth in Mexico become bilingual without teaching in and through the medium of their own languages - the knowledge is not transferred to Spanish which does not have the vocabulary for these nuances or the discourses needed (see Luisa Maffi's doctoral dissertation, 1994; see also Nabhan 2001). I was told a recent example by Pekka Aikio, the President of the Saami Parliament in Finland (29 November 2001). Finnish fish biologists have just "discovered" that salmon can use even extremely small rivulets leading to the river Teno as spawning ground - earlier this was thought impossible. Pekka said that the Saami have always known this - the traditional Saami names of several of those rivulets often include the Saami word for "salmon spawning-bed". This is ecological knowledge inscribed in indigenous languages.

In order to adapt to the massive changes in today's globalisation, people need adaptability, fitness, that requires creativity. I summarize my own views on the relationship between linguistic and cultural diversity, biodiversity, and creativity, using Baker's (2001) summary of Chapter 2, from Baker's review of my latest book:

> Ecological diversity is essential for long-term planetary survival. All living organisms, plants, animals, bacteria and humans survive and prosper through a network of complex and delicate relationships. Damaging one of the elements in the ecosystem will result in

---

[6] See the article on linguistic diversity in the UNEP volume, written by Luisa Maffi, and myself (Terralingua's President and Vice-president), with an insert by Jonah Andrianarivo, Maffi, et al. 1999; see also Maffi 2000b, Harmon 2002, and articles in Maffi (ed.) 2001.

unforeseen consequences for the whole of the system. Evolution has been aided by genetic diversity, with species genetically adapting in order to survive in different environments. Diversity contains the potential for adaptation. Uniformity can endanger a species by providing inflexibility and unadaptability.

Linguistic diversity and biological diversity are [...] inseparable. The range of cross fertilisation becomes less as languages and cultures die and the testimony of human intellectual achievement is lessened.

In the language of ecology, the strongest ecosystems are those that are the most diverse. That is, diversity is directly related to stability; variety is important for long-term survival. Our success on this planet has been due to an ability to adapt to different kinds of environment over thousands of years (atmospheric as well as cultural). Such ability is born out of diversity. Thus language and cultural diversity maximises chances of human success and adaptability" (from Colin Baker's review of Skutnabb-Kangas 2000, Baker 2001: 281).

Thus, biocultural diversity (= biodiversity + linguistic diversity + cultural diversity) is essential for long-term planetary survival because it enhances creativity and adaptability and thus stability. Today we are killing biocultural diversity faster than ever before in human history. We also need to think of the role of indigenous peoples. Most of the world's mega-*bio*diversity is in areas under the management or guardianship of indigenous peoples. Most of the world's *linguistic* diversity resides in the small languages of indigenous peoples. Much of the detailed knowledge of how to maintain biodiversity is encoded in the languages of indigenous peoples. Indigenous peoples are/have the key to our planetary survival. Indigenous self-determination is a necessary prerequisite for the survival of the planet. The governments participating in the Johannesburg World Summit on Sustainable Development could have ensured that indigenous peoples, their languages, cultures and knowledges could survive, on their own lands, under their own control. They did not do anything.

2. The European Charter, Part III, Art. 8. International comparisons, who scores low?[7]

If we think that all indigenous and minority languages should be maintained, knowing that formal education is one of the worst culprits in killing languages, we can look at one of the possible tool for supporting educational linguistic human rights. Today's human rights instruments in general give very little support to minority languages in general, and especially to educational rights, as I and others have shown in countless publications (summarised in Skutnabb-Kangas 2000, Chapter 7; see also May 2001, Thornberry 1997, de Varennes 1996 - see also Fishman 1994 for some caveats). Next, I will look at just one instrument with specific relevance for educational linguistic human rights, namely the *European Charter for Regional or Minority Languages*, in force since 1999, and specifically its Article 8 on education. First two preliminaries.

---

[7] This subsection is mainly based on Skutnabb-Kangas 2000, 2002b, in press a, and Skutnabb-Kangas and Phillipson 2001.

Max van der Stoel, the former High Commissioner on National Minorities of the OSCE[8] (1999: 8-9; see also Rothenberger, compiler, 1997, for his other speeches), discusses negative and positive rights (or *toleration-oriented non-discrimination prescriptions and promotion-oriented rights*; see Skutnabb-Kangas and Phillipson 1994), as the two human rights pillars: The negative rights have to do with "the right to non-discrimination in the enjoyment of human rights"; and positive rights with "the right to the maintenance and development of identity through the freedom to practise or use those special and unique aspects of their minority life – typically culture, religion, and language". He lists the various rights as follows (ibid.):

> The first protection can be found, for instance, in paragraph 31 of the Copenhagen Document, Articles 2(1) and 26 of the ICCPR, Article 14 of the ECHR, Article 4 of the Framework Convention, and Article 3(11) of the 1992 UN [Minorities] Declaration. It ensures that minorities receive all of the other protections without regard to their ethnic, national, or religious status; they thus enjoy a number of linguistic rights that all persons in the state enjoy, such as freedom of expression and the right in criminal proceedings to be informed of the charge against them in a language they understand, if necessary through an interpreter provided free of charge.
>
> The second pillar, encompassing affirmative obligations beyond non-discrimination, appears, for example, in paragraph 32 of the Copenhagen Document, Article 27 of the ICCPR, Article 5 of the Framework Convention, and Article 2(1) of the 1992 UN Declaration. It includes a number of rights pertinent to minorities simply by virtue of their minority status, such as the right to use their language. This pillar is necessary because a pure non-discrimination norm could have the effect of forcing people belonging to minorities to adhere to a majority language, effectively denying them their rights to identity. (OSCE High Commissioner on National Minorities 1999: 8-9)

Thus it is important to see how much positive protection of the kind that van der Stoel deems necessary to avoid forced assimilation Article 8 of the European Charter grants (and see "The Hague Recommendations Regarding the Education Rights of Minorities" for what these should be; see also Max van der Stoel's introduction to them, 1997).

Secondly, we can assess the "respect" that various states show in relation to human rights in general, firstly, by listing which basic human rights instruments they have signed and ratified, and, secondly, to what extent and how they implement them. It is interesting to see that in many cases those countries which are policing the global human rights performance of other countries, especially the united States of America, in fact show minimal respect for both multilateral and even domestic human rights themselves. I have placed all 193 UN member states in a hierarchical order, depending on how many of the 52 basic Universal Human Rights Instruments they had ratified by 31st May 2000 (see UNESCO 2000, the latest UN document on this; the document itself has not counted the number of

---

[8] See the list of abbreviations at the end.

ratified documents but has only listed them), the United States occupies, together with 4 other countries, a shared 161st-164th position of 193 in this Human Rights Olympics - hardly a morally convincing record (still down from May 1998 when it held a 156th – 161st position). The USA does not recognise the authority of international law over US law, something that can be exemplified by the fact that "American representatives on the United Nations Security Council vetoed a resolution calling on all governments to observe international law" as Noam Chomsky notes (1991: 16, as quoted in Pilger 1998: 27). Another example: the United States was the only state voting against the *Declaration on the Right to Development*, adopted by the UN General Assembly in 1986 (General Assembly

Table 5. Signatures and ratifications of the European Charter for Regional or Minority Languages

1. Signed and ratified	2. Signed only but not ratified	3. Neither signed nor ratified
Armenia, Austria, Croatia, Cyprus, Denmark, Finland, Germany, Hungary, Liechtenstein, Netherlands, Norway, Slovakia, Slovenia, Spain, Sweden, Switzerland, United Kingdom	Azerbaijan, Czech Republic, France, Iceland, Italy, Luxembourg, Malta, Moldova, Romania, Russian Federation, Macedonia, Ukraine	Albania, Andorra, Belgium, Bosnia and Herzegovina, Bulgaria, Estonia, Georgia, Greece, Ireland, Latvia, Lithuania, Poland, Portugal, San Marino, Turkey

resolution 41/128 of 4 December 1986)[9]. The Declaration "provides in its Article 8(1) that States shall undertake, at the national level, all necessary measures for the realization of the right to development and *shall ensure* inter alia, *equality of opportunity for all in their access to basic resources, education* ... employment and the fair distribution of income" (Eide 1995: 39; emphasis added). It is also interesting to see where the states called "rogue states" by some USA sources are placed in this Human Rights Olympics (Iran between 141-145, Iraq 104-111, Libya 53-57 and North Korea 173-175). All others except North Korea show a far better record than the USA.

As a prerequisite for asking other states to play a fair game in the international arena, states ought to follow the commonly agreed rules, rather than being rules onto themselves. We need to assess *all* states with the *same* yardstick – everything else is pure hypocritical power politics and against basic democracy.

---

[9] See, e.g. the United Nations publication *The Realization of the Right to Development. Global Consultation of the Right to Development as a Human Right,* 1991, Rosas 1995: 248-249.

After these introductory remarks, I present the ratifications of the European Charter. Table 5[10] shows the signatures and ratifications as of 15th August 2002. I have ranked the countries in three categories only. 17 countries, including the UK, have both signed and ratified[11]. 12 countries have only signed but not ratified, and 15 countries, including Ireland, have neither signed nor ratified. Next we shall look at which alternatives three countries have chosen. The important issues for our purposes here are in Part III, the Education Article 8, specifically the right to mother tongue medium education. In general, the formulations in the Charter include a range of modifications, including 'as far as possible', 'relevant', 'appropriate', 'where necessary', 'pupils who so wish in a number considered sufficient', 'if the number of users of a regional or minority language justifies it', as well as a number of alternatives, as in 'to allow, encourage or provide teaching in or of the regional or minority language at all the appropriate stages of education'. The opt-outs and alternatives in the Charter permit a reluctant state to meet the requirements in a minimalist way, which it can legitimate by claiming that a provision was not 'possible' or 'appropriate', or that numbers were not 'sufficient' or did not 'justify' a provision, or that it 'allowed' the minority to organise teaching of their language as a subject, at their own cost.

I shall present three countries but only discuss Sweden, in comparison to Finland. Britain takes a position between them. Sweden has signed and ratified the *European Charter* for the following languages: "Sami, Finnish and Meänkieli (Tornedal Finnish) are regional or minority languages in Sweden. Romani Chib and Yiddish shall be regarded as non-territorial minority languages in Sweden when the Charter is applied" (from Sweden's ratification, February 2000; several notes have more details). Sweden does not grant any educational rights whatsoever to speakers of Romani or Yiddish, whereas the other three languages all have the same rights

First we have to present the alternatives in the Education Article (Part III, Art. 8). The right to mother tongue medium education can be discussed at all levels, (a) pre-school, (b) primary, (c) secondary, (d) technical and vocational and (e) university and higher education levels. There is a sliding scale in the Charter going from (i) to (iv), which can be exemplified in relation to primary education, (b):

i. to make available primary education in the relevant regional or minority languages, or
ii. to make available a substantial part of primary education in the relevant regional or minority languages; or
iii. to provide, within primary education, for the teaching of the relevant regional or minority languages as an integral part of the curriculum; or
iv. to apply one of the measures provided for under i to iii above at least to those pupils whose families so request and whose number is considered sufficient.

[10] The Table is based on both UNESCO 2000 and updatings from the relevant web-site http://www.conventions.coe.int/treaty/EN/cadreprincipal.htm), downloaded 15th August 2002.

[11] I have not considered reservations and declarations here – in a more detailed assessment these should obviously be considered.

All of the other provisions follow the same pattern for the first alternative, (i), which is *education through the medium of the language.* For pre-school, secondary and vocational levels, (ii) is, as above, *a substantial part of the education through the medium of the relevant language,* whereas (ii) at university level only offers teaching in the languages as subjects.

Table 6. Choices made in Education Article 8 for preschool (a)

Country	i	ii	iii	iv
Sweden Saami, Finnish and Meänkieli			X	
Finland Saami Swedish	X X			
UK Welsh Scottish-Gaelic Irish	X X		 X	

Table 7. Choices made in Education Article 8 for primary school (b)

Country	i	ii	iii	iv
Sweden Saami, Finnish and Meänkieli				X
Finland Saami Swedish	X X			
UK Welsh Scottish-Gaelic Irish	X X			 X

Table 8. Choices made in Education Article 8 for secondary school (c)

Country	i	ii	iii	iv
Sweden Saami, Finnish and Meänkieli				X
Finland Saami Swedish	X X			
UK Welsh Scottish-Gaelic Irish	X X			 X

Table 9. Choices made in Education Article 8 for technical and vocational education (d)

Country	i	ii	iii	iv
Sweden Saami, Finnish and Meänkieli				X
Finland Saami Swedish	X	X		
UK Welsh Scottish-Gaelic Irish				X X X

Table 10. Choices made in Education Article 8 for university and higher education (e)

Country	i	ii	iii	iv
Sweden Saami, Finnish and Meänkieli			X	
Finland Saami Swedish	X	X		
UK Welsh Scottish-Gaelic Irish			X X X	

For secondary and vocational levels, (iii) is the same as above for primary education, *teaching of the language as a subject*, whereas (iii) for pre-schools only suggests that the state should 'apply some of the measures' and is identical with (iv) for primary education. For pre-schools and universities, (iv) makes only a vague commitment to 'encourage and/or allow' some study if none of the other provisions apply.This means that the only provisions where there is *mother tongue medium teaching*, fully or to some extent, are (i) and (ii) for pre-schools, primary, secondary and vocational education, and (i) for universities. *Sweden has not chosen any of these provisions for any of the languages* (see Tables 6-10). Likewise, *teaching minority languages as a subject* is for primary, secondary and technical education in alternative (iii) and for universities provision (ii). For pre-schools it does not exist. *Sweden has not offered this provision to any of the languages either* (see Tables 6-10).

One might argue that the positive provisions are impossible to implement for 'small' languages. Therefore I compare Sweden with Finland. The number of Swedish speakers in Finland is some 5.6% of the population, and might already be smaller than the number of Finnish speakers in Sweden. The Swedish language in Finland is not officially a minority language. Swedish has in Finland the same rights as the majority language, Finnish: both are official languages at the same level. Nevertheless, Finland has ratified the Charter for Swedish, choosing maximal provision, (i), for all the educational levels a) to e) discussed here. Swedish in Finland thus has maximal rights, whereas Finnish in Sweden in the Swedish ratification of the Charter has no right to mother tongue medium education or the teaching of the language as a subject.

We could also compare the ratifications of the two countries in relation to the Saami language(s). There are fewer Saami in Finland than in Sweden. Finland has chosen the maximum, provision (i), for pre-schools and for primary and secondary education and provision (ii) for vocational and university education. Sweden has chosen the lowest provisions, (iv) and (iii), respectively, for Saami. The law which implements the Charter in Sweden gives pre-school children, in 4 municipalities for Saami and 5 municipalities for Finnish and Meänkieli, some rights to at least partial mother tongue medium care, but no rights in the rest of the country where the bulk of the Finnish speakers live. Primary, secondary, vocational and university education are not even mentioned in the relevant Swedish law (Prop. 1998/99: 143: 6-10).

So far we have looked at issues which can be assessed completely objectively: ratifications. I also want to present a couple of quotes about what some governments themselves say about their own implementation, from information given by the various OSCE governments to Max van der Stoel (OSCE's High Commissioner on National Minorities) in a large-scale inquiry about the linguistic rights of persons belonging to national minorities in the OSCE area (1999).In general, the government replies showed a fair degree of ignorance about basic language rights and educational issues. Many governments "need to be *better aware of the content of the international standards* in these various areas" as van der Stoel diplomatically puts it in his conclusions (1999: 37).

Here I have chosen one quote from the British government. I have added a few comments (in italics) to replies; all emphases are mine. The replies show that there is a long way to go, in terms of awareness of language rights.

> In public administration, the Government's policy is to deal with Irish speakers on a basis of courtesy and respect for the linguistic preference. People writing to northern Ireland Departments in Irish will have their letters translated and will receive a reply (in English) in the normal way. However, it is not the Government's policy to move towards a bilingual administration. This could be politically *divisive* and would undermine progress in recent years in extending interest in the Irish language to the wider Northern Ireland Community (reply to question 1, UK).

My comment is: Is it "courtesy and respect" to reply in the language that people have NOT preferred to use? How can using a language that people understand be divisive? Compare this with Norway and Hungary below – and then Sweden:

> [...] any person who contacts a local public body in the administrative area in Sami language has the right to get a reply in Sami (reply to question 2, Norway[12]).

---

[12] In Sweden, getting a written reply from the authorities in the designated minority languages even in those few municipalities where the languages have maximal

The State recognizes the minority languages as a major *cohesive*
factor for their communities (reply to question 1, Hungary).
*My comment: In Sweden, getting a written reply from the authorities in the
designated minority languages even in those few municipalities where the
languages have maximal rights according to the Swedish ratification of the
European Charter for Regional or Minority Languages, is conditional and can be
refused (Prop. 1998/99: 143; 7, 9).*

If you compare what Finland has chosen for the three Saami languages where
two of them have a population of fewer than 500 each and still fewer speakers, with
what Britain has chosen for much larger groups (and which groups it has left
completely outside) and what the attitudes of the UK government are, there may be
conclusions to draw. My general conclusion here is that much official rhetoric of
the EU and its member states endorses a commitment to linguistic diversity, but
in practice many of the member states are perpetuating linguistic hierarchies in
ways that counteract multilingualism and linguistic diversity, and represent a
threat to many languages. Swedish policies look deceptively good, but even if
linguicism is in operation here in sophisticated, i.e. not visibly brutal ways,
Sweden certainly conforms to this pattern. What about Britain?

Next I shall look at the treatment of one specific group of languages, the Sign
languages.

3. Good Friday Agreement and Sign languages – are Sign languages "languages" to be included in the European Charter?

3.1. Good Friday Agreement – "linguistic minorities" or "ethnic communities"?

No country has so far ratified the European Charter for any Sign language. When
representatives of various countries ask for advice from the relevant Council of
Europe office, they are being told that Sign languages are not minority languages
in the sense of the Charter (this was, for instance, the advice to the Danish
Ministry of Foreign Affairs, in April 2001, just prior to the Danish ratification,
according to the Ministry's letter to the Danish Association of the Deaf; told me
by the Secretary of the Association, Helle Skjoldan). Still, Sign languages do
objectively fulfil all the criteria set forth in the Charter's definition of minority
languages. Wrong information and myths prevail. Even in several of the articles
at the first Belfast conference, "Language and Politics", there are many examples
of them. I'll start by showing to you some quotes from the various articles in the
conference book that make the inclusion of Sign languages in the Good Friday
Agreement more difficult or that show ignorance about Sign languages and
bilingual education research. After that, I deconstruct the incorrect arguments
which have been and are being used to exclude Sign languages from the
European Charter.

The first question for an outsider like me is: what does the Good Friday
Agreement text actually say? Compare the following alleged quotes from it:

---

rights according to the Swedish ratification of the *European Charter*, is conditional
and can be refused (Prop. 1998/99: 143; 7, 9).

All participants recognise the importance of respect, understanding and tolerance in relation to linguistic diversity including, in Northern Ireland, the Irish language, Ulster-Scots and the languages of the various *linguistic minorities,* all of which are part of the cultural wealth of the island of Ireland" (Seán Farren, 2000: 121; emphasis added).

My comment is that this could include Sign languages because their Deaf users constitute linguistic minorities (see 3.3 below).

But what Seán Farren renders as "linguistic minorities", is replaced in the same book by at least two eminent people, Tom Hadden (2000: 115-116) and Dauvit Horsbroch (2000: 137), by "the languages of the various *ethnic communities*" (emphasis added). *My comment is that this would exclude Sign language. While their users ARE linguistic minorities, they are NOT ethnic communities.*

My questions to you are, then: what does the Good Friday Agreement ("Guid Fryday Greement", Horsbroch 2000: 137) in fact say? And why has the disagreement between the two renderings not been pointed out? Both texts cannot be correct - still the difference makes all the difference for Deaf users of Sign.

Secondly, four quotes about BSL, the British Sign Language, from Bob McCullough (2000) that are worryingly uninformed:

1. I also feel that BSL has been given a mystical status that tends to absorb too much of some deaf people's time and prevents them buckling down to education so that they may acquire the qualifications needed for progress in the real world. (p. 93).

2. BSL is a language of communication and cannot be recognized as an official language because it has no written form (p. 93).

3. Advocates of BSL say it is a language in itself with its own structure, its own idioms and its own linguistic history. I do not argue with this. But I do insist that it is a language without books and incapable in itself of enabling deaf people to achieve the potential which their intelligence and natural ability equips them (p. 94).

4. I welcome BSL interpreters in educational settings and for communication with doctors and other officials. But I cannot see us having any meaningful part in higher office until English is recognized as our first and most essential language (p. 94).

Even when McCullough has some good suggestions too, the quotes are insidious and dangerous. They glorify English, stigmatize British Sign Language, and rationalize the relationship between them in a way that completely invalidates Sign language so that it is seen as not fit for being the mother tongue, the first and most essential language of the Deaf, or an official language. It seems fit only for some transitional purposes and not much time should be used on it. In McCullough's opinion, Deaf children in school should be allowed some interpretation rather than using the Sign language as the main medium of education (which is obviously the only alternative that is supported by research).

Most of this is counterfactual or unscientific, and constitutes a serious violation of Deaf people's linguistic human rights. These arguments are surprisingly similar to the false arguments used to exclude Sign languages from the European Charter, as you will see when I present these. At the same time as I deconstruct these, I also deconstruct McCullough's arguments.

3.2. What are the arguments for excluding Sign languages from the European Charter for Regional or Minority Languages?[13]

Verena Krausneker quotes in her MA-thesis 'Sign Languages in the Minority Languages Policy of the European Union'' (1998: 22) a written statement on Sign languages and the European Charter by Mr. Fernando Albanese. He was the Director of Environment and Local Authorities in the Secretariat General of the Council of Europe at the point when the European Charter was being negotiated. Mr. Albanese does:

> not think on the basis of the information in my possession that the Charter applies to Sign Languages. In any case, such a problem was never raised during the negotiations of the Charter.

The 'information' that Mr. Albanese claims to possess is in fact serious misinformation and completely false. He claims that:

> the Sign Languages are connected with a handicap and not with the membership to a group, ethnically, religiously or linguistically different from the majority of the population of a state.

A 'regional or minority language' for the purposes of the Charter requires that this language be:

> different from the official language(s) of the State; it does not include either dialects of the official language(s) of the State or the languages of migrants (Article 1(a)ii)

Mr. Albanese then uses the following argument to exclude Sign languages. He thinks that the essential element required by the definition, namely

> the difference in respect of the official language(s) of the State' is missing, because 'If I understand it correctly, Sign Languages are means of communication within any language (Krausneker 1998: 22; emphasis added).

I shall next deconstruct the arguments. Mr. Albanese has claimed two things:

1. The Deaf do not fulfil the requirements of being a minority
2. Sign languages do not fulfil the requirements for being regional or minority languages.

3.3. Deconstructing the arguments: are the Deaf a minority?

The Deaf do objectively fulfil most of the criteria for being a minority, regardless of which definition of a minority is used. The problem is that many of the bureaucrats responsible for the interpretation and management of various Charters and Conventions do not seem to know enough about the characteristics of the Deaf communities in order to assess to what extent the various criteria are fulfilled (see Capotorti 1979 for the difficulty of defining minorities; see also Andr_sek 1989, Packer 1993). There is no definition of a minority that would be universally accepted in international law, but most definitions are very similar indeed. 'Most definitions use as defining characteristics a combination of the following:

---

[13] Subsections 3.2-3.4 follow very closely the English version of what is published in German as Skutnabb-Kangas 2002a.

1. Numbers[14];
2. Dominance is used in some but not others ('in an inferior and non-dominant position', Andr_sek 1989: 60; 'in a non-dominant position', Capotorti 1979: 96);
3. Ethnic or religious or linguistic traits, features or characteristics, or cultural bonds and ties which are (markedly) different from those of the rest of the population (in most definitions);
4. A will/wish (if only implicit) to safeguard, or preserve, or strengthen the patterns of life and behaviour, or culture, or traditions, or religion, or language of the group is specifically mentioned in most definitions (e.g. Capotorti 1979: 96). Language is included in most but not all definitions (e.g. not in Andr_sek's definition 1989: 60).
5. Citizenship/nationality in the state concerned is required in most definitions in charters and covenants as part of the definition, i.e. minorities are defined so as to give national or regional minorities more rights than to immigrants and refugees (who, by definition, are considered non-national and non-regional). In contrast, academic definitions for research purposes often make no mention of nationality as a criterion.' (Skutnabb-Kangas 2000: 489-490).

As an example of a broad definition, I present my own definition (from Skutnabb-Kangas and Phillipson 1994: 107, Note 2; Skutnabb-Kangas 2000: 491), which is based on my reformulation of the definition by the Council of Europe Commission for Democracy through Law (91) 7, Art. 2[15].

> A group which is smaller in number than the rest of the population of a State, whose members have ethnic, religious or linguistic features different from those of the rest of the population, and are guided, if only implicitly, by the will to safeguard their culture, traditions, religion or language.
>
> Any group coming within the terms of this definition shall be treated as an ethnic, religious or linguistic minority.
>
> To belong to a minority shall be a matter of individual choice.

I have in this definition omitted the requirement of citizenship ('who are nationals of that State'), because a forced change of citizenship to my mind cannot be

---

[14] It has to be remembered that these definitions are for the purposes of international law, so that it is possible to see which groups are entitled to protection that is granted to minorities. If a group is a majority in terms of numbers but in a dominated position, they may have rights on the basis of other characteristics, e.g. status, class, gender, or the like, but they are not a minority. From a sociological point of view, we may then speak about a minorized majority, i.e. a majority that suffers from a similar type of discrimination that minorities often face.

[15] This Draft was never accepted by Council of Europe, and the one that replaced it and became the *Framework Convention for the Protection of National Minorities* does not define minorities.

required in order to be able to enjoy basic human rights[16]. Besides, most Deaf are citizens of the state where they live.

As we can see, the Deaf fulfill all the criteria:

1. they are as a group 'smaller in number than the rest of the population of a State;
2. they 'have ... linguistic features different from those of the rest of the population'; and
3. they have, through their organizations, shown 'the will to safeguard their culture, traditions ... or language.'

Therefore, the Deaf are a national linguistic minority to whom the European Charter should apply. If an individual claims that she belongs to a national minority, and the State claims that such a national linguistic minority does not exist, there is a conflict, and the State may refuse to grant the minority person or group rights which it has accorded or might accord to national minorities. In many definitions of minority, minority rights thus become conditional on the acceptance by the State of the existence of a minority in the first place. According to my definition (and this part was suggested by Council of Europe itself!), minority status does NOT depend on the acceptance of the State, but is either 'objectively' ('coming within the terms of this definition' or subjectively verifiable ('a matter of individual choice'), or both, as is the case here for the Deaf. This interpretation has been confirmed by the UN Human Rights Committee in 1994. They reinterpreted Article 27 of the *UN International Covenant on Civil and Political Rights* (1966, in force since 1976) in a General Comment of 6 April 1994 (UN Doc. CCPR/C/21/Rev.1/Add.5, 1994. Article 27 is still the most far-reaching Article in (binding) human rights law granting linguistic rights:

> *In those states in which ethnic, religious or linguistic minorities exist, persons belonging to such minorities shall not be denied the right, in community with other members of their group, to enjoy their own culture, to profess and practise their own religion, or to use their own language.*

Until the reinterpretation, the Article was mostly interpreted as:

1. excluding (im)migrants (who have not been seen as minorities);
2. excluding groups (even if they are citizens) which are not recognised as minorities by the State;
3. only conferring some protection against discrimination (= "negative rights") but not a positive right to maintain or even use one's language;
4. not imposing any obligations on the States.

The UN Human Rights Committee sees the Article as:

1. protecting all individuals on the State's territory or under its jurisdiction (i.e. also immigrants and refugees), irrespective of whether they belong to the minorities specified in the Article or not;
2. stating that the existence of a minority does not depend on a decision by the State but requires to be established by objective criteria;
3. recognizing the existence of a "right";

[16.]This interpretation has since been borne out by the UN Human Rights Commission's April 1994 General Comment on Article 27.

4. imposing positive obligations on the States.

For Deaf people this means that various countries minimally have to see the Deaf as a (linguistic) minority, protected by Article 27. Likewise, the reinterpretation means that minorities, including the Deaf, are supposed to have positive language rights, not only the negative right of protection against discrimination. The states where Deaf live, i.e. all states in the world, thus do have positive obligations towards the Deaf as a linguistic minority.

In addition, the Deaf can of course also be seen as a group with a handicap, if they so choose, but whether they choose this or not has no consequences for their minority status: they ARE national linguistic minorities.

3.4. Deconstructing the arguments: are Sign languages minority languages?

A 'regional or minority language' for the purposes of the European Charter requires that this language be:

> *different from the official language(s) of the State; it does not include either dialects of the official language(s) of the State or the languages of migrants* (Article 1(a)ii).

As we remember, Mr. Albanese did not think that Sign languages were different from the official languages because 'Sign Languages are means of communication *within any language*' (Krausneker 1998: 22; emphasis added). In April 2000 the Danish Ministry of Foreign Affairs, rejecting the demand by the Danish Association of the Deaf that Sign language be included when Denmark ratifies the Charter, quoted Council of Europe's legal department and argued that Sign Language did not fulfill the criteria for being a minority language; it is a 'means of communication' (*kommunikationsmiddel*) rather than a (historical) language, also because the Danish Deaf use the Danish language in its written form as their written language. Here we can recognize McCullough's argument too.

Firstly, Sign languages are completely independent languages and have nothing to do with the official (or other) oral languages of the countries where they exist. Mr. Albanese may be thinking of *Signed languages* or *Manual Sign Codes* like Signed Swedish, Signed English, Signed German, etc, but these are NOT Sign languages, only manually coded oral languages. Secondly, ALL languages, written, spoken and signed, are 'means of communication', even if there are other means of communication too, like pictures, dress, jewelry, and so on. Using visual signs rather than oral signs as a means of communication does not make a language less of a language. Thirdly, Sign languages are historical languages in the same way as oral languages are, and some of them may have a longer pedigree than many oral languages. And finally, the Danish Deaf using 'the Danish language in its written form as their written language', parallels what practically every Deaf community in the world does, even the ones who have been accorded official minority status by the states they live in. Most Sign languages do not as yet have writing systems that would be easily available for the Deaf. The necessary resources for reducing them to writing have not existed. If languages without (everyday use of) their own writing systems were not seen as languages, some two thirds of the world's oral languages would also "disappear", not be seen as languages, because they do not have writing systems, or, if they have them, they have only been used for very few purposes, mostly for translating (parts of) the Bible and writing a few grammars or elementary textbooks but not for everyday communication. Sign languages thus fulfil all the requirements for being minority languages for the purposes of the European Charter.

All the arguments excluding Sign languages are thus false and based on complete ignorance of languages in general and Sign languages in particular, as any researcher in the area can testify. Today important language status planning decisions are based on this type of false information, even in situations where the correct information is easily available (see, e.g. EUD Update 2001, and the World Federation of the Deaf http://www.wfdnews.org/home.asp) and has in fact been offered to the decision makers. This is unethical.

4. Scots and Meänkieli - parallel development from "dialects" to "languages"?

Next I move to two other cases where historical oppression of a language community has resulted in low status but where this may be about to change. I see a clear parallel between the two situations, even if there are major differences too. I shall, again, only describe the one which I am more familiar with, leaving the drawing out of the similarities between the situations discussed at this conference and that of Meänkieli to my audience, partly because of space but mainly because the details of the development in any part of the world are too subtle for an outsider and I do not want to make the type of blunders that an outsider is always bound to make.

When Sweden ratified the *European Charter for Regional or Minority Languages* on 9 February 2000, Sweden suddenly got a completely new language, Meänkieli ("our language"). Of course the idiom had existed for a long time, but its language status, languageness, was officially accepted and enforced at that date. This is what the Swedish ratification says:

> Sami[17], Finnish and Meänkieli (Tornedal Finnish) are regional or minority languages in Sweden. Sweden´s undertakings pursuant to Article 2, paragraph 2 with respect to these languages are described in the appendix. Romani Chib and Yiddish shall be regarded as non-territorial minority languages in Sweden when the Charter is applied.

Altogether, 42 paragraphs or subparagraphs apply to Meänkieli (45 to Finnish and "Sami").

When writing this paper, I made an internet Google search on "Meänkieli", on 12 August 2002. I got 1010 results – pretty impressive for a language that has "existed" for two and a half years. What follows is based on some of the results and on writings by the EBLUL representative of Meänkieli, dr. Birger Winsa (see bibliography), in addition to my general knowledge and contacts with speakers of Meänkieli over the last 35 years. First some background.

---

[17] The spelling that the Saami themselves prefer is *Saami*. In a long discussion with Ole Henrik Magga, Professor of Saami (and the Chairperson of UN's Indigenous Forum), December 2000, he said that *Saami* was the first preference, the second being *Sámi*. The worst spelling, according to him, is *Sami*, i.e. the one that Sweden uses.

Finnish, a Finno-Ugric language, is spoken by some 200-250,000[18] Sweden Finns, most of them descendants of immigrants from the latter part of the 20th century, scattered all over Sweden, but especially in the capital region and major cities (see Skutnabb-Kangas 1996b). Meänkieli, also called Tornedal Finnish, is also a Finno-Ugric language spoken by some 35-70,000[19] Tornedalians foremost in the northernmost municipalities of Sweden. Some of them are immigrants from the Finnish part of the Torne valley, on the other side of the border river, Torne, but most of them are descendants of Finnish-speaking people who have lived in the area for around 1000 years. The Finnish Torne dialect which is spoken on both sides of the river, is a dialect of the Finnish language. When today's Finland was colonized by Sweden (from around 1150 until 1809), there were few differences in the dialect on both sides of the river. After 1809, when Finland became a Grand Duchy under Russia, a separate development started; obviously Meänkieli shows influences of both contact with Swedish and of the fact that most speakers were unfamiliar with standard Finnish, especially in its written form, and their own dialect was, except for some religious literature, not a written language until the 1980s. Still, Finnish and Meänkieli are, at least speaking personally, completely mutually intelligible - I have no more difficulty in understanding Meänkieli than in understanding lots of varieties, dialectal and sociolectal, of the Finnish language in Finland, meaning no difficulties at all, except for a few words. This is where I think the parallels with the situation discussed at this conference may come in.

From 1809 onwards, assimilationist attitudes prevailed in Sweden, because government representatives were afraid that Russia (and later on, after its independence in 1917, Finland) might make territorial demands on the Swedish Tornedalen if the population was Finnish-speaking. Still, when formal education first started in the North in the 1840s, instruction of the Finnish-speakers was in

---

[18] Nobody knows the numbers; there is no mother tongue question in the Swedish census. Figures of up to 400,000 have been claimed.

[19] Even here the estimates differ considerably. The 5 northern Swedish municipalities where Meänkieli now has official status are Haparanda, Övertorneå, Pajala, Kiruna and Gällivare. The names are here given in Swedish; all of them have Finnish names too, but you would not find them on any maps yet. The last two now have 3 official languages, Meänkieli, Saami and Swedish (and thus they also have official names in Saami). Birger Winsa, himself Tornedalian, estimates that in these 5 municipalities there are some "25-45,000 people who can speak/do speak/understand Meänkieli and Finnish (daily). I do not differentiate the immigrants from Finland and the Swedish Tornedalians, because most of the Finnish immigrants come from the Finnish part of Tornedalen and are thus speakers of the Tornedalian Finnish dialect which is called a language on the Swedish side" (personal communication, 25 November 2001; my translation from Swedish). "In Norrbotten there are an estimated additional 5-15,000 people with competence in Meänkieli. In the rest of Sweden there are probably 5-15,000 people with skills in Meänkieli. Thus, totally 35-75,000. But as I said, all of this is estimates" (ibid.). The official web page of the municipality of Pajala estimates that there are altogether 50-60,000 speakers of Meänkieli in Sweden, Finland, Norway and Russia (www.pajala.se).

Finnish. Swedish did not have much influence on Meänkieli or on the people in Tornedalen before 1888, when the state offered to pay for schools, provided that all the instruction was in Swedish. For the poor northern municipalities this was an offer impossible to resist. Several other regulations, inspired by the nationalist European ideas about one nation - one language, also started to make an impact. Children were punished for speaking their mother tongues, libraries were forbidden to buy or own Finnish-medium literature, and so on (see Skutnabb-Kangas 1984, 2000, for examples from all over the world of this linguistic oppression in education, including in Tornedalen[20]). In the late 1950s, a majority of Meänkieli-speaking parents started to speak Swedish to their children. The prohibitions were only slowly lifted in the 1960s, and standard Finnish, i.e. NOT Meänkieli, became an optional subject in schools at the same time as and partly because immigrant minority languages, initially Finnish, started to get some basic educational rights in connection with the "home language reform" some 25 years ago. At that point Meänkieli had thus almost disappeared as the first and most dominant language of children. Meänkieli has been, since the late 1970s and early 1980s, experiencing a revival. Until 1995, there was very little support for this revival from the Swedish state authorities, and the state argued that Sweden would not ratify the European Charter.

In 1995 and 1996, Sweden appointed two Commissions with instructions to determine whether Sweden can ratify the *European Charter for Regional or Minority Languages* and the *Framework Convention for the Protection of National Minorities*. The reports conclude that all Sámi varieties, all Finnish varieties, and all Romany Chib varieties are historical regional or minority languages in Sweden. However, the subsequent Government bill on minority issues, submitted to the Swedish Parliament in June 1999, proposes that "Sámi, Finnish, Meänkieli, Romani Chib and Yiddish" are the five minority languages.

The 4 northern municipalities of Kiruna, Gällivare, Jokkmokk, and Arjeplog provide public services in both Saami and Swedish. The 5 municipalities of Haparanda, Övertorneå, Pajala, Kiruna and Gällivare are expected to provide these services in Meänkieli and Finnish (and Swedish). Thus, Kiruna and Gällivare have three official minority languages, in addition to Swedish, designated for use by local, regional or national authorities in the region. For these municipalities, the new legislation means that individuals, by virtue of citizenship and residence, have the right to use their own languages *vis-à-vis* administrative authorities and courts, irrespective of their knowledge of Swedish. The individual may write in one of the minority languages, but the authority can respond in Swedish, with a note written in the minority language indicating that an oral version of the content can be provided in the home language of the individual. Thus Sweden has also here, just like in educational provisions (see Tables 6-10), chosen one of the provisions with few rights for the indigenous or minority citizens.

---

[20] There is a lot of literature of the ideologies, regulations and reactions, including fiction, about Tornedalen, most of it in Swedish, some in Finnish, and today also in Meänkieli. I recommend the interested reader to use some of the websites found, for instance, through a Google search. References in the bibliography under Winsa and Wande give some suggestions.

There are some 30 recent book titles written in Meänkieli. The Tornedalian schools recently had as a goal that 70% of the pupils should know Meänkieli, both receptively and productively, when leaving elementary school. After protests from some groups of parents, the goal has been changed. Now it is only that 70% of the pupils should understand Meänkieli, i.e. a receptive competence only. According to the official home page of one of the municipalities involved, Pajala (downloaded in August 2002), "the protests were probably coming out as a rage against something being forced upon the children. Today's parents and their parents were not allowed to use Meänkieli, and [were] forced to speak Swedish. Now their children were to be forced to learn Meänkieli."

My question to you is: can we learn something from the parallels? Is a dialect better off if it calls itself a language and is accepted as such? What are the advantages of being a language? Are there status advantages?

Could there be pragmatic drawbacks? Could there be new hierarchies that are being created because few people know how to write the new language? Does too much of the group's energy go to creating the paraphernalia thought to be needed if an idiom is "a language"? Could the energies and the economic resources be employed more usefully for other tasks? Is the undertaking a desperate search for a historically imagined identity, in a time characterized by growing insecurities? Whom does it benefit? And does it further disadvantage some speakers of the dialect/language?

Or is the languageness finally redressing some of the consequences of the historic oppression?

5. Common worries for Gaelic, Maori, Hawaiian, Skolt Saami, Ánar Saami and other reviving (?) languages: what happens when the majority are second language speakers?

Many reviving languages with few and/or elderly speakers only have similar worries; I shall present a couple of them. The Maori language nests, Kahanga Reo, started in 1981; there were in 1998 almost 700 of them (646 according to King 2001: 122) and almost half of the Maori children who attend any pre-school are in them. The 60 (in 1998, ibid., 122) Maori-medium schools, Kura Kaupapa Maori, cater for almost 5,000 students. Both forms have been a great source of inspiration for many indigenous peoples all over the world (see also May, ed., 1999). Both Hawaiian-medium education (Panana Leo. see Wilson 1999, Wilson and Kamana 2001, No'eau Warner 2001) and several Saami programmes (e.g. Balto and Todal 1997, Huss 1999, Todal 1999), were initially inspired by them. In 1979, very few Maori were estimated to be able to speak Maori fluently, and most of them were elderly. After almost two decades of Maori-medium education, the majority of today's adult Maori population 'speak some Maori (59,6%), but only 26,2% are able to carry out daily conversations in Maori with ease' (according to a new study, quoted in Durie 1999: 77; see also Durie 1997). The *Maori Language Act* (1987) which made Maori an official language in Aotearoa/New Zealand, conferred people, among other rights, 'the right to speak Maori in any legal proceedings regardless of ability to speak English' (ibid., 73). Using an indigenous language thus does NOT signal inability to use the dominant language, something that is still a common interpretation almost everywhere else

Language loss in Hawai'i has been even more dramatic than in Aotearoa: of a population of 1,138,870, of which 220,747 were of Hawaiian ancestry in 1992, only about 500-1000, were native speakers of Hawaiian. Of these, all others were over 70, 'except for those from the island of Ni'ihau, a small community of some 300 individuals that maintains first-language fluency in the language at all ages' (Wilson 1999: 95). In addition to them, there are today more than 1500 'neo-native' speaker children 'aged between 3-16 years who have become quite conversant in Hawaiian through attending private community-based Panana Leo pre-schools and public Hawaiian-medium / immersion schools' (ibid.). The first graduates from the immersion schools (1999) can 'attend a Hawaiian language college and obtain a masters degree in Hawaiian language and literature' (ibid.).

The 11 Saami languages have altogether probably 25,000-35,000 speakers whereas there are some 100,000 ethnic Saami in four countries, Norway, Sweden, Finland and Russia (see, e.g. Helander 1984, Aikio-Puoskari 2001, Magga and Skutnabb-Kangas 2001, on various aspects of their situation). The Saami are the only indigenous peoples in the European Union. All three Saami languages, spoken in Finland, have a regional official status, and the European Charter has been ratified for all three. Of the three, Ánar Saami is spoken in Finland only, Skolt Saami mostly in Finland but also by a few families in Russia (and there are some Skolt families in Norway), and North Saami is spoken in all 4 countries. There are fewer than 500 ethnic Skolt Saami and equally many Ánar Saami. Most of the fairly few fluent native speakers are elders, whereas younger speakers are mostly second language speakers. Satu Moshnikoff (2002a, b) tells in two articles about the status and use of Skolt Saami where a strong revitalisation has taken place since the 1990s. Earlier people with Skolt Saami background were ashamed of their origins, language and culture and tried to hide them. Today there is a Skolt Saami language nest and the language is both used as a medium and taught as a subject in school. Young people are eager to learn aspects of culture and have drawn elders into their activities as teachers. Almost 10 books were published in Skolt in 2000 and 2001; it is used in two churches, and some parts of the New Testament have been translated. Media use of Skolt Saami is negligible. A language nest was started already in 1993, but it continued only half a year; there was no money. In 1997 it started again, this time with European Union support. The 17 Skolt children in the language nest in the autumn 2001 were all second language speakers. The cultural content in the language nests is extremely important; there are long and short excursions, the children participate in and learn about reindeer herding, fishing, traditional foods, etc. and parents and elders participate maximally (Moshnikoff, 2000a, b). The situation of Ánar Saami is similar. Most of the young people who speak the language are second language speakers; even so, a language nest has been started, and one of the children, around a year and 7 months at the time of our conference, is the first native language speaker of Ánar Saami for more than 20 years, with parents whose dominant language is still Finnish but who heard Saami in their childhood and study it actively; the mother is one of the two professional educators in the language nest (field notes, Inari, Finland, November 2001). The situation of Lule Saami in Sweden is much worse.

I have read about and heard and participated in similar discussions about some common challenges for all languages mentioned in the subtitle. I shall only mention a couple of the topics here. It is obviously up to the speakers themselves to discuss further, within the groups/nations, and to find solutions - it is not anything where outsiders' opinions should have much weight.

When people are worried about the future of various related languages/dialects, which either have not been reduced to writing at all, or which have competing orthographies, or which have a writing system but very few written materials, or where there are too few people for all the writing tasks deemed necessary (e.g. educational materials), it is easy to start thinking of various kinds of standardisation, in order to make the group of possible users larger. For instance: should one have one standard written Saami but several spoken languages? (This was suggested by some Saami politicians at the 10th Anniversary of the Saami College, in Guovdageaidnu/Kautokeino, Norway, in December 2000, at a panel where I participated). This could be compared with suggestions in, e.g., South Africa, by Neville Alexander (e.g. 1989, 1992) and several others, about possibly standardising Nguni languages and Sotho languages for written purposes. Peter Mühlhäusler from Australia has (e.g. 1996) insightful discussions about the standardisation involved in the reduction to writing of oral languages, as one way of reducing linguistic diversity, i.e. killing some languages/varieties.

When the young Panana Leo or Hawai'ian immersion children start needing words for new concepts where the vocabulary does not exist in Hawaiian, what is the best way of creating those concepts? Should they be created, or should the issues rather be discussed in English only (these discussions have obviously been intense among several Aboriginal nations in Australia for a long time, with many suggestions about separating "white" knowledge and Aboriginal knowledge, also language-wise; see, e.g. Harris 1990). If they are being created, should one use loanwords from the dominant language, or try to create an indigenous vocabulary that fits the language also spiritually.

How can second language speakers or non-fluent speakers teach the language? For instance, in 1990 only one third of the immersion teachers in Kura Kaupapa Maori and bilingual classes were fluent speakers of M_ori (King 2001: 123).

Is it possible for second language speakers to transfer the language to further generations, both in school, and in homes? Will what they transfer be a language with the same knowledges, distinctions, the same spirit, as in the old language? Or will it, as I heard one Hawai'ian elder describe it, be English spoken with Hawai'ian or Hawai'ian-sounding words (field notes, Johannesburg, South Africa, August 2002). The people I have talked with are not mainly worried about normal change that all languages undergo in terms of vocabulary, and to some extent syntax and morphology (even if that may be a worry too), or words disappearing when some of the phenomena disappear; this happens in all languages. Instead, they are worried about the whole structure of the language. It seems to me that, for those who know about Sign languages, the Hawai'ians and others are speaking of a phenomenon comparable to either using a real Sign language, as Deaf people use it, or using Signed English or Signed Swedish, meaning artificial languages, Manual Sign Codes which "seek to represent the lexical items of an oral/aural language", for instance Swedish or English, "in a gestural/visual linguistic context" (Reagan 1995: 140). Thus these 'languages' are

NOT Sign languages, but manually coded oral languages[21]. It seems to me that it is this kind of "artificial" Hawai'ian that the people I have discussed it with are worried about. On the other hand, they also seem worried about the semantic aspects of the language, its "soul", its "spirit", its multi-layeredness, its many hidden meanings, ambiguities, its connections with rituals. The new "immersion Hawaiian" seems simplified, without real contact with the universe it has developed to represent. What comes to my mind is a parallel to simplified Sanskrit for monolingual foreign beginners where none of the thousands of years of philosophical and spiritual connections and connotations can be expressed in a one-word translation of central concepts - like dharma or samsk_ra[22]. I have heard some people say: "If the fullness of the language cannot be grasped in these two senses by the second language speakers who may at some point be the only ones to transfer the language to the following generations, would it not be better to let the language die?" On the other hand, we have all those people who are desperately seeking for even very incomplete fractions of their ancestors' languages, or even languages which were once spoken on the land where they now live (see e.g. several contributions in Hinton and Hale, eds, 2001, or Amery 1999). The languages were not dead; they were only sleeping, waiting to be awakened (see the initial quote again).

When there is a generation gap where only elders and children/young people speak the language whereas many from the middle generations do not know it or do not use it actively, what does this mean for the authority relations? For parent/child relations? For attitudes, difficult to discuss, of shame, blame, self-blame, bitterness, pride, happiness? Why did you not teach me the language? Why did I not have the chance to learn how to read my own language? Did I do wrong when I did not teach it? I only tried to help my children. Why did these rights and this revitalisation not come earlier? Why did my generation have to suffer? It is your own fault that you did not teach it to your children - why do my grandchildren have to suffer for it now? Stop blaming society, go and relearn it!

Are there parallels to the situations discussed at this conference? Can we learn from common challenges?

6. Conclusion

Just as Europe is genetically the world's most homogenous, i.e. poorest part (Cavalli-Sforza 2001: 23), Europe is also the poorest one on linguistic diversity. If

---

[21] "It is a distinction between, e.g. *Swedish Sign Language* (the language of the Swedish Deaf community, i.e. a language which has evolved 'naturally' among the community, just as oral languages have, with its own grammar, vocabulary, etc), and *signed Swedish*, which uses manual sign codes for a spoken language, i.e. trying to imitate or represent spoken Swedish with manual codes." (Skutnabb-Kangas 2000: 229).

[22] See the explanations of these in Rider 1999. I wonder why nobody has pointed out the partial similarities between Bourdieu's "habitus" and samsk_ra - Bourdieu would be enriched...

we discount recent immigrants[23] but count in ex-Soviet Union, we have only some 3% of the world's oral languages (see Price ed. 2000 for these). Middle East is also extremely poor on linguistic diversity. *The Ethnologue* (14th edition http://www.ethnologue.com/ethno_docs/distribution.asp) downloaded 23-01-02), gives the following figures and distribution: Europe 230 languages, 3%, the Americas (South, Central and North) have 1,013, 15%, Africa 2,058, 30%, Asia 2,197, 32%, and the Pacific 1,311, 19% (Table 11).

Table 11. The distribution of languages (*The Ethnologue*, 14th ed.)

Where?	How many languages?	Percentage of total
Europe	230	3%
The Americas (South, Central, North)	1,013	15%
Africa	2,058	30%
Asia	2,197	32%
The Pacific	1,311	19%

Attitudes originally emanating from Europe are still going strong in trying to make the rest of the world equally poor, by killing the linguistic and cultural diversity that still, just, exists in other parts of the world. Linguists estimate that half of the languages existing 500 years ago have already disappeared (e.g. UNESCO Ad Hoc Expert Group on Endangered Languages, 2002). The Europeanised countries, USA, Canada and Australia have been the worst culprits in the last few hundred years in destroying languages. To me it seems that many of these attitudes are still very strong. This could be seen very clearly at the Johannesburg World Summit for Sustainable Development in August - September 2002. Listening to the various parties there, I was thinking of the post-Second-World-War negotiations in Bretton Woods. Some of the first economic instruments for maintaining the disparity between the US and the rest of the world and for developing today's modern globalisation in order to reach this goal were put in place already at the Bretton Woods hotel in July 1944 when the United Nations Monetary and Financial Conference was held. By the end of the Bretton Woods meeting, the World Bank and the International Monetary Fund (IMF), thereafter called 'the Bretton Woods instruments', had been founded, and the groundwork had also been laid for what later became first GATT and then the WTO (World Trade Organisation) (see also Korten 1996). At this meeting the overt agenda was to create institutions that would secure peace and prosperity globally. At Bretton Woods, the US Cold War planner, George Kennan, expressed the goals of the US foreign policy goals. He wrote in 1948, in the aftermath of the passing of the first parts of United Nations Bill of Rights:

> We have 50 per cent of the world's wealth, but only 6.3 per cent of
> its population. In this situation, our real job in the coming period is
> to devise a pattern of relationships which permit us to maintain this

---

[23] Even the city of London has more languages (over 350) among its school children in state schools (based on data collected from more than 850,000 children in 1998.99) than the number of autochthonous languages in the whole of Europe (Mackey 2001: 438).

position of disparity. To do so, we have to dispense with all sentimentality ... we should cease thinking about human rights, the raising of living standards, and democratisation' (quoted in Pilger 1998: 59).

There are clear parallels between the covert and overt agendas after the second World War and the time after September 11th. If we now look at the US overt agenda of claiming to be fighting terrorism and defending democracy, the rule of law, and human rights, we can see the same US egoism, wanting to grab much more than their fair share, and wanting to go it alone when it suits what it thinks is its interests (see Skutnabb-Kangas 2002a, in press b, for details). Britain is following suit, together with most of the European Union. I am afraid that Pierre Bourdieu's analysis of today's globalisation is very accurate. He describes today's globalisation as

... a pseudo-concept that is both descriptive and prescriptive, which has replaced 'modernisation', that was long used in the social sciences in the USA as a euphemistic way of imposing a naively ethnocentric evolutionary model by means of which different societies were classified according to their distance from the economically most advanced society, i.e. American society. [...] The word (and the model it expresses) incarnates the most accomplished form of the imperialism of the universal, which consists of one society universalising its own particularity covertly as a universal model (Bourdieu 2001, 96-97, translation Robert Phillipson).

It is this universalising of the specifically American, meaning USA, model that the whole era after the second "World" War has been about. And that model is disastrous to the planet.

Now how do education in general and lack of linguistic human rights in education in particular fit into this? If subtractive English teaching continues, at the same time as the results of it are glorified, it will become progressively easier to sell North American and European or more generally western ideologies, in fact outright lies, about the fairness of the present neo-liberal world system of disparities. When mother tongue medium teaching does not exist for indigenous peoples, minorities, and other dominated linguistic groups, the knowledge needed for independent analysis of the world is much harder to get. When transnational corporations, together with the Bretton Woods instruments, dominate not only the form but also the content of education, through textbook production and footing other bills too (see, e.g., Barlow and Robertson 1996 for Canada and Monbiot 2000 for Britain; see also Spring 1998 for a general introduction into the relationships between education and the global economy), it becomes progressively more difficult to analyse the rhetoric of the "free" world. When fewer and fewer alternatives exist, it will be easier to construct the power elites of the world as the benefactors whose only wish is to democratise the world and defend everybody's human rights. It is easier to make people accept as universal the ideologies about the necessity of "free" markets and the benefits of globalisation, at the same time as the prerequisites for life on the planet are diminishing and the ecosystem health is deteriorating because of the decisions made by the power elites. If you, my dear audience, feel as dismayed as I do about the picture that I have painted about how US, Britain, and global corporate/

industrial/ financial/ military elites try to run the world (and I hope most of you do), you also know how important the minority languages protection that we are discussing here is. We need to analyse, understand, and act. I congratulate the organisations of the conference for giving us an opportunity for combining all three.

References

Aikio-Puoskari, U. 2001. *Saamen kielen ja saamenkielinen opetus Pohjoismaissa. Tutkimus saamelaisten kielellisistä ihmisoikeuksista Pohjoismaiden kouluissa* (Teaching of and through the medium of Saami in the Nordic countries. A study of the linguistic human rights of the Saami in Nordic schools). Juridica Lapponica 25. Rovaniemi: Lapin yliopisto.

Aikio-Puoskari, U. and Pentikäinen, M. 2001. *The language rights of the indigenous Saami in Finland under domestic and international law.* Juridica Lapponica 26. Rovaniemi: University of Lapland.

Alexander, N. 1989. *Language Policy and National Unity in South Africa/Azania.* Cape Town: Buchu Books.

Alexander, N. 1992. "South Africa: Harmonising Nguni and Sotho". In ed. N. Crawhall *Democratically Speaking: International Perspectives on Language Planning.* Cape Town: National Language Project.

Alexander, N. 1995a. "Models of multilingual schooling for a democratic South Africa". In eds. Heugh et al. 79-82.

Alexander, N. 1995b. "Multilingualism for empowerment". In eds. Heugh et al., 37-41.

Alexander, N. 2000. "Language policy and planning in South Africa: some insights". In ed. Phillipson. 170-173.

Amery, R. 2000. *Warrabarna Kaurna! Reclaiming an Australian Language.* Series Multilingualism and Linguistic Diversity, 1. Lisse: Swets and Zeitlinger.

Andr_sek, O. 1989. *Report on the definition of minorities.* SIM Special No 8. Utrecht: Netherlands Institute of Human Rights, Studie- en Informatiecentrum Mensenrechten (SIM).

Annamalai, E. 1986. "Bilingualism through schooling in India". In ed. A. Abbi. *Studies in bilingualism.* Delhi: Bahri Publications.

Annamalai, E. 1993. "Planning for Language Survival". *New Language Planning Newsletter* 8:1: 1-2.

Annamalai, E. 1994. "Multilingual development: Indian experience". Paper at the UNESCO-OAU conference, Addis Abeba, 21-25 November 1994 "The definition of strategies for the promotion of African languages in a multilingual environment".

Annamalai, E. 1995. "Multilingualism for all - an Indian perspective". In ed. Skutnabb-Kangas. 215-220.

Annamalai, E. 1998. "Language choice in education: conflict resolution in Indian courts". In eds. Benson et al. 29-43.

Annamalai, E. 2001. *Managing Multilingualism in India.* New Delhi: Sage.

Annamalai, E. and V. Gnanasundaram. 2001. Andamanese: Biological

Challenges for Language Reversal. In ed. Fishman. 309-322.

Baker, C. 2001. "Review Skutnabb-Kangas 2000". *Journal of Sociolinguistics*, 5:2, May 2001: 279-283.

Balto, A. and Todal, J. 1997. "Saami Bilingual Education in Norway". In eds. Cummins and Corson. 77-86.

Barlow, M. and H-j. Robertson 1996. "Homogenization of education". In eds. Mander and Goldsmith. 60-70.

Baugh, J. 2000. "Educational Malpractice and the Miseducation of Language Minority Students". In eds. J. Kelly Hall and W.G. Eggington. *The Sociopolitics of English Language Teaching*. Clevedon: Multilingual Matters, 104-116.

Benson, P., P. Grundy and T. Skutnabb-Kangas eds. 1998. *Language rights*. Special volume. Language Sciences 20:1.

Bourdieu, P. 2001. *Contre-feux 2. Pour un mouvement social européen*. Paris. Raisons d'agir.

Branson, J. and D. Miller. 1998. "Nationalism and the linguistic rights of Deaf communities: Linguistic imperialism and the recognition and development of sign languages". *Journal of Sociolinguistics* 2:1, 1998: 3-34.

Branson, J. and D. Miller. 2000. "Maintaining, developing and sharing the knowledge and potential embedded in all our languages and cultures: on linguists as agents of epistemic violence". In ed. Phillipson. 28-32.

Capotorti, F. 1979. *Study of the Rights of Persons Belonging to Ethnic, Religious and Linguistic Minorities*. New York: United Nations.

Cavalli-Sforza, L.L. 2001. *Genes, Peoples and Languages*. London: Penguin.

Cummins, J. 1996. *Negotiating Identities: Education for Empowerment in a Diverse Society*. Ontario, California: California Association for Bilingual Education.

Cummins, J. 2000. *Language, Power, and Pedagogy: Bilingual Children in the Crossfire*. Clevedon, UK: Multilingual Matters.

Cummins, J. and Corson, D. 1997. *Bilingual Education*. Volume 5. *Encyclopedia of Language and Education*. Dordrecht, Boston and London: Kluwer Academic Publishers.

Desai, Z. 1995. "The evolution of a post-apartheid language policy in South Africa: an on-going site of struggle". *European Journal of Intercultural Studies* 5:3: 18-25.

Desai, Z. 1998. "Enabling policies, disabling practices". Paper presented at the Tenth World Congress of Comparative Education Societies, Cape Town, 16 July 1998. Manuscript.

Desai, Z. 2000. "Mother tongue education: the key to African language development? A conversation with an imagined South African audience". In ed. Phillipson. 174-178.

Desai, Z. 2001. "Multilingualism in South Africa with Particular Reference to the role of African languages in Education". *International Review of Education* 47: 3-4: 323-339.

Durie, A. 1997. "Maori-English Bilingual Education in New Zealand". In eds. Cummins and Corson. 15-24.

Durie, A. 1999. "Emancipatory M_ori Education: Speaking from the Heart". In ed. May. 67-78.

Eide, A. 1995. "Economic, social and cultural rights as human rights". In eds. Eide, Krause and Rosas. 21-40.

Eide, A., Krause, C. and Rosas, A. eds. 1995. *Economic, Social and Cultural Rights. A Textbook.* Dordrecht, Boston and London: Martinus Nijhoff Publishers.

EUD Update 2001. *EUD Update 4: 10, March 2001.* Special Edition: Update on The Status of Sign languages in the European Union. (available from the European Union of the Deaf, eud@planetinternet.be; see also http://www.eudnet.org/).

Farren, Seán. 2000. "Institutional Infrastructure Post-Good Friday Agreement: The New Institutions and Devolved Government". In ed. Kirk and Baoill. 121-126.

Fishman, J.A. 1991. *Reversing Language Shift. Theoretical and Empirical Foundations of Assistance to Threatened Languages.* Clevedon/Philadelphia: Multilingual Matters.

Fishman, J.A. 1994. "On the limits of ethnolinguistic democracy". In eds. T. Skutnabb-Kangas and R. Phillipson. 49-61.

Fishman, J.A. ed. 2001. *Can Threatened Languages Be Saved? Reversing Language Shift, Revisited: A 21st Century perspective.* Clevedon, UK: Multilingual Matters.

Fishman, J.A. and G. Schweid Fishman. 2000. "Rethinking language defense". In ed. Phillipson. 23-27.

Graddol, D. 1997. *The Future of English?* A guide to forecasting the popularity of the English language in the 21st century. London: British Council.

Grin, F. 1995a. "The economics of foreign language competence: a research project of the Swiss National Science Foundation". *Journal of Multilingual and Multicultural Development* 16:3, 227-231.

Grin, F. 1995b. "La valeur des compétences linguistiques: vers une perspective économiqu". *Babylonia* 2, 59-65.

Grin, F. 1996a. *Valeur privée de la pluralité linguistique.* Cahier No 96.04, Département d'économie politique. Genève: Université de Genève.

Grin, F. 1996b. "Economic approaches to language and language planning: an introduction". *International Journal of the Sociology of Language* 121: 1-16.

Grin, F. 1997. "Amémagement linguistique: du bon usage des concepts d'offre et de demande". (Language planning: on the proper use of the concepts of supply and demand). In ed. N. Labrie. *Etides récentes en linguistique de contact* (Recent studies in contact linguistics). Bonn: Dümmler, 117-134.

Grin, F. 1999. "Market forces, language spread and linguistic diversity". In eds. Kontra et al., 169-186.

Grin, F. And F. Vaillancourt. 2000. "On the financing of language policies and distributive justice". In ed. Phillipson. 102-110.

Groombridge, B. ed. 1992. *Global Biodiversity: Status of the Earth's Living Resources.* World Conservation Monitoring Centre. London: Chapman and Hall.

Grosjean, F. 2001. "The Right of the Deaf Child to Grow Up Bilingual". *Sign Language Studies* 1:2, Winter 2001: 110-114.

Hadden, T.. 2000. "Should a Bill of Rights for Northern Ireland Protect Language Rights?". In ed. Kirk and Baoill. 111-120.

"The Hague Recommendations Regarding the Education Rights of Minorities". *International Journal on Minority and Group Rights*. Special Issue on the Education Rights of National Minorities 4:2, 1996/1997.

Harmon, D. 1995. "The status of the world's languages as reported in the *Ethnologue*". *Southwest Journal of Linguistics* 14:1and2: 1-28.

Harmon, D. 2002. *In Light of Our Differences: How Diversity in Nature and Culture Makes Us Human.* Washington, D.C.: The Smithsonian Institute Press.

Harris, S. 1990. *Two-way Aboriginal Schooling. Education and Cultural Survival.* Canberra: Aboriginal Studies Press.

Helander, E. 1984. *Om trespråkighet - en undersökning av språkvalet hos samerna i Övre Soppero* (Trilingualism. A Study of Language Choice among Saamis in Övre Soppero). Umeå: Acta Universitatis Umensis. Umeå Studies in the Humanities 67.

Heugh, K. 1995a. "From unequal education to the real thing". In eds. Heugh et al., 42-51.

Heugh, Kathleen. 1995b. The multilingual school: modified dual medium. In eds. Heugh et al., 79-82.

Heugh, K. 1995c. Disabling and Enabling: Implications for language policy trends in South Africa. In ed. R. Mesthrie. *Language and Social History: Studies in South African Sociolinguistics.* Cape Town: David Philip. 329-350.

Heugh, K. 2000a. *The Case against Bilingual and Multilingual Education in South Africa.* PRAESA Occasional Papers No.6. Cape Town: University of Cape Town.

Heugh, K. 2000b. "Giving good weight to multilingualism in South Africa". In ed. Phillipson. 234-238.

Heugh, K., A. Siegrühn and P. Plüddemann eds. 1995). *Multilingual Education for South Africa.* Johannesburg: Heinemann.

Heywood, V.H. ed. 1995. *Global Biodiversity Assessment.* Cambridge and New York: Cambridge University Press and UNEP.

Hinton, L. and K. Hale eds. 2001. *The Green Book of Language Revitalization in Practice.* San Diego: Academic Press.

Horsbroch, D.. 2000. "*Mair as a Sheuch Atween Scotland an Ulster*: Twa Policie for the Scots Leid?". In ed. Kirk and Baoill. 133-142.

Huss, L. 1999. *Reversing Language Shift in the Far North. Linguistic Revitalization in Scandinavia and Finland.* Acta Universitatis Upsaliensis. Studia Uralica Upsaliensia 31. Uppsala: Uppsala University.

Huss, L., A. Camilleri and K. King eds. (in press). *Transcending Monolingualism: Linguistic Revitalisation in Education.* Series Multilingualism and linguistic diversity. Lisse: Swets and Zeitlinger.

ICSU (International Council for Science) 2002. *Science, Traditional Knowledge and Sustainable Development.* Series on Science for Sustainable Development No. 4. Compiled and edited primarily by D. Nakashima and D. Elias, UNESCO. ISSN 1683-3686. www.icsu.org. No place, no publisher.

Janulf, P. 1998. *Kommer finskan i Sverige att fortleva? En studie av språkkunskaper och språkanvändning hos andragenerationens sverigefinnar i Botkyrka och hos finlandssvenskar i Åbo.* ('Will Finnish survive in Sweden? A study of language skills and language use among second generation

Sweden Finns in Botkyrka, Sweden, and Finland Swedes in Åbo, Finland'). Acta Universitatis Stockholmiensis, Studia Fennica Stockholmiensia 7. Stockholm: Almqvist and Wiksell International.

Jokinen, M. 2000. "The linguistic human rights of Sign language users". In ed. Phillipson. 203-213.

Kamwangamalu, N.M. 1997. "Multilingualism and Education Policy in Post-Apartheid South Africa". *Language Problems and Language Planning* 21:3, 234-253.

King, J. 2001. "Te Kahanga Reo; Maori Language Revitalization". In eds. Hinton and Hale. 119-1128.

Kirk, J.M. and D.P. Ó Baoill eds 2000. *Language and Politics. Northern Ireland, the Republic of Ireland, and Scotland.* Belfast Studies in Language, Culture and Politics 1. Belfast: Cló Ollscoil na Banríona.

Klaus, D. (in press). "The use of indigenous languages in early basic education in Papua New Guinea: a model for elsewhere?". *Language and Education.*

Kontra, M., R. Phillipson, T. Skutnabb-Kangas and T. Várady, Tibor eds. 1999. *Language: a Right and a Resource. Approaching Linguistic Human Rights.* Budapest: Central European University Press.

Korten, D.C. 1996. "The failures of Bretton Woods". In eds. J. Mander and E. Goldsmith , 20-30.

Kouritzin, S. 1999. *Face[t]s of first language loss.* Mahwah, NJ: Lawrence Erlbaum Associates.

Krauss, M. 1992. "The world's languages in crisis". *Language* 68:1, 4-10.

Krauss, M. 1995. Paper at a conference of the American Association for the Advancement of Science, reported in *The Philadelphia Inquirer* 19.2.1995, p. A15.

Krausneker, V. 1998. *Sign Languages in the Minority Languages Policy of the European Union.* MA-thesis, September 1998. Vienna: University of Vienna.

Lane, H. 1992. *The Mask of Benevolence: Disabling the Deaf Community.* New York: Alfred Knopf.

Lee, T. and D. McLaughlin. 2001. "Reversing Navajo Language Shift, Revisited". In ed. Fishman. 23-43.

Lipka, J., with G.W. Mohatt and the Ciulistet Group. 1998. *Transforming the Culture of Schools. Yup'ik Eskimo Examples.* Mahwah, NJ and London: Lawrence Erlbaum Associates.

Lowell, A. and B. Devlin 1999. "Miscommunication between Aboriginal Students and their Non-Aboriginal Teachers in a Bilingual School". In: ed. May. 137-159.

Mackey, W.F. 2001. "Review of Baker, P. and Eversley, J. eds. *Multilingual Capital: The Languages of London's Schoolchildren and Their Relevance for Economic, Social and Educational Policies.* London: Battlebridge Publications". *Journal of Multilingual and Multicultural Development* 22:5, 438-439.

Maffi, L. 1994. *A Linguistic Analysis of Tzeltal Maya Ethnosymptomatology.* Ph.D. dissertation, University of California, Berkeley. [UMI order # 9504901].

Maffi, L. 2000a. "Linguistic and biological diversity: the inextricable link". In ed. Phillipson. 17-22.

Maffi, L. 2000b." Language preservation vs. language maintenance and revitalization: assessing concepts, approaches, and implications for language sciences". *International Journal of the Sociology of Languages* 142. ed. N.C. Dorian. *Small languages and small language communities.* 175-190.

Maffi, L. 2001. "Introduction". In ed. Maffi. 1-50.

Maffi, L. ed. 2001. *On Biocultural Diversity. Linking Language, Knowledge and the Environment.* Washington, D.C.: The Smithsonian Institute Press.

Maffi, L., T. Skutnabb-Kangas and J. Andrianarivo. 1999. "Linguistic diversity". In ed. Posey. 19-57.

Magga, O.H. and Skutnabb-Kangas, T. 2001. "The Saami languages: the present and the future". *Cultural Survival Quarterly.* Special issue on endangered languages, ed. E. Quinn. 26-31; 51.

Mander, J. and E. Goldsmith eds. 1996. *The case against the global economy and for a turn toward the local.* San Francisco: Sierra Club.

Martin, D.S. 2001. "The English-Only Movement and Sign Language for Deaf learners: An Instructive Parallel". *Sign Language Studies,* 1:2, Winter 2001: 115-124.

Martin, I. 2000a. *Sources and Issues: a backgrounder to the Discussion Paper on Language of Instruction in Nunavut Schools.* Department of Education, Nunavut. Manuscript. [imartin@glendon.yorku.ca].

Martin, I. 2000b. *Aajjiqatigiingniq. Language of Instruction Research Paper. A Report to the Government of Nunavut.* Department of Education, Iqaluit, Nunavut, Canada. Manuscript. [imartin@glendon.yorku.ca].

May, S. 2001. *Language and minority rights: ethnicity, nationalism, and the politics of language.* Harlow, Essex, England and NewYork: Longman.

May, S. ed. 1999. *Indigenous community-based education.* Clevedon, UK: Multilingual Matters. Also available as Vol. 11, No. 3 of *Language, Culture and Curriculum.*

McCullough, Bob. 2000. "Language, Discrimination and the Good Friday Agreement: The Case of Sign". In ed. Kirk and Baoill. 91-96.

Mittermeier, Russell A. and Cristina Goettsch Mittermeier (1997). *Megadiversity. Earth's Biologically Wealthiest Nations.* CEMEX: México, D.F.

No'eau Warner, S.L. 2001. "The Movement to Revitalize Hawaiian Language and Culture". In eds. Hinton and Hale. 133-146.

Packer, J. 1993. "On the Definition of Minorities". In eds. J. Packer and K. Myntti. *The Protection of Ethnic and Linguistic Minorities in Europe.* Åbo: Åbo Akademi University. Institute for Human Rights. 23-65.

Monbiot, G. 2000. *Captive state. The corporate takeover of Britain.* London: Macmillan.

Moshnikoff, S. 2001a. *Koltansaamen kielen asema ja käyttö vuonna 2001* [The position and use of Skolt Saami in 2001]. Sevettijärvi, Finland. Manuscript.

Moshnikoff, S. 2001b. *Koltansaamen kielipesä.* [The Skolt Saami language nest]. Sevettijärvi, Finland. Manuscript.

Mühlhäusler, P. 1996. *Linguistic ecology. Language change and linguistic imperialism in the Pacific region.* London: Routledge.

Nabhan, G.P. 2001. "Cultural perceptions of ecological interactions: an "endangered people's" contribution to the conservation of biological and linguistic diversity". In ed. Maffi. 145-156.

Nagai, Y. and R. Lister (in press). "What is our culture? What is our language? Dialogue towards the maintenance of indigenous culture and language in Papua New Guinea". *Language and Education.*

Nuffield Languages Inquiry2000. *Languages: the next generation.. The final report and recommendations of the Nuffield Languages Inquiry.* London: The Nuffield Foundation.

Ogden, C.K. 1934. *The System of Basic English.* New York: Harcourt, Brace.

Phillipson, R. 1992. *Linguistic imperialism.* Oxford: Oxford University Press.

Phillipson, R. 1997. "Review of Claude Piron 'Le défi des langues: du gâchis au bon sens'" (The languages challenge: from waste to common sense). *Language in Society,* 26:1, 143-147.

Phillipson, R. 1998. "Globalizing English: are linguistic human rights an alternative to linguistic imperialism?". In eds. Benson et al. 101-112.

Phillipson, R. (in press). *English-Only Europe? Language Policy Challenges.* London: Routledge.

Phillipson, R. ed. 2000. *Rights to language. Equity, power and education.* Mahwah, NJ: Lawrence Erlbaum Associates.

Phillipson, R. and T. Skutnabb-Kangas. 1994. English - Panacea or Pandemic? In eds. U. Ammon, K.J. Mattheier and P. Nelde. *Sociolinguistica 8. English only? in Europa/ in Europe/ en Europe.* 73-87.

Phillipson, R and T. Skutnabb-Kangas 1995. "Linguistic rights and wrongs". *Applied Linguistics* 16:4, 483-504.

Phillipson, R. and T. Skutnabb-Kangas 1996. "English Only Worldwide, or Language Ecology". *TESOL Quarterly.* Eds. T. Ricento and N.C. Hornberger. *Special-Topic Issue: Language Planning and Policy.* 429-452.

Phillipson, R. and T. Skutnabb-Kangas 1997. "Linguistic human rights and English in Europe". *World Englishes* 16:1, 1997, Special issue, *English in Europe.* Eds. M.G. Deneire and M. Goethals. 27-43.

Phillipson, R. and T. Skutnabb-Kangas. 1999. "Englishisation: one dimension of globalisation". In eds. D. Graddol and U.H. Meinhof. *English in a changing world. AILA Review* 13 Oxford: The English Book Centre. 19-36.

Pilger, J. 1998. *Hidden Agendas.* London: Vintage.

Posey, D. 1997. "Conclusion of Darrell Posey's 'Biological and Cultural Diversity - the Inextricable Linked by Language and Politics'". *Iatiku. Newsletter of the Foundation for Endangered Languages* 4: 7-8.

Posey, D.A. ed. 1999. *Cultural and Spiritual Values of Biodiversity.* New York: UNEP (United Nations Environmental Programme) and Leiden: Intermediate Technologies, Leiden University).

Price, G. 1984. *The Languages of Britain.* London: Edward Arnold.

Price, G. ed. 2000. *Encyclopedia of the languages of Europe.* London: Blackwell.

Rahman, T. 1996. *Language and Politics in Pakistan.* Karachi: Oxford University Press. [Paperback reprint, 1998 and 2000].

Rahman, T. 1999. *Language, Education and Culture.* Karachi: Oxford University Press. [Paperback reprint, 2000].

Rahman, T. 2000. *Unpleasant Essays : Education and Politics in Pakistan.* Lahore: Vanguard Books.

Rahman, T. 2002. *Language, Ideology and Power.* Karachi: Oxford University Press.

Rassool, N. 1999. *Literacy for Sustainable Development in the Age of Information*. Clevedon, UK: Multilingual Matters.

Reagan, T. 1995. Neither Easy to Understand Nor Pleasing to See: The Development of Manual Sign Codes as Language Planning Activity. *Language Problems and Language Planning* 19:2, 133-150.

Rider 1999. *The Rider Encyclopaedia of Eastern Philosophy and Religion*. London: Rider.

Rosas, A. 1995. The right to development. In eds. Eide, Krause and Rosas. 247-255.

Rothenberger, A. compiler 1997. *Bibliography on the OSCE High Commissioner on National Minorities: Documents, Speeches and Related Publications*. The Hague: The Foundation on Inter-Ethnic Relations.

Skutnabb-Kangas, T. 1984. *Bilingualism or Bot: the Education of Minorities*. Clevedon, Avon: Multilingual Matters.

Skutnabb-Kangas, T. 1996a. "Educational language choice - multilingual diversity or monolingual reductionism?". In eds. M. Hellinger and U. Ammon. *Contrastive Sociolinguistics*. Berlin and New York: Mouton de Gruyter. 175-204.

Skutnabb-Kangas, T. 1996b. "The colonial legacy in educational language planning in Scandinavia - from migrant labour to a national ethnic minority?". *International Journal of the Sociology of Language*, Vol. 118. Special Issue, *Language Planning and Political Theory*. Ed. H. Dua, Hans. 81-106.

Skutnabb-Kangas, T. 1999. "Linguistic diversity, human rights and the 'free' market". In eds. Kontra et al. 187-222.

Skutnabb-Kangas, T. 2000. *Linguistic genocide in education – or worldwide diversity and human rights?* Mahwah, New Jersey: Lawrence Erlbaum Associates.

Skutnabb-Kangas, T. 2002a. "Sprache und Menschenrechte" (Language and Human Rights). *Das Zeichen. Zeitschrift für Sprache und Kultur Gehörloser*. März Nr. 59, 2002: 52-63.

Skutnabb-Kangas, T. 2002b. "Linguistic Human Rights in Education: Western Hypocrisy in European and Global Language Policy". In *Hatalom és kultúra. Power and Culture. Plenáris el_adások. Plenary Sessions. V. Nemzetkögi Hungarológiai Kongresszus. The 5ᵗʰ International Congress of Hungarian Studies*. Szerkesztette/eds. T. Lahdelma, Jankovics J., Nyerges J. and P. Laihonen. Jyväskylä: University of Jyväskylä, Faculty of Humanities, Hungarian Studies. 115-156.

Skutnabb-Kangas, T. in press a. "Why should the world's linguistic diversity be maintained". Plenary paper at the International Conference Small Languages in the 21ˢᵗ Century Europe, 19-21 April 2001. Riga, Latvia. In press, in conference publication, ed. by Ina Druviete.

Skutnabb-Kangas, T. in press b. "Language Policies and Education: the role of education in destroying or supporting the world's linguistic diversity". Keynote Address at the World Congress on Language Policies, 16-20 April 2002, Barcelona, Spain. In press in Spanish, for the journal of Museo Nacional de Antropologia, Mexico. The English version can be found at http://www.linguapax.org/congres/plenaries/skutnabb.html.

Skutnabb-Kangas, T. in press c. Revitalisation of indigenous languages in education: contextualising the Papua New Guinea experience. *Language and Education.*

Skutnabb-Kangas, T. ed. 1995. *Multilingualism for All.* Lisse: Swets and Zeitlinger.

Skutnabb-Kangas, T. and O. García 1995. "Multilingualism for All - General Principles?". In ed. Skutnabb-Kangas. 221-256.

Skutnabb-Kangas, T. and D. Harmon, David 2002. Review of Nettle, Daniel 1999. *Linguistic Diversity. Language Policy* 1:2. 175-182.

Skutnabb-Kangas, T., L. Maffi and D. Harmon 2002. *Sharing A World of Difference: The Earth's Linguistic, Cultural, and Biological Diversity.* An educational booklet prepared in coordination with the Education Sector of UNESCO; UNESCO, Terralingua and WWF [World Wide Fund of Nature].Paris: UNESCO.

Skutnabb-Kangas, T. and R. Phillipson 1994. "Linguistic human rights, past and present". In eds. T. Skutnabb-Kangas and R. Phillipson. 71-110.

Skutnabb-Kangas, T. and R. Phillipson 1997. "Linguistic Human Rights and Development". In ed. C.J. Hamelink. *Ethics and Development. On making moral choices in development co-operation.* Kampen, The Netherlands: Kok. S. 56-69.

Skutnabb-Kangas, T. and R. Phillipson 1998. "Linguistic human rights". In ed. C.J. Hamelink. *Gazette. The International Journal for Communication Studies.* Special volume, *Human Rights* 60:1. 27-46.

Skutnabb-Kangas, T. and R. Phillipson. 2001. "When the world came to Sweden". In eds. S. Boyd and L. Huss. *Managing Multilingualism in a European Nation-State. Challenges for Sweden.* Clevedon, UK: Multilingual Matters. 70-86. Also Special volume, *Current Issues in Language in Society* 7: 1. 70-86.

Skutnabb-Kangas, T. and J. Cummins eds. 1988. *Minority Education: from shame to struggle.* Clevedon: Multilingual Matters

Skutnabb-Kangas, T. and R. Phillipson eds. in collaboration with M, Rannut 1994. *Linguistic Human Rights. Overcoming Linguistic Discrimination.* Contributions to the Sociology of Language, 67. Berlin/New York: Mouton de Gruyter.

Spring, J. 1998. *Education and the Rise of the Global Economy.* Mahwah, NJ: Lawrence Erlbaum.

Stairs, A. 1988. "Beyond cultural inclusion. An Inuit example of indigenous education development". In eds. Skutnabb-Kangas and Cummins. 308-327.

Thomas, W.P. and Collier, V. (2002). *A National Study of School Effectiveness for Language Minority Students' Long-Term Academic Achievement Report: Project 1:1.* Fairfax, Virginia: VREDE, George Mason University. www.crede.ucsc.edu.

Thornberry, P. 1997. Minority Rights. In ed. Academy of European Law. *Collected Courses of the Academy of European Law.* Volume VI, Book 2. The Netherlands: Kluwer Law International. 307-390.

Todal, J. 1999. "Minorities with a Minority:; Language and the School in the Sámi Areas of Norway". In ed. May. 124-136.

UNESCO Ad Hoc Expert Group on Endangered Languages. 2002. *Language Endangerment.* Draft. Paris: UNESCO Intangible Cultural Heritage Unit.

UNESCO 2000. *Human Rights. Major International Instruments. Status as at 31 May 2000.* Prepared by Symonides, J. and Volodin, V.. Paris: Unesco, Division of Human Rights, Democracy and Peace.

van der Stoel, M. 1997. "Introduction to the Seminar". *International Journal on Minority and Group Rights. Special Issue on the Education Rights of National Minorities* 4:2, 1996/1997: 153-155.

van der Stoel, M. 1999. *Report on the Linguistic Rights of Persons Belonging to National Minorities in the OSCE area. + Annex. Replies from OSCE Participating States.* The Hague: OSCE High Commissioner on National Minorities.

de Varennes, F.1996. *Language, Minorities and Human Rights.* The Hague, Boston, London: Martinus Nijhoff.

Wande, Erling (1984). Two Finnish Minorities in Sweden. *Journal of Multilingual and Multicultural Development* 5: 225-242.

Wande, E. 1988. "Från 1809 till 1988. Svenska Tornedalens språk- och utbildningspolitiska historia". [From 1809 to 1988. The language and education policy history of the Swedish Torne valley]. In eds. I. Svanberg and M. Tydén. *Multiethnic Studies in Uppsala.* Uppsala Multiethnic Papers 13. Uppsala: Centre for Multiethnic Research, Uppsala University. 121-140.

Wande, E. 1996. "Tornedalen". In ed. F. Horn. *Finska språkets ställning i Sverige och svenska språkets ställning i Finland.*[The status of the finnish language in Sweden and the Swedish language in Finland]. Juridica Lapponica 14. Rovaniemi: Rovaniemen Yliopisto.

Wande, E. and Winsa, B. 1995. "Attitudes and behaviours in the Thorne [sic!] Valley". In eds. W. Fase, K. Jaspaert and S. Kroon. *The state of minority languages. International perspectives on survival and decline.* European Studies on Multilingualism, 5. Lisse: Swets and Zeitlinger. 267-292. [should be 'Torne'].

Williams, E. 1998. *Investigating bilingual literacy: Evidence from Malawi and Zambia.* Education Research No. 24. London: Department For International Development.

Wilson, W.H. 1999. "The Sociopolitical Context of Establishing Hawaiian-medium Education". In ed. May. 95-108.

Wilson, W.H. and Kamana, K. 2001. "'Mai Loko Mai O Ka 'I'ni: Proceeding from a Dream': The Aha Panana Leo Connection in Hawaiian Language Revitalization". In eds. Hinton and Hale. 147-176.

Winsa, B. 1997. "Från ett Vi till ett Dem - Torne älv som kulturgräns" [From a We to a They - Torne river as a cultural boundary]. In Korhonen, O. and Winsa, B. *Språkliga och kulturella gränser i Nordskandinavien. Två uppsatser* [Linguistic and cultural borders in Northern Scandinavia. Two essays]. Kulturens frontlinjer. Skrifter från forskningsprogrammet Kulturgräns Norr, 7. Umeå: Kulturgräns Norr. 5-52.

Winsa, B. 1999a. *Attitudes form Collective Identity: The effects of linguistic policy and practice in the Swedish Torne Valley.* Canberra: Applied Linguistics Association of Australia.

Winsa, B. 1999b. "'Monolingual' and 'Homogeneous' Sweden has Five Minority Languages". Terralingua Discussion Paper 13. http://www.terralingua.org

Wong Fillmore, L. 1991. "When Learning a Second Language Means Losing the

First". *Early Childhood Research Quarterly* 6: 323-346.
Wurm, S.A. ed. 2001. *Atlas of the World's Languages in Danger of Disappearing.* Second edition. Paris: UNESCO Publishing.

Abbreviations

EBLUL: The European Bureau for Lesser Used Languages.
European Charter: (Council of Europe's) European Charter for Regional or
    Minority Languages
ECHR: European Convention on Human Rights and Fundamental Freedoms
Framework Convention: (Council of Europe's) Framework Convention for the
    Protection of National Minorities
ICCPR: UN International Covenant on Civil and Political Rights
ICESCR: UN International Covenant on Economic, Social and Cultural Rights
OSCE: Organisation for Security and Co-operation in Europe
UN Universal Declaration: United Nations Universal Declaration_of Human
    Rights
UN Charter: United Nations Charter of Human Rights
UN (Minorities) Declaration: UN Declaration on the Rights of Persons Belonging
    to National or Ethnic, Religious and Linguistic Minorities.

English for Emerging or Submerging Multiple European Identities?

Robert Phillipson

My affiliation to Copenhagen Business School does not mean that I occupy the Carlsberg Chair of Fluid Communication nor the Tivoli Chair of Cross-border Studies. My employer receives my salary from the Danish state, my institution has several language departments in an Arts Faculty, and the business that occupies me is English worldwide, how and why English is expanding, what the implications are for (speakers of) other languages, and how language policy can be given a higher profile in the EU system and in member states.

The internationalisation and commodification of European higher education mean that Danish universities are increasingly expected to run like businesses, to profile and market themselves competitively. One symptom of this is an increasing use of English. This trend in communication in the university world dovetails with comparable developments in commerce, politics, the media, and youth culture, due to the impact of the interlocking processes of Americanisation, globalisation and europeanisation. The expansion of English is central to these processes, and influences local, national and international linguistic identities. I shall explore some of the implications of this by reporting on some historical aspects of European unification and Americanisation, some of the intrinsic paradoxes of language policy in Europe, which account for its relative neglect, whether the expansion of English constitutes a threat to other languages, and the need for more pro-active language polices that strengthen linguistic diversity.

One of the motive forces behind bringing the economies of European states together was to establish forms of interdependence that would render military aggression impossible. This was to be achieved by settling territorial disputes between France and Germany and by ensuring that the re-industrialisation process after the destruction of the 1939-45 war should address the needs and mutual suspicions of these countries and of the countries that the Nazis had occupied. Investment from outside Europe was essential for this, and could only come from one source, namely the USA. The Marshall Plan was part of a strategy to position America as the pre-eminent force globally through the Bretton Woods agreements on trade, the World Bank and the International Monetary Fund, the United Nations, and NATO. A successful economy in western Europe was seen as an essential bulwark against the communist bloc.

American goals have been explicit and consistent since World War II. In 1948, the State Department's senior imperial planner, George Kennan, wrote: "We have 50 per cent of the world's wealth, but only 6.3 per cent of its population. In this situation, our real job in the coming period is to devise a pattern of relationships which permit us to maintain this position of disparity. To do so, we have to dispense with all sentimentality... we should cease thinking about human rights, the raising of living standards and democratisation". President Bush II is visibly cast in this mould, as clearly articulated by Condoleezza Rice, his foreign affairs adviser: "The rest of the world is best served by the USA pursuing its own interests because American values are universal"[1].

The formation of the first EU institutions thus involved a mixture of American and European motives. Some on both sides of the Atlantic in the 1940s had plans for a "United States of Europe", an idea which pacifist visionaries like Victor Hugo had mooted a century earlier. The USA insisted, as a condition for Marshall aid, on the economies of European states being coordinated and integrated. American pressure was therefore decisive for the form of European collaboration that was put in place from the late 1940s, the *European Coal and Steel Community* (1952), and the *European Economic Community* (1958). The first sketch of a *European Political Community*, with an Executive Council, a Court of Justice, and a Parliament was produced in 1953.

The principle of parity for the languages of the participating states was established at this time, initially four, and now eleven. The relative strength of French in EU affairs is attributable to its earlier use in international relations, to the location of EU institutions in cities in which French was widely used, Brussels, Luxembourg, and Strasbourg, and to speakers of French, along with the Germans, occupying the political high ground in shaping the new Europe.

The British were ambivalent about joining the EU because of their imperial links, and their belief that they have a special relationship with the USA. De Gaulle blocked British entry in the 1960s because he saw Britain as a Trojan horse for American interests. When President Pompidou agreed to Britain "joining Europe" in 1972, it is reported that one condition he insisted on was that the pre-eminence of French as the dominant language of EU institutions should remain unchallenged. Although nominally there was parity between the EEC official languages, French was *primus inter pares*. Pompidou's worries about the risk of the French language being eclipsed by English were fully justified, as English is growing like a linguistic cuckoo in the main EU nests. The promotion of English worldwide has been central to British and American global strategy since 1945[2], the British Council playing a key role in maintaining the position of English in postcolonial states, and in the post-communist world where globalisation was preached through the trinity of the market economy, human rights, and English. As the Annual Report of the British Council for 1960-61 states:

> Teaching the world English may appear not unlike an extension of
> the task which America faced in establishing English as a common
> national language among its own immigrant population.

You scarcely need reminding of the consequences of US language policy for immigrant and indigenous languages, or that policies internally within the US also determine American global strategies, and that English is central to both. This has, of course, also been true of the United Kingdom over several centuries.

According to some senior Americans, the world can simply dispense with all languages other than English. In 1997 the US ambassador to Denmark, who came straight from the corporate world, where else, was rash enough to say in my

---

[1] Strategy paper "Campaign 2000: Promoting the national interest", cited in the Danish daily paper *Information*, 14 June 2001.

[2] Phillipson, R. 1992. *Linguistic imperialism.* Oxford: Oxford University Press

wife's hearing at a luncheon at the University of Roskilde: "The most serious problem for the European Union is that it has so many languages, this preventing real integration and development of the Union." A 1997 CIA report states that the following five years would be decisive in the establishment of English as the sole international language[3]. The very idea that there is a single international language is of course nonsense. There are literally hundreds of international lingua francas in use, but the myth of the global use of English is widely believed in, especially by those who benefit from their proficiency in English, including academic cheerleaders of linguistic globalisation.

George Monbiot's book, *Captive state: The corporate take-over of Britain* (Macmillan, 2000), documents the many ways in which corporate power determines national and local government policy in countless fields, including agriculture, energy, the environment, urban planning, the health system, university research, and general education. The consolidation of an EU common market and monetary union has put into effect the wishes of the corporate world, coordinated by the European Round Table of Industrialists, an association of the chief executives of 46 of the biggest companies in Europe (op.cit., 320). This lobbying group is also directly involved in setting the terms for the enlargement of the EU with countries of eastern and central Europe (ibid., 324). In negotiations on admission, all documents from applicant states have to be provided exclusively in English. The Transatlantic Business Dialogue brings together American and European corporations, and dovetails with the G8 and related heads of state networks. There is increasingly a single state-corporate structure. There are plans for a single market incorporating Europe and North America, a Transatlantic Economic Partnership, which will develop "a worldwide network of bilateral agreements with identical conformity procedures" (cited ibid., 329). Monbiot summed up these developments two years before then Johannesburg Earth Summit, and nothing has changed to disprove his analysis (ibid., 329-330):

> Before long…only a minority of nations will lie outside a single, legally harmonised global market, and they will swiftly find themselves obliged to join. By the time a new world trade agreement has been negotiated, it will be irrelevant, for the WTO's job will already have been done. Nowhere on earth will robust laws protecting the environment or human rights be allowed to survive. Elected representatives will, if these plans for a new world order succeed, be reduced to the agents of a global government: built, coordinated and run by corporate chief executives.

Despite this powerful trend, in which English is pivotal, multilingualism is endorsed in countless EU pronouncements. Decisions emanating from Brussels, agreed on by the fifteen member states (and 70-80 per cent of national legislation involves implementing decisions taken in Brussels), are disseminated in the eleven languages. There are comprehensive interpretation and translation services in EU institutions that attempt to ensure that speakers of each of the official languages has equal voice and effect. An ever-expanding range of topics is being

---

[3] Reported by Hervé Lavenir de Buffon, founder of the organisation "Comités pour le français, langue européene". *RO Magazine* 34, 22 June 2002.

added to the EU's remit, including culture. In theory the EU does not legislate on education, but it is deeply involved in agenda-setting, funding countless schemes and research, and the reform and standardisation of higher education. This raises the question of how far language policy is still the preserve of the individual state, or can now be considered a matter for the Union. Can a member state do what it pleases, provided it pays at least lip-service to the language rights expressed in conventions, charters and EU treaties?

Such questions, as well as the management of multilingualism internally in EU institutions, have been subjected to astonishingly little scholarly research. A recent doctoral study in international law in the US concludes that French language protection measures (the Loi Toubon) are in conflict with the Maastricht Treaty and the principles of a common market with the free movement of goods, services, labour and capital. Corporate lawyers may therefore soon choose to challenge national language legislation on precisely these grounds. The American doctoral student has a solution to all that linguistic diversity:

> It is worthwhile to consider whether the EU should answer the call for uniformity on the issue of language business transactions and further protect itself against the potential onslaught of language regulation by each individual Member State. One potential action the EU might take would be to declare a common language in the EU market[4]

Feld argues along predictable lines: rapid access to information, efficiency, saving money on translation, eliminating "national technical obstacles", all arguments that relate to the producer rather than the consumer. She pleads for the termination of the "cultural protectionism of nations", invokes the strong role of English in the world marketplace, and English as a widely learned foreign language (which is correct), English as the "common linguistic denominator" of all European countries (which is rubbish), and "U.S. advances in the areas of technology and science" (which we in Europe are supposed to be grateful for). The EU should act so as to prevent "one nation from frustrating the fundamental principles of the supranational governing body" (a comment which reveals little insight into the principles of EU decision-making). Her parting shot is that adopting a single language would serve, "to unify, rather than divide, Member States." (op.cit., 202). Here is the monolingual worldview of Americanisation being subtly marketed as europeanisation under cover of globalisation.

Now it may well be that European governments are not waiting to follow this advice. Several have introduced or are contemplating legislation to resist the advance of English. However, the *Vanderbilt Journal of Transnational Law* is presumably read by American corporate lawyers, who might choose to test the principle in court, and the outcome of any litigation in the European Court of Justice is unpredictable. But it appears that the Commission may be saving them the trouble and expense.

In July 2002 the Commission sent a "formal notice of complaint"[5] to the French government stating that the national requirement that food products

---

[4] Feld, S.A. 1998. "Language and the globalization of the economic market: the regulation of language as a barrier to free trade. *Vanderbilt Journal of Transnational Law*, 31: 153-202. The citation is from page 199.

[5] French "lettre de mise en demeure".

should be labelled in French (following French legislation) is in conflict with Eurolaw[6]. There has as yet been little litigation in this area, and the decisions are far from unambiguous, as indeed is the relevant Council directive[7] on the harmonisation of member states' legislation on the labelling and packaging of food products. European case law is seen as holding that national law cannot require use of a specific language if the message can be expressed by other means, which can be another language that is easily comprehensible to the purchaser, possibly supported pictorially. The Commission's intervention suggests that it is possible that the transition from a single market to a single marketing language has begun.

The Commission's action is seen by many in France as the thin edge of the wedge. According to L'Allíance pour la souveraineté de la France, in a press communiqué[8] entitled "Europe is attacking the well-informed housewife", the Commission is working to "impose anglo-american" throughout the EU... "the construction of Europe means its destruction for the benefit of mercantile America". A body called "Défense de la langue française"[9] is planning a public demonstration in January 2003, even though the French government has revised its regulations so as to conform to Eurolaw requirements. It has resolved the issue by issuing a new ministerial order that maintains the obligation that products are described in French, but stipulates that other languages can be used in addition[10]. That will not be the end of the affair.

This example of a dispute between the Commission and a national government epitomises how inadequately language policies are handled. A second example that hit the headlines was a proposal to change one of the internal translation procedures in the Commission in Brussels, as part of a cost-saving exercise. The plan was leaked to the French government, as a result of which a joint letter was sent by the Ministers of Foreign Affairs of France and Germany, Hubert Védrine and Joschka Fischer, to Romano Prodi, the President of the Commission, on 2 July 2001. The letter accused the Commission of attempting to introduce "monolingualism" in EU institutions, which was a coded reference to English being installed as the sole in-house working language, and that this represented an unacceptable departure from the current system. Prodi's reply, dispatched in French and German, asserts that multilingualism is of cardinal importance to the EU, that nothing had been decided, but that efficiency and savings in the language services need to be looked into. The impending enlargement of the EU made action even more important.

By this stage, press coverage had identified a "plot to impose English on the EU" (*Irish Times*), "Fischer and Védrine against more English" (*Frankfurter Allgemeine Zeitung*), "Kinnock"s language plan riles the French" (*The*

---

[6] See the article by John Lichfield in *The Independent*, 19 August 2002, which predictably pokes fun at the French and does not address the issue of language rights.
[7] 2000/13/EF, of 20 March 2002.
[8] On 8 July 2002, <www. souverainete.france.org>, see also www.voxlatina.com .
[9] www.langue-francaise.org .
[10] Décret no 2002-1025 du 1 août 2002 art 1, Journal Officiel du 2 août 2002. It is known as the "Decret Dutreil".

Independent), and so on. Much of the press coverage contains inaccurate statements about the present system and its costs, and engages in fanciful and nationalistic interpretation[11]. The exchange of letters and the press reports clearly reveal that an existential nerve had been touched. The two disputes are perfect examples of the recurrent underlying tension between national interests and supranational ones, and the absence of adequate procedures and principles for resolving the issues.

I fear this is generally the case at the supranational level, and often nationally, even in countries which have given some thought to language policy, like France. French efforts have influenced the endorsement of linguistic diversity in EU proclamations, but there tends to be more special pleading for French rather than for rights for all relevant languages[12].

Many factors account for language policy not being handled more smoothly and competently.

1. There are major differences in the ideologies underpinning the formation of states, and in the role ascribed to language in these (the national romantic tradition, *jus sanguinis*, Herder, as in Germany, and the republican tradition, *jus soli*, citizenship, as in France). Language issues are therefore understood differently in different countries, including such basic notions as language and dialect, this impeding a shared understanding of language policy issues.

2. Levels of awareness about language policy issues range widely between and within each EU country. They tend to be relatively high in, for instance, Finland and Greece, but often with a very selective focus, and low in Denmark and England.

3. There is a poor scholarly infrastructure at European universities and research institutes for the analysis of language policy, multilingualism, and language rights, reflecting a lack of investment in this field.

4. Responsibility for language policy in each country tends to be shared between ministries of foreign affairs, education, culture, research, and commerce. They each tend to have little expertise in language policy, and between them there is inadequate coordination, if any. In countries with a federal structure, responsibility is even more diffuse.

5. As English is used extensively by native and non-native speakers from different parts of the world, there is no simple correlation between English and the interests of a particular state. The connection of English to the dominant economic system, and its entrenchment as the most widely learned foreign language in schools (much more successfully in northern than southern Europe), and to global networking remains.

A *laissez faire* policy thus involves major risks for all languages other than English. Leaving language policy to market forces, nationally and in the

---

[11] A prime example is the editorial "Organic is healthier" in *The Daily Telegraph* of 16 August 2001. Another is Ian Black's "EU learns to conduct its business with an English accent", *The Guardian Weekly*, April 4-10, 2002

[12] French has for centuries been regarded as a uniquely significant language, and France as "la mère des arts, des armes et des lois" (Joachim du Bellay, 1525-1560).

supranational institutions, is a recipe for more English and less of the other languages.

Clarifying whether the advance of English entails submerging other languages would require exploration of a range of language functions and contexts. As eleven languages are being used and developed in parallel in EU institutions, one can argue that all are being strengthened internationally, though not necessarily in equal measure, and without the hierarchy of languages being challenged.

I won't go into the tricky question of the functioning of the translation or interpretation services, but merely mention that they are generally branded as excessively costly, whereas they in fact currently account for only 0.8 per cent of the total budget for all EU institutions, meaning 2 euros per year for each European citizen (which is peanuts compared with agricultural subsidies). This is a modest price to pay for a principle that use of the languages of each member state is an obligation, especially when preparing and agreeing on a constant stream of documents with the force of law in each member state.

The parity of the 11 official languages of the EU is a complex question[13], which journalistic coverage of language issues, typically triggered by a crisis of some sort, seldom does justice to[14]. Language policies in Europe reflect many unresolved and interlocking paradoxes and tensions:

1. a legacy of "nation" states, *"national"* interests and languages, BUT *supranational* integration, and the *internationalisation* of many domains, commerce, finance, education, science, politics, and civil society in EU member states;

2. the formal *equality* of EU member states and their languages, BUT a *pecking order* of states and languages, currently visible in the shift from French to English as the primary working language in EU institutions. The figures for draft documents reflect a dramatic shift over the past twenty years from mainly French to mainly English[15];

3. the onward thrust of americanisation, cultural homogenisation ("McDonaldisation"), and the *hegemony of English*, BUT the celebration of European linguistic diversity, *multilingualism*, cultural and linguistic hybridity, and some support for minority and national language rights;

4. languages seen as purely *technical*, pragmatic tools, BUT languages as *existential* identity markers for individuals, cultures, ethnic groups, and states;

5. language policy as a matter of *practical* functioning, BUT language policy as *"politically sensitive"*, a coded way of politicians, eurocrats and diplomats acknowledging that they do not know how to reform the present regime, or

---

[13] Irish is not an official language but is a treaty language. It can be used at the European Court of Justice.

[14] For instance, *The Guardian* on 20 March 2002: "The French language meets its Waterloo. Enlarging the EU is good news for the English language, confirming its victory over French as the classic medium of European integration".

[15] A further symptom is that publications in other languages are being dropped, e.g. the Annual Reports on competition policy were available in all official languages until 1995, the 1996 report was published in Dutch, English, French and German, and it is now published exclusively in English. <http:/europa.eu.int/comm/competition/annual_reports>.

improve EU internal and external communication, an issue which enlargement complexifies;

6.   *Germany* as a demographically and economically dominant force in Europe, BUT *German* progressively marginalised in scholarship, commerce, youth culture, and in the global linguistic marketplace, in similar ways to a reduction in the power of French internationally. The emergence of English as the foremost foreign language in Europe, because of its obvious functional utility, entails the submergence of other languages as foreign languages, and few education systems are seriously addressing the question of ensuring diversity in language learning, whether of foreign, regional minority or neighbouring languages;

7.   *English* being promoted as a linguistic *panacea*, BUT of the 378 million citizens of the member states, only 61 million speak English as a mother tongue, less than half of the rest are proficient in English as a foreign language, and the proportion speaking it confidently varies greatly from country to country[16]. It is ironic that states invest heavily in the learning of a language that symbolises cultural imperialism, and awareness of the forms and mechanisms of cultural and linguistic imperialism is very patchy and often non-existent.

Clarity when discussing EU language policy is elusive because many of the central concepts are muddled and used inconsistently. I will give you three examples:

1.   In theory all eleven languages have the same status as official and working languages. In practice there tends to be a restriction of "*working language*" to French and English, and for certain purposes, German too. This terminological confusion (which is present in the letter written to Romano Prodi by the French and German foreign ministers referred to earlier) is symptomatic of an acceptance of a hierarchy of languages. Some languages are more equal than others.

2.   Secondly, "*lingua franca*" tends to be used as though there is equality between users of the relevant language, but is it likely that native and non-native speakers of French or English perform on a level linguistic playing-field? The innocuous label conceals the power dimension that privileges some and disadvantages others. Use of the mother tongue does not, of course, guarantee intelligibility. People who function regularly in several languages are more likely to be sensitive in their use of language in intercultural communication than monolinguals.

3.   Thirdly, the designations "*native/non-native*" take some users of the language as being authentic and infallible, and stigmatise others as not being the real thing. Work has begun in English as a Foreign Language teaching circles to describe and upgrade the English of continental Europeans, for several reasons[17]. English is used effectively by countless people for whom it is not a first language, so the "ownership" of English is changing, and perhaps these users should be seen as fluent users of a non-national, post-national language rather than as

---

[16]   See Eurobarometer Report 54 of 15 February 2001 for a representative study of foreign language competence in all member states. These reports are on http://europa.eu.int/comm/dg10/epo/eb.html.

[17]   Seidlhofer, B. 2001. "Closing a conceptual gap: the case for a description of English as a lingua franca", *International Journal of Applied Linguistics* 11/2: 133-158.

deficient users of mother-tongue English (Seidlhofer 2002). This is an attractive principle, but whether it has any implications for language pedagogy is unclear. The assumed virtues of native speakers currently give them a colossal advantage, not least on the job market, and not only as language teachers. The Commission and the Council of Europe have been taken to task for illegitimately favouring native speakers of English when advertising posts that all EU citizens should have had equal access to. Monitoring this practice should be undertaken by the EU Ombud institution, but as yet its powers are tightly constrained..

So some of our basic concepts in language policy are misleading. Permeating the structural and ideological factors that snarl up analysis at the supranational level of language policy, there is the banal reality of people talking at cross-purposes, with or without the assistance of interpreters. The unresolved paradoxes remain. The challenge of more equitable, visionary language policies has yet to be met.

Participation in EU activities by vast numbers of civil servants, experts, academics, teachers, and NGOs, adds a supranational linguistic identity to the existing national linguistic identities. Confident users of English and French, whether as a first or second language, are in a privileged position. And needless to say, foreign languages can be learned successfully, even by Brits[18]. In continental Europe, English has traditionally been learned additively, and until recently it has been difficult to imagine that speakers of German or Swedish run any risk of their mother tongues being marginalised or atrophying at the individual or group level. This picture may well be changing. This is due to the inroads English is making in many domains.

The cover of the European edition of *Business Week* of 13 August 2001 asked in a banner headline "Should everyone speak English?". The inside story was flagged as "The Great English divide. In Europe, speaking the lingua franca separates the haves from the have-nots". The cover drawing portrays twin business executives: one communicates successfully, the English speaker; the other is mouthless, speechless. Competence in English is here projected as being imperative throughout Europe in the commercial world. By implication, proficiency in other languages gets you nowhere. The article describes how more and more continental European companies are switching over to English as the in-house corporate language. It also describes how English for business is big business for English language schools. It has been described as second in importance to the British economy after North Sea oil.

English as the Tyrannosaurus Rex of scientific communication[19], is no extinct beast. In some faculties in Norway, scholars are rewarded for publications in English by a large bonus, whereas anything in the local language triggers a paltry

---

[18] I well recall the good advice given to me by the admissions tutor of the university which gave me a place to read "modern", meaning foreign languages. My tutor approved of me immersing myself in France and Germany for months before going up, but advised strongly that I should read as much English literature as possible. How could one expect to acquire a profound familiarity with foreign cultures and languages if one is not securely grounded in one's own group's cultural history? In bilingual education terms, learning should be additive not subtractive.

[19] This is John Swales's term, in an article in *World Englishes* in 1997.

one. The tendency is for "international" publication to be seen as intrinsically superior, even in countries with a long history of national scholarship, and this influences employment criteria and choice of research topic. The dominance of English as a language of science, both in publications and in postgraduate training, is increasingly under scrutiny, with alarm bells ringing in Austria[20], Denmark[21], Germany[22] and elsewhere.

The Nordic Council of Ministers commissioned research in 2001 on possible domain loss in the Nordic languages, a laudable exercise, because while everybody seems to have an opinion on language policy, there is often a dearth of hard data actually documenting trends. The Swedish government established a parliamentary commission to evaluate whether Swedish was under threat from English, and to elaborate an action plan to ensure that Swedish remains a complete language, learned and used well by its first and second language speakers, and retains its full rights as an EU official and working language. The plan also aims to ensure that Swedes are equipped to function well in foreign languages, particularly English, and that Swedes from a minority language background enjoy language rights. A massive national consultation process is currently under way, aiming at legislation in 2003. This nation-state is apparently shifting from monolingualism to a differentiated spectrum of multilingualism.

There is nothing new about functional differentiation among several languages. Christian Wilster, a poet who was the first person to translate Homer's *Iliad* and *Odyssey* from Greek into Danish, wrote in 1827: "Every gentleman who took his education seriously only put pen to paper in Latin, spoke French to the ladies, German to his dog, and Danish to his servants." Since that time we have experienced the heyday of the monolingual nation state throughout Europe, a stranglehold that is being eased apart by Americanisation and Europeanisation. This fluid situation is eroding the monopoly of a unifying and stratifying national language in nation-states, and raises many language rights issues. It is possible that access to the dominant international language will be the key distinction marking out haves and have-nots in continental European countries, in a much broader sense than *Business Week* intended. Broadly speaking this is the role of English intranationally in postcolonial states, where English opens doors for the few and firmly closes them for the many. In much of Europe, competence in English is becoming a prerequisite for access to higher education and employment, in tandem with preferred forms of communication in the national language. States are adjusting to globalisation, which impacts on language policy overtly and covertly. It is not at all clear to what extent states are deciding on national language policy, or whether the initiative has already passed to EU institutions, the boardrooms of transnational corporations, to universities in countries that call themselves "English-speaking", and English-using gatekeepers in countless domains.

---

[20] See the Vienna Manifesto, appendix 5 of *English-only Europe? Language policy challenges,* Robert Phillipson, London: Routledge, 2003.
[21] Jarvad, P. 2001. *Det danske sprogs status i 1990'erne med særlig henblik på domænetab.* Copenhagen: Dansk Sprognævn, 2001.
[22] Gawlitta, K. and F. Vilmar (eds.) in press. *Sprache: Herrschaftsmittel oder geistiges Band? Der Kampf gegen die sprachliche Amerikanisierung.*

The EU has basically steered clear of the issue, apart from needing to address the functioning of its institutions internally and externally in a selected set of languages. The Danish Presidency has a brief from the summit in Sevilla in June 2002 to "study the question of the use of languages in the context of an enlarged Union and practical means of improving the present situation without endangering basic principles. In particular the Council is asked to produce an initial report to the European Council in Copenhagen in December 2002... The discussion on the language regimes in EU is expected to be a lengthy process covering more than one Presidency"[23]. These are essentially concerned with activity at the supranational level, but clearly language policies here interlock with and influence what happens at the national and sub-national levels too.

The Convention on the Future of Europe is unlikely to have language policy as a high priority, even if the goals of recent EU reforms aim at increased accountability, and better communication between EU institutions and citizens. But the Convention has been asked to take language policy on board by a number of bodies. These are typically either concerned with a single official language which is seen as being marginalised (I am familiar with approaches by protagonists of French[24], German[25] and Italian[26]) or the exclusion of minority languages (where efforts are spearheaded by the Catalans). The submission to the Convention "Linguistic proposals for the future of Europe", by the Europa Diversa[27] group, pleads for more active policies to strengthen linguistic diversity, for funding for all autochthonous European languages, for the subsidiarity principle to ensure that power and self-regulation in language affairs should be as decentralised as possible, and for a public debate on reform of the language regime in EU institutions. They suggest that experts and users should identify the specific functions performed by different languages, and that a clear distinction should be made between:

1. "binding documents and political representation", at least one official language for each state must be included, but interpretation and translation services would support a range of specified, necessary functions, depending on need, and in a more flexible but restrictive way than at present,

2. "languages of service to the citizens of Europe", more of which would be used in interaction with the general public and in publications, including the lesser used languages recognised by member states in the European Charter for Regional or Minority Languages, and

---

[23] Personal communication from Poul Skytte Christoffersen, Ambassador of the Kingdom of Denmark to the European Union, 8 August 2002.

[24] See the petition on www.voxlatina.com on "Pour la liberté de vivre en français".

[25] "Für ein Sprachstatut in der Verfassung der EU", Offener Brief europäischer Sprachschützer an Giscard d'Estaing, see appendix to Gawlitta and Vilmar (eds.), in press (see note 22).

[26] The association "La bella lingua" has promoted a resolution in defence of the Italian language, with the support of members of parliament. There is collaboration between protagonists of French, German and Italian.

[27] Fourth draft, 1 July 2002, approved by an international conference convened by five Catalan bodies in Barcelona, May 31-June 1.

3. the internal working languages of the EU institutions, which should be restricted to 3 or 4.

This is a sociolinguistically informed document, the main value of which is to point to a way of addressing and potentially solving some of the current problems of linguistic hierarchies and inefficiency, while also bringing autochthonous languages into mainstream EU communication. Implementation along the lines proposed would serve to consolidate the efforts that the EU currently puts into functioning multilingually, but could make the institutions more communicatively effective and efficient. This exercise might also serve to show how hollow a lot of the rhetoric of total multilingualism and linguistic equality is.

There is in fact nothing odious about a restricted number of languages being used by permanent employees of an institution that brings together people from different backgrounds. Eurocrats can be expected to function in three languages, the mother tongue and two others, and this should be demanded particularly of those who have French or English as their mother tongue. In such employment, a higher level of proficiency can be expected in reading and listening than in writing or speaking. By contrast, it is unreasonable to expect representatives of member states, national politicians, civil servants and experts, to function as well in a foreign language as in their mother tongue. In theory they are not expected to do so, since interpretation and translation serve to facilitate interaction across language borders, and often do so impressively, but in practice there are many logistic problems in drafting complex texts in parallel in several languages, and having texts ready on time.

Change must tackle the fundamental paradoxes in EU language policy, clarify the criteria that can lead to equitable multilingual communication, and implement policy and practice that respect linguistic human rights and strengthen linguistic diversity. There is therefore an urgent need to bring together all the relevant stake-holders in language policy. There is a lot of relevant experience worldwide, though far too little is known to decision-makers nationally and supranationally. Most of the books by social scientists on European integration devote very little space to language policy and reveal gross ignorance. They tend to regard an expansion of English as unproblematical. The issues are, in my view, so complex that they need book-length treatment. My book *English-only Europe? Language Policy Challenges* (Routledge, 2003) attempts to move from describing the past and present of languages in Europe to a set of 45 specific recommendations that are designed to ensure language a higher profile and more competent treatment. They are grouped into four categories covering national and supranational language policy infrastructure, EU institutions, language teaching and learning, and research. But these recommendations remain informed speculation that will hopefully not lie idle until the political will is generated bottom-up and top-down to move away from *laissez faire* and crude national agendas to a more inclusive agenda that converts the EU rhetoric of maintaining diversity into reality. No language is intrinsically evil or good. English can be used to ensure the emergence of a better European linguistic order.

A Response from Ireland

Helen Ó Murchú

Tá idir bhuíochas agus chomhghairdeas ag dul don bheirt chainteoirí clúiteacha seo as a bhfuil curtha acu inár láthair d'fhíricí agus de pholasaithe i gcomhthéacs domhanda. Is eolas agus is ábhar spreagtha é atá go mór *ad rem* dúinne in Éirinn thuaidh agus theas, agus dár gcuid ábhair imní, i gcúrsaí oideachais go príomha. I bhfreagairt ghairid, ní féidir ach díriú ar phointí áirithe uilíocha. Luaim sé cinn ach go háirithe chomh maith leis na himpleachtaí a ghabhann leo. Ar dtús, áfach, seans go mba ábhar spéise don bheirt chainteoirí a chloisteáil gur fhoilsigh Pádraig Mac Piarais paimfléid dar teideal *The Murder Machine* go luath sa bhliain chinniniúnach sin 1916, ag damnú an chórais oideachais a bhí ann lena linn. Ba é an Piarsach a chuir tús leis an oideachas dátheangach in Éirinn, bunaithe ar a raibh feicthe agus iniúchtha aige den chóras i bhFlóndras na Beilge ar a chuairt ansin sa bhliain 1905. Léiríonn an sliocht samplach seo dearcadh agus argóint an Phiarsaigh.

I put it that what education in Ireland needed was less a reconstruction of its machinery than a regeneration in spirit. The machinery, I said, has doubtless its defects, but what is chiefly wrong with it is that it is mere machinery, a lifeless thing without a soul [...] A soulless thing cannot teach; but it can destroy. A machine cannot make men; but it can break men.[1]

1. Cúrsaí cearta

Sna léirithe a rinneadh, cuireadh ar ár súile dúinn an difríocht bhunúsach atá idir **cearta teanga** ar thaobh amháin agus **cearta daonna teanga** ar an taobh eile, coincheap atá i bhfad níos bunúsaí agus ar féidir éilimh i bhfad níos talmhaí agus níos tarraingtí a bhunú air le cur faoi bhráid údarás poilitiúil agus dlíthiúil. Ar ndóigh, níl ceachtar den dá choincheap gan a chuid fadhbanna féin, ní mar choincheapa teibí, ach sa chineál reachtaíochta a bhunaítear orthu. Is ró-mhinic a bhíonn an reachtaíocht easnamhach de thoradh an ró-ghéilleadh don chomhréiteach polaitiúil, mar atá i gceist i gCuid III den Chairt Eorpach do Theangacha Réigiúnacha nó Mionlaigh. Níl an tAcht um Chomhionannas Teangacha Oifigiúla atá ar na bacáin i bPoblacht na hÉireann gan locht ach oiread. Go fiú teideal an Achta seo, níl sé cruinn i gcomhthéacs Bhunreacht na hÉireann agus is ró-bhaol go dtitfidh an tAcht dá bharr.

Is easnamhach iad ar shlí amháin nó ar shlí eile na hionstraim dhlíthiúla atá ann mar chosaint do theangacha agus do phobail teanga. Tá impleachtaí ag an bhfíric sin.

• Is mó dá réir an tábhacht atá le **feidhmiú na n-ionstraimí éagsúla** agus le faire géar a dhéanamh air sin, mar atá déanta ag an eagraíocht *Pobal* i gcás na Cairte.

---

[1] Ó Buachalla, S. 1980. *A Significant Irish Educationalist* . Cork: Mercier Press.

• Beidh stáit ag iarraidh éalú óna gcuid dualgas. Tá an argóint chomhaimseartha acu bunaithe ar an daonlathas liobrálach agus ar na rólanna a bhíonn ag stáit i leith a gcuid saoránach (nuair a oireann). Is **ról neodrach** ceann díobh. Ach ciallaíonn sin ról neamhghníomhach, nó gan aon ní a dhéanamh, rud is ionann ina thorthaí agus ról diúltach. Is **ról éascaitheora** ceann eile díobh, ní ról gníomhaí; is é sin go ngéilltear d'éilimh brúghrúpaí ó am go chéile (*concessionary role*) nó nach gcosctar orthu polasaí áirithe a leanúint, e.g. oideachas dátheangach a chur ar fáil **ar a gcostas féin**. Tá frithargóint mhaith ag Grin[2] sa chur síos a dhéanann sé ar an rud is **maith phoiblí** ann. Dar leis, is ceart agus is cóir don stát idirghabháil a dhéanamh in aon chás a theagmhaíonn don mhaith phoiblí. Is maith poiblí an t-oideachas, maith ba chóir don stát a sholáthar do gach saoránach. Is gá an soláthar sin a chostasú ar bhonn coiteann ar dtús. Má tá costas breise ar oideachas dátheangach a sholáthar, ní cóir an costas iomlán, is é sin an costas coiteann móide an bhreis, a bheith á lua mar argóint i gcoinnibh oideachais dhátheangaigh a sholáthar. Nuair a déantar costasú ceart, faightear fíricí eile amach go minic.

• Tá coincheap an náisiúnstáit, an t-aonteangachas, agus an comhdhlúthú pobail mar aonad polaitiúil amháin an-bheo i gcónaí. Is machnamh é a bhíonn laistiar de na comhréitigh is gá a dhéanamh go minic i gcás reachtaíochta le haghaidh teangacha neamhfhorleathana. Is gá tagairt do *theanga* ní do *phobal teanga,* ar eagla go mbeadh féinrialú nó níos láidre á lorg ag an bpobal sin. Ag an am céanna, tá de pholasaí ag an Aontas Eorpach go mbeidh saoránaigh ag foghlaim (mór)theangacha a chéile. Más fíorEorpaigh atá sna saoránaigh ilteangacha, tá pobail na dteangacha neamhfhorleathana thar a bheith cáilithe. Ach is ceist don Eoraip an stádas céanna a thabhairt do na teangacha sin agus atá ag na teangacha 'oifigiúla', rud a thógfaidh tamall nuair nach bhfuil sé furasta tagairt cheart do theangacha agus do chultúir na hEorpa uile a fháil sa Chairt do Shaoránach atá á dhréachtadh i gcónaí. Ag an am céanna, is ábhar éigin dóchais go bhfuil stádas bainte amach don Mhaltais tar éis na mblianta idirbheartaíochta sna réamhsocruithe ag an tír chun teacht isteach san Aontas .

2. Cluichí cumhachta

Ní hionadh dá réir go dtarraingítear aird ar dhá bhunfhírinne sa taighde a chuir Coimisiún na hEorpa á dhéanamh[3]. Gur **grúpa sóisialta** atá i bpobal teanga – grúpa sóisialta nach bhfuil bunoscionn le normáltacht an stáit *(not deviant from the normativity of the state).* Go mbíonn an-bhaint ag **cúrsaí cumhachta**, go háirithe i dtéarmaí eacnamaíochta, le staid na bpobal teanga seo.

3. Oideachas Dátheangach

Is cuma an do mhionlaigh nó do mhórlaigh a chuirtear oideachas dátheangach ar fáil, tá fírinne amháin do-sheachanta ann. Caithfidh an soláthar a bheith de scoth na cáilíochta chun dátheangachas tairbheach suimitheach a dheimhniú. Tá impleachtaí ag a leithéid de sheasamh.

---

[2] Grin, F. (1999). "Current Problems and Dilemmas of Language Strategies for Europe: An Economist's Perspective". As P. Ó Riagáin & S. Harrington (eag.). *Straitéis Teanga don Eoraip.* Baile Átha Cliath: Bord na Gaeilge.
[3] Euromosaic: the production and reproduction of the minority language groups in the European Union. 1996. Lucsamburg: Coimisiún na hEorpa.

Tumoideachas: I bhformhór cásanna teangacha neamhfhorleathana, ciallaíonn oideachas dátheangach tumoideachas ó aois óg do pháistí arb í an mhórtheanga teanga an teaghlaigh nó na comharsanachta, nó arb í an mhórtheanga ar a laghad an teanga is treise i ngarchomharsanacht an fhoghlaimeora óig. Bíonn impleachtaí dá réir don mhodheolaíocht i gcoitinne agus don chur chuige i gcás na mórtheanga.

Múinteoirí agus Múinteoireacht: Ní mór cumas teangacha agus scileanna múinteoireachta a chinntiú tríd an gcóras réamhoiliúna agus trí chóras leanúnach forbartha ionghairme. Ní hionann cumas sa sprioctheanga agus eolas ar ábhar nó ar ábhair curaclaim agus cumas chun múineadh i gcomhthéacs an ranga dhátheangaigh. Ní hionann múineadh sa rang dátheangach agus eolas ar théarmaíocht ábhair. Ní hionann ábhar agus a théarmaíocht amháin. Bíonn dioscúrsa ar leith ag gabháil le hábhair ar leith. Toisc gurb í an teanga neamhfhorleathan is **dara teanga** ag formhór na ndaltaí sna céadbhlianta den tumoideachas, agus do dhaltaí áirithe tríd an mbunscolaíocht ar fad, ní mór don mhúinteoir agus don dearthóir acmhainní teagaisc/foghlama araon ábhar an churaclaim a chur faoi bhráid daltaí trí mhodheolaíocht dara teanga.

Is tearc iad na samplaí dá leithéid, cé go bhfuil tosú déanta air do phobal Rúisise na hEastóine[4] faoi stiúir Fred Genesee ó Cheanada, a bhfuil obair déanta aige sa réimse atá le foilsiú faoin teideal *Enriched Education*. Is cabhair do mhúinteoirí, a bhfuil an acmhainn sa mhórtheanga acu chun tosaigh ar a n-acmhainn sa teanga neamhfhorleathan, ábhair teagaisc ar leith den chineál seo a bheith ar fáil.

Lena chois sin, ní hionann oideachas dátheangach agus córas atá glan ar dhaltaí le deacrachtaí foghlama nó le riachtanais ar leith teagaisc. Tá bearnaí móra sa soláthar sa réimse seo

An dá theanga: Ní mór a bheith réadúil faoi mhianta fhormhór tuismitheoirí maidir le córas tumoideachais. Tá cumas sa teanga neamhfhorleathan á lorg acu dá bpáistí ach ní ar chostas na mórtheanga. Is comhthéacs iomlán dátheangach a bhíonn le pé machnamh a dhéanann siad. Ní mór freastal air sin chun an córas a choimeád slán. Sna córais tumoideachais in Éirinn thuaidh agus theas, ciallaíonn sin comhchomhairle le tuismitheoirí agus mínithe oideachasúla dóibh ar nádúr an tumoideachais agus ar na roghanna teagaisc a dhéantar, e.g. cúrsaí liteartachta. Ar an taobh eile, ciallaíonn an dátheangachas go ndéanfaí cúram ceart den chaighdeán agus den chineál cumais sa teanga neamhfhorleathan a bheidh ag na daltaí. Ní staid idirtheanga chalcaithe is fearr ach caithfear a bheith feasach ní hamháin ar shealbhú an dara teanga ach chomh maith leis sin ar an ionannú le grúpa agus le nósmhaireachtaí an ghrúpa – leagan teanga ina measc – a tharlaíonn i gcomhluadar na scoile. Tagann ***dílseacht teanga*** sa treis anseo chomh maith,

---

[4] Estonian Language Immersion Centre. 2001. *Annual Report, Year One, October 2001.*

dílseacht don leagan áitiúil, bíodh sin sa Ghaeltacht nó sa chathair, mar a léiríonn taighde a rinneadh i mBéal Feirste[5].

Ceann de na dúshláin is mó a bhíonn le sárú ag an múinteoir sa rang dátheangach is ea an teagasc idirdhealaitheach is gá a sholáthar don rang atá meascetha, ní hamháin mar rang ilchumais, ach mar rang a bhfuil ann samplaí den teanga neamhfhorleathan mar chéad agus mar dhara teanga, den sealbhú agus den saibhriú le chéile. Níl sampla ar fáil dáiríre den oiliúint chuí chuige seo.

Cóilíniú aigne: Ba chóir go mbeadh déchultúrachas ag dul leis an dátheangachas. Mura mbíonn, an fiú an tairbhe an trioblóid? Cuireann Colin Williams[6] fainic orainn ina thaobh.

> [...] the language may survive, but the culture – which is the real source of authenticity and resistance – may die only to be replaced by a dependent, emasculated clone culture [...] which has lost its independence and hence, rationale, to express its *own* values, ideas and ambitions.

4. Teanga agus Canúint

Má ghlactar leis an argóint shíctheangeolaíoch, ó pheirspictíocht na gcainteoirí féin, gur teanga eile ar fad seachas canúint de theanga atá acu, níor mhór do na cainteoirí sin pobal éigin inmhínithe a thaispeáint. Tá a leithéid níos déine de chritéar ná a bheith spleách ar argóintí teangeolaíocha amháin maidir le struchtúr nó le foclóir nó le 'faid' difríochta idir leaganacha.

5. Dara Teanga

Nuair a dhéantar cás na dteangacha neamhfhorleathana éagsúla a iniúchadh go fuarchúiseach, feictear go bhfuil a bhformhór mór ag brath ar chainteoirí dara teanga le creimeadh an phobail dúchais. An féidir pobal a bhunú ar a leithéid? Is ceist í a gcaithfear aghaidh a thabhairt uirthi. Tá de dhifríocht idir na teangacha neamhfhorleathana seo agus cás na hEabhraise go raibh limistéar polaitiúil agus fonnadhaint láidir a chuidigh le buanú na hEabhraise mar dhara teanga. Níl i bhformhór na gcás eile ach gréasáin scaipthe. Ar ndóigh, tá éabhlóidiú ag dul i gcónaí ar choincheap an phobail.

6. Faoi mhíbhuntáiste

Luadh an chomharthaíocht, nó cumarsáid na mbodhar agus na mbalbh. Ag fágain ar leataobh aon argóintí mar gheall ar an gcomharthaíocht mar theanga, a bhfuil cosúlacht áirithe acu leis na hargóintí i leith 'teanga versus canúint', déantar

---

[5] Nic Guidhir, G. 1990. *Our Own Language: An Irish Initiative*. Clevedon: Multilingual Matters.
[6] Williams, C.J. 1994. "Development, dependency and the democratic deficit". As P. Wynn Thomas ed.. *Fifth International Conference on Minority Languages* Clevedon: Multilingual Matters. 101-127.

dearmad ró-mhinic go mbíonn cainteoirí sna pobail teangacha neamhfhorleathana a ndéantar damáiste dúbailte dóibh toisc go gcosctar orthu aon mhodh cumarsáide ach comharthaíocht a bhíonn bunaithe ar chóras éigin den chúpla córas idirnáisiúnta atá in úsáid.

Níl aon amhras ach gurb é cumhacht an Bhéarla sna mórfhorais dhomhanda eacnamaíochta atá ina phríomhbhagairt ar go leor de theangacha an domhain. Ní cabhair ach oiread Airteagal 133 de Chonradh Nice de chuid an Chomhphobail a aithníonn an chumhacht seo trí iarracht a dhéanamh na ballstáit a chur ag oscailt amach a gcuid seirbhísí stáit agus poiblí feasta don mhargadh mór trí phríobháidiú, agus é seo gan plé a bheith ceadaithe faoi i bParlaimint na hEorpa. Ós rud é gur sna seirbhísí stáit go príomha is féidir argóint ar bhonn cearta a bheith á dhéanamh ag cainteoirí teangacha neamhfhorleathana, beidh laghdú ag teacht de réir a chéile ar raon na seirbhísí ar féidir éileamh teanga a dhéanamh ina leith, mar gur san earnáil phríobháideach a bheidh siad.

Conclúid

Leiríodh dúinn sna cainteanna tábhacht an mhórchomhthéacs, idir pholaitiúil, dhíthiúil, dhomhanda agus chomhshaoil. Labhraíodh faoi fhéileacáin na timpeallachta nadúrtha. Ba mhaith liom, mar chríoch, na féileacáin sin a chur ag eitilt thart sa ghairdín teangacha a gcuireann Colin Baker[7] síos air. Is gairdín de bhláthanna áille é gairdín na dteangacha, ilghnéitheach ildaite, le bláthanna de gach toise ag cur le háilleacht a chéile. Ach ní mór aire a thabhairt don ghairdín, chun nach dtachtfaidh fás rábach bláthanna áirithe beatha bláthanna eile agus chun a chinntiú nach múchfaidh an fhiaile an t-iomlán. Nach ansin atá cás teangacha an domhain?

Abstract

This response includes brief discussion of six points arising out of the papers presented: The question of rights, the issue of differential power, bilingual education and issues arising therefrom, e.g. immersion, teacher lifelong education and methodology, the two languages on the curriculum, mental colonisation, language and dialect, second language, and disadvantage. Conclusion evokes Baker's image of the language garden.

---

[7] *Report on new-style Workshop 5A: Bilingual Education in the Primary Sector – Working in two languages. Trinity College, Carmarthen, Wales, 1991.* Strasbourg: Council of Europe

Alba: Luchd an Aona-Chànanais agus Buaidh na Cairt Eòrpaich

Wilson McLeod

Ged a tha grunn chànan gam bruidhinn ann an Alba, is e cumadh-inntinn aona-chànanach a tha aig a' mhòrchuid de dh'Albannaich — gu h-àraidh am measg na feadhna (luchd-poileataigs is eile) a tha a' riaghladh agus a' stiùireadh na dùthcha. Gu ìre mhòir tha muinntir na h-Alba gam faicinn fhèin mar phàirt de shaoghal na Beurla, agus tha na beachdan aca air ceistean cànain gu math coltach ri beachdan luchd Beurla anns an fharsaingeachd. Gu tric, chan eil an t-uabhas sgil no ùidh aca ann an cànain eile, agus tha iad riaraichte gu leòr gu bheil a' Bheurla a' faighinn làmh an uachdar air feadh na Roinn Eòrpa oir (chanadh iad) bhiodh a h-uile duine a' tuigsinn a chèile agus bhiodh a h-uile rud na b'
Thàinig an tuigse seo am bàrr bho chionn ghoirid an lùib iomairt làn-fhollaisich aig Riaghaltas na h-Alba an aghaidh gràin-chinnidh. Gu do-chreidsinneach, agus iad ri brosnachadh an ioma-chultarais, is ann anns a' Bheurla a-mhàin a tha làrach-lìn na h-iomairt, www.onescotland.com *One Scotland, One Language*: sin mar a tha e, agus sin mar bu chòir dha bhith, a rèir urracha mòra na dùthcha.
Mar sin, ged a thog Robert Phillipson ceistean air leth cudromach anns an òraid aige, is gann gu bheil deasbad sam bith ri chluinntinn ann an Alba air poileasaidh cànain an Aonaidh Eòrpaich agus air na tha an dàn do chànain na Roinn Eòrpa anns an fharsaingeachd.

A'Chairt Eòrpach ann an Alba

Is dòcha gu bheil cùisean ag atharrachadh beagan ri linn Cairt Eòrpach air Mion-chànain agus Cànain Roinneil, a chaidh a dhaingneachadh le Riaghaltas na Rìoghachd Aonaichte ann an 2001. Air sàilleabh na Cairt, tha poileasaidhean cànain Riaghaltas na RA (a' gabhail a-steach Riaghaltas na h-Alba) fo smachd lagh eadar-nàiseanta ann an dòigh ùir. Is ann a rèir shlatan-tomhais eadar-nàiseanta a mheasar na poileasaidhean seo a-nis agus tha seo a' toirt chothroman do luchd-iomairt na Gàidhlig agus nam mion-chànan eile (Dunbar 2000, 2001).
Gu mì-fhortanach, chan eil an Riaghaltas a' coimhead air daingneachadh na Cairt Eòrpaich mar thoiseach linn ùir; is e sealladh ro-chaomhnach, ro-chumhang a tha aca. A rèir na Cairt b'fheudar don Riaghaltas co-dhiù 35 paragrafan (a-mach à 65) a shònrachadh ann an Cuid III na Cairt mu choinneimh gach cànan a dh'ainmich e (.i. a' Chuimris, a' Ghàidhlig agus a' Ghaeilge). Shònraich an Riaghaltas 52 pharagraf mu choinneimh na Cuimris, 39 mu choinneimh na Gàidhlig, agus 36 mu choinneimh na Gaeilge. Gu ìre mhòir mhòir, ged-tà, cha do leasaich an Riaghaltas na bha iad a' solarachadh; is ann gun do thagh iad paragrafan a rèir na bha ann mar-thà. Mar sin cha d'fhuaras atharrachadh susbainteach a thaobh phoileasaidhean Gàidhlig ri linn daingneachadh na Cairt; an aon rud ùr a chaidh a chur an gnìomh is e riaghailt ùr ann an siorramachdan Loch nam Madadh, Phort Rìgh, agus Steòrnabhaigh, a tha a' toirt cead do dh'agartaich a tha an sàs ann an cùisean-lagha catharra Gàidhlig a chleachdadh

anns a' chùirt (Dunbar 2001: 246-7). A rèir aithrisean chan eileas a' cur na riaghailt seo gu feum idir: tha na cùirtean seo cho aona-chànanach 's a bha iad riamh.

Tha an tuigse ro-chumhang seo ri fhaicinn anns a' Chiad Aithisg Ùinich (First Periodical Report) a thaobh buileachadh na Cairt anns an RA, a chaidh a chur gu Comhairle na h-Eòrpa anns an Iuchar 2002. Bha e follaiseach nach robh Riaghaltas na RA, no na h-ùghdarrasan ann am Béal Feirste, Caerdydd agus Dùn Èideann a bha an sàs ann an deasachadh na h-Aithisg, a' tuigsinn feallsanachd na Cairt agus cudrom nan cùmhnantan aice. Is e aithisg gu math lapach a tha ann agus tha luchd na Gàidhlig an dùil 's an dòchas gun tèid an Riaghaltas a chàineadh le Comataidh nan Eòlaichean (luchd-sgrùdaidh na Cairt) an dèidh turas rannsachaidh na Comataidh ann an 2003.

An laigse as motha a thaobh na Cairt bho shealladh na Gàidhlig, ged-tà, is e nach eil i a' toirt buaidh air na prìomh dhuilgheadasan a tha a' bualadh air iomairt na Gàidhlig an-dràsta. Mar a chualas aig a' cho-labhairt seo, ged a tha e coltach gu bheil an Riaghaltas a' coilionadh na Cairt tro bhith a' tabhann foghlam tro mheadhan na Gàidhlig aig ìrean bun-sgoile, àrd-sgoile agus àrd-ìre, tha luchd-leasachaidh na Gàidhlig a' gabhail iomagain mu cheistean eile: gainnead luchd-teagaisg, cion cùrsa-trèanaidh airson tidsearan Gàidhlig, cion adhartais a dh'ionnsaigh sgoiltean làn-Ghàidhlig an àite aonadan Gàidhlig, cion leudachaidh foghlam tro mheadhan na Gàidhlig anns an àrd-sgoil, agus eile. Mar eisimpleir, tha e fìor gu bheil an Riaghaltas a' tabhann foghlam tro mheadhan na Gàidhlig air ìre àrd-sgoile (ann an co-rèir ri Airteagal 8, earrann 1(c)(i) na Cairt); ach tha dìreach beagan a bharrachd air 200 sgoilear anns an dùthaich air fad an sàs ann, mar as trice chan eil na clasaichean tro mheadhan na Gàidhlig a' dol an dèidh S2, agus tha an siostam fhathast fo sgàile aithisg mhì-chliùitich a chuir an cèill nach robh e "miannaichte no comasach" grunn chuspairean a theagaisg tron Ghàidhlig anns an àrd-sgoil (Luchd-Sgrùdaidh na Banrigh airson Sgoiltean 1994: 3). Tha beàrn mhòr eadar na geallaidhean farsaing anns a' Chairt Eòrpaich agus na tha tachairt "air an talamh".

Nàdar na Coimhearsnachd Ghàidhlig

Chuir Tove-Skutnabb Kangas cudrom air foghlam tro mheadhan a' chànain mhàthaireil — cuspair a tha air leth cudromach ann an tòrr choimhearsnachdan air feadh an t-saoghail. Ann an Alba, ged-tà, tha nàdar na coimhearsnachd Ghàidhlig a' sìor atharrachadh, agus chan eil "ceist a' chànain mhàthaireil" aig cridhe an deasbaid. Ged a tha luchd-ionnsachaidh na Gàidhlig fhathast air leth gann — 5% den iomlan, is dòcha — tha e coltach gu bheil a' mhòrchuid den chloinn a tha an sàs ann am foghlam tro mheadhan na Gàidhlig ag ionnsachadh na Gàidhlig mar darna cànan.[1] Fiù am measg na cloinne a fhuair Gàidhlig anns an

---

[1]Chan eil fiosrachadh deimhinne ri fhaighinn air a' cheist seo. Ann an Dùn Èideann, mar eisimpleir, tha e coltach gu bheil dìreach a' chòigeamh cuid den chloinn a tha an sàs ann am foghlam tro mheadhan na Gàidhlig anns a' bhaile a' faighinn Gàidhlig aig an taigh. Is dòcha gur e seo an àbhaist taobh a-muigh nan sgìrean far a bheil a' Ghàidhlig na cànan coimhearsnachd, ach bhiodh an ìre gu math nas àirde ann an Innse Gall.

dachaigh mus tàinig iad chun na sgoile, chan eil a' Bheurla na "cànan coimheach" dhaibh oir bidh a' Bheurla aca cuideachd mus ruig iad an sgoil (mar as trice, anns an latha an-diugh, mar phrìomh-chànan). Mar sin cha bu chòir foghlam tro mheadhan na Gàidhlig ann an Alba anns an latha an-diugh a thuigsinn mar oidhirp a bhith a' dìon luchd-labhairt mion-chànain bho bhogadh ann an cànan nach tuig iad, cleachdadh a tha cumanta ann an iomadach dùthaich (mar a dh'innseas Tove Skutnabb-Kangas anns na sgrìobhaidhean brìoghmhor aice (e.g. Skutnabb-Kangas 2000)) agus a bha cumanta air Gaidhealtachd na h-Alba mus robh dà-chànanas na àbhaist am measg nan Gaidheal (Smith 1948; Scottish Council for Research in Education, Committee on Bilingualism 1961). Gu ìre mhòir mhòir is e iomairt ath-bheòthachadh cànain (no fiù's aiseirigh cànain) a tha ann am foghlam tro mheadhan na Gàidhlig, ged nach eil deasbad fiosraichte, innleachdail ga chumail am measg luchd-labhairt na Gàidhlig air na dùbhlain a thig an lùib ath-bheòthachadh cànain, gu h-àraidh a' bheàrn eadar dealbhachadh sealbhachaidh (*acquisition planning*, .i. ionnsachadh sgilean cànain) agus dealbhachadh cleachdaidh (*usage planning*, .i. ciamar a thèid na sgilean seo a chur gu feum gu làitheil).

Ged a tha luchd na Gàidhlig dà-chànanach anns an latha an-diugh — mar a tha a' mhòr-mhòrchuid de luchd-labhairt mion-chànain na Roinn Eòrpa air fad — gu tric chan eil luchd-poileataigs agus luchd-riaghlaidh na h-Alba a' tuigsinn suidheachadh na coimhearsnachd Ghàidhlig agus iad a' cumail a-mach (os àird no os ìosal) gum bu chòir seirbhisean Gàidhlig a thabhann dìreach don fheadhainn nach eil comasach anns a' Bheurla.[2] Chan eileas a' tuigsinn prionnsapalan còraichean cànain, gum bu chòir *roghainn cànain* a bhith ann — ach is dòcha gun atharraich sin mar thoradh air buaidh na Cairt Eòrpaich; tha e soilleir, a rèir aithisgean sgrùdaidh Comataidh nan Eòlaichean nach eil e gu diofar sam bith gu bheil luchd nam mion-chànan comasach anns a' chànan oifigeil cuideachd, gu bheil uallach air na h-ùghdarrasan feumalachdan nan coimhearsnachdan dà-chànanach a fhrithealadh.

A' Chairt Eòrpach: Duilgheadasan mìneachaidh

Chan eil e furasta poileasaidh / ro-innleachd Riaghaltas na RA a thaobh daingneachadh na Cairt a thuigsinn, gu h-àraidh a thaobh Airteagal 8 den Chairt, a tha a' buntainn ri foghlam. Ged a tha e follaiseach nach ann air sgàth adhbharan prionnsapail gun do shònraich an Riaghaltas tuilleadh pharagrafan mu choinneimh na Cuimris seach na Gàidhlig agus na Gaeilge, ach dìreach air sgàth 's gu bheil an ìre solarachaidh a thathas a' tabhann mar-thà nas àirde, tha duilgheadasan àraid a' nochdadh an lùib a' chlòdha bhig. Mar eisimpleir, shònraich an Riaghaltas deich paragrafan ann an Airteagal 8 mu choinneimh na

---

[2]Mar eisimpleir, a rèir Seirbhis Eadar-theangachaidh Comhairle Dhùn Èideann "Gaelic [is] a language of choice as opposed to one of need", agus mar sin tha iad a' diùltadh eadar-theangachadh a dhèanamh às leth duine sam bith aig a bheil a' Bheurla. An dèidh gearan bhon bhuidhinn-iomairt Ghàidhlig FÀS (Dùn Èideann) anns an Damhair 2002, thèid ath-sgrùdadh a dhèanamh air a' phoileasaidh spìocach seo.

Gàidhlig ach dìreach naoi airson na Cuimris (agus na Gaeilge), ged a tha an ìre solarachaidh a thaobh foghlam tro mheadhan na Cuimris fada nas àirde.[3]

Duilgheadas nas cudromaiche a thaobh Airteagal 8 is e gun do shònraich an Riaghaltas fo-earrannan 1a (i), 1b (i) agus 1c (i) mu choinneimh na Gàidhlig agus earrannan 1a (iii), 1b (iv) agus 1c (iv) mu choinneimh na Gaeilge. A rèir coltais tha fo-earrannan (i) nas treasa agus nas fharsainge na (iii)/(iv). Tha na fo-earrannan (i) a' cur an cèill gu bheil uallach air an Riaghaltas "to make available pre-school / primary / secondary education in the relevant regional or minority languages" (.i. anns a' Ghàidhlig), agus tha na fo-earrannan (iii)/(iv) a' cur an cèill gum feumar foghlam anns a' mhion-chànan a thabhann "at least to those pupils whose families so request and whose number is considered sufficient." Chan eil e buileach soilleir dè dìreach a tha fa-near an lùib fo-earrannan (i) — chan eil mìneachadh ùghdarrasach ann, agus cha bhi, oir cha tig a' Chairt fo chomhair cùirt làn-chumhachdach — ach tha e coltach gur e solarachadh gnàthach, "prìomh-shruthach" a tha san amharc. Tha e furasta gu leòr a thuigsinn carson a thagh an Riaghaltas fo-earrannan (iii) agus (iv) a thaobh na Gaeilge, oir tha riaghailtean teann aig na h-ùghdarrasan foghlaim ann an Èirinn a Tuath a thaobh fosgladh sgoiltean/aonadan Gaeilge: chan e solarachadh gnàthach a tha ann idir. Ach tha suidheachadh foghlam tro mheadhan na Gàidhlig gu math coltach ri suidheachadh foghlam Gaeilge. Chan eil solarachadh foghlam tro mheadhan na Gàidhlig idir na àbhaist (mar a tha teagaisg matamataig, can): cha tig aonad ùr Gàidhlig às aonais iomairt, coiteachadh agus spàirn. Chan eil foghlam Gàidhlig idir air a ghnàthachadh, fiù am measg nan ùghdarrasan as taiceile, leithid Comhairle na Gaidhealtachd. Mar sin faodar argamaid a thogail nach eil an Riaghaltas a' coilionadh na Cairt a thaobh fo-earrannan 1a (i), 1b (i) agus 1c (i); tha nàdar an t-solarachaidh aca gu math nas fhaisge air fo-earrannan 1a (iii), 1b (iv) agus 1c (iv). Gu dearbh, is dòcha gur e sin na bha fa-near don Riaghaltas anns a' chiad dol-a-mach, oir tha a' Chiad Aithisg Ùineach aig Riaghaltas na RA a' cumail a-mach gur iad 1a(iii), 1(b)(iv) agus 1(c)(iv) na fo-earrannan a tha a' buntainn ris a' Ghàidhlig. Tha mearachd ann gun teagamh, ach an ann anns a' Chiad Aithisg Ùinich a tha i, no anns an Ionnstramaid Daingnichidh thùsail?[4]

Tha grunn cheistean eile ann an lùib coilionadh na Cairt a thaobh foghlam Gàidhlig: mar eisimpleir, an co-cheangal ri fo-earrann 1(h) tha uallach air an Riaghaltas "to provide the basic and further training of the teachers required to implement those of paragraphs a to g accepted by the Party", ach tha gainnead an

---

[3]An diofar is e nach do shònraich an Riaghaltas earrann 8(2) mu choinneimh na Cuimris; tha an earrann seo a' cur an cèill "With regard to education and in respect of territories other than those in which the regional or minority languages are traditionally used, the Parties undertake, if the number of users of a regional or minority language justifies it, to allow, encourage or provide teaching in or of the regional or minority language at all the appropriate stages of education." Is mathaid gur e an tuigse a tha air cùlaibh seo gu bheil an Riaghaltas den bheachd gu bheil Galldachd na h-Alba na "territory other than those in which the regional or minority languages are traditionally used", agus do bhrìgh sin gu bheil solarachadh foghlam Gàidhlig air a' Ghalldachd a' coilionadh na h-earrainn seo.

[4]Tha mi glè bhuidheach de Robert Dunbar (Oilthigh Ghlaschu), a thug fiosrachadh agus comhairle air leth luachmhor dhomh air na puingean seo.

luchd-theagaisg — gainnead a tha a' leantainn air bho bhliadhna gu bliadhna gun fhuasgladh freagarrach bhon Riaghaltas — a' ciallachadh nach eil aonadan Gàidhlig a' fosgladh a dh'aindeoin iarrtas nam pàrant. Faodar argamaid a thogail nach eil an Riaghaltas a' dèanamh gu leòr an lùib seo, nach eil iad a' riarachadh na tha "required to implement" na geallaidhean aca a thaobh solarachadh na Gàidhlig. Gu deimhinne, cha b'urrainnear a ràdh gum biodh riaghaltas a' coilionadh a dhleastanasan tro bhith a' trèanadh dithis thidsearan nuair a tha 200 a dhìth; ged nach eil a' bheàrn idir cho mòr sin ann an Alba, feumaidh ceist a bhith ann a thaobh gèilleadh Riaghaltas na RA ris an fho-earrann seo.

Co-dhùnadh

Ged a tha i lag ann an iomadach dòigh, tha a' Chairt Eòrpach gu math cudromach don choimhearsnachd Ghàidhlig ann an Alba. Tha poileasaidhean an Riaghaltais a' tighinn fon phrospaig ann an dòigh ùir, agus is ann a rèir shlatan-tomhais eadar-nàiseanta agus a rèir sgrùdaidhean le eòlaichean eadar-nàiseanta a thèid na poileasaidhean seo a mheasadh. Chan e seo an "inbhe thèarainte" a tha luchd-iomairt na Gàidhlig a' sireadh, ach tha àrainneachd ùr ann a-nis agus tha seo a' toirt chothroman ùra don choimhearsnachd Ghàidhlig argamaidean a dhealbhadh agus iomairtean a thogail.

Liosta Sgrìobhaidhean

Dunbar, Robert (2000). "Implications of the European Charter for Regional or Minority Languages for British Linguistic Minorities". *European Law Review Human Rights Survey*, 25, 46-69.

Dunbar, Robert (2001). "Minority Language Rights Regimes: An Analytical Framework, Scotland, and Emerging European Norms", ann an *Linguistic Politics: Language Policies for Northern Ireland, the Republic of Ireland, and Scotland*, deasaichte le John Kirk agus Dónall Ó Baoill, 231-54. Béal Feirste: Cló Ollscoil na Banríona/Queen's University Press.

Luchd-Sgrùdaidh na Banrigh airson Sgoiltean (1994). *Solarachadh na Gàidhlig ann am Foghlam ann an Albainn*. Dùn Èideann: Roinn Foghlaim Oifis na h-Alba.

Scottish Council for Research in Education, Committee on Bilingualism (1961). *Gaelic-Speaking Children in Highland Schools*. Lunnainn: University of London Press.

Skutnabb-Kangas, Tove (2000). *Linguistic Genocide in Education — Or Worldwide Diversity and Human Rights?* Mahwah, NJ: Erlbaum.

Smith, Christina A. (1948). *Mental Testing of Hebridean Children in Gaelic and English*. Lunnainn: University of London Press.

Abstract

The monolingual mindset is strong in Scotland and debates about language policy are generally conducted at a low level. In most ways Scotland identifies itself and functions as part of the English-speaking world, and like other English-speakers, many Scots do not seem particularly troubled about the increasing use of English in Europe and beyond.

The European Charter for Regional or Minority Languages has important ramifications for the Gaelic community in Scotland, even if it will not necessarily advance resolution of the key problems relating to Gaelic education (shortage of teachers, inadequate teacher training systems, the desire for all-Gaelic schools instead of Gaelic units, etc.). The precise policy of the UK Government with regard to the Charter, although clearly disappointingly narrow and minimalist, is somewhat confusing. Most strikingly, the Government designated three key paragraphs in the Charter (Article 8, sections 1a (i), 1b (i) and 1c (i)) that do not seem to correspond with actual provision for Gaelic; but its First Periodical Report (submitted in July 2002) proceeded on the assumption that it had actually signed up to three less demanding paragraphs (Article 8, sections 1a (iii), 1b (iv) and 1c (iv)).

Despite these difficulties, the fact that the Government's provision for Gaelic will now be judged by international criteria and assessed by international experts is highly significant and will create new opportunities to Gaelic campaigners and the Gaelic community in general.

Privileging Indigeneity

Anthea Fraser Gupta

Ideology of Language Planning

It is inevitable that in any nation, organisation, or even family, some languages will be privileged at the expense of others. This privileging is typically based on a mixture of functionality and ideology. Those of us who analyse these decisions bring to the analysis our ideologies, which may in turn feed into the development of new or old ideologies. My first paper in the field of language planning (Gupta 1985) was an exploration of the link between policies and politics – what was the goal of a language planning decision? what was its likely outcome? In more recent papers and presentations (1997, 2001a, 2001b) I have taken issue with some of the arguments of the Language Rights Movement, mostly in connection with the promotion of native languages in education. I have argued that the concept of native language is not a useful one in many multilingual settings, and that traditions of certain languages being associated with education in some places need to be respected. I have consistently argued that English is not the property of certain locations (such just those where its traditional native speakers are), but a tool for the world. Today I am going to look at the ideology behind the identification of 'Regional or Minority Languages' in Europe.

My own linguistic ideology comes from a stance associated with Le Page's Acts of Identity (e.g. Le Page & Tabouret Keller 1980), which casts speakers as active creators of their own sociolinguistic identity. I also believe that as a linguist I need to respect the dynamic of language change, which is part of the inevitable change in all human behaviour. In language, as in sexual behaviour, directing behaviour is not an exact science. A further motivating political ideology for me is my rejection of a genetically based nationalist ideology.

With unfortunately almost no reference to the sociolinguistic literature, De Swaan (2001) has examined the economics of language choice in way I find very powerful, discussing the 'political economy of language' (2001:18) and making clear how choice operates at the level of the individual as well as in wider contexts. The 'Q value' of a language is its communication value, a measure based on the 'prevalence' and 'centrality' in a certain 'constellation' (p33ff). The most *central* languages are those which have large numbers of speakers who are also competent in some other language(s), and which are therefore highly *connected*. De Swaan shows how individuals make choices about language learning and use, defends their rights to choice, and shows how governmental decisions on language can only succeed if they correspond with Q-value. Prospective speakers compare language repertoires. The promotion of minority languages in locations with a strong majority language is hampered by their having low Q values of the languages. The fact, for example, that virtually all adult speakers of Scots Gaelic speak English, and that few speakers of Gaelic are non-native speakers, lowers the Q value of Gaelic. A lowered Q-value would also accrue 'insider' languages such as Scots, which it may be unacceptable for an outsider to attempt at all.

In some respects de Swaan's analysis revisits the ground covered many years ago by Greenberg (1956) and Stewart (1968) (Stewart is not quoted by de Swaan), though in a more politically informed way. One thing I find especially valuable in De Swaan's analysis is his moral neutrality to language shift. People engaged in language shift may be portrayed as victims, perhaps seen as damaged or even morally reprehensible. I have argued elsewhere (Gupta 1997 etc.) that language shift, creolisation, and ethnic mixing are in themselves morally neutral, and not evidences of wrongful destruction, as is sometimes implied (or inferrable) in the discussion of language shift.

Indigeneity

In this paper I would like to turn to something that I find worrying in a number of guises, and that is the ideology that sees the 'indigenous' as more worthy than the imported. In the narrative of political and linguistic management indigeneity has been problematic.

When the concepts of ecology are transposed to languages, languages fill the role of the organisms, and can be imagined as killers, as murder victims, or as sick. Mühlhäusler (1996:2) describes the metaphor as "particularly productive", although not without problems. The biological metaphor lends itself to considering some behaviours as natural and encouages a perspective that sees 'indigenous' or 'autochthonous' groups as a natural part of an ecology, and therefore as especially worthy of protection. Skutnabb-Kangas (2000:487ff) problematises the concept of indigeneity and includes other non-dominant linguistic groups in her remit, but Nettle and Romaine (2000) seem to take the term as a given and do not define it. Indigeneity makes links between languages, genetic heritage, and territory.

Some cultures, such as Europe a millenium ago, or India 500 years ago, operate with a division between classical, learned languages on the one hand, and vernaculars on the other. The classical language (Latin, Sanskrit, Persian, for example) is typically spoken as a native language by few or none but linked a literate elite across a wide geographical area. Vernaculars (English, Urdu, Bengali) flourish orally and develop writing systems -- in these contexts vernaculars are often the first languages of literacy. Not all vernaculars are equal -- de Swaan's Q-value operates here too, as some vernaculars do not develop writing systems, while others become regionally strong languages of education, and are used by non-native as well as native speakers.

Historically some of these classical languages had been languages of political or religious conquest. In a colonial setting the conquerors are typically seen as superior to the conquered -- and the 'natives' and their language as superior to that of the natives. In India, English, after Macaulay's famous Minute of 1835 (quoted by Mahmood 1895:50f) did not displace the vernaculars, but the classical languages. But a colonial situation is not static. As can be seen with Latin in Europe, a language can persist after the conquerors have left, to become both a culturally based language, and also, in many parts of Europe, developing into new vernaculars. This has already happened with English.

Nor are peoples static. Since humans left Africa people have moved from place to place. Some of these people adopted new languages as they moved.

Others brought their languages to new places. All of us will have ancestors who were involved in language shift, whether that is known to us or too far back in our ancestry to have been transmitted. Historical linguists have long known that languages are not transmitted with DNA.

All of us have ancestors too who have been on both sides of the colonising and conquering shifts down the millenia. The 'indigenous' of a place can only ever be relative to the more recent arrivals. Sometimes, as with those who brought the Celtic languages to the British Isles, the process took place prehistorically. In the case of those who brought the Germanic languages we know much more about the processes, while the introduction of the Romani languages is also in historical times. Furthermore, groups do not remain discrete, but merge, especially through marriage. Migration, language shift, and intermarriage are long established human practices. They have not stopped. It is dangerous to solidify this fluidity into policy.

Myths of origin are valuable in the construction of national and ethnic identity, and these myths must have some point of contact with historical reality. Many nations operate with a myth of indigeneity, which is attached to people as well as to languages. The myth of indigeneity served the British Empire well. In a colonial setting it is quite likely that indigeneity may be equated with inferiority, and that those seen as indigenous, or 'native' may be without power. But it is also possible to establish the indigenous as having rights to the territory which those not seen as indigenous do not have. This casts the indigenous as superior and is ethically no different from casting the indigenous as inferior. An ideology of indigeneity establishes certain groups of people (usually determined by ancestry) as having a particular link with a piece of territory. A language linked to these people is in turn seen as an indigenous language. It is perfectly possible that the superior rights of the indigenous and their inferior characteristics may be linked, as they were, for example, in colonial Malaya.

The myth of indigeneity was forcefully promoted by the colonial powers in a number of places. The eighteenth century British scholars who argued that the Malays were indigenous to the Malay peninsula and archipelago did not argue indigenousness on the basis of the greatest antiquity. Marsden (1812b:xix f) argues for Malay being regarded as indigenous to the region despite its not being the most ancient language of the region. He compares the indigeneity of Malay in the Malay archipelago to the indigeneity of English in Great Britain (also displacing other languages), and concludes that as Malay has 'wide dissemination and high degree of antiquity .... In this restricted sense it is that we are justified in considering the main portion of the Malayan as original or indigenous.'

Swettenham, former governor of the Straits Colony and High Commissioner for the Federated Malay States, takes the Malays indigeneity as given, and develops it into a justification of empire which positions the Chinese as co-developers of the colony with the British. Chinese 'energy and enterprise have made the Malay States what they are today, and it would be impossible to overstate the obligation which the Malay Government and people are under to these hard-working, capable, and law-abiding aliens' (Swettenham 1907:232). On the other hand the part played by the Malays 'was mainly negative' (p233).

> There are people who have no patience with the Malays, who
> say they are lazy and useless and have already received far too

much consideration... They do not strive for riches, but they are probably as happy and contented as other people who regard life differently, and it is questionable whether we should deserve their thanks if we could teach them the tireless energy, the self-denying frugality of the Chinese... You cannot make people virtuous by Act of Parliament, and you cannot graft the Chinese nature on to the Malay body. The Malays are 'the people of the country'; we went to the Malay States for their benefit, and we have somehow managed to give them an independence, a happiness and a prosperity which they never knew before; and while it is not Malays alone who have thus benefitted, but all classes and nationalities, the credit is due to a few British officers who strove ceaselessly for that object which Lord Curzon puts first amongst the lessons taught him by Eastern administration. (Swettenham 1907:304f).

This centrality of the Malays is the central theme of Swettenham's life work, and he returns to it in the closing words of his book, arguing that 'time will not change the Malay character or alter the fact that the Malays are 'the people of the country' whose confidence we have gained by making their interests our first consideration.' Shamsul (1997) discusses the way in which ethnographic studies by the colonists were made to serve the requirements of colonialism , and emphasises how seldom the social categories that emerged from this ethnography are questioned today:

[...] suffices to say that the social category 'Malay' (for that matter Chinese, Indian, Kadazan and Iban, too) has always been used, first, as something given and taken-for-granted and, second, in analytical terms, as tool for analysis used automatically in pair or cluster with other social categories, such as Chinese or Indian. This in turn has resulted in 'essentialising' the Malays (and simultaneously the Chinese, Indian and Others, too) giving it a set of ideal-typical attributes for the sake of analysis thus encouraging the obviously simplistic perception that Malays as a social group is a homogenous one. What seems to be an analytical convenience, in fact 'orientalist' in spirit, has developed into a 'scientific approach' thus 'Malay' or 'Malayness' as a social category has never been problematised or perceived as something constructed, invented, artificial despite the fact that 'what it means' and 'what it is' have always been altered, redefined, reconstituted and the boundaries expanded according to specific social-historical circumstances, especially after the introduction of colonial 'racism' and 'racial category' into the realm of authority-defined and everyday-defined social reality in British Malaya [...].

The myth of the indigenous Malay was used to legitimise colonial rule; and in modern Malaysia is is used to legitimise the bumiputra policy (related concepts also motivate political discourse in Brunei, see for example Gunn 1997). In modern Singapore indigeneity serves a national myth of striving meritocrats building on nothing to create a prosperous city, but also feeds into policies and discourse based on ethnic stereotyping.

Policies of privileging indigeneity have given separate treatment to groups identified as indigenous in many places, including Fiji, Malaysia and Israel. In all cases the priviliging of the group has negative consequences on members of other groups, even if they know the language which is privileged. Privileging *a language*, by contrast, does not confer an exclusive advantage on those who speak it, or who comes from its congruent ethnic group, unless those who do not speak a priviliged language are denied access to its learning (as is the case in modern Singapore, where those who are not ethnic Chinese are denied access, in the school system, to both Chinese and Japanese). So the privileging of Malay in Malaysia does not disadvantage those who are not Malay, as access to learning Malay is facilitated for all.

In modern Malaysia, there is constant negotiation about which privileges are to be given to those groups regarded as 'bumiputera' -- 'princes of the earth' / 'sons of the soil'. There are also constant negotiations about which groups can so name themselves. Can the mixed people that developed in Malaysia (for example, the Straits Chinese, and the Malacca Eurasians) call themselves indigenous (at the moment the answer is 'no')? Can those whose ancestors came from parts of the Malay Archipelago which are now in Indonesia (at the moment the answer is 'yes')? Israel identifies Jewish people as being entitled to a particular territory -- again there is the negotiation of definition of how 'Jewish' is to be defined. In both Fiji and Malaysia, part of the motivation for privileging 'indigenous' groups was a perception that they were economically disadvantaged compared to other groups, mostly the descendants of people from India and China. The other part was an assertion of power by a group who were in a narrow majority. In Israel too, there had been a history of oppression, though the oppressors were not the ancestors of those competing for the territory. All three examples, I would argue, show how the oppressed can take on the role of the oppressor.

The motivations for privileging indigeneity are many, and are often concerned with the redressing of previous oppression. Privileging a language is not enough to redress this history of oppression, as anyone can learn any language. So the group must be privileged. But if one group is privileged other groups are inevitably downgraded. It remains important to analyse the ideology of privileging indigeneity and to assess the ethics of any such privileging.

Regional or Minority Languages in Europe

The European Union defines languages in a hierarchy, which, as I have said, is inevitable in any organisation. At the top are the 11 official languages of the EU: Spanish, Danish, German, Greek, English, French, Italian, Dutch, Portuguese, Finnish and Swedish (the order in which they appear on the front cover, which, except for Español, is in the alphabetical order of their names in themselves -- Spanish appears to be in the alphabetical order of 'Castiliano'). Some of these are more official than others, inevitably, but that issue is not relevant to my argument. These languages are official languages of member states, but a member state with more than one official language can be represented by only one of them, something which especially affects Luxembourg and the Republic of Ireland: the 11 official languages, plus Irish and Luxembourgish were promoted as languages to be learnt in the European Year of Languages (European

Community 2000). The runners up in the EU hierarchy are *Regional or Minority Languages*:

> The customary definition of regional or minority language is that used in *European Charter for Regional or Minority Languages*, an international treaty supervised by the Council of Europe and adopted by many EU Member States, i.e. languages traditionally used by part of the population of a state that are not dialects of official languages of the state, languages of migrants or artificially created languages. (*Regional or Minority Languages of the European Union*)

This is a rewording of the Charter. In the Charter itself the key words which are vague in meaning but not defined are 'traditionally' and 'migrant' -- the traditional use of a language by nationals of a State is the crucial part of definition. It is not clear whether the categories of 'migrant' and 'national of the state' are exclusive or overlapping terms (*European Charter* 1992, Article 1). Potentially the European Charter's definitions could be interpreted as including the languages of the descendants of recent migrants who have are now nationals, if they then become 'traditional'. That is not how the Charter has been interpreted -- rather the terms 'indigenous'and 'autochthonous' tend to be used to refer to the languages covered by the Charter, and the term 'immigrant' appears to include the native-born children and grandchildren of immigrants. In the UK the languages currently within the scope of the Charter (and ratified to some extent or another in the Charter) are Welsh, Scottish-Gaelic, Irish (in that order) and, to a lesser extent Scots and Ulster Scots, and (Council of Europe 2002).

The same indigenous / immigrant rhetoric is used by the Summer Institute of Linguistics *Ethnologue*:

> **Immigrant languages**. All languages spoken in a country are not necessarily listed as separate entries in the Ethnologue, especially immigrant languages which are still spoken in the country of origin and apparently have no significant dialect differences between the two locations. Known immigrant languages are listed in the introduction at the beginning of each country's listing, with population estimate if known. They are not included in the language statistics for that country. Information about immigrant languages is incomplete, and may be incorrect. Corrections are requested. Some languages listed in the country introductions may not be immigrant languages, but if the only unique thing known about a language in a given country is its presence, or its population, and it is listed with more information in another country, then it may also be listed only in the country introduction. This is especially true for the countries of the former USSR. ('Introduction')

Ethnologue can't possibly follow this definition through. So we find, for example, English listed as one of the languages of the US, Australia, and India. In the UK, which Ethnologue currently identifies as having 12 living and 2 dead languages, the definition appears to have been in terms of a 'language' having originated in the UK. There are also problems of the definition of a 'language' – some of these languages aren't, by any reasonable definition, languages, but are partial lexicons, or dialects (Polari, Yinglish). Yinglish, by the way, is described as 'a language of USA', which suggests it's an immigrant language (from the US?). Why should it be there and not Hinglish, London Jamaican / Patwa? (known in Ethnologue as 'Southwestern Caribbean Creole English'). If Polari and Traveller Scottish are UK languages, why isn't Shelta (because it's 'a language of Ireland' – but Ethnologue itself claims 30,000 speakers of it in the UK and 6,000 in Ireland!). Languages spoken by large numbers of UK nationals are classed as immigrant languages (e.g. Gujarati, Greek).

Just as in Malaysia groups lobby for the right to be indigenous, so in the EU languages lobby for the right to be identified as a 'Regional or Minority' language. In the UK Cornish has recently argued for its acceptance as a recognised language for minority status, and BSL is another potential candidate. But Gujarati and Greek can make no such case.

Many of the recognised Regional and Minority Languages have been subject to considerable attack from speakers of the majority languages that surround them and were often the subject of concerted efforts at eradication. They have typically lost speakers as a process of language shift, as speakers make the kind of pragmatic decisions discussed by de Swaan. However, those who speak the minority languages, or who are the descendants of speakers of them, are not necessarily *now* among the most underprivileged members of society. The privileging of these languages is not based on a need to ameliorate an underprivileged *group of people*, but on a sense of the cultural and affective importance of the *languages*. Ó Riagáin (2001:45) also makes the point that the Charter is carefully addressed at languages.

The rhetoric of indigeneity fits well with a recent trend in European politics to emphasise the European and the Judaeo-Christian tradition. This emphasis has shown electoral success in a number of European countries, and, in 2002, has seen the Netherlands attempting to impose a Dutch language policy on mosques, and a British Minister, David Blunkett, regretting that in 30% of Asian British families, English was not used at home, and advising Asian British parents to use English in the home in order to "overcome the schizophrenia which bedevils generational relationships" (Blunkett 2002). Ironically, However, in the prevalent discourse, both the 'indigenous'and 'immigrant' languages are typically not seen as suitable to be learnt by those who do not come from the community with which they associated. For example, Welsh (so important in Wales) cannot be taught as part of the National Curriculum in England, while languages such as Gujarati and Urdu, which *can* be part of the national curriculum (ages 11-16) are taught as 'Modern Foreign Languages' to a very small proportion of children, most of whom are native speakers of the languages.

I am sympathetic to efforts to redress the injustices and oppression of the past; to efforts to benefit underprivileged groups and to efforts to answer the linguistic needs of as many members of society as practicable. But these aims are not answered by making a distinction between 'indigenous' and 'migrant' languages, which can only be based entirely on a quasi-genetic territorial system that gives a high values to the indigenous. I do not see that there can be any human rights or linguistic justification for prioritising groups defined as indigenous over groups not so defined.

Languages are Human Behaviours

We often have to work with the concept of 'a language'. But we should never forget that languages are not things -- they are aspects of human behaviour.

The ideology of indigeneity is often linked to notions of language preservation. Since the ecological analogy was made in the 1970s this metaphor has largely been used in connection with discussions of language death, and, increasingly, by those concerned with the loss of languages and language types, which is seen as analogical to the loss of species and genotypes. (Nettle & Romaine 2000, Skutnabb-Kangas 2000). Ways of (for example) classifying nouns may be seen as analagous to individual genes.

However, analogy is what this is. Languages are not tangible, like white-handed gibbons (and their genes) or like artefacts such the Ring of Brodgar or the Taj Mahal. Instantiations of languages exist concretely as text, and the rules that generated or could generate such texts can be inferred from text and from introspection. But languages are abstractions. We have no purely linguistic definition of 'a language' or 'a dialect' but must refer to cultural understandings for a usable concept. (We do have reasonable definitions of 'language', by comparison.)

Languages are human constructs of human behaviour. Some cultural behaviours carry moral values, e.g. mating practices, styles of dress. What practices are worth celebrating and what should we strive to eradicate? Candidates for the undesirable for me would include: exposure of infants, foot binding, sati, corporal and capital punishment. Other people have different evaluations. Few cultural behaviours seem to be universally seen as ethically neutral (notions of manners in eating perhaps?). In language, however, most things seem ethically neutral. To what extent should their loss be deplored? Old English had a three way number distinction -- should it have been preserved? Does its loss matter? If no-one spoke a language with the middle voice would there have been a loss we should mourn? Would the world be a worse place without uvular fricatives? Should we decide what is worth preserving in behaviour (as opposed to in text)? Does that mean we have to try to influence language behaviour?

If the motivation of a language policy is to preserve a language, does that imply a purist tradition, which will prevent the appearance of new loanwords, or of regular linguistic change?

Like Mühlhäusler (1996:4f) I find it hard to see languages as anything other than social constructs, and I place human behaviour at the centre of language, rather than some external entity called 'a language' (Harris 1980, Le Page & Tabouret-Keller 1985). I do accept that it is sometimes necessary to talk about languages as named entities which have a social meaning in a community, but I do not accept languages as things that need or deserve protection, though I can agree that there are circumstances in which groups of people may need to take action to enable themselves to continue performing language in a desired way. I certainly don't think that grammatical rules are things worthy of preservation. The axiom that languages change is an absolute.

Conclusion

The privileging of the indigenous is in the context of a discourse which analogises languages as part of an ecology. A biological ecosystem may work smoothly for the benefit of all in it, or may favour some organisms at the expense of others. But under any real ecosystem lies a long history of conflict. When we come to humans, we need to question the ethics of the notion that some humans are a natural part of a physical territory, while other humans are an intrusion that disturbs the natural, like Himalayan balsam in Yorkshire or water hyacinths in Bengal. The ethics and the pragmatics of privileging some languages must be explored. If language shift and language change are both inevitable (perhaps natural?) aspects of human behaviour, then efforts to direct linguistic behaviour will benefit from exploiting the pragmatic and ideological motivations of the people whose behaviour they wish to change, but must also recognise the inevitability and moral neutrality of language shift and language change.

References

Blunkett, David. 2002. "What does citizenship mean today?" [Integration with Diversity: Globalisation and the Renewal of Democracy and Civil Society. In *Rethinking Britishness*. The Foreign Policy Centre.] Reference to preprint version of essay, 15 September 2002, *The Observer Comment* <www.observer.co.uk/comment/story/0,6903,792223,00.html> [accessed September 2002]

Council of Europe. 2002. "List of declarations made with respect to treaty no. 148. European Charter for Regional or Minority Languages". <conventions.coe.int/Treaty/EN/cadreprincipal.htm> Complete chronology on: 06/10/02

de Swaan, Abram. 2001. *Words of the World*. Cambridge: Polity.

European Charter for Regional or Minority Languages. Strasbourg, 5.XL.1992. Council of Europe ETS no. 146 [accessed August 2002] <conventions.coe.int/treaty/en/Treaties/Html/148.htm>

European Communities. 2000. "A Community of Languages". <www.europarl.eu.int/language/default_en.htm> [accessed August 2002]

Greenberg, Joseph H. 1956. The measurement of linguistic diversity. *Language* 32: 109-115

Gunn, Geoffrey C.. 1997. *Language, Power and Ideology in Brunei Darussalam*. (Monographs in International Studies, Southeast Asia Series Number 99) Athens, Ohio: Ohio Centre for International Studies

Gupta, Anthea Fraser. 1985. "Language Status Planning in the ASEAN Countries". In ed. David Bradley *Pacific Linguistics: Papers in Southeast Asian Linguistics* No. 9. *Language policy, language planning and sociolinguistics in Southeast Asia*. 1-14

Gupta, Anthea Fraser. 1996. "English and Empire: teaching English in nineteenth century India". In eds. Neil M Mercer & Joan Swann *Learning English: Development and Diversity*. London/New York: Routledge/ Open University. 188-194

Gupta, Anthea Fraser. 1997. "When mother-tongue education is *not* preferred". *Journal of Multilingual and Multicultural Development* 18(6): 496-506

Gupta, Anthea Fraser. 2001a. (9 June) "English in the linguistic ecology of Singapore". *GNEL/MAVEN: The Cultural Politics of English as a World Language* (Freiburg) [on line version from <www.leeds.ac.uk/english/staff/afg>]

Gupta, Anthea Fraser. 2001b. "Realism and imagination in the teaching of English". *World Englishes* 20 (3): 365-381

Harris, Roy. 1980. *The language myth*. London: Duckworth

Le Page, R B & Andrée Tabouret-Keller. 1985. *Acts of Identity: creole-based approaches to language and ethnicity*. Cambridge: CUP

Mahmood, Syed. 1895. *A History of English Education in India*: its rise, development, progress, present condition and prospects being a narrative of the various phases of educational policy and measures adopted under British the rule from its beginning to the present period (1781 to 1893). Muhammadan Anglo-Oriental College, Aligarh: Aligarh

Marsden, William. (1812). *A Grammar of the Malayan Language*. London: Longman

Mühlhäusler, Peter. 1996. *Linguistic ecology: language change and linguistic imperialism in the Pacific regions*. London / New York: Routledge

Nettle, Daniel & Suzanne Romaine. 2000. *Vanishing voices: the extinction of the world's languages*. Oxford: OUP

Ó Riagáin, Dónall. 2001. "Language rights / human rights in Northern Ireland and the Role of the European Charter for Regional or Minority Languages". In eds. John M Kirk & Dónall P Ó Baoill. *Linguistic Politics*. Belfast: Cló Ollscoil na Banríona. 43-54

"Regional and minority languages of the European Union". European Communities 1995-2002 <europa.eu.int/comm/education/langmin/regmin.html> [accessed August 2002]

Shamsul Amri Baharudin. (1997). "Ethnicity, class or identity? In search of a new paradigm in Malaysian Studies". <www.gv.net.my/massa/shamsul.htm> [accessed July 1999]. [printed in *Akademika*, No. 53 (July): 33-59.]

SIL International. 2002. *Ethnologue: Languages of the World and a whole lot more!* <www.sil.org/ethnologue>

Skutnabb-Kangas, Tove. 2000. *Linguistic genocide in education – or worldwide diversity and human rights?* Mahwah, NJ: Lawrence Erlbaum

Stewart, William A. 1968. "A sociolinguistic typology for describing national multilingualism". In ed. Joshua A Fishman. *Readings in the Sociology of Language*. The Hague: Mouton. 531-545

Swettenham, Frank A. (1881). *Vocabulary of the English and Malay Languages*. Singapore: Government Printing Office

Swettenham, Frank. (1907). *British Malaya: An Account of the origin and progress of British Influence in Malaya*. London / New York: John Lane The Bodley Head

Language, Culture and Development:
The Gaeltacht Commissions 1926 and 2002

John Walsh

1. Introduction

The aim of this paper is to examine the theoretical assumptions about development, and the role of culture in socio-economic development, which can be identified in the reports of two government Commissions (1925-6 and 2000-2) established to make proposals concerning the Gaeltacht. The reports of both Commissions, and the government responses to them, provide insights into the developmental approach to the Gaeltacht being employed at two different periods in the State's history. Following a description of both reports and consideration of the principal assumptions contained therein, this study will then examine the theoretical bases of the approaches to development employed by both Commissions.

2. Definition

2.1 Development

Development Studies did not emerge as a distinct academic discipline until after the Second World War and has since then been applied predominantly to what became known as the Third World. However, the concept of development remains highly contested, as it means different things to different people. Therefore, any definition of development as a concept must include reference to this conflict. The following definition is proposed, emphasising the vision of development favoured by the author but acknowledging the fact that different meanings are assigned to it: 'development is a process which increases living standards of groups of people through (a) the provision of regular, satisfying employment, (b) education appropriate and relevant to a community's cultural or linguistic circumstances, (c) protection of culture of the group in question, (d) participation in political decision-making and (e) avoiding environmental degradation. The process reverses the poverty, exclusion and socio-cultural and economic inequality associated with underdevelopment. It is acknowledged, however, that the concept of development is highly contested and that the elements listed above are not universally accepted as being important in the development process' (Kirby, 1997; Martinussen, 1998).

2.2 Culture

"Culture" is an equally contested concept. It is proposed here, however, to limit considerations of culture to two categories, that of (a) distinctive way of life and (b) critique of other cultures. The following definition is suggested: 'Culture is the sum of the constantly changing elements of life which have symbolic meaning or value for a specific group of people, usually national, linguistic or ethnic groups. A specific culture may also act as a critique of other cultures containing opposing values' (Eagleton, 2000).

3. Gaeltacht Commission 1925-6

3.1 Background and context

Following 1922, a country which was emerging from the shadow of the large British colonial economy was bound to be faced with severe developmental challenges: although Irish growth rates were average for western Europe, there were high levels of internal deprivation, poverty and underdevelopment, particularly in the areas which were to be designated as Gaeltacht.[1]

Replacing the economic nationalism which had characterised much of political debate prior to independence, the Cumann na nGaedheal government was highly conservative on the economy and stuck rigidly to the orthodoxy of *laissez-faire* and free trade. This policy had been eulogised by predominantly British classical and neoclassical economists for over a century prior to this, and such influences on Ireland did not dissipate following independence. Economic policy was largely non-interventionist: with its eye on balancing the books, the government of W.T. Cosgrave rejected state-led industrialisation through import-substitution (ISI) and protectionism and instead placed its hopes in the agricultural sector, mostly dairying and livestock, as the bedrock for future development. The result was that industry was relegated to second place behind agriculture (Lee, 1989: 112).

3.2 Establishment and terms of reference

Following the establishment of the Gaelic League in 1893, elements of the language revival movement began idealising the Irish-speaking districts as the repositories of pure Irishness, upon which the future existence of Ireland depended (Ó Torna, 2000: 61). There is ample evidence, however, that such idealised accounts of peasant life were in sharp contrast with the severe economic reality. Much of the Irish-speaking western seaboard was coterminous with the areas designated in 1891 as Congested Districts by the British government, due to severe over-population and subsequent economic collapse.

In 1922, one of the new state's first tasks in relation to the Irish language was to define the boundaries of Irish-speaking districts. In 1925, the government established a Gaeltacht Commission, which had two aims: (1) to map the areas which were Irish-speaking and (2) to recommend how they could be improved economically and how the use of Irish could be extended in them (Gaeltacht Commission, 1926: 1).

---

[1] Land Valuation statistics compiled in the Gaeltacht Commission report of 1926 illustrate a direct correlation between increasing percentages of Irish speakers and decreasing land value.

3.3 Principal findings

The Commission decided that Irish speaking communities totalling 257,406 people remained in 12 of the 26 counties of the Free State (Donegal, Sligo, Mayo, Galway, Roscommon, Clare, Limerick, Kerry, Cork, Waterford, Tipperary and Kilkenny). However, it reported an alarming decrease of 31 percent in the number of native speakers between the Census of 1911 and 1925. Two categories of Gaeltacht were recommended by the Commission: "Fíor-Ghaeltacht" (full Gaeltacht), where 80 percent or more of the population were Irish speaking and "Breac-Ghaeltacht" (partial Gaeltacht), where between 25 and 79 percent could speak the language. No distinction was made between ability to speak Irish and actual use of the language, and the Commission's findings have been disputed by generations of scholars (Ó Cuív, 1950: 27-31; Ó Gadhra, 1989: 6-7). However, the maps and interviews with priests, teachers, fishermen and public officials were highly significant because they illustrated the potential which existed in the 1920s to build an extensive native Irish-speaking community over a considerable area of the west of the country.[2]

The Commission's second main objective was to make recommendations about the use of Irish across various areas of life. The report includes 82 recommendations, most of which (26) deal with education. 23 deal with the use of Irish in administration and 24 concern 'economic matters'.

4. Gaeltacht Commission 2000

4.1 Background and context

The Gaeltacht Commission of 2000-2 found itself dealing with a vastly changed situation, both socio-economically and linguistically. Following the conservatism of Cosgrave, Fianna Fáil in 1932 had embarked upon an ambitious programme of import-substituting industrialisation (ISI), based on protectionism through stringent tariffs. In another dramatic policy shift, ISI was abandoned by Seán Lemass in the 1950s and replaced by a combination of export-led industrialisation (ELI) and foreign direct investment. The radical new policy opened the Irish economy to an unprecedented extent, leaving it highly dependent on foreign industrialists.

As was the case in 1926, there was little difference between Gaeltacht industrial policy and national policy. Both Gaeltarra Éireann and its successor, Údarás na Gaeltachta, concentrated on attracting external companies to invest in the Gaeltacht, either from elsewhere in Ireland or from abroad. Industrialisation came to be associated with the spread of English (Ó Cinnéide *et al*, 1985: 7-8). Other areas were ignored, however, and high levels of underdevelopment persisted in parts of the Gaeltacht (Comharchumann Forbartha na nOileán, 1979; Ó hAodha, 1971).

---

[2] For detailed extracts of the Commission's evidence, see Walsh, John, 2002. *Díchoimisiúnú teanga: Coimisiún na Gaeltachta 1926*. Dublin: Cois Life.

Exceptional growth in the 1990s led to claims of a "Celtic Tiger" economy. Between 1993 and 2001 the annual growth rate was more than double the average recorded over the previous three decades. GDP per person moved to the EU average and from 1990 to 2002, employment increased by an annual average of 3 percent (Clinch *et al*, 2002: 24-27). Yet despite the boom, the Gaeltacht lagged behind: GDP per capita was at three-quarters of the national average and outward migration by young adults continued (Ní Bhrádaigh, 2001: 3).

By this stage, the Gaeltacht had shrunk considerably. The borders had been redrawn in 1956, resulting in many areas losing Gaeltacht status. At the same time, a government department to co-ordinate Gaeltacht affairs, Roinn na Gaeltachta, was set up. This was followed in 1957 by the establishment of the first state agency for the Gaeltacht, Gaeltarra Éireann, which took responsibility for the development of Gaeltacht industry. A Gaeltacht Civil Rights Movement in the 1960s and the emergence of Gaeltacht-based co-operatives in the 1970s, led to the establishment in 1980 of Údarás na Gaeltachta, part of whose board was to be chosen directly by Gaeltacht residents in elections (Walsh, 2002: 23-31). The socio-economic development of the Gaeltacht has, however, been accompanied by declining percentages of Irish speakers. An analysis of the Census of 1996 revealed that of the official Gaeltacht population of 86,039, only 20,813 adults speak Irish each day (Ó hÉallaithe, 1999: 12).

4.2 Establishment and terms of reference

In 2000, the government established another Gaeltacht Commission to investigate the causes of decline and to make recommendations about how they could be tackled. The Minister of State at the Department of Arts, Heritage, Gaeltacht and the Islands, Éamon Ó Cuív, expressed disappointment that the language was not being examined in a scientific way, as in other European countries.[3] Given these remarks, it is interesting that the Commission chose an image of an abandoned boat on a beach for its website (http://www.coimnagael.ie). It seems that the association of the Gaeltacht with symbols of loss and decay did not end in 1926.

4.3 Principal findings

Based on the results of the 1996 Census, the Commission reports that only 18 of the 154 district electoral divisions (DEDs) in the Gaeltacht returned more than 75 percent of daily Irish speakers. 12 of these are in Galway, four in Donegal and two in Kerry. The Commission was in no doubt that much of the official Gaeltacht, as it appears on maps, is on the point of expiring (Government of Ireland, 2002: 10). The Commission issued 19 recommendations covering legislation, education, state services, research and the restructuring of Údarás na Gaeltachta (Government of Ireland, 2002: 16-17).

---

[3] Full Minister's speech available on Coimisiún na Gaeltachta's website at http://www.coimnagael.ie/aith.html (read 23.08.2001)

Having described briefly the main findings of both reports, the assumptions about development, and the role of culture in development, will now be identified. Theoretical bases for the assumptions will then be explored.

5 Theoretical Assumptions of Gaeltacht Commission Reports

5.1 Gaeltacht Commission 1925-6

Four assumptions concerning development have been identified in the context of the Commission report of 1926: (a) interventionism; (b) industrial development; (c) idealisation of Gaelic culture and (d) anti-urban bias.

5.1.1 Interventionism

The 1926 Commission report is strongly interventionist in tone, sharply criticising the previous British administration and the current Free State government for their policy towards the Gaeltacht. The Commission urged state intervention in favour of the language across a wide range of areas. Most of the 82 recommendations required a direct financial commitment by government.

The extent of intervention urged by the Commission is noteworthy given the strong *laissez-faire* economic policies of Cumann na nGaedheal (Lee, 1989; Girvin, 1989: 12-18; Ó Gráda, 1997: 227). It was unsurprising, therefore, that an administration which adhered fervently to *laissez-faire* nationally did not welcome a document which urged it to abandon such a policy in its dealings with the Gaeltacht (Government of Ireland: 1929).

In a governmental White Paper, certain measures were adopted but most were rejected, most notably the proposal that a permanent Gaeltacht Commission be established to co-ordinate all aspects of state policy towards these districts. The government instead instructed the Minister for Fisheries to act as co-ordinating authority for Gaeltacht services. While it is true that the state introduced a state introduced a grants system[4] and new housing legislation for the Gaeltacht,[5] it did little else to underpin socio-economic development and most of the financial measures were unrelated to language maintenance (Government of Ireland, 1929).

Such a low level of practical political and financial commitment to the Gaeltacht was in stark contrast to the lofty rhetoric of Cosgrave in his letter to the chairman of the Gaeltacht Commission, General Richard Mulcahy, only four years earlier. Cosgrave spoke of the centrality of the language to Irish nationality, and of the need to do everything possible to develop it (Government of Ireland, 1926: 3). Such rhetoric is entirely absent from the White Paper. The government states in vague terms that the Gaeltacht is important and that its case

---

[4] Scéim Labhairt na Gaeilge (Scheme for speaking of Irish), 1932. A £2 grant was provided for each child in Gaeltacht families who was deemed to be fluent in Irish. For an interesting insight into the operation of the scheme in one Gaeltacht area, see Hindley (1994).

[5] Gaeltacht Housing Act, 1929

was considered seriously but, through its failure to accept or implement most of the recommendations, its concern rings hollow.

5.1.2 Industrial development

The Commission's treatment of industrial development in the Gaeltacht reflects government policy as a whole: industrialisation is subordinated to agriculture. The report devotes 67 paragraphs to 'Economic Conditions', most of which deal with agriculture or fisheries. Only 13 paragraphs discuss 'Rural Industries' or 'Home Industries', mostly homespun wool, lace-making, embroidery and knitting. The exclusive choice of 'rural' or 'home' to denote Gaeltacht industry reflects the revivalist perception of these regions as pre-modern or inimical to urban life. Only one paragraph is devoted to industrial policy (Government of Ireland, 1926: 54).

5.1.3 Idealisation of Gaelic Culture

The first Commissioners were operating in the early years of independence following a period of nationalist revival and renewed interest in Irish. In common with elements of the language revival movement which preceded it, the Commission engages in rhetorical idealisation of the Gaeltacht as the bedrock for the state's future development. The Commission's views are unsurprising given that five of the twelve eleven members were closely associated with the language movement.[6] The Commission chairman, former Minister for Defence, General Richard Mulcahy, was also a passionate supporter of the Irish language (Valiulis, 1992: 239). This explains the Commission's emphasis on the rural, Gaelic idyll and on its reluctance to consider anything other than existing traditional industry. It views modernisation with suspicion and idealises the Gaeltacht as the dwindling source of an ancient unchanging culture superior to that of the English-speaking masses (Gaeltacht Commission, 1926: 24).

The government's response was more complex. Its own roots were in the same romantic rhetoric about the Gaeltacht and - although toned down in the leaner economic atmosphere of 1929 - the sense that the Gaeltacht was untouchable remains pervasive. After all, the state itself had been founded on a belief that the Irish-speaking districts were the cultural well from which the future of the nation flowed. Its harsh economic policy, however, contradicted this cultural view.

---

[6] Pádraig Ó Siochfhradha (An Seabhac), Séamus Ó hEochadha (An Fear Mór), Pádraig Ó Cadhla, Risteárd Ó Foghludha (Fiachra Eilgeach) and chairman Richard Mulcahy were all past or present Gaelic League activists. The questions of one such member, Pádraig Ó Siochfhradha ("An Seabhac") to witnesses often contained statements about the superiority of Gaelic culture. See An Seabhac's questioning in the evidence of 17 April, 5 May, 3 June, 6 October, 9 October (all 1925). Furthermore, claims by sceptical witnesses that the Gaeltacht was smaller than claimed by the Commissioners were met with hostile responses. See the evidence of 3 June and 6 October 1925.

5.1.4   Anti-urban Bias

An implicitly anti-urban bias is also apparent in the report. There is a strong emphasis on re-settling Irish speakers from severely congested areas to other rural districts elsewhere in the country. It recommended that priority be given to Irish speakers in the resettlement of the Western grasslands, particularly in the Gaeltacht, and that English speakers have their claims satisfied elsewhere. The rationale for such preferential treatment for Irish speakers is couched in romantic rhetoric:

> These people are not only uneconomic holders, but they are the Evicted Tenants of the Race. Through all their particular vicissitudes they have, in preserving the National language as their traditional speech, carried with them an undeniable title and claim to a footing in the soil of their country (Government of Ireland, 1926: 42)

Although the Commission recognised the importance of Galway, itself classified as Breac-Ghaeltacht, in aiding the restoration of Irish generally, it devotes only one paragraph of its 68 page report to the city, and makes no specific recommendation in its regard.

5.2 Gaeltacht Commission 2000-2

The 2002 report also contains certain assumptions about development which have been classified as follows: (a) interventionism; (b) theoretical framework and (c) development and modernisation. The most notable difference is the absence of idealisation, surely due to the linguistic crisis now facing the Gaeltacht.

5.2.1   Interventionism

The greatest similarity between the Commissions of 1926 and 2002 is the strong pro-intervention ethos of both reports. Each of the 19 recommendations of the 2002 report has significant financial implications for government ranging from the enactment of legislation and publicity campaigns to the implementation of a sociolinguistic research unit and increased investment in Gaeltacht infrastructure. However, similar to the report of 1926, the 2002 Commission fails to produce costings for its proposals despite being requested to do so in the terms of reference. In both cases, therefore, government has been spared the potentially embarrassing situation of being shown clearly what expenditure is required to implement a comprehensive programme for Irish in the Gaeltacht and elsewhere.

5.2.2   Theoretical framework

Compared to 1925-6, the Commissioners of 2000-2002 had access to a vastly expanded corpus of academic research in the fields of language rights, language planning, bilingualism, sociolinguistics and in the discipline of development itself, some of which are reflected in their findings. However, none of the Commissioners were specialists in sociology, economics or development. Therefore it is perhaps not surprising that the Commission avoids choosing one specific theoretical framework to analyse its findings, focussing instead on very general theories about linguistic diversity.

The influence of academic research in relevant fields from 1926 to 2000 can be detected in the Commission's report: bilingualism and multilingualism (Sections 3.1 and 5.2), language rights (Sections 3.1, 3.2 and 5.1) and language planning (Section 5.7). However, it appears that the Commission had no specific analytical framework in mind while preparing its report. Given that the Gaeltacht has become associated historically with the anti-modern, it is surprising that the Commission fails to analyse the tradition-modernity dialectic.[7] It provides information about the state of bilingualism in a global context and about European Union policy in this field but no reference is made to the key European Commission report on linguistic diversity, *Euromosaic* (1996), or to the updated version being prepared at present. Other pioneering work by researchers or minority language organisations into bilingual and multilingual situations is not referred to either.[8] The Commission requested experts in the National University of Ireland, Galway to carry out additional research, but the findings are entirely empirical in nature (Ó Cinnéide *et al*, 2001).

---

[7] See, for instance: Commins, P. 1988. "Socioeconomic development and language maintenance in the Gaeltacht". *International Journal of the Sociology of Language*, 70: 11-28; Johnson, N. 1997. "Making Space: Gaeltacht policy and the politics of identity'. In ed. B. Graham. *In Search of Ireland: A Cultural Geography*. London: Routledge; Ó Cinnéide, M., M. Keane and M. Cawley. 1985. "Industrialization and Linguistic Change among Gaelic-Speaking Communities in the West of Ireland". *Language Planning and Language Problems*, 9 (1): 3-15; Ó Riagáin, P. 1992. *Language Maintenance and Language Shift as Strategies of Social Reproduction: Irish in the Corca Dhuibhne Gaeltacht 1926-1986*. Dublin: Institiúid Teangeolaíochta Éireann; Ó Tuathaigh, G. 1986. "Aistriú pobail Ghaeltachta go háiteanna eile in Éirinn: Cúlra an pholasaí". In ed. M. Ó Conghaile. *Gaeltacht Ráth Cairn: Léachtaí Comórtha*. Béal an Daingin: Cló Iar-Chonnachta; Ó Tuathaigh, M.A.G. 1990. *The Development of the Gaeltacht as a Bilingual Entity*. Dublin: Institiúid Teangeolaíochta Éireann.

[8] For example, see: Tucker, V. 1997. "A Cultural Perspective on Development". In ed. V. Tucker. *Cultural Perspectives on Development*. London: Frank Cass; Casson, M, P. Cooke, R. Merfyn Jones and C. Williams. 1994. *Quiet Revolution? Language, Culture and Economy in the Nineties*. Aberystwyth: Menter a Busnes; Dafis, Ll. ed. 1995. *Economic Development and Lesser Used Languages: Partnerships for Action*. Llanbedr Pont Steffan: Cwmni Iaith; Price, A. 1997. *The Diversity Dividend: Language, Culture and Economy in an Integrated Europe*. Brussels: European Bureau for Lesser Used Languages; Grin, F. 1996. "The economics of language: survey, assessment and prospects". *International Journal of the Sociology of Language* 121: 17-44; Nelde P., M. Strubell and G. Williams G. 1996. *Euromosaic: The Production and Reproduction of the minority language groups in the European Union*. Luxembourg: European Commission; Nelde, P. 1999. "Multilingualism and the Economy as Issues in European Language Policy". In eds. K. Heberts and J.G. Turi. *Multilingual Cities and Language Policies*. Åbo: Åbo Akademi University Social Science Research Unit.

5.2.3 Development and Modernisation

Perhaps reflecting more than 50 years of development thinking, the Commission report contains several references to the "development" of the Gaeltacht. However, its treatment of "development" reveals an imprecise understanding of the concept, and it fails to provide a definition of what it considers the development process to entail.

There are hints at the type of Gaeltacht development favoured, when the Commission outlines new sectors, including the social economy and cultural tourism, which are the main opportunities for employment growth (Government of Ireland, 2002: 14). Citing "job creation" (14) as its main criterion for development is revealing, and will be explained later.

The Commission also expresses concern that the Irish language appears weakest in areas in which the most development has taken place and adds: "it is essential that the language be linked to development and to a modern approach" (14). This statement infers that, in the view of the Commission, development is synonymous with modernisation and that, to date, the Irish language has been absent from this process.

The association of development with modernisation is significant, as it provides a link to one of the most influential paradigms of the 20th Century, modernisation theory. Various theories of modernisation, which have been profoundly influential on modern development thinking, will now be examined. Both economics and sociology will be considered in order to elucidate how both disciplines have contributed to understandings of modernisation and development, and of the place of culture in this process. The assumptions which have already been outlined will be traced back to these economic and sociological theories, in order to illustrate the influence which they have exercised on the understandings of development favoured by the Commissioners and by government.

6. Economic theories of modernisation

6.1 Adam Smith and the Scottish Enlightenment

The Scottish philosopher Adam Smith (1723-1790) is credited with creating modern economic thought in the West through his key work *An Inquiry into the Nature and Causes of the Wealth of Nations* (1776). In order to increase the wealth of nations, Smith argued that society should exploit the natural drives of all humans, rather than suppress them. He wrote: "It is not from the benevolence of the butcher, the brewer, or the baker, that we expect our dinner, but from their regard to their own interest" (quoted at Buchholz, 1999: 20-1). Smith's emphasis on individual entrepreneurship, guided by the free market, was to become a resounding theme for generations of future economists. The renowned reference to the butcher, brewer and baker and the distinction drawn between benevolence and self-interest forms the backbone of much of influential contemporary economic thought.

For Smith, this "invisible hand" was the true source of social harmony: the free market. The key concept of *laissez-faire* - that government intervention with industry inappropriate and harmful and that the market would take care of society's needs - was established. It also represented the triumph of rationality over chaos and, by extension, the triumph of modernity over tradition (Heilbroner, 1967: 62-4).

This point is particularly important because Smith was Scottish, and because the Scottish Enlightenment with which he was so closely associated was itself located at the centre of conflicting identities in Scotland at the time. The Enlightenment emerged following the Union of 1707 and looked south to London. Many of its leaders allied themselves with emerging concepts of Caledonia and North Britain, and turned their backs on the Gaelic Highlands.

Leading figures in the Scottish Enlightenment had strong views on Gaelic culture, which in the eighteenth century remained strong throughout much of the Highlands and Western Isles. The Enlightenment's views on progress and rationality were expressed in the 'stages of history' theory, which posited the development of society through four distinct stages: savage, barbarian, agricultural and commercial. In the Scottish context following the Act of Union in 1707 and the Jacobite defeat at the Battle of Culloden in 1746, the doomed or obsolete race were the Gaels who remained stuck in the first two stages of development.[9] Following Culloden, the Gaelic clan system in the Highlands was in retreat. Smith and his followers believed that such a society, based on kinship, familiarity and sentiment was anaethema to the reason and individualism of *laissez-faire*, which held that the rising tide would lift all boats (Herman, 2001: 95).

The emphasis on rationality was a formative influence on economics as a distinct discipline. The result was that the foundations of economic theory were based on a premise that human freedom and an individual's value were dependent on material possessions (Kirby, 1997: 101-2). These conclusions about empirical rationality in economics have significant implications for that discipline's relationship with culture. If certain cultures were viewed as traditional or custom-bound - as was clearly the view of some Scottish Enlightenment figures towards Gaelic - and if economic development was based on the natural advance of industry and science, these cultures were intrinsically anti-development. It follows from this, of course, that the Lowlands culture shared by Smith and his contemporaries was superior, through its links with London as the centre of the English-speaking world.

6.2 David Ricardo, utilitarianism and Classical economics

While Smith laid the foundations, classical economics is deemed to have begun with David Ricardo, the British-born son of a Jewish immigrant from Holland who in 1803 began publishing his views on the economy. Ricardo refined and developed Smith's theories, but the strong anti-interventionist message remained unchanged: as a Member of Parliament, Ricardo became one of the staunchest critics of the 'Corn Laws' of 1815, which prohibited the import of cheap grain in order to protect British farmers (Heilbroner, 1967: 73).

---

[9] 'Doomed race theory' has been employed most recently in the case of aboriginal communities in Australia. See http://www.jcu.edu.au/aff/history/reviews/mcgregor.htm (read 15.8.2002)

Ricardo was also a fervent adherent to utilitarianism, a doctrine which subordinated society to individuals, supported the maximisation of individual freedom and opposed government interference in the personal sphere (Rubin, 1979: 236). Such an approach was in opposition to the collective bonds of traditional society, where individual freedoms were severely curtailed. Therefore, traditional cultures had no place in the modernisation project.

The neoclassical school of economics, developed by Alfred Marshall after 1890, developed the non-interventionist message even further. Marshall took a gradualist approach to the economy: the world could improve, but only cautiously and slowly. Marshall stridently opposed any attempts to dramatically reorganise society, describing government intervention as "evil" (quoted at Dasgupta, 1985: 120). At the time that Marshall was writing, the Irish language revival movement was in full swing.

6.3 Conclusions

Three main conclusions can be drawn about the ways in which theories of classical and neo-classical economics understood the links between economics and culture.

(a) Scottish Enlightenment

The first is that the Scottish Enlightenment movement, critical to the origins of classical economics, was linked to a long-standing clash of cultures in Scotland between, in general terms, Gaelic Highlands and non-Gaelic Lowlands. On the one hand was the defeat of Culloden in 1746, and the subsequent association of Gaelic culture with the savage and primitive: on the other were the Act of Union of 1707, the reorientation towards London, the emergence of concepts of North Britishness and, through Enlightenment ideals, the association of progress and development with industry, commerce and trade. Therefore, Smith, through his association with Highland figures such as Adam Ferguson and anti-Gaelic polemicists such as David Hume, were turning their backs on irrational, traditional and savage Scotland in order to embrace a universal, rational, utilitarian notion of progress.

(b) Economic theory and culture

The second conclusion is the extent to which the economy theory which we have examined assumes that its own cultural frame of reference is the only valid one. Despite the absence of overt references to culture, the classical and neo-classical theories outlined above are themselves deeply cultural. Instead, what these theorists share is an antipathy for culture or cultures which they view as traditional or anti-modern, because of their custom-bound or collective nature. Most leading figures in the development of modern economics were from either Britain or the United States, where English-speaking modernising élites had long become dominant over other indigenous, traditional cultures. As these cultures became vanquished, their world views were deemed irrelevant to economics, because the cultures of the economists themselves were not threatened with extinction and instead were part of the onward march towards progress for all.

The conflict amounted to the culture of modernisation eclipsing other cultural viewpoints.

(c) Anti-interventionist ethos

The final conclusion is that the strong anti-interventionist ethos first hinted at by Smith, and developed by classical and neoclassical economists, has had a profound impact on government policies which stretch far beyond the purely economic realm. This point has been amplified by Irish sociolinguist, Seán Ó Riain, who refers to "*laissez-faire* teanga" ["linguistic *laissez-faire*"] in a key historical survey of language planning in Ireland. He concludes that, in economic terms, the result of such a policy was the weakening of poorer nations: by extension, *laissez-faire* attitudes to language have had detrimental effects on weaker languages while the languages of the powerful and wealthy thrive (Ó Riain, 1994: 100).

In the context of the 1926 report, it is clear that a central component of government policy on national development, including that of the Gaeltacht, was a belief in *laissez-faire* as preached by generations of classical and neo-classical economists, from Smith through to Ricardo and Marshall. Through its rejection of most of the Commission's economic recommendations and by failing to suggest alternatives, the government applied *laissez-faire* to the Gaeltacht. The fact that no separate government ministry for the Gaeltacht was established until 1956 is further evidence of this view. The Cosgrave government cannot be accused of implementing unadulterated modernisation theory: as has already been pointed out, its policy was often contradictory and contained conflicting elements of nationalism and economic modernisation. However, the fact that its *laissez-faire* views led the Commission to be rejected is evidence that economic modernisation theory was a key influence on its assumptions.

Although economic thought has evolved in the seventy-five years since the first Commission presented its report, Western policy-making has remained predominantly under the influence of modernisation theory throughout much of this period. Rationality, material progress, individualism and free trade remain key components of the dominant economic paradigm. It is unsurprising, therefore, that the Commission of 2002 also displays these influences. As already stated, the report links development to modernisation. It also presents development of the Gaeltacht in terms of "employment growth" alone (14), reflecting modernisation theory's emphasis on the standard indices of growth, employment and GNP/GDP rates, rather than on other factors such as literacy, health standards, environmental protection or educational levels. As in the case of the report of 1926, it cannot be argued that the Commission of 2002 faithfully reproduces every facet of theories of economic modernisation. However, many of the assumptions already identified can be traced back to such theories.

The emergence of theories of sociology, in particular those concerning modernity and modernisation, will now be considered. It will be argued that a combination of sociological theories of what constitutes the modern, coupled with economic views on the almost sacred nature of markets, has had far-reaching effects on language policy in Ireland since independence.

7. Sociological theories of modernisation

7.1 Émile Durkheim and the division of labour

From the 1890s on, French sociologist Émile Durkheim emphasised the importance of social roles as a major difference between traditional and modern society. The main change which accompanied industrialisation was an increase in a society's division of labour. In pre-industrial societies, roles were diffuse, in that workers undertook a variety of tasks in order to ensure survival. Furthermore, such roles were allocated by society, or dictated by the person's social standing at birth. In contrast, Durkheim argued that in industrial society, each worker specialised in a single activity in which he or she became fully skilled. This complex 'division of labour' allowed various tasks to be accomplished simultaneously. Furthermore, workers gained greater individual freedom to achieve the roles which they desired, rather than remaining bound by custom or tradition. Specialised societies were 'organic societies', according to Durkheim, while 'mechanical societies' were homogenous and non-differentiated (Kirby, 1997: 46; Tovey & Share, 2000: 9; Ní Riain, 2002: 13-17).

Therefore, in common with classical and neo-classical economic theories, early sociological theories of modernisation placed considerable emphasis on individual rather than collective rights. Furthermore, Durkheim emphasises the importance of common norms and values which hold society together and prevent social dissolution. Durkheim's concept of *anomie*, as he termed such social dissolution, was his most significant contribution to sociology. Max Weber, a contemporary of Durkheim's, further developed the importance of ideas and values in the process of social change.

The key concepts of the sociology of modernisation, therefore, are on the one hand the pursuit of individual aims but on the other the parallel necessity for societal rules to prevent *anomie*. Both elements have significant implications for culture. An emphasis on individual rights is problematic for concepts of culture which are based on collective rather than individual goals: in the case of Ireland, the socio-economic concept of *meitheal* (working party) is a prime example of a society in which individual members sacrificed personal gain and co-operated to achieve global goals of self-sufficiency. The second element, social norms to avoid *anomie*, is also problematic, as it raises the question: who decides the values which are deemed to hold society together, and on what basis? If norms are decided and implemented by powerful social actors, cultural groups whose norms are different, or who form minorities within, for instance, a state's borders, will suffer through the implementation of such norms. A concept of modernisation based on the achievement of individual goals irrespective of social or cultural differences does not hold as an aim the advancement of weaker cultures sharing territory with cultures of status. This raises the possibility that modernisation theory is itself a culture, existing in opposition to other views of the world which do not share its values.

7.2 Ferdinand Tönnies and the urban/rural divide

A further element of sociological theories of modernisation concerns the association of modernisation with urbanisation. The concentration of factories in towns and the resultant urban sprawl was criticised by early sociologists, among them German Ferdinand Tönnies, who believed that urban society was not instilled with a sense of community. The 'close personal relationships' (*Gemeinschaft*) of traditional, mainly rural society were replaced by 'impersonal calculative relationships' (*Gesellschaft*) of modern, industrial society.

The distinctions drawn by Durkheim, Weber and Tönnies can be seen clearly in the 1926 report. To the Commission and government alike, the Gaeltacht represented Durkheim's 'mechanical' society, the *Gemeinschaft* of Tönnies and the custom-bound irrational society of Weber. The modernisation project could advance elsewhere, but the traditional Gaeltacht was to be frozen in time. Ignoring the Gaeltacht economically while eulogising it culturally can be traced to a belief, inherent in the modernisation process, that weaker cultures have a lesser value than dominant cultures. This can be seen in the Scottish Enlightenment's hostility to the Gaelic Highlands and in their association of progress with a greater, universal, rational culture. It can also be seen in the utilitarianism of David Ricardo, which elevated the importance of the individual above society, thereby rendering worthless traditional cultures based on collectivity. And it can be seen in Weber's concept of instrumental rationality, which described how society moved towards accumulating surplus and away from traditional notions of subsistence economy.

7.3   Talcott Parsons and contemporary modernisation theory

From the late 1940s onwards, the work of sociologist Talcott Parsons began to influence American sociological thought. 'Parsonian sociology', as it would be called, was to become one of the most significant influences on 20th Century social theory. Parsonian sociology has its roots in scientific theories of evolution: the belief that organisms could adapt and change regardless of their environments and move from lower to higher forms of life. Taking his biological model, Parsons argued that societies too could advance to the higher stage and modernise autonomously through following processes of differentiation and cultural change, universally applied.

'Evolutionary universals' such as money, markets, bureaucratic structures, government and legal systems were identified by Parsons as the key components in modern society (Robertson, 1991: 9).   Another key element of Parsonian sociology was his theory of 'pattern variables', or sets of options from which social actors could choose. These choices, between traditional and modern ways of life, show clearly the influence of Durkheim, Weber and Tönnies (Hamilton, 1983: 102).

In common with other theorists of modernisation, Parsons also placed significant emphasis on the diffusion of common social values and his own cultural background played a key role in his work. Parsonian versions of modernisation were infused with concern for the cultural core of the American socio-cultural system (Robertson, 1991: 9-14).

The influence of Parsons has already been alluded to, and it can be argued that his views also affected Irish social research. Following 1966, the Irish Economic and Social Research Institute (ESRI) employed many researchers who had received their training in the United States. The same situation applied to many Irish universities. Add to this the factor of a common language, and it is likely that Parsons' views exerted an influence on sociological enquiry in Ireland. Furthermore, it has been pointed out that modernisation theory has become so ingrained in modern sociological thought, that it is unquestioningly accepted as common sense, frequently unknown to its adherents (O'Dowd, 1995: 168; Tovey & Share, 2000: 20, 50).

7.4 Conclusions

Any conception of society which views the past with suspicion and hostility has profound implications for the treatment of culture. The modernisation thesis was developed to a greater extreme by one of the most vocal proponents of modernity in the 20th Century, Massachusetts-born economist and philosopher Clarence Ayers (1891-1972). In his *Theory of Economic Progress* (1944), Ayers contrasts 'dynamic' modern society with tradition and the past, which hinder progress:

> This [scientific] conception of truth and of human values generally is at variance with all tribal legends and all tribal authority; and since the technological revolution is itself irresistible, the arbitrary authority and irrational values of pre-scientific, pre-industrial cultures are doomed ... The only remaining alternative is that of intelligent, voluntary acceptance of the industrial way of life and all the values that go with it (quoted at Barry, 1987: 9)

The conclusion which can be drawn here is not that traditional culture exists in opposition, or in subservience to modernity, but rather that anything other than "the industrial way of life" is doomed to extinction. There can be little doubt but that Ayers is one of the most stridently pro-modernity and anti-tradition voices in modern sociological thought.

Therefore, it is an integral part of modernisation theory that linguistic differences fade away as modernity develops and that modernisation brings about cultural homogenisation. Such an understanding has significant implications for developmental efforts in the Gaeltacht.

8. General conclusions

With seventy-five years separating them, it is unsurprising that the contents of the two Gaeltacht Commission reports are considerably different. Influenced by nationalism and by the sociological theories of Durkheim, Weber and Tönnies, the Commission of 1926 displayed reticence about the modernisation process, inferring that Irish in the Gaeltacht could be maintained only within its traditional domains. Therefore, many of the 'economic' recommendations made by the Commission were limited to 'traditional' industries such as agriculture, fisheries, weaving and seaweed-processing. Its insistence on extensive government intervention can also be seen as opposing the dominant economic policy of *laissez-faire*, which was a central component of the modernisation project as developed by classical and neoclassical economists. This position was unsurprising given national policy at the time: agriculture was elevated over industry by Cumann na nGaedheal and, given the presence of pro-government

TDs on the Commission, it is to be expected that this view be reflected in the final report.

The government engaged in the same idealism of the language movement but ensured that it never moved beyond the realm of rhetoric. It may have proclaimed a vision of the Gaeltacht which was close to Durkheimian or Weberian classifications of traditional society, but it chose to pursue a policy of non-interventionism in Gaeltacht affairs. Such a decision can be linked to the *laissez-faire* policies of Cumann na nGaedheal in the country as a whole, and the attendant economic views on modernisation which revered the magic of the market over state planning and which favoured individual needs over those of society.

Faced with seventy-five years of decline and state neglect, the Commission of 2002 avoided idealisation of the Gaeltacht. It chose instead to focus on theories of bilingualism, language rights and language planning although these were addressed in a haphazard fashion. Its vision of development for the Gaeltacht is language-centred, but it also reveals assumptions which can be traced to the influence of modernisation theory. Conversely, its support for widespread state intervention is in opposition to a central tenet of modernisation theory, and its support for involving "the people of the Gaeltacht as stakeholders in the process" (14) recognises the importance of various community-based initiatives which have attempted to stem the tide of language decline since the 1960s.

For the moment, the following tentative conclusion can be drawn from this paper: since independence, Irish government policy contains assumptions which can be traced to modernisation theory, with its attendant hostility to traditional culture and its distaste for intervention in socio-economic planning. However, a central pillar of government policy throughout this period has been the revival of the traditional culture associated with the Irish language, a highly complex task requiring high levels of careful planning and intervention. It is argued, therefore, that the modernisation bias of government policy has militated against creating an effective strategy for increasing the range of domains in which Irish is used regularly, and has fostered a perception that the Irish language is important only in a symbolic, and not a practical sense. Consideration of new theoretical work linking language, culture and development may help social actors forge strategies which move beyond existing perceptions of culture as merely exotic decoration and place language at the centre of the development process.

References

Barry, F. 1987. "Between Tradition and Modernity: Cultural Values and the Problems of Irish Society". Dublin: University College Dublin, Centre for Economic Research, Department of Political Economy, Policy Paper No. 23

Buchholz, T. 1999. New ideas from dead economists: an introduction to modern economic thought, 2nd edition. London and New York: Penguin

Casson, M., P. Cooke, R. Merfyn Jones and C. Williams. 1994. *Quiet Revolution? Language, Culture and Economy in the Nineties.* Aberystwyth: Menter a Busnes

Clinch, P., F. Convery and B. Walsh. 2002. *After the Celtic Tiger: Challenges Ahead.* Dublin: The O'Brien Press

Comharchumann Forbartha na nOileán. 1979. *Community Education Project, Ceantar na nOileán, Connemara (West of Ireland): Submission for Grant Aid to van Leer Foundation.*

Dafis, Ll. ed. 1995. *Economic Development and Lesser Used Languages: Partnerships for Action.* Llanbedr Pont Steffan: Cwmni Iaith

Dasgupta, A.K. 1985. *Epochs of Economic Theory.* Oxford and New York: Basil Blackwell

Gaeltacht Commission. 1926. *Gaeltacht Commission: Report.* Dublin: The Stationery Office

Gaeltacht Commission. 2002. *Coimisiún na Gaeltachta 2002: Tuarascáil/Report.* Dublin: Department of Arts, Heritage, Gaeltacht and Islands

Government of Ireland. 1929. *Statement of Government Policy on Recommendations of the Commission.* Dublin: The Stationery Office

Grin, F. 1996. "The economics of language: survey, assessment and prospects". *International Journal of the Sociology of Language* 121: 17-44

Hamilton, P. 1983. *Key Sociologists: Talcott Parsons.* London & New York: Routledge

Hamilton, P. ed. 1985. *Readings from Talcott Parsons.* London & Chichester: Ellis Horwood & Tavistock Publications

Heilbroner, R. 1967. *The Worldly Philosophers: the Lives, Times, and Ideas of the Great Economic Thinkers,* 3rd edition. New York: Simon and Schuster

Herman, A. 2001. *The Scottish Enlightenment: The Scots' Invention of the Modern World.* London: Fourth Estate

Hindley, R. 1994. "Clear Island (Oileán Chléire) in 1958: a Study in Geolinguistic Transition". *Irish Geography,* 27 (2): 97-106

Johnson, N. 1997. "Making Space: Gaeltacht policy and the politics of identity". In ed. B. Graham. *In Search of Ireland: A Cultural Geography.* London: Routledge

Kirby, P. 1997. *Poverty amid Plenty: Irish and World development reconsidered.* Dublin: Trócaire

Lee, J.J. 1989. *Ireland 1912-1985: Politics and Society.* Cambridge: Cambridge University Press

Nelde, P. 1999. "Multilingualism and the Economy as Issues in European Language Policy". In eds. Heberts, K. and J.G. Turi. *Multilingual Cities and Language Policies.* Åbo: Åbo Akademi University Social Science Research Unit

Nelde, P., M. Strubell and G. Williams. 1996. *Euromosaic: The Production and Reproduction of the minority language groups in the European Union.* Luxembourg: European Commission

Ní Bhrádaigh, E. 2002. "Entrepreneurship in the Gaeltacht - its patterns and evolution: a study of entrepreneurship in a peripheral and minority language region". Unpublished research paper, Trinity College, Dublin

Ní Riain, I. 2002. *Carraig & Cathair: Ó Díreáin.* Dublin: Cois Life

Ó Cinnéide, M., M. Keane and M. Cawley. 1985. "Industrialization and Linguistic Change among Gaelic-Speaking Communities in the West of Ireland". *Language Planning and Language Problems,* 9 (1): 3-15

Ó Cinnéide, M., S. Mac Donncha and S. Ní Chonghaile. 2001. *Polasaithe agus Cleachtais Eagraíochtaí Éagsúla le Feidhm sa Ghaeltacht*. Galway: Research Centre in Social Sciences, National University of Ireland, Galway

Ó Cuív, B. 1950. *Irish Dialects and Irish-Speaking Districts*. Dublin: Institute of Advanced Studies

Ó Gadhra, N. 1989. *An Ghaeltacht (Oifigiúil) - agus 1992?* Dublin: Coiscéim

Ó hAodha, B. 1969. *An tSuirbhéireacht ar Ghaeltacht na Gaillimhe/The Galway Gaeltacht Survey*. Galway: The Social Sciences Research Centre, University College Galway

Ó hÉallaithe, D. 1999. "Uair na Cinniúna don Ghaeltacht". *Cuisle*, February 1999

Ó Riagáin, P. 1992. *Language Maintenance and Language Shift as Strategies of Social Reproduction: Irish in the Corca Dhuibhne Gaeltacht 1926-1986*. Dublin: Institiúid Teangeolaíochta Éireann

Ó Riain, S. 1994. *Pleanáil Teanga in Éirinn: 1919-1985*. Dublin: Carbad/Bord na Gaeilge

Ó Torna, C. 2000. "Cruthú Constráide agus an Turas Siar: An Ghaeltacht i dtús an fichiú haois". *An Aimsir Óg* (2000): 51-65

Ó Tuathaigh, G. 1986. "Aistriú pobail Ghaeltachta go háiteanna eile in Éirinn: Cúlra an pholasaí". In ed. M. Ó Conghaile. *Gaeltacht Ráth Cairn: Léachtaí Comórtha*. Béal an Daingin: Cló Iar-Chonnachta

Ó Tuathaigh, M.A.G. 1990. *The Development of the Gaeltacht as a Bilingual Entity*. Dublin: Institiúid Teangeolaíochta Éireann

O'Dowd, L. 1995. "Development or Dependency? State, Economy and Society in Northern Ireland'. In eds. Clancy, P., S. Drudy, K. Lynch and L. O'Dowd. *Irish Society: Sociological Perspectives*. Dublin: IPA and Sociological Association of Ireland

Price, A. 1997. *The Diversity Dividend: Language, Culture and Economy in an Integrated Europe*. Brussels: European Bureau for Lesser Used Languages

Robertson, R. ed. 1991. *Talcott Parsons: theorist of modernity*. London: Sage

Rubin, I.I. 1979. *A History of Economic Thought*. London: Ink Links (translation of 2nd revised Russian edition, 1929)

Tovey, H and P. Share. 2000. *A Sociology of Ireland*. Dublin: Gill & Macmillan

Tucker, V. 1997. "A Cultural Perspective on Development". In V. Tucker ed. *Cultural Perspectives on Development*. London: Frank Cass

Valiulis, M.G. 1992. *Portrait of a Revolutionary: General Richard Mulcahy and the founding of the Irish Free State*. Dublin: Irish Academic Press

Walsh, J. 2002. *Díchoimisiúnú Teanga: Coimisiún na Gaeltachta 1926*. Dublin: Cois Life

War Zone Language:
Language and the Conflict in Northern Ireland

Cordula Bilger

Introduction

Like flags, parades, colours, or music, language plays an important role in the constitution of community identities. I am interested in how people from different communities or people with different political backgrounds speak 'different languages'. My study[1] of the discourses used in the context of Northern Ireland is based on ideas developed by Critical Linguistics, which I consider a useful and practical approach for the analysis of all kinds of texts. In his book *Language in the News: Discourse and Ideology in the Press*, Roger Fowler defines Critical Linguistics as:

> an inquiry into the relations between signs, meanings and the social and historical conditions which govern the semiotic structure of discourse, using a particular kind of linguistic analysis (Fowler 1991: 5).

In other words, Critical Linguistics tries to describe the relations between social structures, ideological processes, and language. It claims that every act of linguistic expression is somehow 'ideologically' motivated, that there is always a reason why somebody says or writes something in one particular way and not in another. I have studied examples from all the groups involved in Northern Ireland, and I am going to illustrate the ideas by looking at how the British and Irish Governments managed to find sets of words on decommissioning acceptable to the republicans, but still carrying the other parties along.

One of the key claims of Critical Linguistics is that language does not only *encode* power structures in society, but that language is *itself* instrumental in enforcing power differences. Language is never a *mirror* of reality. Rather, in Roger Fowler's words, it is "a refracting, structuring medium" (Fowler 1991: 10), because presenting anything through language always involves selection. In his book *Linguistic Criticism*, Fowler argues:

> Linguistic codes do not reflect reality neutrally; they interpret, organize, and classify the subjects of discourse. They embody theories of how the world is arranged: world-views or ideologies. (Fowler 1986: 27)

World-views and ideologies, as well as the circumstances of the situation in which speech or writing appears, determine which 'aspects of reality' speakers or writers *do* express and which they do *not*. This selection does not only happen on the level of terminology, but also in syntax. Syntax determines the perspective in a statement. As Roger Fowler puts it, "syntax analyzes actions and states, casting

---

[1] Bilger, Cordula. 2002. "War Zone Language: Language and the Conflict in Northern Ireland". Unpublished PhD. thesis, University of Zurich.

people into roles and assigning responsibility to persons mentioned" (Fowler 1991: 41).

2. Syntagmatic Models

Critical Linguists distinguish between different syntagmatic models which describe the interrelation of objects and events. In the transactive model, an action or process is presented as passing from the agent across to the affected. An example from *Time* magazine is:

1) *Now Northern Ireland's paramilitaries must decommission their weapons* [...]. [2]

The agent in this sentence is 'Northern Ireland's paramilitaries', the process is 'decommission', and the affected is 'their weapons'. In the non-transactive model, on the other hand, only one entity – an agent *or* an affected – is directly involved in a process, as in the next two examples:

2) *Many people died in the conflict* [3]
3) *The issue of all arms must be resolved.* [4]

There is no agent in example 3, we do not know *who* is supposed to resolve the issue of arms. If speakers or writers are concerned with clearly establishing the causes of an incident and identifying who exactly is responsible for it, they will prefer to use the transactive model. If, however, they do not consider it important to state clearly who does or did what to whom – or if they want to conceal the real facts –, the non-transactive model will serve them best. By choosing the focus in a statement, a speaker or writer channels and narrows the hearer's or reader's perception (cf. Hodge and Kress 1993: 21).

2.1 Passivisation

For example, choosing a passive sentence construction enables a speaker or writer not to mention the agent in a process at all. In the sentence:

4) *Much has been achieved for the people of Northern Ireland with the ending of violence.*[5]

---

[2] www.time.com/time/europe/magazine/1999/126/, 6-12-99.

[3] Adams, Gerry. 1994. *Presidential Address by Gerry Adams, Sinn Féin Ard Fheis, 26 February 1994*. Belfast: Sinn Féin, p. 2.

[4] cain.ulst.ac.uk/events/peace/docs/ga221001.htm, in a speech made by Sinn Féin leader Gerry Adams on 22 October 2001.

[5] Northern Ireland Information Service. 1995. *Building on the Peace*. Belfast: Northern Ireland Information Service, cover.

we do not know who has achieved much. Is it the British Government who published the booklet in which the sentence appeared? Or the paramilitary groups who had called a ceasefire? Or the people of Northern Ireland in general? The non-transactive sentence is vague. Another feature of passivisation is that – in relation to the corresponding active sentence structure – it inverts the order of agent and affected. In an active sentence structure, the theme of the sentence – that is, 'what the sentence is about' or, in other words, the piece of given information to which new information is added – is the agent. In a passive sentence construction, by contrast, the theme of the sentence is always the affected.

2.2 Nominalisation

Whereas in a passive sentence, the focus is shifted from the agent to the affected, in a nominalised sentence, the focus is on the process itself. For instance, using euphemistic language, republicans often call for the:

5) *demilitarisation of the conflict* [6].

This nominalised phrase encodes the republican view that not only paramilitary groups must give up their weapons, but all sides in the conflict, that is, also the security forces, and that, moreover, the British Army must be withdrawn from Northern Ireland. But as the sentence does not explicitly say *who* is supposed to demilitarise, this meaning remains implicit. Like passivisation, nominalisation often involves agent deletion.

2.3 Other Agency Obscuring Techniques

Apart from passivisation or nominalisation, there are other, more complex techniques that allow a speaker or writer to be vague about 'who did what to whom'. On 16 July 2002, the IRA issued an apology for killing and injuring what they call 'non-combatants' during all the years of the conflict. The first sentence of the statement read as follows:

6) *Sunday July 21 marks the 30th anniversary of an IRA operation in Belfast in 1972 which resulted in nine people being killed and many more injured.* [7]

Containing two passives, this non-transactive sentence *does* say that the IRA carried out an operation and that the result of the operation was that nine people were killed and many were injured. But – even though this might be dismissed as splitting hairs – the statement does *not* explicitly say that 'it was the *IRA* who killed and injured people'. I would claim that this sentence structure encodes the

---

[6]   *Captive Voice/An Glór Gafa*, winter 1993: 1; *An Phoblacht/Republican News*, 27-1-94: 5, quoting Sinn Féin leader Gerry Adams.

[7]   cain.ulst.ac.uk/events/peace/docs/ira160702.htm, in a statement by the IRA on 16 July 2002.

republican ideology that while the IRA – which republicans see as a 'military force that was at war with the British, who occupy the northern part of Ireland' – did not deliberately kill innocent people, it *had to* carry out this operation to resist that occupation, and that – unfortunately – the operation 'resulted in victims'. Other examples where writers with a republican background describe acts of violence carried out by the IRA but leave the relation between agent and process vague are the following:

7) *Volunteers from South Armagh Brigade Oglaigh na hÉireann carried out an attack on British forces guarding their main helicopter base in Bessbrook on Wednesday evening 12 February. One of the British soldiers on duty was hit by a single shot and died.*[8]

8) *A number of British soldiers have been killed in IRA operations at the main gate of the base [...].*[9]

9) *The North Armagh Brigade of the IRA have said they carried out yesterday's ambush on an RUC patrol in Lurgan, Co. Armagh in which two RUC men were shot dead.*[10]

3. Vagueness and (Constructive) Ambiguity

Vagueness and ambiguity have played a crucial role in the Northern Ireland peace process. Ambiguous language is used by the political parties, the leaders of loyalist and republican paramilitary groups, and the British and Irish governments alike.

3.1 The Issue of Arms Decommissioning
A central issue in the Northern Ireland peace process has been the decommissioning of paramilitary arms. Not surprisingly, decommissioning has been the central point of controversy in the Good Friday Agreement and in other documents. The crucial passage in the Good Friday Agreement reads as follows:

10) *All participants accordingly reaffirm their commitment to the total disarmament of all paramilitary organisations. They also confirm their intention to continue to work constructively and in good faith with the Independent Commission, and to use any influence they may have, to achieve the decommissioning of all paramilitary arms within two years following endorsement in referendums North and South of the agreement and in the context of the implementation of the overall settlement.*[11]

---

[8]   RM Distribution, a republican electronic news service, 26-2-97, in a statement by the IRA.

[9]   *An Phoblacht/Republican News*, 24-3-94: 2.

[10] RM Distribution, a republican electronic news service, 17-6-97.

[11] Great Britain. Northern Ireland Office. 1998. *The Agreement: Text of the Agreement Reached in the Multi-Party Negotiations on Northern Ireland.* 10 April 1998. Belfast: HMSO, chapter 7.

The two sentences of this passage are extremely complex. Both sentences contain nominalised phrases: 'the total disarmament of all paramilitary organisations' and 'the decommissioning of all paramilitary arms'. Both of these phrases lack an agent; it is not made explicit *who* is supposed to disarm paramilitary organisations or *who* is to decommission arms. The second sentence merely says that the parties who signed the agreement confirm that they intend to use any influence they may have to achieve that *somebody* will decommission all paramilitary arms. It is of course obvious who the agent of that process is. But the authors of the sentence must have felt that a vague formulation that does not bluntly state that 'the IRA and other paramilitary groups must or will hand in their arms' would alienate the sympathisers of such groups less. Historian and journalist Jack Holland was right when he claimed in an article in the *Irish Echo* that "[t]he words of the agreement never mention anyone delivering arms to anybody" (Vol. 74, No. 29, 18–24 July 2001, www.irishecho.com/news/article.cfm?id=9536).

When the Ulster Unionist leader David Trimble and his party colleagues realised that the final draft of the Good Friday Agreement did not in fact force the IRA to hand in its arms before Sinn Féin could enter the government, they turned to Prime Minister Tony Blair, who wrote a 'side-letter' to Trimble, in which he tried to deal with their doubts concerning the agreement's terms on decommissioning. The crucial passage in the letter read as follows:

11) *Furthermore, I confirm that, in our view, the effect of the decommissioning section of the agreement, with decommissioning schemes coming into effect in June, is that the process of decommissioning should begin straight away.*[12]

This formulation is again very complex, and the statement is vague. Blair did *not* actually say that, in his view, decommissioning had to begin straight away. All he said was that 'in his view', the agreement had an 'effect', namely that a 'process' 'should' begin straight away. And that 'process' is not necessarily decommissioning itself but just something which would finally lead to it. I would claim that in this sentence, the relations between agents, processes, and affected are completely obscure. We do not know *who* is supposed to start this process nor *who* is supposed to decommission arms. Blair was deliberately ambiguous about who was meant to do what to whom.

In April 1999, Prime Minister Blair and his Irish colleague Bertie Ahern issued a declaration on how to break the impasse on the decommissioning of paramilitary weapons. The document – commonly referred to as the Hillsborough Declaration – proposed that before devolution and the establishment of the Northern Ireland Executive,

12) *a collective act of reconciliation will take place. This will see some arms put beyond use on a voluntary basis, in a manner which will be*

---

[12] www.ireland.com/newspaper/opinion/1999/0630/opt1.htm, 30-6-99, quoting British Prime Minister Tony Blair.

verified by the Independent International Commission on
Decommissioning [...]. [13]

Like the term 'decommissioning', the phrase 'to put arms beyond use' is
euphemistic in that it neither clearly denotes to 'hand over weapons' nor to
'destroy weapons'. The authors of the declaration again chose non-transactive
sentence constructions that enabled them not to mention the agent of a potential
act of decommissioning. Using a nominalised phrase, they proposed that 'a
collective act of reconciliation will take place', without stating who would
actually do this. The authors continued, 'this will see some arms put beyond use
on a voluntary basis'. This complex passivised sentence is also vague. The agent
of the process of putting arms beyond use is deleted, and the sentence merely says
that 'this will see' some arms put beyond use. The whole formulation is very
unclear.

On 6 May 2000, the IRA issued a statement in which it said that

13) *the IRA leadership will initiate a process that will completely and
verifiably put IRA arms beyond use* [14].

As in earlier statements by the IRA, the agent of a potential act of
decommissioning is not the organisation itself but 'a process'. A year later, when
there was still no sign of an IRA arms decommissioning, David Trimble claimed
that "[f]ourteen months ago the IRA promised to put its weapons completely and
verifiably beyond use" (www.thetimes.co.uk/article/0,,525-2001263502,00.html,
2-8-01). But that was simply not the case. It only promised to *initiate a process*
that would put IRA arms beyond use. On 5 December 2000, the IRA leadership
released another statement:

14) *The leadership of Óglaigh na hÉireann want to reiterate our commitment to
the resolution of the issue of arms and our view that this is a necessary step
in a genuine peace process. We remain prepared to initiate a process which
would completely and verifiably put IRA arms beyond use [...]*. [15]

Using an agentless nominalised phrase, the IRA said that it remained committed
to 'the resolution of the issue of arms'. But the authors of the statement remained
silent about *who* they thought should resolve the issue of arms. And they again
stated that they 'remained prepared to initiate a process which would put IRA
arms beyond use'. There was not a single transactive sentence in the whole

---

[13]   cain.ulst.ac.uk/events/peace/docs/bi1499.htm, in a declaration of British
      Prime Minister Tony Blair and Irish Prime Minister Bertie Ahern at
      Hillsborough Castle on 1 April 1999.

[14]   RM Distribution, a republican electronic news service, 6-5-00, in a statement
      by the IRA.

[15]   209.68.13.153/aprn/current/news/07iras.html, in a statement by the IRA on 5
      December 2000.

statement that said that 'the IRA will decommission its arms'. Similarly, in a statement on 9 August 2001, the IRA confirmed that it:

15) *has agreed a scheme with the IICD which will put IRA arms completely and verifiably beyond use.*[16].

This time, the agent is 'a scheme'. When the IRA finally *did* put some arms beyond use in October 2001, it did not say that 'we have put some arms beyond use', but that:

16) *in order to save the peace process we have implemented the scheme agreed with the IICD in August* [17].

And five months later, on 8 April 2002, the IRA released another statement, which contained the following sentence:

17) *The leadership of Oglaigh na hEireann has taken another initiative to put arms beyond use.*[18]

I would argue that the IRA leadership uses such vague, non-transactive sentence structures to reduce the danger that a more hardline republican base would see the acts of putting arms beyond use as a defeat or surrender on the part of the IRA.

But the British and Irish governments and the pro-agreement parties have *also* been careful not to alienate republicans by portraying an IRA weapons hand-over or destroyal as a defeat of the IRA. They have therefore been talking of paramilitary disarmament in vague, euphemistic terms. For instance, neither the word 'decommissioning' nor the phrase 'to put arms beyond use' clearly denote 'handing weapons over' or 'destroying weapons'. As we have seen, this vagueness or ambiguity does not only appear on the level of terminology, but also in syntax. A term that is often mentioned in this context is 'constructive ambiguity'. Because arms decommissioning is such a controversial issue, the Good Friday Agreement and other documents had to leave it unresolved and used ambiguous language in reference to it, so that as many sides as possible could support the agreement. In his article "Irreversible Peace in Northern Ireland", Jonathan Stevenson talks about constructive ambiguity on the issue of decommissioning and argues that it is likely that:

> absolute clarity would have produced a political stalemate and no implementation at all. Perhaps, without the room ambiguity afforded each side, neither would have been willing to try (Stevenson 2000: 12).

---

[16] cain.ulst.ac.uk/events/peace/docs/ira090801.htm, in a statement by the IRA on 9 August 2001.

[17] cain.ulst.ac.uk/events/peace/docs/ira231001.htm, in a statement by the IRA on 23 October 2001.

[18] cain.ulst.ac.uk/events/peace/docs/ira080402.htm, in a statement by the IRA on 8 April 2002.

3.2 The Issue of a 'Permanent Ceasefire' and an 'Unequivocal Renunciation of Violence'

Another example that illustrates the use of ambiguous language in the context of the conflict in Northern Ireland is the following. When the IRA declared its second ceasefire in July 1997, it did not announce a 'permanent ceasefire', but merely a 'complete cessation of military operations':

18) *We want a permanent peace and therefore we are prepared to enhance the search for a democratic peace settlement through real and inclusive negotiations. So, having assessed the current political situation, the leadership of Oglaigh na hEireann are announcing a complete cessation of military operations from 12 o'clock midday on Sunday the 20th July 1997. We have ordered the unequivocal restoration of the ceasefire of August 1994.* [19]

There was much controversy over the meaning of the word 'complete'. People were wondering whether it meant 'permanent', or whether the IRA merely announced a tactical ceasefire. The authors of the statement *did* use the word 'permanent', but only in connection with the word 'peace', not in connection with the ceasefire itself. They said that 'we want a permanent peace'. However, when republicans refer to 'permanent peace' or 'lasting peace in our country', they do not mean 'the absence of paramilitary violence', but the establishment of a united Ireland. Further, the IRA *did* use the word 'unequivocal'. Not, however, in relation to the renunciation of violence itself but only to the *restoration* of the ceasefire of August 1994 – a ceasefire which itself was not unequivocal, as we know. I would claim that the aim of this statement was to say different things to different people. The IRA wanted to win the trust of moderate nationalists, unionists, and the British and Irish governments, who expected the IRA to finally commit itself to peaceful, democratic means. On the other hand, the IRA leadership wanted to reassure the hard-line republican base that it was still committed to achieving a united Ireland.

3.3 The Issue of a North/South Body

Yet another example that illustrates the use of vague, ambiguous language is the following. A major point of controversy in the all-party talks at Stormont was the nature of the new North/South body that was to be established. Unionists had warned Prime Minister Tony Blair not to use the word 'executive' in reference to such a body, because they feared that it could become something like an all-Ireland government. Nationalists, by contrast, had likewise contacted Blair to tell him that whatever language was finally used in the agreement, the body had to be p r o v i d e d   w i t h   e x e c u t i v e   p o w e r   (c f . www.ireland.com/newspaper/front/1998/0112/fro1.htm, 12-1-98). What the two

---

[19] RM Distribution, a republican electronic news service, 19-7-97, in a statement by the IRA.

governments finally proposed in the *Propositions on Heads of Agreement* in January 1998 was:

19) [a] *North/South Ministerial Council to bring together those with executive responsibilities in Northern Ireland and the Irish Government in particular areas* [20].

A similar formulation was later used in the Good Friday Agreement. As expected, the authors of the document avoided the phrase 'a North/South body with executive powers' because that would probably have caused the unionists to leave the talks. Still, the word 'executive', which nationalists and republicans were anxious to see, was there. Not, however, in reference to the powers of the North/South Ministerial Council but only in reference to the responsibilities of the politicians who were to meet in that council. The authors of the document obviously tried to please nationalists and unionists simultaneously by means of using ambiguous language.

References

Bilger, Cordula. 2002. "War Zone Language: Language and the Conflict in Northern Ireland". Unpublished PhD thesis, university of Zürich

Fairclough, Norman. 1989. *Language and Power*. Language in Social Life Series. London: Longman

Fowler, Roger. 1986. *Linguistic Criticism*. Oxford: Oxford University Press

Fowler, Roger. 1991. *Language in the News: Discourse and Ideology in the Press*. London: Routledge

Fowler, Roger et al. 1979. *Language and Control*. London: Routledge and Kegan Paul

Hodge, Robert and Gunther Kress. 1993. *Language as Ideology: The Politics of Language*. 2nd ed. London: Routledge

Stevenson, Jonathan. 2000. "Irreversible Peace in Northern Ireland?" *Survival* 42.3: 5–26

---

[20]   British and Irish Governments. 1998. *Propositions on Heads of Agreement*. 12 January 1998. Belfast: Northern Ireland Office.